Religion in Revolutionary England

Manchester University Press

This volume is dedicated
in gratitude for the life of
Chris Durston
1951–2005
Scholar, Colleague, Friend

Religion in Revolutionary England

edited by
CHRISTOPHER DURSTON
and
JUDITH MALTBY

Manchester University Press

Manchester and New York

distributed exclusively in the USA by Palgrave

Published by Manchester University Press
Oxford Road, Manchester M13 9NR, UK
and Room 400, 175 Fifth Avenue, New York, NY 10010, USA
www.manchesteruniversitypress.co.uk

Distributed exclusively in the USA by
Palgrave, 175 Fifth Avenue, New York,
NY 10010, USA

Distributed exclusively in Canada by
UBC Press, University of British Columbia, 2029 West Mall,
Vancouver, BC, Canada V6T 1Z2

British Library Cataloguing-in-Publication Data
A catalogue record for this book is available from the British Library

Library of Congress Cataloging-in-Publication Data applied for

ISBN   0 7190 6404 X *hardback*   EAN   978 0 7190 6404 3

ISBN   0 7190 6405 8 *paperback*   EAN   978 0 7190 6405 0

First published 2006

15 14 13 12 11 10 09 08 07 06   10 9 8 7 6 5 4 3 2 1

Typeset by
Carnegie Publishing, Lancaster
Printed and bound in Great Britain
by Cromwell Press, Trowbridge, Wiltshire

Contents

An appreciation of the work of Christopher Durston
Jacqueline Eales   vii
Preface   xiii
Notes on contributors   xv

Introduction: religion and revolution in seventeenth-century England
Christopher Durston and Judith Maltby   1

Part I   Theology in Revolutionary England

1   Living with the living God: radical religion and the English Revolution   *J. C. Davis*   19

2   The toleration controversy during the English Revolution
John Coffey   42

3   The legacy of mothers and others: women's theological writing, 1640–60   *Elizabeth Clarke*   69

Part II   Inside and outside the Revolutionary national Church

4   'The public profession of these nations': the national Church in Interregnum England   *Ann Hughes*   93

5   A ministry of the gospel: the Presbyterians during the English Revolution   *Elliot Vernon*   115

6   English Catholics at war and peace   *William Sheils*   137

7   Suffering and surviving: the civil wars, the
     Commonwealth and the formation of 'Anglicanism',
     1642–60   *Judith Maltby*   158

8   Freedom to form: the development of Baptist movements
     during the English Revolution   *Mark Bell*   181

Part III   Local impacts of religious revolution

9   'Preaching and sitting still on Sundays': the Lord's Day
     during the English Revolution   *Christopher Durston*   205

10 'So many sects and schisms': religious diversity in
     Revolutionary Kent, 1640–60   *Jacqueline Eales*   226

11 The experience of defeat revisited: suffering, identity
     and the politics of obedience among Hertford
     Quakers, 1655–65   *Beverly Adams*   249

Index   269

An appreciation of the work of Christopher Durston

Chris Durston's unexpected death in August 2005 at the age of fifty-four has cut short an important contribution to the academic profession and to the study of early modern history in particular. From 1976 until 2004 he was based at St Mary's College, Strawberry Hill in Twickenham, where he and Susan Doran founded the Centre for Religious History in 1996 and jointly organised a series of highly successful international conferences, mainly on early modern religion. In 2002 his work at St Mary's and his academic reputation were recognised by his appointment to a personal chair. Chris was also a strong advocate for the academic study of History and worked with the Higher Education Funding Council for England as a subject reviewer and more recently as an institutional auditor, approaching these tasks with the aim of protecting the academy's professional integrity. This spirit was also reflected in his long service as a member of the steering committee of the History in the Universities Defence Group (HUDG), now known as History UK (HE). In 2004 Chris was a popular choice as co-convenor of HUDG with Virginia Davies and at about the same time he also took up a new post at the University of Plymouth.

Chris's career as an historian began with the study of Modern History at Hertford College, Oxford, from 1969 to 1972. He then undertook postgraduate study at Reading University under the supervision of Anne Pallister and completed his doctorate on 'Berkshire and its County Gentry 1625–1649' in 1977. Along with Clive Holmes' work on the Eastern Association, this was one of the first studies to challenge the assumption in Alan Everitt's 1966 book on Kent that the county gentry were intrinsically insular in political and social outlook in the early Stuart period. The thesis was never published in its entirety, but it formed the groundwork for his future research, and articles based on it were published in the early 1980s. Chris's obituary in *The Independent* described his research as resulting in 'an impressively wide-ranging yet well-integrated body of work'.* The themes which unified his research and publications were clearly set out in his first book, *The Family in the English Revolution* (Basil Blackwell, 1989), in which he noted with approval the shift of historical attention away from 'high politics and international diplomacy' towards a greater interest in the 'beliefs and institutions which helped to shape the social and cultural experiences of our less exalted ancestors'. Chris was profoundly interested in the radicalism of the civil war period, but also wished to explain why the reform programmes of 1640–60 proved to be 'so short-lived and abortive'. *The Family in the English Revolution* contributed to the growing literature on the early modern family by analysing these decades in depth. It provided an overview of the attempts made by the state and by individuals to abolish or remodel the family and emphasised how radical religious beliefs also led to the questioning of its patriarchal structure. Chris concluded that adherence to traditional culture, as represented by the institution of the family, helped to subvert the puritans' reforms, including the introduction in 1653 of the secular registration of marriage, which many couples chose to supplement with a traditional religious ceremony.

Allied to Chris's insights into the lives of the wider population and the ways in which the revolutionary impulses of the 1640s and 1650s were resisted, was his keen interest in human psychology, which also strongly informed his work. He recognised that in the early modern period religious writing was a unique medium for the expression of psychological experience and he explored this aspect of people's lives in a number of his publications. His interests in the religious history of the period are evident in the book that he co-authored with Susan Doran, *Princes, Pastors and People: The Church and Religion in England 1529–1689* (Routledge, 1991), which not only explained central changes in religious policy from the Reformation to the Glorious Revolution, but also analysed their impact on the lives of the English people. His own Catholic faith provided him with an empathy for the religious groupings of the past, but never prevented him from being impartial in their study.

Psychological motivation also played a supporting, but illuminating, role in Chris's interpretation of the reigns of James I and Charles I, in two publications in the Lancaster Pamphlets series in 1993 and 1998 respectively, which represent a cogent introduction to the events and

---

* Obituary by Professor Ralph Houlbrooke and Dr Frank Tallett, *The Independent*, 24 August 2005.

historiography of the early Stuart period from a post-revisionist stand-point. Although Chris argued that James' reign should not be seen as part of a 'high road' to civil war and that the blame for war lay squarely with his son, whom he characterised as weak, stubborn and insecure, he also acknowledged the importance of religion as an ideological factor in the conflict.

The religious cultural divide of the early modern period was similarly the theme of the collection of essays, *The Culture of English Puritanism, 1560–1700* (Macmillan, 1996), which we edited together. Chris's strengths as a collaborator and his enjoyment of working with colleagues in the field were important ingredients in the publication of this volume. He also brought his earlier experience of co-authorship to the writing of an extended introduction, which reflected both of our interests without any loss of focus. Chris brought energy, attention to detail and a calm sense of purpose to the process of assembling and editing the work of the eight contributors, who included Margaret Aston, Patrick Collinson, Ralph Houlbrooke, Martin Ingram, Peter Lake and John Spurr. His own chapter allowed him to develop further his analysis of the failure of the puritan cultural revolution of the years 1645–60 and drew together a body of ideas developed in a number of his earlier publications, including articles in *The Seventeenth Century* on the programme of fasts introduced during the English Revolution and in *History Today* on the puritan attempt to eradicate traditional Christmas celebrations. Chris believed that the impo-sition of puritan religious and cultural reforms met widespread resistance from a population attached to more deeply rooted and familiar customs. This analysis has been further extended in Chris's own essay on sabbath observance during the English Revolution in the present volume and in two articles for the *Journal of Ecclesiastical History* and *Historical Research*, which were in the press when he died.

In the late 1990s Chris started to publish his major work on the Cromwellian major-generals. Two articles in *English Historical Review* and *History* were followed by the publication of his most significant monograph, *Cromwell's Major-Generals: Godly Government during the English Revolution* (Manchester University Press, 2001). Chris himself referred to the difficulties of writing about the topic, remarking at the start of the book on the number of distinguished historians who had failed in the attempt to write a detailed history of this aspect of Cromwell's rule. The major-generals were in office for little over a year, from late 1655 to January 1657, but the scope of the research required to analyse the experiment and the reasons for its failure is apparent from a reading of the finished book. Chris not only wrote about the nineteen major-generals and their deputies, whose remit covered the whole of England and Wales, but he also analysed the structures put in place to support them. This included the personnel and work of the next tier of local governors, the commissioners for securing the peace of the Commonwealth and their relationships with the traditional forms of local government in the localities. The major-generals were also involved in the work of the recently appointed ejectors, who had powers to remove scandalous clergy and schoolmasters, and triers, who approved all new appointments of clerics. They were also responsible for the oversight and taxation of the royalist enemies of the Cromwellian regime. In keeping with his earlier work, the book revealed how the major-generals' aims to create a godly nation were resisted by considerable numbers of the people they were meant to control. The major-generals met hostility not only from the surviving royalists and Anglicans, but also from a wider population who resented the imposition of moral and other reforms, including the suppression of unlicensed alehouses, which took up much of the energies of the major-generals. This nationwide study was based perforce on the analysis of an array of local sources and Chris's achievement in mastering and interpreting this huge body of material resulted in a book of immense scholarship and authority.

The energy and enthusiasm which Chris brought to his research is reflected in the fact that when he died he had four articles in the press, as well as his contribution to this volume. He was also working on a third monograph, which would have been on the subject of religious change in the English parishes from 1620 to 1670. This last project would have allowed him to explore in further detail the religious changes introduced during the English Revolution and the ways in which they clashed with so many of the traditional forms of Elizabethan and Jacobean worship. Chris was an outstanding scholar, who wrote with great clarity and avoided modish forms of expression and enquiry in his work. To paraphrase one of the civil war puritan ministers whom he studied, his work was 'solid, and tended unto edification'. As a result, his books on the family in the English Revolution and Cromwell's major-generals will continue to be the standard works on these subjects and all of his publications will remain important points of reference for those in the field for many years to come.

Jacqueline Eales

Publications by Christopher Durston

Books

The Family in the English Revolution (Basil Blackwell, Oxford, 1989)

Co-author with Susan Doran, *Princes, Pastors and People: The Church and Religion in England 1529–1689* (Routledge, London and New York, 1991, 2nd edn, 2003)

James I (Routledge, London and New York, 1993, Lancaster Pamphlet)

Co-editor with Jacqueline Eales, *The Culture of English Puritanism, 1560–1700* (Macmillan, Basingstoke, 1996); co-author of Introduction, 'The puritan ethos, 1560–1700', and author of essay, 'Puritan rule and the failure of cultural revolution, 1645–1660'

Co-author with Barry Coward, *The English Revolution: An Advanced Sourcebook* (John Murray, London, 1997)

Charles I (Routledge, London and New York, 1998, Lancaster Pamphlet)

Cromwell's Major-Generals: Godly Government during the English Revolution (Manchester University Press, Manchester, 2001)

Co-editor with Judith Maltby, *Religion in Revolutionary England* (MUP, 2006); co-author of the Introduction, and author of the essay 'Preaching and sitting still on Sundays: the Lord's Day during the English Revolution'

Articles and essays

'London and the provinces: the association between the capital and the Berkshire county gentry of the early seventeenth century', *Southern History*, 3 (1981)

'Henry Marten and the high shoon of Berkshire: the Levellers in Berkshire in 1648', *Berkshire Archaeological Journal*, 70 (1981)

'"Wild as colts untamed": radicalism in the Newbury area during the early modern period', *Southern History*, 6 (1984); reprinted in Barry Stapleton (ed.), *Conflict and Community in Southern England* (Sutton, Gloucester, 1992)

'"Lords of misrule": The Puritan war on Christmas 1642–60', *History Today*, 35 (1985)

'"Let Ireland be quiet": opposition in England to the Cromwellian conquest of Ireland', *History Workshop Journal*, 21 (1986)

'Signs and wonders and the English Civil War', *History Today*, 37 (1987)

'"Unhallowed wedlocks": the regulation of marriage during the English Revolution', *Historical Journal*, 31 (1988)

'"These dangerous times": England's phoney war in the summer of 1642', *History Today*, 42 (1992)

'"For the better humiliation of the people": public days of fasting and thanksgiving during the English Revolution', *The Seventeenth Century*, 7 (1992)

'The fall of Cromwell's Major-Generals', *English Historical Review*, 113 (1998)

'"Settling the hearts and quieting the minds of all good people": the Major-Generals and the Puritan minorities of Interregnum England', *History*, 85 (2000)

'Assessing students in seminars', in A. Booth and P. Hyland (eds), *The Practice of University History Teaching* (Manchester University Press, Manchester, 2000)

'"Moses and the milksop": the religious relationship between Oliver Cromwell and Charles Fleetwood', *Cromwelliana* (2003)

'Cromwell's Major-Generals', *Cromwelliana* (2004)

Twelve articles in the *Oxford Dictionary of National Biography* (2004), including entries on the regicides Sir John Bashstead, George Fleetwood, William Goffe, John Hewson, John Oakey and Edward Whalley

'Edward Fisher and the defence of Elizabethan Protestantism during the English Revolution', *Journal of Ecclesiastical History*, 56 (2005)

'Winstanley', in Susan Doran and Thomas Freeman (eds), *The Tudors and Stuarts on Film: Historical Perspectives* (Palgrave, Basingstoke, 2006)

'By the book or with the spirit: the debate over liturgical prayer during the English Revolution', *Historical Research*, 79: 203 (2006)

'Policing the Cromwellian Church: the activities of the county ejection committees, 1654–1659', in Patrick Little (ed.), *The Cromwellian Protectorate* (Boydell and Brewer, forthcoming)

'James I and Protestant heresy', in Ralph Houlbrooke (ed.), *James VI & I: Ideas, Authority and Government* (Ashgate, Aldershot, forthcoming)

Preface

The editors conceived this volume as a means of bridging the historio-graphical gap between a number of existing volumes of essays dealing with aspects of religion in England in the pre-1640 and post-1660 periods, in particular Kenneth Fincham's *Early Stuart Church, 1603–1642* (Basingstoke, 1993) and Mark Goldie, Tim Harris and Paul Seward's *The Politics of Religion in Restoration England* (Oxford, 1990). It is thus our hope that it will find a wide readership and prove helpful to both undergraduate and postgraduate students following courses on the seventeenth century and the English Revolution, as well as to more experienced academics working in these fields.

To meet the different needs of these readerships, the volume brings together a range of essays of somewhat varying levels and complexities covering a broad spectrum of religious expression and experience in the 1640s and 1650s. Several contributions, such as those by John Coffey and Mark Bell, summarise and make more readily available the results of important monographs published by the authors in the last few years. Beverly Adams and Elliot Vernon's essays similarly highlight some of the major findings of their recent doctoral theses. Other contributions, those of Elizabeth Clarke, Judith Maltby, William Sheils, Christopher Durston and Jacqueline Eales, address key aspects of the English people's reli-gious experiences in the midst of revolution in a nuanced but accessible manner that it is hoped will appeal to a student readership. While the remaining couple of essays by J. C. Davis and Ann Hughes are rather more controversial and perhaps demand of their readers a somewhat greater acquaintance with the realities of seventeenth-century religious *mentalités* and structures, both break important new ground in their respective areas and make significant contributions to the evolving academic debate on mid-seventeenth-century religion. While it is too much to suggest that the volume has 'something for everyone', we do believe the volume will prove of benefit to both 'experts' and 'non-experts' alike.

Earlier versions of the essay by Judith Maltby appeared in Stephen Platten (ed.), *Anglicanism and the Western Christian Tradition: Continuity, Change and the Search for Communion* (Norwich, 2003), and R. N. Swanson (ed.), *The Church and the Book*, Studies in Church History, 38 (2004).

As most of the contributors completed their essays before the appearance of the *Oxford Dictionary of National Biography* in the autumn of 2004, they frequently give references to entries in the old *Dictionary*. Readers should remember that, where this is the case, an updated biography is now also available in the new version.

Christopher Durston and Judith Maltby

Notes on contributors

Beverly Adams completed a PhD on Hertford Quakers at Queen Mary College, University of London, in 2000. Since then she has been working as a Research Fellow on the House of Lords Section of the History of Parliament Trust, working on the episcopate between 1660 and 1715.

Mark Bell is the author of *Apocalypse How: Baptist Movements during the English Revolution* (2000).

Elizabeth Clarke is Reader in English Literature at the University of Warwick. She is the author of *Theory and Theology in George Herbert's Poetry* (1997) and co-edited *'This Double Voice': Gendered Writing in Early Modern England* (2000). She is currently working on a monograph, *Re-writing the Bride: Politics, Authorship and the Song of Songs in Seventeenth Century England*.

John Coffey is Reader in Early Modern History at the University of Leicester. He is the author of *Politics, Religion and the British Revolutions: The Mind of Samuel Rutherford* (1997), *Persecution and Toleration in Protestant England, 1558–1689* (2000), and *John Goodwin and the Puritan Revolution* (forthcoming).

J. C. Davis is Professor of History at the University of East Anglia. His many publications include *Utopia and the Ideal Society* (1981), *Fear, Myth and History: the Ranters and the Historians* (1986), and *Oliver Cromwell* (2001).

Christopher Durston taught early modern history at the University of Plymouth until his death in 2005. He was the author and editor of a number of books and essays on mid-seventeenth-century religion, including *The Culture of English Puritanism* (1996, with Jacqueline Eales), *Cromwell's Major-Generals* (2001), and *Princes, Pastors and People: The Church and Religion in England 1500–1700* (2003, with Susan Doran).

Jacqueline Eales is Professor of Early Modern History at Canterbury Christ Church University. She has published extensively on the English civil wars and is currently working on clerical marriage in seventeenth-century England.

Ann Hughes is Professor of Early Modern History at Keele University. Her publications include *Politics, Society and Civil War in Warwickshire, 1620–60* (1980), *The Causes of the English Civil War* (1998), and *Gangraena and the Struggle for the English Revolution* (2004).

Judith Maltby is Chaplain and Fellow of Corpus Christi College, Oxford, and Reader in Church History in the University of Oxford. Her publications include *Prayer Book and People in Elizabethan and Early Stuart England* (1998). She is currently undertaking research on Church of England loyalists during the civil wars and Interregnum.

William Sheils is Reader in History at University of York. His major publications include *The Puritans in the Diocese of Peterborough 1558–1610* (1979), *The English Reformation* (1989), and *A History of Religion in Britain: Practice and Belief from Roman Times to the Present* (1994, with S. Gilley).

Elliot Vernon completed a University of Cambridge PhD thesis on 'The Sion College Conclave and London Presbyterianism during the English Revolution' in 1999.

Introduction: religion and revolution in seventeenth-century England

Christopher Durston and Judith Maltby

I

Religion and the English Revolution are deeply and inextricably linked, for the years between 1640 and 1660 witnessed some of the most remarkable and important events in the entire history of English religion. The 1640s saw a full-scale civil war fought principally over divergent visions of the future of the national Church. The victorious Long Parliament abolished episcopacy and attempted to replace it with a Presbyterian governmental structure based on the classis, elder and synod. It outlawed the set prayers of the Book of Common Prayer and introduced *A Directory for Public Worship* containing guidelines for a new extemporised liturgy; and it imposed a strict moral code with draconian penalties for blasphemy, sabbath-breaking and sexual misconduct. The following decade witnessed the ending of the state Church's monopoly with a constitutional guarantee of toleration to large numbers of law-abiding trinitarian Protestants, and the resultant emergence and rapid growth of a range of new denominations, some of which, such as the Baptists and Quakers, were to play a prominent role in the subsequent religious development of both England and the wider world. Many contemporaries regarded these developments as a 'second Reformation', and, taken together, they may well have done more than the earlier sixteenth-century Reformation to shape the subsequent multi-denominational reality of England, ensuring that by 1800 it would be one of the most pluralist Christian states in Europe.

Twenty years ago John Morrill famously claimed that the English civil war was 'the last of Europe's wars of religion'.[1] At the time this was a controversial statement because for much of the twentieth century many of his fellow seventeenth-century historians had been reluctant to concede that religion could be a sufficiently strong force to motivate the English people to take up arms either for or against their sovereign. Religion was simply too unfashionable an explanation among late twentieth-century historians to account for the English Revolution. A century earlier Victorian historians, such as Samuel Rawson Gardiner, had been happy to see the conflict as the struggle of England's Protestant vanguard, or puritans, to free themselves from the ecclesiastical and constitutional tyranny of a high-church, absolutist Stuart monarchy. Christopher Hill, the colossus who presided over civil war studies from the 1940s to the 1980s, also knew a great deal about the early modern puritans and he, too, believed they were largely responsible for plunging the country into armed conflict. But for Hill, they were not so much determined agitators for spiritual and moral reform and renewal as England's first capitalists in disguise, who, while ostensibly pursuing deep and genuine religious objectives, were in fact unconsciously promoting the substructural economic interests of their nascent bourgeois class.[2] If only a few of Hill's contemporaries fully endorsed his uncompromising Marxist analysis of the origins of the civil war, most of them were sufficiently influenced by him to agree that genuine religious concerns lacked the power to provoke so momentous and catastrophic an event.

We live now, however, in a new century and a different world, both historiographically and politically. Marxism's materialist star has waned with the downfall of the Soviet empire, and Hill too has recently left us. Moreover, the events of 11 September 2001 and the subsequent emerging conflict between western governments (some of which are influenced by evangelical Christian attitudes) and groups of Islamist radicals in the Middle East and Asia have dramatically highlighted how ideological differences centred around contrasting religious world-views can indeed generate enmity, conflict and sickening violence. At least partly as a result of this changed modern climate, most early twenty-first-century historians of the civil war would now agree that religious concerns played a major role in causing the breakdown of political stability and the slide towards full-scale internal war in England.

II

The Protestant Church of England established by Elizabeth I in the mid-sixteenth century had begun life as an awkward mongrel, within which a Reformed theology of salvation was combined with an episcopalian governmental structure and a liturgy that retained many points of continuity with the old Catholic past. Given this hybrid nature, it inevitably had many critics, but on the whole it worked and achieved one of its founder's main aims of providing an orthodox centre-ground with wide boundaries, within which the great majority of the English people would be prepared to worship. After a long Elizabethan 'carrot and stick' campaign, involving education, evangelisation, propaganda and coercion, by 1600 a Church which had initially struggled to establish a clear identity and win over adherents had begun to put down deep roots and, as Judith Maltby has recently demonstrated, firmly embedded itself in the affections of large sections of the population.[3]

Following his accession in 1603, James I wisely did little to upset this religious applecart. Having previously promoted a reinvigorated Protestant episcopate in his Scottish domain, he saw much to admire in the established Church of his newly acquired kingdom. Like his predecessor, he thus followed policies aimed at preserving the comprehensive nature of the established Church and isolating those religious extremists who wished to pull it down and replace it with a more conservative or radical alternative. The accession of his son, Charles I, in 1625, however, signalled a divisive move away from this inclusive 'Elizabethan' approach to the state's religion. Charles shared the religious sensibilities of a small 'Arminian' or 'Laudian' minority within the Church, whose adherents upheld a number of beliefs that were fundamentally at odds with those of a great many of their fellow English Protestants. In particular, they were uncomfortable with the more rigid interpretations of the Reformed doctrine of predestination, they considered set prayer and the sacraments to be of greater spiritual value than preaching, and they elevated the status of the clergy to heights not seen since before the Reformation. Famously and perhaps most controversially, they also promoted 'the beauty of holiness', or the reintroduction into church interiors of decorative features such as east-end altars, paintings and statues, and the reincorporation into worship of a number of ceremonies and rituals which to their critics appeared uncomfortably close to popery.[4]

Charles's decision wholeheartedly to back this Laudian clerical faction and to help them to gain control of most of the important offices in his Church by the mid-1630s was to have fateful consequences both for himself and his people. Although some historians have argued that the Laudians managed to achieve some degree of popularity for their programme, the bulk of the evidence supports the view that they failed effectively to reform the religious sensibilities of the grassroots.[5] Unquestionably, and catastrophically, they also profoundly alienated large numbers of hitherto conformist puritans. Until the late 1620s moderate puritans had felt able to remain within what they regarded as the half-reformed English Church. Whatever scruples they might have had about the institution of episcopacy, they had taken comfort from the facts that its bishops were soundly predestinarian in the core matter of salvation and that the Prayer Book's impure liturgy was not totally without spiritual benefit to those who experienced it. Their responses to the sudden deterioration in the spiritual environment after 1630, and what they saw as the tainting of the essentially sound 'Elizabethan' features of the national Church, included recourse to more radical expressions of faith, emigration to the New World, outspoken criticism of the Laudian bishops – a tactic which frequently resulted in severe punishment or a grudging and often deeply resentful conformity to the new status quo. While the opposition of those who followed this last path was covert and passive, and their thoughts and attitudes not always therefore readily accessible to historians, it seems clear that many of them spent the 1630s waiting, hoping and praying for an opportunity to turn the tables on their new ecclesiastical masters.

Their chance came when in 1637 Charles attempted to impose a new Laudian Prayer Book upon his staunchly Calvinist subjects in Scotland, a kingdom he had left as a small child and returned to only once in 1633. It was a policy that resulted in a Covenanter uprising, a war inauspiciously called the Bishops' War, and a disastrous military defeat that led directly to the recall of an English Parliament that had not met for more than ten years. Between 1640 and 1642 the members of the Long Parliament legislated to rid the Church of its Laudian features, dealing harshly with the movement's clerical and lay ringleaders and orchestrating a nation-wide campaign to dismantle decorative innovations, such as altar-rails and stained glass. Spurred on by the downfall of their Laudian enemies and the progress of provincial iconoclasm, some puritan MPs then started promoting and supporting calls for the abolition of both the Book of Common Prayer and episcopacy. But such novel and radical demands alarmed many of their more conservative colleagues who, if they had had little time for the disgraced Laud, still retained a strong attachment to the institution of episcopacy and the traditional Prayer Book liturgy. It was these deep divisions over the future of the Church, coupled with the profound mutual distrust between King and MPs, which eventually doomed to failure all attempts to reach a compromise constitutional and religious settlement. During the summer of 1642, many of those MPs who retained an attachment to the Prayer Book and to an episcopacy purged of its Laudian accretions answered Charles I's summons to join his royalist forces in the north, while most of those looking for further wholesale reform of the Church defied him and remained at Westminster. In August 1642 Englishmen thus found themselves fighting a bitter and deeply divisive civil war, and one with religious discord at its centre.[6]

III

The first three essays in this volume consider some of the theological debates and speculations which emerged during the ensuing revolutionary years. Many English men and women on both sides of the civil war divide saw the conflict in primarily religious terms and claimed to have the backing of the Almighty for their cause. Royalists saw themselves as upholding God's anointed and his Church against the sacrilegious assault of heretical and rebellious parliamentarians. Many puritan clergymen, meanwhile, preached in eschatological terms, portraying the war as an apocalyptic struggle between the parliamentarian forces of light and the Antichristian Stuarts. In the wartime climate of confusion, crisis and uncertainty, discerning the will of the all-powerful God became a major preoccupation. This frantic search to uncover the will of a God who was widely recognised to be interventionist, capricious, and frequently wrathful and vengeful is the subject of J.C. Davis's contribution to this volume. Davis's essay stresses the extreme difficulties faced by those, such as Oliver Cromwell and many of his associates, who claimed explicit divine approbation for their actions. They knew that straying away from the divine will was a fatal error, certain to lead to failure. But staying on message with a hyperactive deity who was constantly interfering in human affairs, who appeared to favour 'unceasing and dynamic change' and who was no respecter of human institutions, no matter how prestigious or long-established, was a far from simple task and one that required constant prayer, fasting and study of scripture. Even then, nobody could ever be certain that his purposes had been accurately discerned, and, as Davis shows, the resultant anxiety about one's standing with one's Maker was for many a deeply troubling aspect of life in revolutionary England.

Another key feature of the post-1642 religious landscape was the breakdown of the disciplinary structures of the national Church and the subsequent appearance and proliferation of a variety of religious groups who claimed the right to worship as they saw fit without outside interference. The lengthy, wide-ranging and often heated debate over the issue of toleration that their emergence prompted is the subject of John Coffey's essay. Underlying all the arguments in what Coffey describes as this 'bitter family quarrel among puritans' was the question of how much power the civil magistrate should possess in religious matters – a fundamental issue which had also caused much tension and conflict in the puritan colonies of New England. In revolutionary Old England the protagonists were divided into three camps: anti-tolerationists, such as the Presbyterians, Thomas Edwards and Samuel Rutherford, who were opposed to allowing any opt-out from the state Church; conservative tolerationists, such as the

Independents, Jeremiah Burroughs and John Owen, who believed that all mainstream puritan denominations should possess the right to worship in their own way, but that some limits to toleration had to be imposed to prevent blasphemy and irreligion; and radical tolerationists, such as the Seeker Roger Williams and the Leveller William Walwyn, who believed that all persecution on religious grounds was fundamentally unchristian. According to Coffey, in the course of their arguments these men developed 'new ways of speaking about religion and politics', and their collective efforts represented 'a seminal controversy' with profound implications for the subsequent history of English politics and religion.

As Elizabeth Clarke's essay shows, the heady, liberating atmosphere which accompanied the destruction of the old religious order after 1642 also provoked a small number of women to share their theological deliberations with a wider public. Clarke explains how before 1640 the few female authors who addressed religious themes had been obliged to side-step contemporary male objections to their involvement in public discourse by presenting their religious beliefs as 'mothers' legacies' – ostensibly private documents which fulfilled women's appropriate role of educating their children. She goes on to show, however, how in the exceptional environment of the revolutionary period some women broke out of this constricting mould and began to demand the right to engage in public theological debate on equal terms with their male contemporaries. Women such as Katherine Chidley, Elizabeth Warren, Elizabeth Richardson, Mary Pope, Elizabeth Poole and An Collins all took advantage of the greater press freedoms of the revolutionary years to publish a wide variety of theological opinions, ranging from Richardson's defence of the old Prayer Book Church to Chidley's support for religious toleration and trenchant denunciation of Presbyterian intolerance. All of them had to fight hard to have their voices heard, and when their work did see the light of day the response from a predominantly male readership was overwhelmingly hostile and condescending. The radical Independent Katherine Chidley encountered a particularly fierce backlash after she dared to challenge Thomas Edwards over his attack on the London gathered churches, and she was furious that Edwards refused to engage in debate with her, preferring instead to defend himself against other male Independent authors. Clarke characterises the combined efforts of these women as a 'brief flowering' which ultimately came to little, concluding that 'even in the liberating years of the English Revolution, a woman's commitment to religion was judged more by her obedience to orthodoxy, than by her personal engagement with theology'. For all that, the very fact that this 'brief flowering' occurred at all is surely further testament to the extraordinary nature of the years between 1640 and 1660.

IV

Between 1642 and 1646 both sides in the civil war conflict were preoccupied by the military struggle in progress. This did not, however, prevent the Long Parliament giving a great deal of its attention to the question of the future of the Church. By the terms of the alliance it entered into with the Scots in 1643 – the Solemn League and Covenant – Parliament's leaders committed themselves to major ecclesiastical reform. Towards that end, they established the Westminster Assembly of Divines, a body of around a hundred leading English ministers and a smaller number of laymen and Scots advisers, entrusting it with the task of devising a new liturgy and governmental structure for the Church. In early 1645, on the recommendation of the Assembly, Parliament replaced the set liturgical forms of the Book of Common Prayer with the extempore prayers of the *Directory for Public Worship*. Ministers were henceforth forbidden to use the Prayer Book and obliged instead to compose their own liturgical prayers within the theological guidelines laid down in this *Directory*, which remained the official liturgy of the Church for the next fifteen years. Parliament also accepted the Assembly's plans for a new national Presbyterian structure, within which parishes would be grouped into classes and local associations, and ecclesiastical decision-making handed over to a network of provincial synods. Episcopal government of the Church had effectively come to an end in the early stages of the war as a result of the imprisonment of some bishops and the decision of the others to survive, as one of them put it, by imitating tortoises and hiding in their shells. The episcopal office was officially brought to an end in late 1646 following the eventual parliamentarian victory over Charles I, and during the late 1640s a few areas, such as London and Manchester, witnessed the creation of an embryonic network of Presbyterian classes and associations.

In the aftermath of their military victory, a majority of Long Parliament MPs remained firmly committed to the Assembly's vision of a national Presbyterian Church. A minority of MPs, however, and more importantly the great majority of both the rank-and-file soldiers and the officers of the New Model Army that had won the war for them, were fervently opposed to the implementation of this compulsory system and favoured instead the ending of the state Church's monopoly and the establishment of toleration for those who wished to form their own gathered churches. The direction and character of religious change thus became one of the important issues of contention in the bitter power struggle between army and Parliament that developed in the late 1640s. At the end of 1648 the New Model Army finally ended the impasse and imposed its will on its opponents. In December of that year it forcibly expelled from Parliament all

those MPs it regarded as obstructionist. The following month this purged
House of Commons put Charles I on trial and publicly executed him for
waging war against his own people. In the aftermath of these dramatic
revolutionary events, power fell to a military regime firmly committed to
a degree of religious toleration and opposed to the compulsory national
system advocated by the Presbyterians and episcopalians alike.

Between 1649 and 1660 Interregnum England remained under the
control of a succession of military, godly regimes. But, despite their
sectarian inclinations, these regimes did not entirely do away with the
national Church. The centuries-old parochial structure remained in place,
and the great majority of the English people – probably somewhat in excess
of 90 per cent – continued to worship regularly at their parish churches,
just as they had before the civil war. Furthermore, while a majority of the
nine thousand or so ministers who officiated in these parishes were now
broadly Presbyterian in outlook, numbers of clerics who retained a preference for the old pre-war Church had managed to hang on to their cures
and continued clandestinely to provide services based on the old Prayer
Book. Under questioning by the authorities, some claimed that pressure
from their flocks forced them to use the old Prayer Book. When John
Bowles, rector of St Aldates, Oxford, was cited by the Oxford University
visitors in 1648 and asked if he used the *Directory*, he replied that he did
but that he was also forced 'on his conscience' to use the Prayer Book, as
most of his parishioners had threatened to desert his church if he refused
to do so.[7]

Despite the sense of continuity that these realities undoubtedly fostered,
the context of religious worship had nonetheless radically changed. Some
men and women who took their religious duties particularly seriously now
regularly supplemented their attendance at Sunday worship with participation in semi-official weekday services organised by their Independent
or Congregationalist parish ministers. At Bray in Berkshire during the
mid-1650s, for example, the Independent minister, Ezekias Woodward,
held religious exercises in his house for those of his parish he considered
the most morally and spiritually sound – though the numbers attending
apparently dropped off after he rather tactlessly told them that probably
only about half of them could be counted among the elect predestined for
heaven.[8] Moreover, a minority of men and women now broke all links with
the established Church and worshipped instead in the gathered churches
of sects such as the Baptists, Seekers, Fifth Monarchists and Quakers.
Equally significantly for the first time in English history their right to
do so was enshrined in the constitution. In 1650 the Act for the Relief of
Peaceable People rescinded the legal requirement on all adults to attend
their parish church on Sundays, and a few years later the two documents

that underpinned the Cromwellian Protectorate – the 1653 Instrument of Government and the 1657 Humble Petition and Advice – both explicitly stated that all law-abiding, trinitarian Christians (with the exception of the adherents of 'popery and prelacy') who opted out of the national Church should not be discriminated against or persecuted.

V

The nature of the Interregnum state Church and the beliefs and practices of those who remained outside it are the subject of the second set of essays in this volume. Ann Hughes' and Elliot Vernon's contributions focus on the characteristics of the post-civil war national Church – or 'public profession' – and, contrary to the verdict of other past and present historians, both claim that its level of achievement was highly creditable. Hughes argues that the Interregnum saw a number of important and welcome ecclesiological developments, including a determined effort by the regime to augment clerical stipends and the establishment of committees of the triers and ejectors. The triers were a central body given responsibility for vetting new candidates for the ministry. The ejectors took the form of local county committees which were charged with investigating complaints of scandal and insufficiency against clerics already in post. Hughes maintains that both these groups carried out their work efficiently and reasonably sensitively, and that they were responsible for a significant improvement in the calibre of the parochial clergy. She also stresses the inclusive nature of the public profession and illustrates how substantial numbers of Independents and even some moderate Baptists found a home in the religious 'big tent' of Cromwellian England. She further claims that in supervising the Interregnum Church, Cromwell was open, flexible and responsive to the needs and concerns of local communities. Hughes concludes by arguing that, while the Interregnum national Church may have appeared an 'overall failure in principle', the reality on the ground was one of productive pragmatism creating 'real opportunity in practice'.

This positive assessment of the Interregnum Church is confirmed by Elliot Vernon's researches into the grassroots' impact of Presbyterian evangelisation in Lancashire and London during the late 1640s and 1650s. Vernon claims that many Presbyterian ministers within the public profession laboured tirelessly to bring about the spiritual and moral regeneration of their flocks, their principal tools in this work being preaching, catechising, and their insistence on the strict observance of the sabbath and on examination prior to receipt of the sacrament. He pays special attention to the practice of the morning exercise, whereby parishioners were encouraged to attend a month-long series of daily sermons and prayer sessions prior to beginning work. While Vernon acknowledges that these evangelical strategies, particularly sabbath observance and sacramental examination, were often resented and resisted by the laity, he insists that the clergy pressed on regardless and that they 'laboured, often heroically, to use the parochial structure as a means for the further Reformation of the English people'. The degree of success achieved by the governmental initiatives and evangelical campaigns described by Hughes and Vernon is, of course, difficult to assess precisely. Hughes, however, argues that many historians have condemned the public profession of the 1650s for failing to meet an unrealistically high achievement threshold, and Vernon suggests that the ultimate proof that the Presbyterian ministry achieved a significant measure of success was the tenacity of post-Restoration nonconformity.

VI

Whether or not the public profession was adequately meeting the spiritual needs of the majority of English men and women, some individuals undoubtedly found it wholly inadequate or unacceptable and sought alternative vehicles for their spiritual sustenance. Included in this category were both conservatives, such as Catholic recusants and Prayer Book Protestants, and religious radicals, such as Baptists and Quakers. Of these three groups – Catholics, Baptists and Quakers – most refused to have anything to do with the public profession, but some, such as the diarist John Evelyn, who hankered after the old Prayer Book form of Christianity, were rather more accommodating. Numbers of them dutifully attended their parish church even when the minister was not of their persuasion, supplementing what was for them an unappetising religious diet by participating in covert – or at times not so covert – illegal Prayer Book services. Ironically, the situation that these Prayer Book loyalists found themselves in during the late 1640s and 1650s was very similar to that of the conformist puritans within the pre-war established Church.

The first of three studies of these 'outsiders' is William Sheils's piece on the fortunes of the English Catholic community between 1640 and 1660. He begins by considering the extent of active Roman Catholic support for the Stuarts during the 1640s and early 1650s. After emphasising that the picture is a complex one, subject to marked regional variations, he concludes that, while Catholics were not 'an army in waiting' in 1642, they did rally to the king's cause in proportionately somewhat greater numbers than their Protestant neighbours. He goes on to consider how, both during the war years and after 1646, both armed and neutral Catholic landowners fared at the hands of the parliamentarians. Here again he stresses the individual and local variations and argues that they suffered least in those parts of the country, such as the North Riding of Yorkshire, where they remained well connected to the governing local elites, and most in those areas, such as East Anglia, where the success of a century of Protestant evangelisation had been more effective in excluding them from power and distancing them from their gentry neighbours. He concludes by pointing out that, although the Interregnum was a period of trial and retrenchment for the English Catholic community, it was also one that saw the emergence of important political, intellectual and spiritual developments that would prove significant in the long-term history of English Catholicism.

In her essay on the fortunes of Prayer Book Protestants during the English Revolution, Judith Maltby discusses another important disenfranchised group, and one that was far less used than the Roman Catholic community to finding itself excluded from the religious establishment. She shows how many of them, such as John Evelyn, refused to abandon the old Book of Common Prayer even after its outlawing in 1645, and how throughout the late 1640s and 1650s they continued to attend clandestine Prayer Book services, either in the own homes or in the churches of sympathetic clerics. The inclusion of services to mark the major feasts of the Christian year had been a prominent feature of the old liturgy, and Maltby goes on to argue that the decision by the Long Parliament to proscribe the celebration of Christmas, Whitsun and Easter proved both unpopular and unenforceable, and in some areas, such as Kent in 1647, it prompted a nostalgic call for a return to both the old pre-war liturgy and royal government. But despite this groundswell of support for the old liturgy, there was never any serious prospect that a Prayer Book counter-revolution would threaten the new puritan establishment, and even just a few months before the return of the King in 1660 the hopes of those who favoured the Elizabethan vision of the English Church over the more godly version then prevailing seemed destined to remain unfulfilled. Maltby describes how Prayer Book Protestants spent a great deal of time in the late 1640s and 1650s trying to understand why God had apparently so decisively turned against them, and how some of them concluded that their misfortunes were a divine punishment for the sacrilegious appropriation of so much ecclesiastical land and property during the Reformation of the previous century. She ends her piece by suggesting that the 'exile' experience of the 1650s helped to forge a clearer direction and identity for the episcopalian Church of England that – miraculously to its supporters – returned with the monarchy in 1660.

From the other end of the religious spectrum, radical Baptists and Quakers also strained the tolerationist instincts of the Interregnum regimes. Mark Bell's survey of the three strands of the mid-seventeenth-century

Baptist movement (General, Particular and Seventh Day) discusses the core beliefs shared by these influential sectarian groups, and shows how, in addition to their central determining belief in adult believers' baptism, it was their intense biblicism and preoccupation with the need for purity which made it impossible for the great majority of them to cooperate with the established public profession. He then goes on to outline their take on the politics of the revolutionary period and to explain how they managed to steer around the dangers they encountered through guilt by association with first the Levellers in the late 1640s and then the Fifth Monarchists in the late 1650s and early 1660s. It was by carefully dissociating themselves from these movements, both of which presented a direct challenge to the governments and social order of their day, that the Baptist leaders, he argues, managed to assure their survival into the post-Restoration period when so many other contemporary sects disappeared.

VII

The final three contributions to this volume move the spotlight away from the arguments and actions of the various competing religious interest groups discussed above, to consider instead how the upheavals of the 1640s and 1650s affected the consumers of religion: the mythical men and women in the streets of revolutionary England. Christopher Durston's piece focuses on the attempt by successive governments and the clergy of the public profession to force the nation to observe Sunday as a day entirely given over to public and private religious devotions. He discusses first the literary debate between the advocates of this whole-day Christian sabbath and those who argued instead that Sunday was a day of celebration and that the people should therefore be allowed to indulge in harmless pastimes and leisure activities after attending a Sunday morning service. He goes on to chart the passage in 1644, 1650 and 1657 of the increasingly rigorous sabbatarian legislation promoted by the Long, Rump and Protectorate Parliaments. He then considers the impact of these acts at the grassroots, arguing that while successive governments achieved a nominal conformity to their will, they never persuaded the nation to embrace with enthusiasm their particularly austere vision of Sunday. In conclusion, he claims that the unpopularity of the sabbatarian legislation only succeeded in further alienating the mass of the population from their new godly masters and thereby contributed to their emphatic repudiation in 1660.

Jacqueline Eales's essay attempts to pull together many of the themes discussed by the volume's previous contributors by presenting a case study of religious developments within Kent, a county, as she shows, with a long history of involvement with religious heterodoxy in the two centuries preceding 1640. She first reveals how, during the two years before the outbreak of fighting, the pent-up religious frustrations of the Caroline Personal Rule burst out into the open, producing sustained agitation against the bishops and the Book of Common Prayer, which in turn provoked rival petitioning campaigns in their favour. The radical assault on these two cornerstones of the established Church was led by several prominent Presbyterians in the county. As the 1640s progressed, however, the religious centre-ground was to shift steadily to the left, and by the end of the decade the Presbyterian firebrands of the pre-war period had become conservative establishment figures struggling desperately to hold together some form of national Church in the face of the separatist aspirations of the county's growing number of gathered churches. Eales goes on to illustrate the growing religious radicalism in some quarters of the county by citing a number of individual 'pilgrims' progresses', and showing how some men and women traversed the whole spectrum of religious experience on offer during the revolutionary years. By the late 1650s significant numbers of these 'seekers' had found a home in the burgeoning Quaker movement which developed quickly in Kent after 1655. While carefully delineating the growth of Protestant dissent in Kent, Eales is also keen to stress that, throughout the period from 1640 to 1660, many other Kentish men and women retained a strong attachment to the old Prayer Book Church and, despite their official proscription, secretly continued to observe its feasts, often within their own households.

The final essay in this volume, Beverly Adams's study of the development of Quakerism in the borough of Hertford from the mid-1650s to the mid-1660s, considers the impact of religious radicalism at the local level before and after the Restoration. It reveals how the movement spread quickly in a town with a long tradition of support for radical Protestantism, and how it won over a number of well respected and influential members of the urban community. Adams takes issue with many earlier accounts of Quaker persecution or 'sufferings', which have claimed that Friends remained passive and defenceless in the face of harassment by the authorities. She argues instead that Hertford's Quakers employed a range of legal devices in an attempt to challenge vigorously the validity of the punitive measures taken against them, and that, while they refused to compromise their core beliefs, they did not actively seek martyrdom and indeed did all they could to retain their status within the community. She further points out that this Quaker defiance was expressed in both spiritual and civic forms. On the one hand, they were determined to uphold the rights of the individual conscience and to demand a personal liberty to worship their God as they saw fit. On the other, they vigorously upheld their civic rights as free members of the Hertford borough, and objected strongly to the attempts of the county magistracy to erode their rights as citizens.

VIII

If the picture of diversity and a degree of religious pluralism which characterised the revolutionary years remains attractive to many modern readers, the subsequent restoration of the monarchy and of an episcopal Church of England should remind us that to many contemporaries the 1650s was a decade of spiralling governmental and spiritual chaos, marked by the further erosion of ancient liberties. The death of Oliver Cromwell in 1658 and his replacement by his far less able son, Richard, amplified this perception and many a 'parliament man' of the 1640s turned royalist as the only way to restore stability to the country. By 1660 republicanism had failed and the political nation as well as the general population embraced its default setting of 'Church and King'.

Like the monarchy, however, the 'restored' Church of England was not a carbon copy of its namesake before the civil war. Although a number of significant posts were held by sympathisers with the 'beauty of holiness' agenda of the 1630s – not least the early Restoration archbishops of Canterbury, William Juxon and Gilbert Sheldon – the Restoration Church of England was not a victory from the grave for William Laud. Respected Presbyterians, such as Edward Reynolds, accepted episcopal and other ecclesiastical preferment, no doubt hoping they would be forces of moderation and act as a bridge between the new emerging Anglicanism and the more conservative forms of what would become Protestant nonconformity. In a sense, the Restoration settlement also closed a chapter on a struggle between Church and state which had been going on since the Middle Ages and which had come to a head in fight over the 'Laudian' canons of 1640, for Parliament was now to be the 'governing body' of the Church of England. Henceforth, the ultimate authority to change the rules by which Church life was governed, canon law, was firmly established as lying with the two Houses of Parliament. Further, as John Spurr has argued, the post-Restoration Church did not so much defeat puritanism as absorb it, or at least aspects of it. The emergence of religious associations, such as the Society for the Promoting of Christian Knowledge (SPCK) as well as missionary societies, often with significant lay leadership, is evidence of a devotional shift in the established Church of England. All of this was a long way from the clericalist expansionism of Archbishop Laud.[9]

Whatever optimism there was from leading puritans at the beginning of Charles II's reign, it quickly evaporated. The dominant senior clergy and Tory MPs helped to ensure a religious settlement which could not be embraced except by those on the more traditional wing of Presbyterianism – and not even by some of them. The Act of Uniformity of 1662 led to the expulsion of around one thousand clergy who could not in conscience subscribe to the restored episcopal Church and Prayer Book. Ejecting clergy in large numbers was a practice well established by the parliamentary and Interregnum governments and the 1662 ejections must be seen in this context. A cluster of parliamentary acts, commonly called the Clarendon Code after Charles II's chief minister, harassed, suppressed and humiliated the King's nonconformist subjects, closing off to them (on paper at least) opportunities for education and public office. Despite their support for Charles I in the civil wars, toleration for Roman Catholics was simply not up for discussion.

Nonetheless, the genie was out of the bottle, and there was no way back to the Elizabethan and Jacobean consensus; no way back to the ideal of a single national Church which belonged to everyone and to which everyone belonged. The Clarendon Code, its fury fuelled in part by the sufferings of proto-Anglicans in the 1640s and 1650s, was an admission that the Church of England no longer held the religious monopoly. The *national* Church of England had become the *established* Church, merely enjoying certain privileges over its competitors in the religious marketplace. The Toleration Act of 1689, which hardly provided 'toleration' in the modern sense, was nonetheless a grudging admission that England's Christian pluralism was a reality in the religious life of the nation. This pluralism had been fostered and released by the remarkable two decades between 1640 and 1660, when the religious climate was characterised by extraordinary diversity, rapid change, and intense and often bitter animosity and conflict. No one volume can hope to portray every detail of this scene or to do full justice to its complexity or significance. Taken together, however, the following essays address many of the most crucial religious questions that exercised and divided the men and women of revolutionary England. In doing so, they throw new light on one of the most complicated, contentious, yet compelling chapters in English religious history.

Notes

1 John Morrill, 'The religious context of the English civil war' (first published in 1984), reprinted in John Morrill, *The Nature of the English Revolution* (Harlow, 1993).

2 For this analysis, see, among Hill's many books, *Puritanism and Revolution* (London, 1958), and *Society and Puritanism in Pre-Revolutionary England* (London, 1964).

3 Judith Maltby, *Prayer Book and People in Elizabethan and Early Stuart England* (Cambridge, 1998).

4 For more details on the Laudian project, see Peter Lake, 'The Laudian style', and Kenneth Fincham and Peter Lake, 'The ecclesiastical policies of James I and Charles I', both in Kenneth Fincham (ed.), *The Early Stuart Church* (Basingstoke, 1993).

5 For the popularity of the Laudians, see Christopher Haigh, *English Reformations: Religion, Politics and Society under the Tudors* (Oxford, 1993), and Alexandra Walsham, 'The parochial roots of Laudianism revisited: Catholics, anti-Calvinists and "parish Anglicans" in early Stuart England', *Journal of Ecclesiastical History*, 49 (1998).

6 See John Morrill, 'The Church of England, 1642–1649' (first published in 1982), and 'The attack on the Church of England in the Long Parliament' (first published in 1985), both in Morrill, *Nature of the English Revolution*.

7 A.G. Matthews, *Walker Revised* (Oxford, 1948), pp. 295–6.

8 For Woodward, see Bodleian Library, Oxford, Walker MS, C2, fol. 457.

9 John Spurr, 'From puritanism to dissent, 1660–1700', in Christopher Durston and Jacqueline Eales (eds), *The Culture of English Puritanism, 1560–1700* (Basingstoke, 1996); John Spurr, *The Restoration Church of England 1646–1689* (New Haven, CT, 1991).

PART I
Theology in Revolutionary England

1

Living with the living God: radical religion and the English Revolution

J. C. Davis

'Many of you have been witnesses of the finger of God, that hath been seen amongst us of late years.'
'God owned it by pleading their causes and fighting their battles for them ...'
[on the authority of Parliament 1648–53]
'The thing was more of God than of men.'
[on the execution of Charles I]
>   Colonel Thomas Harrison, extracts from his speech at his execution,
>   13 October 1660

'Will you make God the author of your treasons and murders?'
>   The Court to Thomas Harrison at his trial, 11 October 1660[1]

I

On 22 January 1655 Oliver Cromwell dissolved his first protectoral parliament with an extraordinary, angry and frustrated speech. The MPs had proven unwilling to build on the hard work done by the protectoral council, in drafting and approving ordinances before Parliament met. More particularly, he grieved at Parliament's failure to accept their role as instruments chosen to do God's work in the three nations of England, Scotland and Ireland. His earnestness was fired, he said, 'because I speak for God and not for men'. Looking back over the last fifteen years, they must realise that God was working his will among, and, if possible, through, them. 'We know the Lord hath poured this nation from vessel to vessel, till he poured it into your lap.' Power had been theirs 'by divine providence and dispensation'. Cromwell was well aware that a more cynical interpretation was being made of events since his expulsion of the Rump Parliament in April 1653, but 'To say that men bring forth these things, when God doth them, judge you if God will bear this.' There could be no excuse for the blasphemy of attributing the revolution and its consequences to the cunning of men rather than to God, even less so because 'We in this land have been otherwise instructed, even by the Word and Works and Spirit of God.' To ignore the teaching of scripture, providence and the Holy Spirit was to enter the most dangerous of territory; 'every sober heart' should 'take heed how he provokes, and falls into the hands of the living God by such blasphemies as these'.

Not satisfied with this dire message, Cromwell went on to evoke a more extreme penalty and, astonishingly, confirmed it by speaking for Christ. Deliberately to deny God's sovereignty over events in the world, imputing them to men when God had been instructing nations and men otherwise, was a blasphemy too far. And it provoked God more than normally: 'What then? Nothing but *a fearful falling into the hands of the living God.*'[2] Yet, more was to come. Such egregious blasphemy would lead God to withdraw the benefits of Christ's redemptive sacrifice; 'they speak against God, and they fall under his hand without a Mediator.' In denying 'His works in the world, by which he rules kingdoms', 'we provoke the Mediator'. 'And he may say, I'll leave you to God, I'll not intercede for you, let him tear you to pieces; I'll leave thee to fall into God's hands; thou deniest me my sovereignty and power committed to me, I'll not intercede nor mediate for thee; thou fallest into the hands of the living God.'[3]

There is a political theology invoked here which has been barely recognised. Cromwell was no theologian and we must be careful not to read too much into this outburst. Nevertheless his message that the very essence of a Trinitarian God, with the Father redeeming and reconciling fallen humanity to him through the sacrifice of his son, might be set aside by a living God whose angry interventionism could lead to the withdrawal of redemptive mediation was clear. To deny God's control of political and military events was to risk not only rebuke or temporary anger but being cast permanently into outer darkness, bereft of hope. Behind the redemptive God was an angry and potentially savage deity and Christ himself could be provoked to partake of that character. If we are to understand the political mind set of mid-seventeenth-century England, we, like our ancestors if in a different way, need to acknowledge the living God. What can we learn about him?

II

He was above all a controlling God, not only omniscient and omnipotent but ceaselessly intervening in the events of this world. He had laid out the framework of history from the creation, through the Fall, the trials and tribulations of Israel, his Incarnation and redemptive sacrifice, to the Second Coming and Last Judgement. But, in between those milestones, he was a constant, participatory presence. The exact chronology of the key staging posts yet to come might only be visible through a glass darkly but, for those with eyes to see and ears to hear, the shaping influence of the living God in contemporary history could be starkly apparent. Modern historians may attribute Parliament's unexpected victories in the first and second civil wars to factors such as greater resources, strategic advantage, superior organisation, greater political support, leadership qualities, or even the de facto construction of a military/fiscal state. At the time, however, victory was commonly and even officially attributed to the virtually unaided efforts of an interventionist, ceaselessly active, arbitrary, judgemental and, to a surprising degree, capricious God. He both gave victory and inflicted defeat. Rejecting the title of king on 13 April 1657, Cromwell reflected on God's harsh dealings with the Stuarts. 'God in his severity has not only eradicated a whole family and thrust them out of the land for reasons best known to himself, [but] has made the issue and close of it to be the very eradication of a name or title ... God has seemed providentially not only to strike at the family but at the name.'[4] But backsliding by God's chosen could also expose them to divine displeasure. Cromwell acknowledged the defeat of his 'Western Design' at Hispaniola in April 1655 as just such a rebuke. 'We have cause to be humbled at the reproof God gave us at San Domingo, upon the account of our sins, as well as others.'[5]

Human initiative, vision and creativity, however important they might be, were dwarfed by divine will. The living God required the submission of individuals, institutions and nations to be obedient instruments of this will. To act otherwise was sinful, or a tempting of a God whose dynamism obliged his servants to accept that they were always *disposable* instruments, servants for only as long as they were useful and accepted their servitude as perfect freedom. One implication of this was the futility of any personal or national reliance on secular or ecclesiastical institutions, the inanity of being wedded and glued to forms rather than to God's evolving will. From this perspective, the civil wars were 'wars of religion' in the most unmediated sense. They were conflicts in which the Lord of Hosts was the principal protagonist and ultimate victor. The destruction of the ancient constitution in the revolution of 1648–9 and the subsequent conquest of Ireland and Scotland by God's armies reinforced this point of view and gave it official status. But this nexus between the living God and the human beings available as possible instruments of his will was pregnant with irony, particularly but not exclusively, for his parliamentarian servants.

For the living God could be capricious and wilful rather than a follower of rules, a breaker rather than an observer of forms. God could be, as Alexandra Walsham has described him, 'a God who behaves more like a feudal warlord jealously engaged in a personal vendetta than a stern but benevolent Father and Redeemer'.[6] Those who bridled at the arbitrariness of monarchs (or even of parliaments) and strove to maintain the limits on their powers had to swallow what looked remarkably like the arbitrary, even tyrannical, demands of divine sovereignty. God was also ubiquitous, functioning with alarming variations of enthusiasm on all sides and at all levels of society. He was, or so it was claimed, available to Roman Catholics, Protestants, 'Arminians' and 'puritans', manifest equally in elite and popular cultures. He made appearances as the God of royalists as well as of parliamentarians.[7] His intervention could be responsible for the sting of a bee or a spider falling into a bowl of porridge, but he also shaped political and international events on all sides and for all nations. The audience for printed news of his doings was voracious and widespread, reaching well beyond the godly elites.[8] Just as Cromwell saw the triumphs of the New Model Army as God's victories and his mercies, so royalists could eventually hail the Restoration as God leading Israel out of exile.[9] Readings of providence might inform the image of Cromwell as a latter-day Gideon, but they also underpinned the cult of Charles the Martyr.[10] The living God, and demonstrations of his support, became the greatest recruiting sergeant and the shaper of military culture for a generation locked into what in the most important respects was a holy war.

For servants of the living God perhaps the most troubling ambiguities were raised when the pursuit of his will seemed to run counter to his instructions recorded in his words in scripture. God's ire could obviously be raised by failure to meet the standards of the ten commandments. This applied equally to the first table (Commandments 1 to 4), with its warnings against idolatry, blasphemy and the worship of false gods, and the second table's requirements regarding conduct towards others (Commandments 5 to 10). Reformation itself could be seen to be about preventing failures under either table, striving for purity of religion and the reformation of manners. In either case, reformation, or the warding off of God's anger, could be an urgent matter of both personal safety and national security. Opening his second protectoral parliament on 17

September 1656, Cromwell urged members to join with him in securing the nation against threats from within and the international threat of a resurgent Catholicism led by Spain. Armed preparation and reformation were to be the twin props of such security: 'they are scarcely distinct'. 'So in my conscience, if I were to show at this hour, where the security of the nations will lie, forces, arms, watchings, parts, your being and freedom, be as politic and vigilant as you can be, I would say in my very conscience, and as before Almighty God I speak it, I think your reformation, if it be honest and thorough, and just, it will be your best security.'[11] In the final analysis, reformation took priority over rearmament.

Fear of idolatry, which enraged God, thereby exposing individuals and the nation to danger, was a theme of both provincial and metropolitan sermons.[12] The problem was that attaching primacy to anything but the direct will of the living God could come to seem idolatrous.[13] Texts themselves could become idols.[14] To uphold any obstacle to God's will became both idolatrous – an offence against the first table – and, because by enraging God it endangered others, also a sin against the second table. So John Cooke, prosecutor at the trial of Charles I, could argue that the regicide was justified because monarchy had become morally equivalent to murder or adultery in its defiance of God's will.[15] Here, in particular, was a point of extreme difficulty for those committed to realising the will of God. Not only did the killing of the King run counter to the standard injunctions of Romans 13 (condemning resistance to the powers that be) and 1 Peter 13–14 (submission to governors), it also breached the oath of the Solemn League and Covenant made 'in the presence of Almighty God', which committed those taking it to defend the King's 'person and authority' and 'power and greatness'. It was a difficulty with which Cromwell wrestled in his famous letters to his cousin Robert Hammond on 6 and 25 November 1648, on the eve of the military purge of Parliament and the regicide. The answer was to 'look into providences', the promptings of the living God, and in this case the driving force of his will brushed aside even his own scriptural injunctions and oaths sworn in his name.[16]

Such tensions and their differing responses to them, as well as divergences over how to deal with idolatry and sin, drove wedges between the godly, fracturing their unity, and leading to competing claims as to the will of the living God. By the 1650s he appeared to be prompting his chosen in many different, particularised and contrasting ways. One response to this was to accept at least a temporary plurality, 'leaving every man free to the Grace of God and to the work of the Spirit, who worketh all things in the Hearts of the Sons of Men, according to the Counsel and Good Pleasure of His own Will'.[17] But such provisional liberty of conscience, waiting for God to steer consciences towards unity, was anathema to those who saw the immediate will of God with blinding clarity. For John Rogers, for example, anything short of replacing the present decay with the apocalyptic prospect of the Fifth Monarchy of Christ was apostasy and defiance of God's will.[18] However much the persistence of such disunity grieved the hearts of the faithful, it was the living God who would bring it to an end. The regicide Colonel John Barkstead reflected on this in his speech at his execution on 19 April 1662. 'Indeed as to those that fear the Lord in the nation, I could wish that the Lord would settle them, and make them of one mind; but that is the work of the Lord, and it must lie there; and truly he will do it in his time.'[19]

III

In his classic essay 'God and the English Revolution', Christopher Hill argued that there were three 'Gods' at work in the English Revolution.[20] The first of these was a god of authority and tradition who blessed the established order. The second was a god of justice, rather than of continuity − a justice to be found and tested by the study of scripture. Finally, there was a god to be found in every believer: the Spirit. This was the source of claims for religious equality and of religious radicalism in the period. If the 1640s began with almost universal fidelity to the first of these gods, it ended with the apparent success of the second and only partially successful moves to discipline the third. But was the living God a stabilising or destabilising force? The problem with Hill's model is that all variants suggest versions of divinely acceptable equilibrium or stability, achieved either by recognising God's endorsement of continuity, by the decoding and implementation of scripturally revealed rules, or by an assertion of spiritual equality.

There is something to each of these aspirations, but the living God escapes them all. What if God, this side of the last judgement, was a perpetual destabiliser, and obliged to be so, in part by the imperfections of the human instruments at his disposal? What if he was not a God of order and equilibrium, but a God of unceasing and dynamic change, a God of seemingly arbitrary and inconsistent will rather than of rules? Of course, as true faith was a vital bulwark against the vicissitudes and contingencies of a fragile security in this brief life and the principal hope of salvation thereafter, the right kind of religious order was a priority. But to engender such a stability was difficult. The blunt instruments of an enforced religious uniformity had been tried and for many of the godly in the 1640s had been found wanting. Attempts to produce a coherently godly society through binding it with oaths and covenants or through the casuistical discipline of informing and tutoring consciences also proved flimsy means of salvaging some remnants of stability in face of the living God.[21]

IV

In important respects, the civil wars were a prolonged struggle for sustained instrumentality under divine providence.[22] Part of that struggle was played out in days of fasting, humiliation, prayer, contemplation of the ways and words of the Lord, and repentance. Within days of its opening, the Long Parliament had declared a national fast day. As the crisis deepened, these became more regular. Between February 1642 and February 1649 the MPs observed eighty-five monthly fasts with additional days at moments of special crisis or thanksgiving. In response, Charles I ordered regular fast days for all his loyal subjects, to be held on the second Friday of each month, beginning on 10 November 1643. At their most basic, days of fasting and humiliation were a means of diverting or assuaging divine anger.[23] More profoundly, they were exercises in retuning to the wavelengths of the living God with the purpose of assuring continued personal and group instrumentality, a theme well illustrated by the sermons preached on these occasions and frequently published.

Twin means towards succeeding in that purpose, leitmotivs of the fast sermons, were reformation and the excision of idolatry. From the first, the sermons emphasised the linkage of these themes. God, the MPs were told, always began his reformations by punishing idolatry. The unleashing of iconoclasm was the counterpart to fasting and humiliation. William Dowsing, the iconoclast *par excellence* of this period, possessed an almost complete set of the published fast sermons.[24] While the fear of being an 'unhumbled people' did not go away, there were few doubts as to God's responsiveness. Ralph Josselin, for example, duly noted that victory in Ireland at the battle of Rathmines in August 1649 had come the day after a public fast.[25] Obliging God to respond through repeated fasts could, George Fox thought, become a 'burthen to the Lord'.[26]

What was the character of this active, and sometimes harassed, living God as revealed in the fast sermons? Just before Christmas 1641, at the end of a year's legislative activity limiting the King's prerogatives and erecting barriers to royal absolutism, Edmund Calamy evoked a God operating on a very different basis. Kings might be limited but God had 'an independent and illimited Prerogative over all Kingdoms and Nations to build them, or destroy them as he pleaseth'. 'If God's power over Kingdoms be so large and so absolute; let all the world stand in awe, and not dare to sin against such a mighty and terrible God.'[27] The struggle against absolute monarchy, as against absolute parliaments, was waged in large part by men who firmly believed in total submission to an absolute God. On the first of Parliament's fast days, Stephen Marshall stressed the fluidity, the changeableness of God's will. He could abandon a wayward people with the consequence that 'all their strength is gone, as Sampson was when his Lockes were cut off'. To avoid such a fate, the nation must 'bee on God's side in all causes' wherever that might lead them.[28]

Such an aspiration meant that unceasing attention must be paid to God's doings in this world. Adaptation to God's providential will meant, first of all, taking it seriously. The Westminster Assembly, an Anglo-Scots body charged with reforming the Reformation, led by example. In December 1645, with victory in the civil war beginning to look assured, its committee on providence warned against complacency and noted signs of induration of heart. In its Large Catechism, developed in the early summer of 1647, the Assembly dealt with the Lord's Prayer phrase by phrase. 'Thy will be done' drew admonitions against the tendency to repine against God's providence. 'Give us this day' meant not only expectation of material provision but 'waiting upon the providence of God from day to day'. On the second commandment, with its warning against idolatry, the Catechism noted 'God's sovereignty over us, and property in us, his fervent zeal for his own worship and his revengeful indignation against all false worship ... accounting the breakers of this commandment his enemies and such as hate him'. The third commandment, taking the Lords name in vain, included 'murmuring and quarrelling at, curious prying into, and misapplying of God's decrees and providences'.[29]

Given the omnipotence, interventionism and potential for anger of the living God, the appropriate posture for his saints was submission, the surrender of autonomy and acceptance of dependence. According to Jeremiah Burroughs, preaching in September 1641, it was 'the greatest happiness on earth to be instrumentall for God'. Divine activity achieved things. Human activity achieved nothing. Human instruments were virtually passive in God's hands.[30] At most, their agency consisted in readiness and watchfulness, observing and following God's promptings. But they could never claim credit. 'This is that day', proclaimed Cornelius Burgess in his sermon for November 1641, 'wherein our God came riding to us in his Chariot of Triumph, and made himself fearful in praises, by doing wonders, and leaving us no more to doe, but to praise his Name.'[31]

This sense of the controlling will of the living God and of human instrumentality was deepened for many by the experiences of war. Cromwell was not alone in attributing the outcomes of battle to God but he was particularly graphic and particularly insistent that in the end God's will was shrouded in inscrutability. Reporting on the storming of Drogheda in 1649, he wrote, 'it was the Spirit of God, who gave your men courage, and took it away again; and gave the enemy courage, and took it away again; and gave your men courage again, and therewith this happy success. And therefore it is good that God alone have all the glory.' It was the wilfulness of God that explained the ebb and flow of battle.[32] In July 1653, opening the Nominated Assembly, he noted the 'strange windings and turnings of providence: those very great appearances of God, *in crossing and thwarting the purposes of men.*'[33] Earlier, in a letter to Oliver St John after the battle of Preston, he mused on the involuntary instrumentality of men to God. 'They shall, will they, nill they, fulfil the pleasure of God, and so shall serve our generation.'[34] John Milton likened Christians to soldiers with providence as their drum.[35] There was though something too regular implied by this metaphor; for, however much one focused on God's great design, his favour was too provisional, his will too ephemeral, to be identified with any certainty. The Scots minister George Gillespie, preaching to the Westminster Assembly in March 1644, could point only to negatives as encouragement for his Anglo-Scots audience. What united them was fear of the Last Days and of the living God. 'God would not have England say, "Mine own hand hath saved me" Judg. vii 2; neither will he have Scotland to say, "My hand hath done it": but he will have both to say, His hand hath done it, when we were lost in our own eyes.' He was equally clear that God would not be bound by his own prophecies.[36]

If the living God provided so little scope for the independent wills of men and nations, he was equally impervious to their institutions and laws. As the crisis of late 1648 unfolded, the preachers of fast sermons warned MPs of the irrelevance of human constitutions and formalities. On 29 November, a bare week before Pride's Purge, George Cokayn preached a sermon with a deftly summative title: *Flesh Expiring and Spirit Inspiring in the New Earth: or God himselfe supplying the room of withered Powers, judging and inheriting all Nations.* Only a month before, Peter Sterry had warned MPs of the futility of clinging to hope in constitutional arrangements given the imminence and immanence of the living God. 'Who is not amazed to see the changes that are made in the Garment of this Earth? One day we see it, as a field Flourishing with fair Hopes; another Day, that Field vanish't, and in its Place, as a City on Fire, or a Sea of Blood. He that now discerns not the Light of Heaven, the Brightness of the Godhead, which is Christ coming upon us and thus changing us; what manner of Night is He in? sure a Night, as black as the Shadow of Death.'[37]

The day after the King's execution, John Cardell preached the sermon *Gods Wisdom Justified and Mans Folly Condemned, Touching all manner of Outward Providential Administrations.* He reminded the MPs that 'God by his *Providence* brings his People into *straits*, and *difficulties* and *dangers*, on *purpose* many times to take *occasion* from thence to *magnifie* his own *great Power*, and *Wisdom*, and *Goodness* towards them in their *Deliverance.*' 'Duty belongs to us, events to God.'[38] Certainly, for the revolutionaries the regicide and the destruction of the ancient constitution remained the work of God rather than of men. At most, Milton conceded, it was done by the people acting as God's instruments and under his guidance.[39] For Sir Henry Vane the younger, it was a matter of acknowledging the sovereignty of the living God over both nations and individuals. 'Christ the Son of God, is king *de jure*, over the whole world, but in particular, in relation to these three kingdoms. He ought not to be kept out of his throne, nor his visible government, that consists in the authority of his word and laws, suppressed and trampled under foot, under any pretence whatsoever.' Vane's war against King Charles, he argued, was not treason but 'the duty I owed to God the universal King'. It was that universal King who, according to Vane, brought about his spiritual awakening when he was fourteen or fifteen, destroyed the monarchy in England, and brought him in the end to the scaffold.[40] Among others executed at the Restoration, Colonels Scroop and Okey also believed that God had brought or sent them to the scaffold.[41] At the opening of Cromwell's second protectoral parliament, John Owen had preached a sermon in which he called on all present to acknowledge that God had founded Zion in England despite all opposition.[42] With remorseless logic, those who survived to the Restoration had to acknowledge that what God had built through them as his instruments, he had also brought crashing down.

V

It would be a mistake, however, to identify these beliefs solely with military and religious zealots, or with a hard-core, revolutionary vanguard. Both international, 'scientific' networks and individuals examining their own experiences, for example, shared many of the same preconceptions.

The cosmopolitan European network of correspondents associated with Samuel Hartlib blended interest in the advancement of natural science and progressive schemes for social and economic improvement with concern for the international Protestant cause and with the living God's plans, both immediate and apocalyptic.[43] Typical in this respect was a letter from John Beale to Hartlib in August 1657 which mixed the quotidian and the apocalyptic. It began with a discussion of the preservation of beer, suddenly and matter-of-factly switched to the apocalypse, and concluded with some comments on the fermentation of liquids and the possibility of a universal language.[44] A petition to Parliament among Hartlib's papers concerning fishing and colonial settlement in North America concludes by reminding MPs of the imminence of Christ's Second Coming.[45] Writing from Paris in the summer of 1659, Henry Oldenburg discussed affairs in the Ottoman Empire and the state of libraries in Abyssinia but ended by asking for further information about books on the apocalypse.[46] From the early 1630s, when the correspondence begins, the network saw the '*apocalipsis*' in a European-wide context, emerging from a struggle between Christ and Antichrist which moved from the Netherlands to Austria to Poland to Sweden to Germany.[47] For Hartlib and his associates, England was not the peculiar or the exclusive theatre of God's holy war.

There were, on the other hand, those in the correspondence network who were sceptical of too close a reading of millennial expectancy. John Dury was keen to dissociate the question of the admission of the Jews to a Christian commonwealth from that of the millennium: 'we are very much inclined to mistake in conjectures of that nature.'[48] From Zurich in December 1654 he wrote to Hartlib: 'The millenary men in due time God will beat off from extravagancies and what I can contribute shall not be wanting if God give life and leisure.'[49] By contrast, John Beale, again writing to Hartlib in the later 1650s, retained his millennial enthusiasm. God was in constant 'Conferences with the spirite of Man'. This was an age in which 'Light is Broake foorth'.[50] In January 1658 he was warning against those who 'make too much haste to set up a fifth Monarchy by carnall weapons, and by a carnall attempt against Civill Government. But surely there is a day in which the God will bring gold for brasse, for iron, silver etc.'[51] His faith in the coming apocalypse undimmed, Beale could see no role for violence; the work was to be done by God himself.

God's appearance and intervention in the world was essential even to the advancement of scientific knowledge. In his notebooks for 1640, Hartlib recorded his conviction that the advancement of learning aspired to by Francis Bacon could not be achieved 'till God himself reveals those *principia rerum* out of which everything was made up, unto us'.[52] Possibly in October 1652, Hartlib received a letter from Morgan Lloyd [Llwyd]. Writing from Wrexham, Lloyd explained that, although he did not know Hartlib, he was contacting him because he was famous and appeared to have had prophetic status conferred on him by God. Like others, Lloyd was waiting for 'the kingdome of God and the salvation of Israel'. Perhaps Hartlib could confirm the rumour of the appearance of environmental signs of Christ's imminence: 'the truth of the signe of the son of man in Germany or Poland in the clouds'. In closing, Lloyd excused himself for badgering Hartlib on the grounds of the importance of 'so great a matter as that of the appearance of Jesus'.[53]

Nevertheless, disappointed hopes pulled people back to the here and now. In the spring of 1655, as the Protectorate began to appear at least a constitution with medium-term prospects, Moses Wall wrote to Hartlib, who was he knew still looking for 'Apocalypticall truths', 'time passeth, and there are revolutions, yet not the thing we wait for, that is, when he shall come who is the desire of all nations'. In the meantime, he counselled, they must work for order since God is a God of order and not of confusion.[54] As the new year of 1659 opened, Wall wrote again to Hartlib reflecting on prospects and retrospects. The present outlook was a dismal one of 'God's withdrawing himself from us'. Wall looked nostalgically back to the civil war when the issues were clear: 'god was among us, he showed himself plainly, he roused himself like a mighty giant, and was ready to give more of himself, and to open his bosome to receive us'. All was shattered when Cromwell led the nation into reliance on constitutional and institutional contrivances, and usurped the throne of King Jesus: 'god withdrew and hid himself, and the body of the Nation proved apostaticall'. Wall had retired to the country to clear his mind. A first revival of hope came with Oliver's death, God's 'seasonable taking away of the late greate man'. Still, he felt

> at a loss in apocalypticall prophecyes; for many hopes from thence have been given us, but every vision faileth; we believed that the times of refreshing therin mentioned wold have come before now, and still darkness is upon us. Some will say, what would you have? Are not the Saints exalted in this our age? What would you have? I answere, Saints so called, or that call themselves so, are exalted, but by what arts? Againe, what is to have formall saints, out-side professours to be exalted to live, after the flesh, and to enjoy the great things of a polluted, and dark world, what is this to seeing and enjoying god, and to performing that greate and comfortable promise ... Jehovah the Lord lives among them and in them.[55]

In 1651 Edward Lane challenged John Dury's preface to a new edition of Joseph Mede's *Clavis Apocalyptica* on the basis that Dury attached too much importance to the visible Church in these latter days. What is interesting about their correspondence in this dispute is how much common ground they shared. Dury acknowledged that there was no perfect Church on earth: 'our present condition is a wilderness of confusion and desolation' and 'we have not yet any permanent Citie on earth'. The perfection that was 'to come before the Church on Earth be taken up into Heaven' was that prophesied in the books of Daniel and Revelation, and that was in the hands of King Jesus. For his part, Lane agreed that one should not be too critical of the existing visible churches for fear of giving comfort to Antichrist, but like Dury he knew that such perfection as the Church might enjoy could come only with God's fulfilling of His own prophecies.[56]

The dynamic, living God whose promises formed the only glimpses available of the post-apocalyptic society, and whose goading was designed to spur humanity towards the denouement of history, was a God who undermined all attempts to set up an ideal society or an ideal Church on earth by human contrivance. God was a destroyer, not a sanctifier of carnal forms; hence the deep ambivalence here about re-*form*-ation.[57]

VI

How to discern the doings of the living God and his immediate will were primary concerns to those charged with considering the affairs of the nation, to those interested in international power struggles, and even to those involved in the development of natural philosophy. But what about the living God's relationship with private individuals? Was this not the age of the birth of 'bourgeois individualism', of 'the rise of the spirit of individualism', of the emergence of autobiography as 'a written articulation of the self' produced 'in order to make the self heard and known' – in short the age of puritan individualism? Until very recently, a key to the forging of that individualism was held to be the rise of the spiritual autobiography, asserting and charting 'freedom for the individual to work out his own salvation in his own way'.[58] Such assertions, the basic building blocks of a liberal, rational society, were seen as fuelled by puritan introspection, encouraged and exemplified by the spiritual journals or autobiographies written by the godly. This was an interpretation which held sway until the 1960s, if not beyond, but has subsequently come to seem beleaguered. Even while the links are being asserted, doubts surface. The editors of *Her Own Life: Autobiographical Writings by Seventeenth-Century Englishwomen* note the absence of 'the personal anatomizing that we might expect to find in autobiography'. In one case, the autobiographer 'creates herself', but only as 'an extreme model of feminine passivity'.[59] There are signs of editorial frustration here that are echoed in John Stachniewski and Anita Pacheo's recent edition of John Bunyan's *Grace Abounding*. Bunyan's need to conform to an 'elect paradigm *distorts* what the autobiography does contain'. 'Bunyan was *lumbered* with the belief that God was the author of the story he was trying to write.'[60] 'Distort' and 'lumbered' are not the language of editorial confidence and should alert us that something is wrong.[61]

There can be no doubt that the daily record of spiritual experience kept by individuals was a key feature of seventeenth-century English Protestant piety. An impressive number of such accounts survive, either as spiritual diaries or as retrospective narrative accounts, but we should be cautious about their uniqueness, ubiquity and their character as spiritual autobiographies.[62] Not all seventeenth-century diaries, memorials and 'autobiographies' were works of spiritual introspection; diaries, such as those of Samuel Pepys, Robert Hooke and even William Laud, demonstrate more prosaic preoccupations. But the keeping of journals as aids to 'daily direction' was widespread from the mid-Elizabethan period onwards. It is these spiritual journals, and what they tell us about the relationship of individuals and the living God, which will concern us here. In looking at that relationship, it is immediately apparent that one function of the journals was to keep a daily record of 'providences' or 'mercies', but we are looking for some indications of a more profound relationship.[63]

The most famous and influential classic of the genre was John Bunyan's *Grace Abounding to the Chief of Sinners*, first published in 1666 and substantially expanded in its third (1674) and fifth (1680) editions. From its very beginning, even on the title page, Bunyan made clear that the narrative centre of the text was not Bunyan himself but God. *Grace Abounding* is 'A Brief Relation of the exceeding mercy of God in Christ to his poor servant *John Bunyan*'. It is the story of 'the work of God upon my own Soul ... for he woundeth and his hands make whole'. It is not an account of either Bunyan's self-development or development of self, but a narration of 'the merciful working of God upon my Soul', of 'the goodness and bounty of God towards me'. The story is not of Bunyan's discovery of himself but of 'the Father in his Son'.[64] Throughout the work Bunyan refers to the parallel experience and loss of personal autonomy of St Paul, and the text is constructed as a collage of scriptural references. As far as possible, that is, the account was cast in the words of holy writ rather than those of John Bunyan.

Personal autonomy, the agency of the self, is indeed hard to find in this classic of spiritual 'autobiography'. Rather we are presented with a series of divine actings on the blank canvas of Bunyan's personality and experience. It was God who moved his parents to send him to school when their relative poverty might have precluded them from doing so. God sent him childhood dreams. God stayed with him even in a youthful phase of carelessness towards sin. God twice saved him from drowning, once from a poisonous snake, and then again from injury when he was a soldier in the civil war. God brought about his marriage to a woman who, providentially, brought two important spiritual books to the marriage. Again and again, God shaped Bunyan's life and experience, sending voices to him and using agents like the ungodly woman who reproved him for swearing or the godly women who, sitting in the sunshine in Bedford, conversed of godly things and inspired him.[65] God stopped him from falling in with the Ranters, kept him worrying about his spirituality, sent him dreams of redemption, inspired him to reread the whole Bible to see if anyone who trusted in the Lord was ever confounded, and time and time again God sent key scriptural references into his head when they were needed.[66] If we are what we remember, it is important to recognise that in *Grace*

Abounding memory is a field of divine agency. The Bunyan depicted there is endlessly reconfigured and redirected by God, by 'Grace Abounding'. Indeed, at one level, the text operates as a warning against personal autonomy. At the moments when Bunyan is tempted to take responsibility for his own salvation, then he is in most danger, 'going about to establish my own righteousness, [I] had perished therein, had not God in mercy shewed me more of my state by nature'.[67]

Bunyan's sainthood does not come then through his own agency. Equally his spiritual authenticity rests not on any sense of selfhood, not in any partnership with himself, but in the denial of self and in total reliance on a living and ever-active God. 'It would be too long for me here to stay, to tell you in particular how God did set me down in all the things of Christ, and how he did, that he might so do, lead me into his words, yea and how he did also open them up unto me, make then shine before me, and cause them to dwell with me, and comfort me over and over, both of his own being, and the being of his Son and Spirit, and Word and Gospel.'[68] God guided what Bunyan read, how he read it, what he wrote and how he wrote it. When he became a preacher, it was God who made him into a pastor of his congregation. 'I thank God, he gave unto me some measure of bowels and pity for their souls.'[69] It was God who not only led him away from taking pride in his skills as a preacher but directed him away from preaching Hell and damnation to expounding a gospel of greater comfort.[70] In all of these ways, and other more worldly ones such as preventing him from having carnal relations with women other than his wife, 'the Lord did lead me'.[71] Perhaps most graphically, in his later account of his imprisonment, Bunyan saw himself not at the disposition of his gaolers but in the hands of the living God. 'I lie waiting', he wrote in his confinement, 'the good will of God, to do with me as he pleaseth ... they can do no more, nor go no farther than God permits them.'[72] Even his persecutors were captives in the hands of the living God and shaped by his will. For Bunyan, narrativity with the self as the focal point was an impossibility. This life was a wilderness.[73] The pilgrim's progress through it had to be guided every step of the way by God. In other words, only God's doings, not man's, could generate a narrative pattern.[74]

This sense of life not as a sequence of choices through which the self is actualised but as a series of divinely construed occasions and situations by which God subdues, contains and even eliminates the self is the leit-motiv of seventeenth-century spiritual 'autobiography'. Richard Norwood, who wrote his 'Confession' in the 1630s when he was approaching fifty, had been a teacher of mathematics and surveyor of Bermuda. But in his account this potentially fascinating story becomes merely the shadowy background to God's shaping of his life. Like Bunyan, Norwood was saved by God from drowning in childhood. It was the Lord who used his parents and teachers to plant some knowledge of Christianity in him. God gave him the opportunity to study mathematics and sent Mr Topsall to him as instructor. God caused him to quarrel with the stage players who otherwise might have led him astray. 'The Lord can change the disposition of my heart', 'I conceived and understood him to be who giveth all things not only their beings but also their well beings, whose mercy is over all his works, who hath a care of all his creatures giving them food in due season and whatsoever true contentment, loveliness, comfort or joy there is in anything in this world it is not from Satan ... but from God.'[75] The alternative to divine guidance was not personal autonomy, not selfhood, but paralysis and collapse or, yet worse, the guidance of Satan. John Crook, writing in the 1630s, recalled how the rigorous piety he had practised from his youth had excited the admiration of others but had left him discontented and with a sense of hypocrisy. Rather than being a self-dependent individual, he saw himself as 'a cast-away', until he heard a voice saying 'Fear not ... I will help thee' and calling for his submission in all things to the will of God.[76]

Agnes Beaumont's story of the persecution she suffered both as a nonconformist and a woman, is an account of how God guided her through all her troubles, on one occasion sending John Bunyan on horseback past her home so that she could ride behind him to a religious meeting. 'The Lord hath made troublesome times for me; praying times, humbling and mourning, and heart searching times.'[77] Beaumont's experience of being shaped by an ever-active and watchful God was shared by other women who recorded their lives in diaries or narratives. An Collins introduced her *Divine Songs and Meditations* (1653) with the assertion:

> I chiefly aim that this should be
> Unto the praise of God's most blessed name.

At those moments when she was tempted to rely on herself, she had found herself fearful, distempered and dismayed. Nothing would give peace and content 'But saving graces and God's holy word'.[78] The *Report and Plea* (1654) of the prophetess Anna Trapnel showed her times of spiritual crisis as moments of struggle between the truth of God's word and her 'self'. Peace came when she abandoned self and submitted to God's providential control. 'For in all that was said by me, *I was nothing*, the Lord put all in my mouth and told me what I should say, and that from the written word, he put it in my mouth: so that I will have nothing ascribed to me, but all honour and praise given to him whose right it is, even to Jehovah, who is the King that lives for ever.'[79]

Defending herself as an excommunicant from an Independent congregation in 1659, Susanna Parr argued that it was not her will but God's that had led to the impasse. 'Weakness is entailed upon my sex in general, and for myself in particular, I am a despised woman, a woman full of natural and sinful infirmities, the chiefest of sinners and the least of saints.'[80] Alice Thornton's intention was, as her editors noted, 'to record and remind herself of God's goodness in saving her from losses and grief and leading her to salvation through suffering'. She entitled her record *A Book of Remembrances of all the remarkable deliverances of myself, husband and children.*[81] Sarah Davy's *Heaven Realised* (1670) followed a similar pattern: the redemptive interventions of a sometimes harsh but always caring and merciful God in the life of an intrinsically worthless individual. 'I abhor myself in dust and ashes.' 'I am a poor weak nothing, not able to do anything if thou [God] shouldst leave me, never so little.'[82] In this sense there was no narrative, no history without God's sovereignty. One last example may suffice. Anne Wentworth would not even have felt able to write her *Vindication* (1670) without divine instruction. 'Nor durst I ... put myself into this work, without his express command concerning it.' Her narrative, like so many others of its type, is one of the deconstruction, rather than the configuration, of a self. It was the story of God '*breaking* me all to pieces in myself, and making me to become as *nothing* before him ... *bowing* my own will and fitting me for his service'. 'I was as a thing that *is* not.'[83]

VII

This essay has stressed the importance of the living God in shaping early modern thinking about the affairs of the nation, the world and individual experience. Of course, we must place our understanding of this in a wider context of tensions between the dramatic and the mundane, between divine mystery and reason, and between scripture and providence as revelatory of God's will. Not everyone was preoccupied all of the time with the controlling intentions of the living God. George Herbert bemoaned the tendency of country folk to think that nature operated independent of the immediate intervention of divine will.[84] Marchamont Nedham thought that in civil society God ruled only mediately.[85] Ironically, as a writer he was often in the pay of men who thought God's intervention in the world, the affairs of the nation and their own lives was much more immediate. Thomas Hobbes thought an individual's primary religious duty was to honour an unimaginable or incomprehensible God, yet he also acknowledged that God sometimes commanded and directed men and women immediately even if these were his '*peculiar* Subjects'.

Like Abraham, men were bound not only by unchanging moral laws but by such special commands as God should deliver to them.[86] Even James Harrington, whose reliance as a political thinker was on material forces engendering the structures of power and on political architecture sustaining those in authority, conceded something to the living God: 'a commonwealth is not made by men, but by God, and they who resist his holy will, are weapons that cannot prosper.'[87] Engagement with the living God was 'an indispensable constituent of political decision-making' in the English Revolution, hindering the construction of a viable constitutional settlement and dominating the key players' interpretations of their actions and their consequences.[88]

Of all the cultural contexts of the past perhaps the most important for this period and one of the most difficult for us to track is that of Almighty God, the living God. To his adherents, he transcended time, even though he incessantly expressed his omnicompetence by moulding it, reshaping it at will, and rending the veil between the eternal and the time bound. He drove individuals and nations on then held them back, encouraging and chastising, building and destroying, revealing and withdrawing himself, forever retaining his mystery, his inscrutability and above all his wilfulness. The issue for us is not only what difference the living God might have made to the behaviour and self-perception of individuals, groups, communities and nations in shaping the English Revolution. It is also a question of how we, as a predominantly secular culture, are to assess their achievement. A common and apparently defensible judgement of the English Revolution is that it was a failure, at heart because its political and constitutional contrivances lacked stability and sufficient consensual backing. More debatably, its legacy might have been an antipathy to religious enthusiasm and the establishment of a platform for the 'rise of individualism'. But, what difference does it make to our assessment of the Revolution if we acknowledge that these assumed aspirations and outcomes were never the core, mainstream concerns of those who rode the military/fiscal machine and the absolutist regime that the pressures of war had inadvertently created; but rather that their overriding objective was to be instruments in the hands of the living God?

Notes

1 William Cobbett (ed.), *Complete Collection of State Trials* (15 vols, London, 1809–12), vol. 5, cols. 1025, 1231, 1235. For background on the themes of this essay, see Blair Worden, 'Providence and politics in Cromwellian England', *Past and Present*, 109 (1985), 58–99; Alexandra Walsham, *Providence in Early Modern England* (Oxford, 1999); J. C. Davis,

'Cromwell's religion', in John Morrill (ed.), *Cromwell and the English Revolution* (London, 1990), pp. 181–208; reprinted in David L. Smith (ed.), *Cromwell and the Interregnum* (Oxford, 2003), pp. 139–66.

2 Cromwell is here referring to Hebrews 10:31; Cromwell's emphasis.

3 W. C. Abbott (ed.), *The Writings and Speeches of Oliver Cromwell*, 4 vols (Cambridge, MA, 1937–47), vol. 3, pp. 591–2.

4 *Ibid.*, vol. 4, p. 473.

5 Cromwell to Major-General Fortescue, October 1655, *Ibid.*, vol. 3, p. 858; Blair Worden, 'Oliver Cromwell and the sin of Achan', in Derek Beales and Geoffrey Best (eds), *History, Society and the Churches* (Cambridge, 1985), pp. 125–45. The gap between Cromwell's perception and that of modern historians is illustrated by Austin Woolrych's insistence that Cromwell should have focused less on sin and more on 'inadequate planning, under-provision of troops, poor commissariat, and gross ignorance of the needs of soldiers campaigning in the tropics': Austin Woolrych, *Britain in Revolution, 1625–1660* (Oxford, 2002), p. 634.

6 Walsham, *Providence*, p. 90. See also J. C. Davis, 'Against formality: one aspect of the English Revolution', *Transactions of the Royal Historical Society*, 6th series, 3 (1993), 265–88.

7 G. C. Browell, 'The politics of providence in England, 1640–1660', unpublished PhD thesis, University of Kent (2000), p. 9, and chapters 2 and 3 for royalist providentialism.

8 Walsham, *Providence*, pp. 20, 31, 50. For a providential bee sting, see Alan Macfarlane (ed.), *The Diary of Ralph Josselin, 1616–83* (Oxford, 1991), p. 19, entry for 5 September 1644. For the spider in the bowl of porridge, see Francis J. Bremer, *John Winthrop: America's Forgotten Founding Father* (New York, 2003), p. 98. The incident took place on 15 December 1610.

9 Jonathan Sawday, 'Re-writing a revolution: history, symbol and text in the Restoration', *The Seventeenth Century*, 7 (1992), 183.

10 Andrew Lacey, *The Cult of King Charles the Martyr* (Woodbridge, 2003), pp. 2, 50.

11 Abbott (ed.), *Writings and Speeches*, vol. 4, p. 270.

12 Jacqueline Eales, 'Provincial preaching and allegiance in the first English civil war, 1640–46', in Thomas Cogswell, Richard Cust and Peter Lake (eds), *Politics, Religion and Popularity in Early Stuart Britain* (Cambridge, 2002), pp. 189, 191–2. See also Julie Spraggon, *Puritan Iconoclasm during the English Civil War* (Woodbridge, 2003).

13 See for example Jonas Dell, *Forms the Pillars of Antichrist* (London, 1656) p. 7.

14 Crawford Gribben, *The Puritan Millennium: Literature and Theology, 1550–1682* (Dublin, 2000), pp. 21–2.

15 John Cooke, *Monarchy No Creature of God's Making* (Waterford, 1651), b2; the reference is to 1 Samuel 8.

16 For the text of the Solemn League and Covenant, see S. R. Gardiner (ed.), *Constitutional Documents of the Puritan Revolution, 1625–1660* (Oxford,

1906), pp. 267–71. For the correspondence with Hammond, see Abbott (ed.), *Writings and Speeches*, vol. 1, pp. 676–8, 696–9.

17 *A Declaration Inviting the People of England and Wales, to a Day of Solemn Fasting and Humiliation* (March, 1654), in Abbott (ed.), *Writings and Speeches*, vol. 3, p. 225.

18 See, for example, John Rogers, *Sagrir* (London, 1653).

19 Cobbett (ed.), *State Trials*, vol. 5, col. 1326.

20 Christopher Hill, 'God and the English Revolution', *History Workshop Journal*, 17 (1984), 19–31. Hill also argued that, because of its emphasis on spiritual individualism, Protestant heterodoxy led to secularism: *Ibid.*, p. 23.

21 David Martin Jones, *Conscience and Allegiance in Seventeenth Century England: The Political Significance of Oaths and Engagements* (New York, 1999). For a recent treatment of religious division in covenanted American colonies, see Michael Winship, *Making Heretics: Militant Puritanism and Free Grace in Massachusetts, 1636–41* (Princeton, 2002). Keith Thomas, 'Cases of conscience in seventeenth-century England', in John Morrill, Paul Slack and Daniel Woolf (eds), *Public Duty and Private Conscience in Seventeenth-Century England* (Oxford, 1993), pp. 29–50; Edward Vallance, 'The kingdom's case: the use of casuistry as a political language, 1640–1692', *Albion*, 34 (2002), 557–83.

22 Walsham, *Providence*, p. 110.

23 For an excellent treatment of fast days in this period, see Christopher Durston, '"For the better humiliation of the people": public days of fasting and thanksgiving during the English Revolution', *The Seventeenth Century*, 7 (1992), 129–49.

24 Spraggon, *Puritan Iconoclasm*, esp. pp. 13, 50–1, 251; Trevor Cooper (ed.), *The Journal of William Dowsing: Iconoclasm in East Anglia during the English Civil War* (Woodbridge, 2001), p. 6.

25 Macfarlane (ed.), *Diary of Josselin*, p. 177.

26 Durston, 'Days of fasting and thanksgiving', p. 144; see also pp. 135, 138.

27 Edmund Calamy, *England's Looking-Glass* (London, 1642) pp. 3, 6. Jonathan Edwards was still describing God as absolute and arbitrary in the eighteenth century; see Philip Greven, 'The self shaped and misshaped: *The Protestant Temperament* reconsidered', in Ronald Hoffman, Michael Sobol and Frederika J. Teute (eds), *Through a Glass Darkly: Reflections on Personal Identity in Early America* (Chapel Hill, 1977) p. 358.

28 Stephen Marshall, *A Sermon Preached ... November 17, 1640* (London, 1641), pp. 15, 16.

29 A. F. Mitchell and John Struthers (eds), *Minutes of the Sessions of the Westminster Assembly of Divines: November 1644 to March 1649* (Edinburgh and London, 1874), pp. 166–7, 388–9, 409–10.

30 Jeremiah Burroughs, *Sions Joy* (London, 1641), A2.

31 Cornelius Burgess, *Another Sermon* (London, 1641), p. 1.

32 Abbott (ed.), *Writings and Speeches*, vol. 2, p. 127.

33 *Ibid.*, vol. 3, p. 53; my emphasis.

34 *Ibid.*, vol. 1, p. 644.

35 John Milton, *The Tenure of Kings and Magistrates*, in Martin Dzelzainis (ed.), *Milton: Political Writings* (Cambridge, 1991) p. 46.

36 Quoted in Gribben, *Puritan Millennium*, pp. 111–15.

37 Peter Sterry, *The Clouds in which Christ Comes* (London, 1648), pp. 38, 47–8.

38 John Cardwell, *Gods Wisdom Justified* (London, 1649), title page, pp. 9, 39 (marginal note).

39 John Milton, *A Defence of the People of England*, in Dzelzainis (ed.), *Milton: Political Writings*, p. 52.

40 Cobbett (ed.), *State Trials*, vol. 6, cols. 181, 183, 194, 197.

41 *Ibid.*, vol. 5, cols. 1300, 1319.

42 John Owen, *God's Work in Founding Zion* (Oxford, 1656), pp. 8–9.

43 The best introduction to this group remains Charles Webster, *The Great Instauration: Science, Medicine and Reform 1626–1660* (London, 1975).

44 For this essay I have used *The Hartlib Papers*, CD-ROM, 2 disks (Ann Arbor, 1995) [hereafter *HP*]. The originals are in the Sheffield University Library and I use their call numbers in citations. 24 Aug. 1657, *HP*, 62/18/1A–4B.

45 *HP*, 64/20/5A–6B.

46 Oldenburg to Hartlib, 5 Jul. 1659, *HP*, 39/3/25A–27B.

47 For example, de la Greve to John Dury, 4 Nov. 1632, *HP*, 69/1A-B: letters from Zurich, 22 Jul. 1654, *HP*, 43/45A–46B; Walter Wells to Hartlib, 15 Jul. [1632?], *HP*, 33/3/9A; 'Ephemerides', 1634, *HP*, 29/2/58A.

48 John Dury, 'Concerning the Question whether it be lawfull to admit Jewes to come into a Christian Commonwealth', *HP*, 68/8/1A–2B.

49 Dury to Hartlib, 16 Dec. 1654, *HP*, 4/3/66A. It is perhaps worth noting that even here it is God who will curb the excesses of the Fifth Monarchy Men and God who will determine Dury's capacity to assist that process.

50 Beale to Hartlib, undated, *HP*, 62/7/2A.

51 Beale to Hartlib, 18 Jan. 1658, *HP*, 51/60A.

52 Hartlib, 'Ephemerides', Feb.–Aug. 1640, *HP*, 30/4/45A–52B.

53 Lloyd to Hartlib, 30 [Oct.] 1652, *HP*, 65/8/1A–2B.

54 Wall to Hartlib, 3 Apr. 1655, *HP*, 34/4/11A–12B.

55 Wall to Hartlib, 9 Jan. 1659, *HP*, 34/4/19A–20B. Typically, Wall then goes on to discuss cures for sick cattle.

56 Lane to Dury, 10 Jun. 1651, *HP*, 1/32/1A–2B; Dury to Lane, 7 Jul. 1651, *HP*, 1/32/3A–6B.

57 Davis, 'Against formality', 265–88; J. C. Davis, 'The millennium as the anti-utopia of seventeenth century political thought', *Anglophonia*, 3 (1998), 57–66.

58 William Haller, *The Rise of Puritanism* (New York, 1957), p. 229; Christopher Hill, *Society and Puritanism in Pre-Revolutionary England* (London, 1964), pp. 483–4, 487–8; C. B. Macpherson, *The Political Theory of Possessive Individualism* (Oxford, 1962); Elspeth Graham, Hilary Hinds, Elaine Hoby and Helen Wilcox (eds), *Her Own Life: Autobiographical*

Writings by Seventeenth-Century Englishwomen (London, 1989); Ian Watt, *The Rise of the Novel* (London, 1957); Michael McKeown, *The Origins of the English Novel 1600–1740* (Baltimore, 1987); John Stachniewski and Anita Pacheo (eds), *Grace Abounding and Other Spiritual Autobiographies* (Oxford, 1998), introduction; A. S. P. Woodhouse (ed.), *Puritanism and Liberty* (London, 1938), introduction.

59 Graham *et al.* (eds), *Her Own Life*, pp. 3, 148.

60 Stachniewski and Pacheo (eds), *Grace Abounding*, p. xii (my emphasis). Cf. p. xxxii.

61 Tom Webster in one of the most sensitive recent treatments of this theme has argued for the categorisation of spiritual journals as 'ego literatures'. For reasons which I hope will become apparent below this is not in my view satisfactory. Tom Webster, 'Writing to redundancy: approaches to spiritual journals and early modern spirituality', *Historical Journal*, 39 (1996), 33–56, esp. 35.

62 Michael Mascuch, *Origins of the Individualist Self: Autobiography and Self-Identity in England, 1591–1791* (Stanford, CA, 1996).

63 As examples of the commonplace nature of providential incidents we might take Joanna Moody (ed.), *The Private Life of an Elizabethan Lady: The Diary of Lady Margaret Hoby, 1599–1605* (Stroud, 2001), p. 173, and Jack Binns (ed.), *Memoirs and Memorials of Sir Hugh Cholmley of Whitby, 1600–1657* (Woodbridge, 2000), pp. 93, 108–9, 153.

64 Stachniewski and Pacheo (eds), *Grace Abounding*, pp. 3–6.

65 *Ibid.*, pp. 6–9, 10–14.

66 *Ibid.*, pp. 16–24; see also pp. 28–9, 40, 55, 58–9, 61.

67 *Ibid.*, p. 14.

68 *Ibid.*, p. 37.

69 *Ibid.*, p. 77.

70 *Ibid.*, pp. 78, 82.

71 *Ibid.*, pp. 76, 86.

72 'A relation of the imprisonment of Mr John Bunyan', in *Ibid.*, p. 105.

73 For the theme of self-reliance as exposing the individual to a moral and spiritual wilderness see, for example, Laurence Clarkson, *The Lost Sheep Found* (London, 1660); Nathaniel Bacon, *A Relation of the Fearfull Estate of Francis Spira in the Yeare 1548* (London, 1638). The latter was a *cause célèbre* in early modern Europe. For commentary on it, see Michael MacDonald, '*The fearefull estate of Francis Spira*: narrative, identity and emotion in early modern England', *Journal of British Studies*, 31 (1992), 32–61; Brian Opie, 'Beyond ideology: apostasy and the horrors of selfhood in some Renaissance texts', *Mentalités/Mentalities*, 2 (1984), 21–33.

74 Cf. Mascuch, *Origins*, p. 92.

75 Text in Stachniewski and Pacheo (eds), *Grace Abounding*, pp. 123–53, esp. pp. 139, 145.

76 *Ibid.*, pp. 160–1, 163.

77 *Ibid.*, pp. 193, 197.

78 Graham *et al.* (eds), *Her Own Life*, pp. 58, 59.

79 *Ibid.*, pp. 73, 84.
80 Susanna Parr, *Susanna's Apology Against the Elders* (London, 1659), in *ibid.*, p. 102.
81 *Ibid.*, p. 148.
82 *Ibid.*, pp. 172, 177.
83 *Ibid.*, pp. 185, 189. For Jeremiah Burroughs' denial of the self's existence, see also Gribben, *Puritan Millennium*, p. 159. As late as 1741, Isaac Backus felt spiritually safe only when he became 'a helpless Creature' and God had 'a right to do with me just as he Pleased'. See Philip Greven, *The Protestant Temperament* (New York, 1977), p. 92.
84 Walsham, *Providence*, p. 23.
85 [Marchamont Nedham], *The Excellencie of Free State* (London, 1656), p. 16.
86 Richard Tuck (ed.), *Hobbes: Leviathan* (Cambridge, 1991), pp. 23–4, 79, 198–9, 276, 280, 322–3. For his continued wrestling with this problem, see pp. 292–4.
87 J. G. A. Pocock (ed.), *The Political Works of James Harrington* (Cambridge, 1977), p. 704.
88 Browell, 'Politics of providence', abstract; cf. Mark Stephen Jendrysik, *Explaining the English Revolution: Hobbes and his Contemporaries* (Lanham, MD, 2002), p. 81.

2

The toleration controversy during the English Revolution

John Coffey

I

One of the defining features of the English Revolution, according to Jonathan Scott, was 'its astonishing intellectual fertility'.[1] In contrast to other contemporary upheavals in Scotland, Ireland, France and Spain, the revolution in England generated an unprecedented volume of print and an extraordinary range of competing ideas. Pamphlet wars were fought over a multitude of issues, but few debates were so fierce, protracted or seminal as the controversy over toleration. After its full-scale eruption in 1644, the toleration controversy surged on throughout the revolutionary years and into the Restoration era. Nowhere else in seventeenth-century Europe, with the possible exception of the Netherlands, produced such a rich literature on religious toleration.

Unsurprisingly, scholars have written a great deal about 'the great English toleration controversy'.[2] During the 1930s the Harvard historian, W. K. Jordan, provided the most comprehensive treatment in his four-volume work, *The Development of Religious Toleration in England*. Volumes 3 and 4 were devoted to the 1640s and 1650s, and Jordan catalogued and summarised hundreds of tracts for and against toleration published during these years. But, rather than stimulating further research, his labours acted as a deterrent to subsequent scholars, who felt that there was little left to be said. Toleration, as Blair Worden has observed, began to seem a quaintly Victorian subject.[3] Only in the late twentieth century, in an era of multiculturalism and religious fundamentalist revival, did toleration once again become a hot topic.[4] In the case of seventeenth-century England, this resurgence of interest has resulted in a steady flow of articles and in Andrew Murphy's impressive book *Conscience and Community: Revisiting Toleration and Religious Dissent in Early Modern England and America.*[5]

This chapter aims to provide a basic taxonomy of the great English toleration controversy. Jordan slotted writers into twelve different categories, defining them as much by their denominational allegiance or religious outlook as by their position on toleration. His groupings were orthodox Presbyterians, moderate Presbyterians, Independents, Baptists, Latitudinarians, Cambridge Platonists, rationalists and sceptics, Erastians, the rank and file, Anglican extremists, moderate Anglicans, and Roman Catholics. Some of these categories work reasonably well, but others are highly problematic. A number of these groups were internally divided over toleration. Jeremy Taylor and Herbert Thorndike may both have been 'moderate Anglicans', but the former promoted liberty of conscience and the latter repudiated it.[6] John Goodwin and John Owen were leading Independent clergy but, as we shall see, they diverged significantly on toleration. The poets John Milton and Abraham Cowley are rather dubiously filed under 'rationalists and sceptics', though one was a radical parliamentarian and the other an Anglican royalist. As for Jordan's 'Erastians' – Henry Parker, William Prynne, James Harrington and Thomas Hobbes – one can only imagine the rancour that would have ensued if these four had been placed together in the same room.

If we cannot hope to match Jordan's comprehensive survey, we can at least clarify the positions of the major parties in the toleration controversy. Although some royalists did address the issue, this was essentially a dispute among parliamentarians, who were deeply divided over the settlement of the Church. To a considerable degree, the toleration controversy was also a bitter family quarrel among puritans. That this was so may appear puzzling; after all they are synonymous in the popular imagination with narrow-minded bigotry and intolerance. Yet the zeal of the godly promoted intransigent nonconformity and fissiparous sectarianism, and thus raised fundamental questions about the viability and desirability of religious uniformity. By the 1640s puritans were becoming deeply divided into competing factions.[7] Presbyterian proponents of religious uniformity clashed with Independent advocates of toleration, and the Independents themselves were torn between conservative and radical tendencies. Consequently, the period saw a three-way tussle among puritan parliamentarians over liberty of conscience. Antitolerationists, led by the Presbyterian clergy, denounced 'pretended liberty of conscience' and 'the accursed toleration' of 'the Independent party'. Conservative tolerationists, including the leading Independent clergy, advocated liberty of conscience for orthodox Protestants whatever their

Church. Finally, radical tolerationists questioned the basic assumption that the magistrate had coercive power in matters of religion, and openly advocated toleration for heresies and false religion. We shall now examine these three broad groupings in turn, exploring how and why they differed.

II

In November 1640 the Scots Presbyterian minister Robert Baillie arrived in London. The Covenanter revolution in his homeland and the resultant Bishops' War had brought the years of Laudian dominance to a grinding halt and forced Charles I to recall the English Parliament. Baillie was on a mission to promote the Covenanter cause and undermine English episcopacy. His letters home capture the exhilaration of the godly in 1640. 'All here are wearie of Bishops', he wrote. 'God is makeing here a new world.' He was well aware that some of the English godly were opposed to 'the Scotts Discipline'; in the City, 'Brownists' and 'Separatists' were a noisy and worrisome minority, while at Westminster several puritan peers, including Lord Saye and Sele and Lord Brooke, as well as 'some leading men' in the House of Commons were suspected of favouring the congregational church polity of New England rather than the presbyteries of Scotland. Yet Baillie was optimistic that 'The farr greatest part are for our discipline'. Congregational ministers such as Thomas Goodwin and Jeremiah Burroughs were 'learned, discreet and zealous men', who would hardly throw the 'Nationall Church' into 'unspeakable confusions' by denying the presbyteries and general assemblies 'power of censure' over individual congregations. When it came to the crunch, he predicted, 'they will joyne to overthrow Episcopacie, [and] erect Presbyterian government and assemblies'.[8]

Baillie's hopes for godly uniformity seemed well founded. Puritans had decried the Caroline regime because it had promoted crypto-popery and oppressed godly consciences, but they did not object to magistrates who advanced godliness and suppressed schisms and heresies. The mainstream godly were embarrassed by the antics of the sects, and insisted that they wanted to maintain a comprehensive and compulsory national Church. As Parliament's Grand Remonstrance explained:

> it is far from our purpose or desire to let loose the golden reins of discipline and government in the Church, to leave private persons or particular congregations to take up what form of Divine service they please, for we hold it requisite that there should be throughout the whole realm a conformity to that order which the laws enjoin according to the Word of God. And we desire to unburden the consciences of men of needless

and superstitious ceremonies, suppress innovations, and take away the monuments of idolatry.[9]

This emphasis on 'discipline', 'government', 'conformity' and 'order' in a national Church reflected the conventional wisdom of early modern Europe. It was widely believed that religious unity was a great blessing – a nation that prayed together, stayed together. Religious diversity, on the other hand, was potentially disastrous for national cohesion, and persecution of religious minorities could thus be justified on essentially political grounds.[10] There was also a powerful theological tradition in support of coercive uniformity. The great theologian of the early Church, St Augustine, had provided a trenchant theoretical defence of the use of force against sects and heresies, and later medieval churchmen had gone beyond Augustine and used his arguments to justify the death penalty for heresy. Dissenting movements such as the Albigensians, Waldensians, Hussites and Lollards were subjected to fierce repression, and in the decades following Luther's Reformation there were over three thousand executions for heresy in Europe, mainly of Protestants and Anabaptists.[11] Yet despite this, mainstream Protestant reformers clung on to the principle of coercive uniformity. Calvin played a key role in the trial and execution of the anti-Trinitarian Michael Servetus in 1553 and subsequently published a learned theological defence of his actions. With a few exceptions, Reformed divines were convinced that magistrates should use their power against heresy, idolatry and schism.

In Protestant England, both the political and the theological case for uniformity were regularly invoked. The Elizabethan regime executed both Catholic priests and Protestant separatists for sedition, and burned anti-trinitarians for heresy.[12] Both Bishop John Jewel and King James I defended the execution of Servetus, and between 1560 and 1640 there was a broad consensus that the magistrate had the power to instruct the population in the public faith, compel them to attend orthodox worship, and restrain false teachers from spreading their ideas or gathering followers.[13] After 1640 the great majority of parliamentarians shared these deep-rooted assumptions. The Solemn League and Covenant, signed by the Scots Covenanters and the English parliamentarians in 1643, bound both sides to a programme of religious intolerance. They agreed to 'endeavour the extirpation of popery, prelacy ... superstition, heresy, schism, profaneness', and more positively, committed themselves to 'the nearest conjunction and uniformity in religion' between the Churches of England, Scotland and Ireland.[14]

In 1643 the Long Parliament established the Westminster Assembly of Divines to advise it on Church reform. Among its 120 members were many of England's most eminent puritan divines, who were soon joined by a group of Scots commissioners, including Baillie, Alexander Henderson, George Gillespie and Samuel Rutherford. At first, the Scots were excited by the prospects for reform. Slowly, however, they saw their best-laid plans unravel before their eyes. While the majority of the assembly did favour a Presbyterian Church settlement, there was an obstructive knot of 'Dissenting Brethren', 'mighty opposites to presbyterial government', who wanted the assembly to recognise and accept the independence and self-government of their gathered congregations.[15] Apprehensive about the Presbyterian juggernaut, in January 1644 these Brethren issued *An Apologeticall Narration*, laying out their 'middle way' between separatism and Presbyterianism, and asking for a limited toleration of orthodox Congregational churches. Its publication signalled the start of England's great toleration debate, and from 1644 onwards, radical Independents released a torrent of books and pamphlets denouncing Presbyterian persecution and demanding liberty of conscience.[16]

The Presbyterians were astonished at this new vogue for toleration. 'If some of those godly ministers who were famous in their time should rise out of their graves and come now among us', wrote Thomas Edwards in 1646, 'they would wonder to see things come to this passe in England, and to meet with such Books for Toleration of all Religions'.[17] With some justification, Presbyterians saw themselves as the heirs and maintainers of the puritan and Reformed tradition, a tradition now under threat from the tolerationists. As they pointed out, toleration was a policy previously associated with Socinians, Arminians, and Anabaptists, all notorious dissenters from Protestant orthodoxy. The agitation for liberty of conscience appeared to them to be part of a general assault on the orthodox Reformed faith.

In their sermons to parliament, the Westminster Assembly Presbyterians denounced 'an illimited toleration of all Religions', and reasserted the need for uniformity.[18] Obadiah Sedgwick called on the House of Commons to pass an act declaring 'your Abhorring of the mentioning, yea, of the very thoughts of Tollerating all Opinions in the Church'.[19] Another leading Presbyterian, Edmund Calamy, reminded Parliament of its duty 'to suppresse these divisions and differences in Religion by your Civil Authoritie, as farre as you are able, lest you be accessory unto them'.[20] In a sermon to the Lords, Samuel Rutherford warned that liberty of conscience would only exacerbate England's woes, and argued that magistrates should employ force 'to curbe the spread of false doctrine'.[21]

Both English Presbyterians and Scots Covenanters also published major works against sects, heresies and toleration. Such heresiographers as Baillie, Rutherford, Edwards, John Bastwick and Ephraim Pagitt tried to discredit the Independent coalition by chronicling the more outlandish beliefs and actions of England's sectaries.[22] Edwards, Rutherford and Gillespie rearticulated the traditional Reformed vision of a magistrate who imitated Old-Testament kings by using his power to crush heresy and suppress schism.[23] Their position was reinforced by William Prynne's major defence of religious coercion, *The Sword of Christian Magistracy Supported*, published in 1647. The sub-title informed the reader that this was *A Full Vindication of Christian Kings and Magistrates Authority under the Gospell, To punish Idolatry, Apostacy, Heresie, Blasphemy and obstinate Schism, with Pecuniary, Corporall, and in some Cases with Banishment, and Capitall Punishments.*[24]

Alongside their books and sermons, the Presbyterian clergy issued a series of declarations against toleration. In January 1645 an official letter of the London ministers expressing abhorrence at 'that great Diana of Independents, and all the Sectaries so much cryed up by them in these distracted times, viz. A Toleration, A Toleration'. Reformation was 'in danger of being strangled in the birth by a lawlesse Toleration that strives to be brought forth before it'.[25] The Scots Covenanters issued their own *Declaration* condemning 'Liberty of Conscience, the Nurse of all Heresies and Schismes'.[26] In December 1647 the London Presbyterian clergy published *A Testimony to the Truth of Jesus Christ, and to our Solemn League and Covenant; as also against the Errours, Heresies and Blasphemies of these Times, and the Toleration of them.* They complained that they were witnessing a 'Deformation' instead of a Reformation, and that rather than calling for the 'Extirpation of Heresie, Schisme, Prophanesse', 'multitudes are not ashamed to presse and plead for a publike, formall and universall Toleration'. After years of travail, England had 'brought forth an hideous Monster of Toleration'.[27] During 1648 a flood of copycat testimonies poured in from godly clergy in one county after another.

The mainstream puritan position was codified in the 1647 Westminster Confession of Faith. Chapter 20, entitled 'Of Christian Liberty, and Liberty of Conscience', averred that 'God alone is lord of the conscience', and rejected 'implicit faith' and 'blind obedience'. But it also insisted that Christian liberty should not undermine order or orthodoxy. Opinions or practices 'contrary to the light of nature, or to the known principles of Christianity' or 'destructive to the external peace and order which Christ hath established in the church' could be 'proceeded against' by church censures and 'the power of the civil magistrate'. This was confirmed in chapter 23, 'Of the Civil Magistrate', which outlined the magistrate's duty 'to take order that unity and peace be preserved in the church, that the truth of God be kept pure and entire, that all blasphemies and heresies be suppressed, all corruptions and abuses in worship and discipline prevented or reformed, and all the ordinances of God duly settled, administered, and observed'. The Westminster Assembly's Larger Catechism, meanwhile, listed 'tolerating a false religion' as a violation of the second of the ten commandments, which condemned idolatry.[28]

In May 1648 Parliament finally satisfied the demands of the Presbyterian clergy by passing 'An Ordinance for the Punishing of Blasphemies and Heresies'. The section on blasphemy prescribed the death penalty for atheism and anti-Trinitarianism, while that on heresy threatened imprisonment for Arminians, universalists, Baptists and antinomians.[29] Had this Blasphemy Ordinance ever been put into effect, the prisons of England would have been bursting at the seams and some individuals might have gone to the stake. It was not, however, to be. A decade that had begun with so much promise ended in disappointment for the Presbyterian clergy, for the Church established by Parliament was in no way to their liking. In Baillie's famous phrase, it was 'a lame Erastian Presbytery', under the control of lay politicians and compatible with gathered congregations beyond the parish system.[30] Independents such as John Goodwin emphasised that they had no objection to this lamb-like parliamentary Presbytery, only to the lion-like 'High Presbyterie' sought by 'the Ministers' and 'Gangraena's Gang'.[31] Following the New Model Army coup of December 1648, even this 'lame Erastian Presbytery' was dead in the water; power fell into the hands of the Independent party, and the cause of religious uniformity was doomed.

III

This triumph of the Independents was extraordinary, for they constituted only a small minority of the godly, let alone of the nation as a whole. Within the Westminster Assembly the Dissenting Brethren had fought a rearguard action against the Presbyterian advance, while in the City of London the gathered congregations had become well established.[32] Within parliament, the Independents also had some influential supporters, for example Lord Saye and Sele in the Lords and Oliver St John and Sir Henry Vane the younger in the Commons. But it was in the army that the Independent cause found its strongest support, thanks to such commanders as Oliver Cromwell. Men such as Cromwell and Vane were deeply hostile to Presbyterian uniformity and powerful patrons of religious Independency and, although they accepted the need for an established Church, they were determined to secure toleration for the gathered congregations.[33]

In supporting a limited toleration for godly gathered congregations, Independents did not necessarily deny that the magistrate had coercive power in matters of religion. Indeed, Dissenting Brethren such as Thomas Goodwin, Philip Nye and Jeremiah Burroughs, together with the rising star John Owen, agreed with the Presbyterians that the Christian magistrate was duty bound to suppress idolatry and heresy.[34] They simply argued, however, that godly evangelical Protestants who differed over matters of ecclesiology should not be classed with heretics and idolaters. Thomas Goodwin explained that, rather than advocating 'liberty of all opinions', 'I plead only for Saints'.[35] By distinguishing between what they regarded as the 'fundamentals' of doctrine and 'secondary matters' of ecclesiology, they hoped to secure toleration for Presbyterians, Independents, Baptists and Calvinist episcopalians, while denying it to Socinians, Catholics and possibly Arminians too.

The position was clearly laid out in 1645 by Jeremiah Burroughs in his *Irenicum*. As in the *Apologeticall Narration*, the Congregational viewpoint was presented here as a middle way between two extremes. On one side were the advocates of rigid uniformity, who insisted that 'nothing should be tolerated'. On the other, were the proponents of 'absolute liberty for all Religions', who declared that 'all things should be tolerated'. Burroughs argued that both policies were deeply divisive and that the radical tolerationists were giving moral support to contemporaries who preached and practised 'horrid blasphemous things'. His own view was that the magistrate should tolerate 'some things conceived errors' but suppress serious heresies and blasphemies. Like the Presbyterians, he affirmed that contemporary Christian rulers had the same power in matters of religion as their Old Testament counterparts.[36] As he explained in response to Thomas Edwards in 1646, he had never pleaded for 'a universall, an unlimited toleration of all Religions' and 'should be loath to live in England if ever it should be here'.[37]

In this respect, the conservative Congregationalists were lining up with their New England brethren.[38] John Cotton, the leading Massachusetts puritan who was regarded as something of an oracle among English Congregationalists, had emphatically defended the magistrate's power in religion against the founder of Rhode Island, Roger Williams. Like the Dissenting Brethren, Cotton distinguished between dissenters who obstinately denied 'Fundamentals' of the faith, and those who dissented on lesser matters: the magistrate could tolerate the latter, but not the former. Cotton was anxious to point out that Massachusetts puritans lived peacefully alongside the pagan natives, and were more tolerant and reasonable than Williams suggested.[39] But he was also four-square behind Augustine's defence of religious coercion, and shared Calvin and Beza's belief that obstinate heretics who persisted in seducing others from the truth could be put to death by the magistrate, as Servetus had been.[40] Another senior

Massachusetts minister, Nathaniel Ward, agreed that 'Tolerations in things tolerable' were acceptable, but that 'laxe Tolerations' were not. On his visit to England in 1647, he was disturbed by 'talke of an universall toleration' among 'Opinionists', and was keen to point out that New England was tough on heresy. He pointed to Augustine's defence of 'just severity', and the example of Christian emperors to prove that 'prosecution scattered Errour'.[41] Such a position was only marginally different from that of the Presbyterians, and it is hardly surprising that Presbyterians and conservative Independents enjoyed a *rapprochement* in the 1650s. When Massachusetts was accused of persecuting Baptists in the early 1650s, Thomas Cobbett responded with *The Civil Magistrates Power in Matters of Religion*, a work recommended as 'very profitable to these times' by the Presbyterian licenser, Obadiah Sedgwick.

On this issue, however, the New England Congregationalists were closer to the Presbyterians than were the English Independents. John Owen's 1649 *Discourse about Toleration* stands in sharp contrast to Cotton's *Bloudy Tenent Washed*, published just two years earlier. Whereas Cotton showed no hesitation in endorsing the defences of religious coercion provided by Augustine, Calvin and Beza, Owen voiced grave doubts about the use of corporal punishment in matters of religion. His tract took aim at both anti-tolerationists and radical tolerationists, but would have pleased the latter more than the former. Although he avoided naming names, he set out to dismantle many of the arguments advanced by Edwards, Rutherford and Gillespie. He argued that the coercive strategy they promoted was 'first invented' by the pagans 'for the extirpation of Truth' and was currently employed by the papists against Protestants. The godly should think twice before they used 'the Broome of Antichrist, to sweep the Church of Christ'. Owen maintained that 'untill Augustine' the early church had opposed the use of 'corporall punishment' in religion, and that he himself was extremely tentative about the use of force against peaceable heretics.[42]

Faced with the rise of Socinianism and other heresies in the 1650s, Owen later sounded a more conservative note. In 1655, he even offered a guarded defence of Calvin's role in the execution of Servetus, suggesting that the Spaniard's 'atheism and blasphemy' were such 'that I must say he is the only person in the world, that I ever read or heard of, that ever died upon the account of religion, in reference to whom the zeal of them that put him to death may be acquitted'.[43] The rather tortuous phrasing here suggests that Owen had not developed a sudden enthusiasm for heresy executions, but had become convinced that the worst heretics had to be restrained by the magistrate. In the Congregationalists' Savoy Confession of 1658, he explained that the Christian magistrate was bound 'to take care that men of corrupt minds and conversations do not licentiously publish and divulge Blasphemy and Errors', but should tolerate secondary differences among Christians.[44]

This limited tolerationist position was accepted by most of the leading Independent politicians. Lord Saye and Sele, for example, maintained that in cases of 'dangerous errors in respect of Infection of others, and seducements', the magistrate ought 'to forbid the outward actings and practise of such things, being in their natures destructive to the foundations of Christian Religion, and not suffer and permit men to uphold them forth in their conversation amongst others ... no more than he ought to suffer a man to run up and down, with a Plague sore running upon him, to destroy others'. He added, however, that the magistrate must not 'force men outwardly to ... practice what is contrary to their consciences'.[45] Henry Ireton, Cromwell's son-in-law, articulated a similar position during the Whitehall debates of 1648. He wanted to secure liberty for 'men that are conscientious' without opening the door to 'anything that any man will call religion'. Like Saye and Sele, he argued that the Christian magistrate had the power to restrain idolaters, heretics and blasphemers, and that the Old Testament magistrate, whose restraining of false religion was 'a perpetual rule', remained a model.[46]

Cromwell himself was a less systematic thinker than his son-in-law, but was in substantial agreement with Ireton and Owen.[47] He often spoke in favour of 'liberty of conscience', and chided those who would not be satisfied 'unless they can put their finger upon their brethren's consciences, to pinch them there'.[48] In response to complaints about lukewarm indifference to heresy, he was reported as saying 'that he had rather Mahumetanism were permitted amongst us, then that one of God's Children should be persecuted'.[49] Yet Cromwell also condemned the notion that the magistrate had no authority to punish blasphemers and heretics, rebuking radical tolerationists for their 'patronizing of villainies'.[50] When one of his advisors complained of 'New England's rigidness and persecution', Cromwell was said to have leapt to the defence of the Massachusetts puritans, stating that 'they acted like wise men'.[51] According to one Socinian, Cromwell also inveighed against anti-Trinitarians, and declared that the magistrate 'must not tolerate such as speak against the God of the Country'.[52]

With Cromwell's support, the conservative Independents became the new establishment in the 1650s. Although the parish system was retained, the old ideal of religious uniformity was abandoned. A parliamentary act of 1650 repealed the penalties traditionally imposed for not attending the established Church, and Independent and sectarian congregations were granted freedom to worship and propagate their beliefs. This was a dramatic break with the past, and with both episcopalian and Presbyterian ideals of a comprehensive and uniform state Church. If England was not exactly an unregulated free market in religion during the 1650s, the state Church did face fierce competition and Congregationalists, Baptists and Quakers were able to put down roots and flourish.

But while the Independents wished to protect godly consciences, they had no time for what they regarded as irreligion or heresy. The 1650 act also declared that 'all and every person within this Commonwealth' must attend some form of religious worship 'upon every Lord's day'. England was still a Protestant nation, and conservative Independents wanted a godly magistracy which promoted true religion and prosecuted heresy. When an English translation of the Socinian *Racovian Catechism* appeared in 1652, the Rump Parliament responded to pressure from Congregationalist clergy and ordered its burning. Owen and other leading Congregationalists were appointed as advisors to the Rump's Committee for the Propagation of the Gospel, and produced *The Humble Proposals*. These recommended that all non-parochial congregations be registered with magistrates and that Parliament suppress 'that abominable Cheat of Judiciall Astrology'. They also drew up sixteen *Principles of Christian Religion*, which defined the 'fundamentals' of faith in trinitarian and evangelical Protestant terms. The ministers proposed that no one 'be suffered to preach or promulgate any thing in opposition unto such Principles'.[53]

Owen's scheme was not, however, implemented, and when Cromwell became Lord Protector in December 1653, the new constitution of the Instrument of Government declared that 'such as profess faith in God by Jesus Christ (though differing in judgement from the doctrine, worship or discipline publicly held forth) shall not be restrained from, but shall be protected in, the profession of the Faith, and exercise of their religion'.[54] To many, this seemed to guarantee a very broad toleration indeed; only popery and prelacy were excluded from this free exercise clause, and even Socinians could happily profess faith in God by Jesus Christ. But Owen and his fellow Congregationalists wished to impose a more restrictive reading on this clause. During the first protectoral parliament of 1654, a parliamentary committee set up to consider the matter nominated a group of divines to determine the fundamentals of religion, which would then demarcate the limits of toleration under the protectorate. The group naturally included the leading Congregationalist divines, but also such Presbyterians as Richard Vines, Francis Cheynell and Stephen Marshall, who welcomed the Congregationalists' desire to get tough on heresy.[55] This time, the divines drew up a list of twenty fundamentals, which was privately published for the benefit of MPs as *A New Confession of Faith*.[56] This new statement of faith was implicitly anti-Arminian as well as anti-

Socinian. Once again, however, it generated controversy and the early dissolution of the parliament meant that it was never implemented.[57]

The conservative Independents were no doubt dissatisfied with this outcome; in their eyes there was too much room for heresy in Cromwellian England. But in some ways the situation captured the ambiguity of their own position on toleration. On the one hand, the godly were enjoying unparalleled freedom of religion; on the other, Socinians and Quakers and other heterodox movements were experiencing frequent harassment and restraint. As we have seen, the leading Independents were prepared to burn heretical books, but unwilling to burn heretical preachers. Unlike Servetus, the Socinian John Biddle did not die at the stake, but met a less heroic fate when he was exiled to the Isles of Scilly. The conservative Congregationalists had no wish to instigate a fiery Inquisition, but they did expect the state to prevent the spread of heresy.

IV

There was, however, a third position in the revolutionary debates over toleration, one adopted by radical Independents, sectaries and republicans. As Thomas Edwards observed, tolerationists could be divided into two camps: while some called for 'a limited and bounded [toleration] of some sects only', others advocated 'a Universal Toleration of all Religions and Consciences'.[58] Baillie also noted that Independents were divided over the idea of 'Toleration for all or any Religion', adding 'Whatever may be the opinion of Io. Goodwin, of Mr Williams and some of their stamp, yet Mr Burrowes in his late *Irenicum* upon many unanswerable arguments explodes that abomination'.[59] Gillespie, too, distinguished sharply between the authors and supporters of the *Apologeticall Narration* and those who taught 'that the magistrate ought not to inflict any punishment, nor put forth any coercive power upon Hereticks or Sectaries, but on the contrary grant them liberty and toleration'.[60] The rift between the two groups was most clearly exposed by the Whitehall debates of 1648, when Ireton and Nye took on the radicals.[61]

As the Presbyterians noted, the arguments of the new tolerationists looked very similar to those of the radical Protestant humanists of the sixteenth century who had condemned the execution of Servetus. Obadiah Sedgwick complained that their arguments could all be traced back to Sebastian Castellio – 'a friend of that monstrous Heretick Servetus' – who had been refuted 'by learned and pious Beza'.[62] Edwards alleged that John Goodwin's ideas were stolen out of Mino Celsi.[63] Goodwin was certainly influenced by a famous tolerationist work by Jacobus Acontius.[64] Some English writers may also have read later tolerationist books by Dutch

Arminians or Polish Socinians. But in England itself, the only radical tolerationist writings prior to 1640 were produced by General Baptists, who had strong links to the Netherlands.[65]

The Dutch connection was significant. Whereas conservative Independents looked admiringly to Massachusetts, radical Independents like Roger Williams were openly critical of the intolerance of the Massachusetts puritans and enthusiastic about the tolerant pluralism of the Dutch republic. In the 1650s, one writer declared that he much preferred the 'free Ayre' of Holland 'where all Religions are permitted', to the enforced conformity of New England.[66] It was thus with some justice that Presbyterians accused radical Independents of trying to turn London into a new Amsterdam.[67] As Baillie explained to a correspondent in the Netherlands:

> Not only [do] they praise your magistrate, who for policie gives some secret tollerance to diverse religions, wherein, as I conceave, your divines preaches against them as great sinners; but avows, that by God's command, the magistrate is discharged to put the least discourtesie on any man, Turk, Jew, Papist, Socinian, or whatever, for his religion.[68]

Baillie was no doubt thinking of a notorious statement by Roger Williams: 'It is the will and command of God that, since the coming of his Son the Lord Jesus, a permission of the most Paganish, Jewish, Turkish, or anti-christian [i.e. Roman Catholic] consciences and worships be granted to all men in all nations and countries.'[69] Williams was a close friend of the radical puritan politician Sir Henry Vane the younger, who shocked the Scots when he 'prolixly, earnestly, and passionately reasoned for a full liberty of conscience to all religions'.[70] Another key radical tolerationist was the Independent pastor John Goodwin, 'a bitter enemie to Presbyterie, [who] is openly for a full liberty of conscience to all sects, even Turks, Jews, Papists, and all to be more openly tolerate than with yow'. Baillie recognised that the Westminster Dissenting Brethren would not endorse this view, but warned that 'this way is very pleasant to very many here'.[71]

Baillie was not mistaken. Numerous radical Protestants in the 1640s and 1650s denied the civil magistrate any coercive power in matters of religion, and argued that the state should maintain a policy of toleration even in cases of heresy and false religion. Among the most significant figures were John Goodwin, who addressed the issue in numerous works, especially *M. S. to A. S.* (1644) and *Hagiomastix* (1647); Henry Robinson, a merchant associated with the Hartlib circle and the author of *Liberty of Conscience* (1644); Roger Williams, founder of the Rhode Island colony, whose *Bloudy Tenent of Persecution* (1644) was perhaps the most influential tolerationist book of the 1640s; William Walwyn, London merchant, religious pamphleteer, Leveller leader, and author of *The Compassionate Samaritan* (1644) and *Toleration Justified* (1646); Richard Overton, a General Baptist and Leveller leader, who published the brilliant satire *The Arraignment of Mr Persecution* (1645); William Dell, army chaplain and later master of Gonville and Caius College, Cambridge, who condemned religious coercion in his sermon to the House of Commons, *Right Reformation* (1646); Sir Henry Vane the younger, who promoted toleration at Westminster and argued against persecution in *Zeal Examined* (1652); John Milton, an admirer of Vane and Williams, whose *Areopagitica* (1644) defended the liberty of the press, and who denounced religious uniformity in poetry and prose; the Particular Baptist Samuel Richardson, author of *The Necessity of Toleration* (1647); Samuel Fisher, General Baptist turned Quaker, who set out his position in *Christianismus Redivivus* (1655); the Socinian John Croope, author of *Conscience-Oppression* (1656) and *Panarmonia* (1659); and Henry Stubbe, a republican protégé of Vane, who promoted civil and religious liberty in *An Essay in Defence of the Good Old Cause* (1659).

Because radical tolerationists were a motley crew, composed of Independents, Baptists, Seekers, Quakers and Socinians, they never issued a joint statement to compare with the Westminster Confession or the Savoy Confession. However, their position was articulated in various petitions and in the programmatic statements of the Leveller movement. The Levellers were willing to accept a national Church, but insisted that it must not be 'compulsive'; their first 'Agreement of the People' of 1647 declared 'That matters of Religion, and the wayes of Gods Worship, are not at all intrusted by us to any humane power, because therein wee cannot remit or exceed a tittle of what our Consciences dictate to be the mind of God, without wilful sinne'.[72] The radical tolerationist position was also incorporated into the General Baptist Confession of Faith of 1660. Echoing Roger Williams, this declared 'That it is the will and mind of God (in these Gospel times) that all men should have the free liberty of their own consciences in matters of Religion, or worship, without the least oppression, or persecution'.[73]

In contrast to the Presbyterians and the conservative Congregationalists, few radical tolerationists were parish clergy. Most were either lay intellectuals (such as Milton, Walwyn and Stubbe) or separatists (such as Williams, Richardson, Fisher, and Croope). As a result, they were strongly anti-clerical, and had good reason to fear a powerful ministry that defined orthodoxy and could call on the state to enforce it. Although they were sometimes willing to accept a non-coercive national Church, most opposed tithes and favoured lay preaching.[74] This was true of John Goodwin, vicar of St Stephen's, Coleman Street, in the City of London from 1633 to 1645 and again from 1649 to 1660. Goodwin was an unusually anti-clerical clergyman who opposed tithes and fostered lay preachers in his gathered church.

Whereas the Presbyterians and conservative Congregationalists promoted strict Reformed orthodoxy, radical tolerationists were often associated with heterodox beliefs. Goodwin was alleged to be unsound on justification and biblical authority, and in the late 1640s he embraced Arminianism. Williams was a conventional Calvinist, but as a Seeker he believed that true apostolic churches would only be revived in the last days. Walwyn was accused of various heresies and seems to have believed in universal salvation and antinomian ideas of free grace. Overton had denied the immortality of the soul in *Mans Mortalitie* (1643). Richardson rejected traditional ideas of divine punishment in *Of the Torments of Hell* (1658). Vane was notorious for his cloudy mysticism. Milton seems to have become an anti-Trinitarian and Arminian in the 1650s. Croope was a Socinian, and Stubbe claimed to be a strict Calvinist in 1659 but ended up as a deist. While radical tolerationism was not necessarily incompatible with orthodox Calvinism, many of its advocates were attracted to toleration because of their enthusiasm for 'new light'.

Their willingness to question traditional ideas was driven by a radical Protestant vision of Church history. Compared to mainstream Protestants, sectarian tolerationists took a much dimmer view of the Western Christian tradition. The former had always detected defection from primitive truth in the rise of papal authority, devotion to Mary, the mass and justification by works. But for radical Protestants, the apostasy went much deeper. Among the corruptions they identified were tithes, clerical authority, infant baptism, and even the doctrine of the Trinity. Above all, these writers argued that the direst consequence of the great apostasy was persecution. The Church had forgotten that the weapons of its warfare were not worldly but spiritual. Whereas mainstream Protestants celebrated Constantine's conversion to Christianity as a triumph, radical tolerationists tended to lament it as a second Fall. 'Christianity', wrote Williams mournfully, 'fell asleep in Constantine's bosom'.[75] The church had been corrupted by Antichrist, and the key mark of its corruption was its willingness to employ the Beast's own engine of persecution.[76]

Radical tolerationists believed that the great mistake of Christian rulers was to model themselves on Old Testament kings, who had been given divine authority to crush idolatry and false religion. The Church's apostasy had been a lapse into 'Judaising' and 'grosse legality'.[77] Williams devoted much of *The Bloudy Tenent* to showing that Old Testament Israel was merely a carnal foreshadowing of the New Testament Church. With the coming of Christ, God had inaugurated a new dispensation and begun to work through a different kind of community: one composed of 'volunteers' rather than conscripts; multi-ethnic rather than national; spiritual rather than carnal; and gentle, not coercive.[78] The Presbyterians found this dispensationalist argument infuriating, but it was also one of the central points of contention with the conservative Independents at the Whitehall debates.[79]

Radical tolerationists believed that, while the Church's fall had ushered in a millennium of apostasy, they were now living through the restoration of primitive Christianity. The first Reformers had made a start, but 'further reformation' would require much more than the implementation of existing programmes. 'We have lookt so long upon the blaze that Zuinglius and Calvin hath beaconed up to us', wrote Milton, 'that we are stark blind'.[80] Reformation was a continuing process. If America, the world's fourth great continent, lay undiscovered for so many ages, suggested John Goodwin, then 'many truths ... may be yet unborne'.[81] But hidden truths would only be brought to light if the Church learned to tolerate its bold explorers. New ideas should be fostered, not suppressed. Theological dogmatism was a roadblock to spiritual progress, and radical tolerationists commended a healthy scepticism about clerical dogmas. In an era of restoration, they suggested, it was often difficult to tell what was heresy and what was orthodoxy. Earlier prophets had been burned as heretics, and those who persecuted ran the risk of fighting against God.[82]

Toleration was essential therefore for two reasons. Firstly, it was a matter of principle. Authentic Christianity was non-coercive; the true Church was often persecuted, but never persecuting. The hallmark of false religion, by contrast, was reliance on force. The second reason was pragmatic. Toleration was the means to an end: the restoration of primitive Truth. Toleration of new ideas was vital if primitive Christianity was to be reconstructed, and clergy who demanded the suppression of 'heresy' were destroying the possibility of full restoration.

If the tolerationist position was generated by a radical Protestant view of history, it could be bolstered by a distinctive use of natural law contract theory. In line with mainstream parliamentarianism, John Goodwin argued that the power of magistrates was derived from popular consent, rather than received directly from God. He went on, however, to explain that God had not given the people the power 'to enslave or subject the consciences of men in matters appertaining unto himself'. Instead, 'God reserves the legislative power over the consciences of men unto himself alone'. Thus the people were simply unable to authorise the magistrate to establish a system of compulsory religious uniformity.[83] The magistrate's power was strictly civil or secular, because it was not possible to make 'a spirituall extraction out of a secular roote'.[84] Indeed, so-called 'Christian magistrates' had the same duties and no greater authority than pagan magistrates. They were to rule by 'the Law of Nature', and punish offences against it.[85] Since the people established government according to natural reason rather than divine revelation, rulers could only punish offences which were contrary to the clear 'light of nature'.[86]

This naturalistic account of the origins and ends of government suggested a limited and essentially secular role for the state. As Williams put it, the ends of government were 'merely civil': 'to conserve the civil peace of people so far as concerns their bodies and goods'.[87] Logically, this implied freedom for all peaceable religions that did not violate natural law. Because magistrates were 'Elected by the World, not by the Church', one pamphleteer reasoned, they 'owe universall protection, ought indifferently to administer Justice to all, without respect of the person or Religion of any'.[88] This natural law argument dovetailed with the radical Protestant convictions explored above. The belief that religious coercion was a mark of Antichrist drove various writers to advocate 'toleration of all religions', including Muslims and Roman Catholics.[89] Henry Robinson declared that compelling papists to attend Protestant worship was 'no more pious an act, then for Papists to use the like compulsion towards Jewes and Protestants in forcing them to heare their sermons, masse or Vespers'.[90] Catholic propagandists exploited the potential of this tolerationist argument in a series of pamphlets published in the 1650s, in which they posed as radical Protestants who were driven by the logic of their own principles to support toleration for papists.[91]

Radical puritans often, however, resisted such logic. Catholics were indelibly associated in their minds with sedition, persecution and idolatry, and Milton used each of these characteristics to justify their exclusion from toleration.[92] For Milton and others, the goal was 'Liberty of conscience to all professing Scripture the rule of their faith & worship'.[93] Their prime concern was to defend other radical Protestants who were stigmatised as 'Hereticks and Sectaries'. Whereas Owen and his allies drew the line at the intolerable heresy of Socinianism, radical tolerationists stood up for anti-Trinitarians such as Paul Best and John Biddle. Atheism, by contrast, was generally excluded from lists of tolerable opinions on the grounds that the denial of a Creator flew in the face of natural reason. Walwyn was almost unique in urging toleration for atheists.[94] Moreover, radical tolerationists agreed that adultery, fornication, drunkenness and other forms of 'licentiousness' were sins against the light of nature. The General Baptists, for example, made it clear that 'all wicked lewdness, and fleshly filthiness ... ought to be punished'.[95] Religious liberty would not open the door to irreligion, anarchy or licentiousness.

Despite drawing clear limits to liberty, radical tolerationists attempted to push the boundaries of toleration much further than most of their contemporaries. In the protectoral parliaments only a few MPs were willing to deny the magistrate's coercive power in matters of religion, and they were heavily outnumbered by Presbyterians and conservative Congregationalists. When Parliament debated the 'horrid blasphemy' of the Quaker James Nayler in 1656, the MPs divided up into hardliners who demanded his execution and 'merciful' men who favoured a lesser punishment.[96] The hardliners, who included both Presbyterians and conservative Congregationalists such as the major-generals, William Goffe, William Boteler and Edward Whalley claimed that blasphemy was against the light of nature, that Old Testament penal laws against blasphemers were still in force, and that a failure to put Nayler to death would dishonour God and provoke His wrath. One speaker even cited Calvin, Rutherford and Cotton to justify the execution of blasphemers. While leading Cromwellians questioned these arguments and spoke against the death penalty and mutilation, they did not make a strong case for toleration. Colonel Holland and Major-General William Packer were exceptional in defending Nayler on the grounds of free exercise of conscience. Packer, a Baptist, emphasised that Christian magistrates did not have the same power as Jewish magistrates in matters of religion, and declared that the duty of Parliament was 'to give every man his native liberty, which is given in Holland, Poland, and other countries, a free exercise of their consciences'. The radical Independent tolerationist Joshua Sprigge also led a party of thirty petitioners who asked Parliament to remit Nayler's punishment and 'leave him to Gospel remedies, as the proper way to reclaim'. Such pleas were unavailing; while he narrowly escaped the death penalty, Nayler was flogged, pilloried and branded as a blasphemer.[97]

Despite the punishment of Nayler and Biddle, John Milton could express satisfaction in 1659 that 'the governors of this commonwealth since the rooting out of prelats have made least use of force in religion, and most have favour'd Christian liberty of any in this Iland before them since the first preaching of the Gospel'. But Milton wanted the nation's rulers to 'enlarge' liberty of conscience, 'if in aught they yet straiten it'.[98] Ever since the Whitehall debates of December 1648 radical Independents had been wary of the restrictive tendencies of their conservative brethren. In 1652 Milton had joined with Williams and Vane in condemning Owen's *Humble Proposals*. He wrote two sonnets, one fulsome in its praise of Vane, the other equivocal in its support for Cromwell, who seemed worryingly close to Owen.[99] Determined to protect and expand religious freedom, other radical tolerationists protested against tithes, condemned the punishment of Biddle, advocated the readmission of the Jews, and challenged the authority of Cromwell's triers and ejectors.[100] In the climactic year of 1659, they published a host of pamphlets in defence of 'civil and religious liberty'.[101]

V

In his *Essay in Defence of the Good Old Cause* of 1659, Henry Stubbe observed that 'Those who are for a free Toleration are the lesse numerous, beyond all proportion', and that without the support of the army they would be powerless. Opponents of toleration, he pointed out, constituted the majority of the population, owned most of the land, and predominated in the ministry and the universities. Given arms and ammunition, Presbyterians and episcopalians would surely destroy 'Sectarian-Toleration'.[102] Stubbe's judgement was sounder than that of W. K. Jordan, who suggested that by 1660 the necessity of toleration was accepted by 'responsible opinion' and 'the mass of men'.[103] In fact, the Restoration settlement proved that support for religious uniformity was very strong among the nation's elites, and during the quarter-century after 1660 England witnessed a persecution of Protestants by Protestants without parallel in seventeenth-century Europe. Dissenters were fined and imprisoned in their thousands for defying the penal laws against non-conformity and holding illegal conventicles.[104]

Yet the toleration controversy did not die; it simply entered a new phase. The main post-Restoration proponents of uniformity were the Anglican royalists rather than the Presbyterians, who now found themselves outside the established Church as the largest group of persecuted dissenters. To their acute discomfort, they now found their own words quoted against them, as Anglicans gleefully republished Presbyterian attacks on tolera-tion, using them to justify the repression of dissent.[105] The experience of persecution sowed seeds of doubt in Presbyterian minds about the wisdom of imposed uniformity in religion, and the Toleration Act of 1689 rein-forced their growing sense that toleration was not such a bad thing after all. By the early eighteenth century, the Presbyterian historian Edmund Calamy was sounding more like John Goodwin than like his own grandfa-ther. Building on the anti-Erastian foundations of earlier Presbyterianism, he defined the two key principles of dissent in ways that would have gladdened the heart of Independents: the right of private judgement with Christ as the sole Lord of conscience, and the spiritual and voluntary nature of the Church with Christ as the sole lawgiver.[106] It was a remark-able turn-around. Within the space of two generations, Presbyterians had moved from denouncing 'accursed toleration' to embracing it. In the eight-eenth century, throughout the English-speaking world they would speak the language of their erstwhile Independent foes.[107]

Anglicans too eventually changed their tune. One of the most intriguing tolerationist works of the revolutionary period was *Liberty of Prophesying*, written in 1647 by a former royal chaplain and future bishop, Jeremy Taylor. The book was very much the product of a particular moment, published at a time when royalists were in negotiations with the Independent party. It argued for a wide-ranging toleration among Christians who differed on secondary matters, and offered a remarkably sympathetic defence of the Baptists. By and large, royalists did not welcome his proposal, and according to one contemporary Charles I himself disapproved of his former chaplain's imaginative proposal.[108] John Reading, another former royal chaplain, rebuked Taylor for giving succour to the Anabaptists and expressed a wish that he would imitate St Augustine by publishing a book of retractions.[109] On this question, Taylor was to be a prophet without honour in his own land, at least in the short term, and he seems later to have distanced himself from his treatise. *Liberty of Prophesying* found its warmest reception among radical puritans such as Roger Williams, who commended the work to an Anglican laywoman, only to be told that she preferred Taylor's defence of the clerical office.[110] Toleration was still perceived as a radical Protestant cause, and it is not surprising to find Samuel Rutherford attacking Taylor alongside Henry Robinson and John Goodwin.[111]

Yet after the Restoration, as some moderate Anglicans began to advocate toleration for dissenters, *Liberty of Prophesying* became one of the most frequently cited tolerationist works by Anglican and dissenter alike, and the former would eventually acclaim a book whose liberality they had once found an embarrassment. It was read by the young John Locke when he was a student under John Owen in Oxford alongside Henry Stubbe.[112] After initially writing against toleration at the Restoration, Locke later changed his mind and in 1689 published his classic *Letter Concerning Toleration*. Although a heterodox thinker and not a representative Anglican, he helped to bring tolerationist ideas into the mainstream of English intellectual culture.

VI

The tolerationists of the revolutionary period pioneered new ways of speaking about religion and politics, and the phrases they popularised would eventually resonate throughout Anglophone Protestant culture. They promoted religious liberty, soul freedom, liberty of conscience, individual judgement, the free exercise of religion, equal freedom without partiality; and they denounced the yoke of bondage, compulsive jurisdiction, ecclesiastical tyranny, dominion over consciences, the magistrate's meddling in matters of religion, coercive power, and persecuting state religion. Some recent historians have been sceptical about the significance of revolutionary writing on toleration, and have suggested that the mentality of these seventeenth-century puritans was far removed from that of Victorian non-conformist Liberals.[113] Yet to read the writings of eighteenth- and nineteenth-century dissenters is to be constantly reminded of the language and arguments of seventeenth-century tolerationists.[114] The great toleration debate of the 1640s and 1650s was a seminal controversy, and one with profound ramifications for England's subsequent religious and political development.

Notes

1   Jonathan Scott, *England's Troubles: Seventeenth-Century English Political Stability in European Context* (Cambridge, 2000), pp. 21, 33.

2   See Perez Zagorin, *How the Idea of Toleration Came to the West* (Princeton, 2003), chap. 6, 'The great English toleration controversy, 1640–1660'.

3   Blair Worden, 'Toleration and the Cromwellian Protectorate', in W. J. Sheils (ed.), *Persecution and Toleration*, Studies in Church History, 21 (Oxford, 1984), pp. 199–200.

4   The resurgence of interest is reflected in a series of books published in the late 1990s: O. P. Grell and R. Scribner (eds), *Tolerance and Intolerance in the European Reformation* (Cambridge, 1996); Cary J. Nederman and John C. Laursen (eds), *Difference and Dissent: Theories of Toleration in Medieval and Early Modern Europe* (Lanham, MD, 1996); C. Berkvens-Stevelinck, J. Israel and G. H. M. Posthumus Meyjes (eds), *The Emergence of Tolerance in the Dutch Republic* (Leiden, 1997); John C. Laursen and Cary J. Nederman (eds), *Beyond the Persecuting Society: Religious Toleration before the Enlightenment* (Philadelphia, 1998); John C. Laursen (ed.), *Religious Toleration: 'The Variety of Rites' from Cyrus to Defoe* (New York, 1999); Alan Levine (ed.), *Early Modern Skepticism and the Origins of Toleration* (Lanham, MD, 1999); and O. P. Grell and R. Porter (eds), *Toleration in Enlightenment Europe* (Cambridge, 1999).

5   Andrew Murphy, *Conscience and Community: Revisiting Toleration and Religious Dissent in Early Modern England and America* (University Park, PA, 2001).

6   Compare Jeremy Taylor, *Liberty of Prophesying* (London, 1647), with Herbert Thorndike, *A Discourse of the Forbearance or the Penalties which a Due Reformation Requires* (London, 1670).

7   See G. Nuttall, *The Holy Spirit in Puritan Faith and Experience* (2nd edn, Chicago, 1992), and M. Watts, *The Dissenters: From the Reformation to the French Revolution* (Oxford, 1978), pp. 1–220.

8   D. Laing (ed.), *Letters and Journals of Robert Baillie*, 3 vols (Edinburgh, 1841–42), vol. 1, pp. 273–4, 283, 287, 311.

9 S. R. Gardiner (ed.) *Constitutional Documents of the Puritan Revolution, 1625–1660* (Oxford, 1889), p. 229.

10 See Conrad Russell, 'Arguments for religious unity in England', *Journal of Ecclesiastical History*, 18 (1967), 201–26.

11 See W. Monter, 'Heresy executions in reformation Europe, 1520–1565', in Grell and Scribner (eds), *Tolerance and Intolerance*.

12 See John Coffey, *Persecution and Toleration in Protestant England, 1558–1689* (Harlow, 2000), pp. 85–104.

13 *Ibid.*, pp. 21–46.

14 Gardiner (ed.), *Constitutional Documents*, pp. 268–9.

15 A. Bonar (ed.), *The Letters of Samuel Rutherford* (Edinburgh, 1984), p. 618.

16 On the tolerationist writings of 1644, see W. Haller, *Liberty and Reformation in the Puritan Revolution* (New York, 1955), pp. 143–88.

17 Thomas Edwards, *Gangraena* (London, 1646), part I, p. 49.

18 See the following sermons preached between September and December 1644: Lazarus Seaman, *Solomon's Choice* (London, 1644), p. 41; Obadiah Sedgwick, *An Arke against a Deluge* (London, 1644), p. 29; William Spurstowe, *England's Eminent Judgements* (London, 1644), p. 28; Edmund Calamy, *An Indictment against England* (London, 1645), pp. 33, 37–8; Thomas Thorowgood, *Moderation Justified* (London, 1645), pp. 10–12.

19 Sedgwick, *An Arke*, p. 29.

20 Calamy, *An Indictment*, p. 37.

21 Samuel Rutherford, *A Sermon preached before the House of Lords* (London, 1645), pp. 33–4.

22 Robert Baillie, *A Dissuasive from the Errours of the Time* (London, 1645); Edwards, *Gangraena*; John Bastwick, *The Utter Routing of the Whole Army of Independents and Sectaries* (London, 1646); Ephraim Pagitt, *Heresiography: or A Description of the Hereticks and Sectaries of these latter times* (London, 1645); Samuel Rutherford, *A Survey of Spiritual Antichrist* (London, 1648). On Edwards, see now Ann Hughes, *Gangraena and the Struggle for the English Revolution* (Oxford, 2004).

23 Samuel Rutherford, *The Due Right of Presbyteries* (London, 1644), pp. 351–86; George Gillespie, *Wholesome Severity reconciled with Christian Liberty* (London, 1645); Thomas Edwards, *The Casting Down of the Last and Strongest Hold of Satan, or A Treatise against Toleration* (London, 1647); Samuel Rutherford, *A Free Disputation against Pretended Liberty of Conscience* (London, 1649).

24 William Prynne, *The Sword of Christian Magistracy Supported* (London, 1647).

25 *A Letter of the Ministers of the City of London ... against Toleration* (London, 1645), p. 6.

26 *The Scots Declaration against the Toleration of Sects and Sectaries, and the Liberty of Conscience* (London, 1647), p. 5.

27 *A Testimony to the Truth of Jesus Christ* (London, 1647), pp. 22, 31, 33.

28 *The Confession of Faith, the Larger and Shorter Catechisms* (Belfast, 1933), pp. 69–71, 81, 153.

29 See *An Ordinance presented to the Honourable House of Commons* (London, 1646); *An Ordinance of the Lords and Commons Assembled in Parliament, for the Punishing of Blasphemies and Heresies* (London, 1648). Although introduced in 1646, the ordinance was only passed in May 1648. It is reprinted in C. H. Firth and R. S. Rait (eds), *Acts and Ordinances of the Interregnum*, 3 vols (London, 1911), vol. 1, pp. 1133–6.

30 Laing (ed.), *Letters and Journals of Robert Baillie*, vol. 2, p. 362.

31 John Goodwin, *Hagiomastix, or The Scourge of the Saints* (London, 1647), sigs bv–br.

32 See Robert S. Paul, *The Assembly of the Lord* (Edinburgh, 1985), and Murray Tolmie, *The Triumph of the Saints* (Cambridge, 1978).

33 For an admirably clear account of the political factions, see David Scott, *Politics and War in the Three Stuart Kingdoms, 1637–49* (Basingstoke, 2004).

34 See A. Zakai, 'Religious toleration and its enemies: the Independent divines and the issue of toleration during the English civil war', *Albion*, 21 (1989), 1–33.

35 Thomas Goodwin, *The Great Interest of States and Kingdoms* (London, 1645), p. 53.

36 Jeremiah Burroughs, *Irenicum, to the Lovers of Truth and Peace* (London, 1645), pp. 18–47.

37 Jeremiah Burroughs, *A Vindication of Mr Burroughes against Mr Edwards ...* (London, 1646), p. 23.

38 A helpful comparative treatment of Congregationalists in England and New England during the revolutionary decades is provided by F. Bremer, *Congregational Communion: Clerical Friendship in the Anglo-American Puritan Community, 1610–1692* (Boston, 1994), pp. 123–201.

39 John Cotton, *The Bloudy Tenent Washed, and Made White in the Bloude of the Lambe* (London, 1647), pp. 5–6, 18, 33, 147–9.

40 See John Cotton, *The Controversie concerning Liberty of Conscience in Matters of Religion* (London, 1646), pp. 13–14; and *The Bloudy Tenent Washed*, pp. 55, 97–100, 173–82.

41 Nathaniel Ward, *The Simple Cobler of Aggawam in America* (London, 1647), pp. 2–8.

42 John Owen, *A Sermon Preached to the House of Commons ... With a Discourse about Toleration* (London, 1649), pp. 58, 61, 65.

43 John Owen, *Vindiciae Evangelicae* (London, 1655), in William H. Goold (ed.), *The Works of John Owen*, 24 vols (Edinburgh, 1850–53), vol. 12, pp. 40–1. Hugh Peter was also alleged to have defended the execution of Servetus: see John Croope, *Conscience Oppression* (London, 1657), p. 52.

44 *A Declaration of the Faith and Order Owned and Practised in the Congregational Churches in England* (London, 1659), pp. 17–18.

45 [William Fiennes], *Vindiciae Veritatis* (London, 1654), p. 147.

46 A. S. P. Woodhouse (ed.), *Puritanism and Liberty* (London, 1938), pp. 142–4, 154–6, 166–8.

47 There is no definitive treatment of Cromwell's position on liberty of

conscience, but see Worden, 'Toleration and the Cromwellian Protectorate', and J. C. Davis, 'Cromwell's religion', in John Morrill (ed.), *Oliver Cromwell and the English Revolution* (London, 1990), pp. 191–9.

48 W. C. Abbott (ed.), *The Writings and Speeches of Oliver Cromwell*, 4 vols (Cambridge, MA, 1937–47), vol. 3, p. 586.

49 Roger Williams, *The Fourth Paper, Presented to Major Butler* (London, 1652), preface.

50 Abbott (ed.), *Writings and Speeches*, vol. 3, pp. 436–7.

51 Bremer, *Congregational Communion*, p. 178.

52 Croope, *Conscience Oppression*, p. 35.

53 *The Humble Proposals of Mr Owen, Mr Tho. Goodwin, Mr Nye, Mr Sympson, and Other Ministers* (London, 1652), pp. 5–6.

54 Gardiner (ed.), *Constitutional Documents*, p. 416.

55 Richard Baxter, *Reliquiae Baxterianae* (London, 1696), part II, pp. 197–9. Baxter, who was also present, objected strenuously, however, to the narrowness of the confession, which he blamed on Owen and Cheynell, the 'over-Orthodox Doctors'.

56 *A New Confession of Faith, or the First Principles of the Christian Religion* (London, 1654). George Thomason acquired a copy, now in the British Library (E.826.3).

57 See S. R. Gardiner, *The History of the Commonwealth and Protectorate*, 4 vols (London, 1903), vol. 3, p. 220.

58 Edwards, *The Casting Down of … Satan*, title page.

59 Baillie, *A Dissuasive*, epistle dedicatory. See also *An Attestation of our Reverend Brethren of the Province of London* (London, 1648), unpaginated, which contrasts Burroughs with Williams, 'that Catholick Advocate and Patron of all irreligious'.

60 Gillespie, *Wholesome Severity*, p. 2. The four writers he had in mind were Williams, Goodwin, Robinson and Walwyn.

61 See C. Polizotto, 'Liberty of conscience and the Whitehall debates of 1648–49', *Journal of Ecclesiastical History*, 26 (1975), 69–82.

62 Sedgwick, *An Arke*, p. 29.

63 Edwards, *The Casting Down … of Satan*, p. 197.

64 John Goodwin, 'Epistle to the reader', in Jacobus Acontius, *Satans Stratagems* (London, 1648), sigs a4–A.

65 Thomas Helwys, *A Short Declaration of the Mystery of Iniquity* (London, 1612); Leonard Busher, *Religions Peace, or a Plea for Liberty of Conscience* (London, 1614); Thomas Helwys, *Persecution for Religion Judged and Condemned* (1615); John Murton, *Objections Answered* (London, 1615); John Murton, *A Most Humble Supplication* (London, 1620).

66 *Freedome of Religious Worship* (1654), p. 26.

67 See for example, *Londons Metamorphosis: or, a Dialogue between London & Amsterdam* (London, 1647). The claim that London was being 'Amsterdamnified by several opinions' occurs as early as 1641: *Religions Enemies* (London, 1641), p. 6.

68 Laing (ed.), *Letters and Journals of Robert Baillie*, vol. 2, p. 184.

69 Roger Williams, *The Bloudy Tenent of Persecution*, ed. E.B.Underhill (London, 1848), p.2.

70 Laing (ed.), *Letters and Journals of Robert Baillie*, vol.2, p.235.

71 *Ibid.*, vol.2, pp.180–1, 184. Baillie was probably commenting on [John Goodwin], *M.S. to A.S. with a Plea for Liberty of Conscience* (London, 1644), pp.53–4.

72 D.Wolffe (ed.), *Leveller Manifestoes of the Puritan Revolution* (New York, 1944), p.227.

73 *A Brief Confession or Declaration of Faith set forth by many of us, who are (falsely) called Ana-baptists* (London, 1660), p.10.

74 See for example, J[ohn] M[ilton], *Considerations touching the Likeliest Means to Remove Hirelings out of the Church* (London, 1659).

75 Williams, *The Bloudy Tenent*, p.154.

76 This point is developed in Christopher Blackwood, *The Storming of Antichrist* (London, 1644), and [Sir Henry Vane], *Zeal Examined* (London, 1652).

77 See Thomas Collier, *The Exaltation of Christ* (London, 1646), pp.93–6.

78 Williams, *The Bloudy Tenent, passim.*

79 Woodhouse, *Puritanism and Liberty*, pp.155–69.

80 John Milton, *Areopagitica* (London, 1644), in D.M.Wolfe (ed.), *The Complete Prose Works of John Milton*, 8 vols (New Haven, CT, 1953–82), vol.2, p.550.

81 John Goodwin, *Imputatio Fidei, or A Treatise of Justification* (London, 1642), sigs b3v–c2.

82 This argument is developed in two of Goodwin's most important tolerationist tracts: *Theomachia* (London, 1644) and *Hagiomastix* three years later.

83 John Goodwin, *Basanistai, or the Triers [or Tormentors] Tried and Cast* (London, 1657), pp.18–20.

84 [John Goodwin], *M.S. to A.S.*, pp.79–80; John Goodwin, *Innocency and Truth Triumphing Together* (London, 1645), pp.89–90.

85 John Goodwin, *Thirty Queries* (London, 1653), pp.3–4, 6.

86 Woodhouse (ed.), *Puritanism and Liberty*, pp.156–7; John Goodwin, *The Apologist Condemned* (London, 1653), pp.7–25.

87 Williams, *The Bloudy Tenent*, pp.131, 40.

88 *Freedom of Religious Worship*, p.43.

89 See J.Coffey, 'Puritanism and liberty revisited: the case for toleration in the English Revolution', *Historical Journal*, 41 (1998), 961–85; N.Matar, 'The toleration of Muslims in Renaissance England: practice and theory', in Laursen (ed.), *Religious Toleration*, pp.129–31; N.Carlin, 'Toleration for Catholics in the puritan revolution', in Grell and Scribner (eds), *Tolerance and Intolerance*, pp.216–30.

90 [Henry Robinson], *A Short Answer to A.S.* (London, 1645), p.35.

91 William Birchley [John Austin], *The Christian Moderator, or Persecution for Conscience Condemned*, 3 parts (London, 1651–3); *Englands Settlement upon the Two Solid Foundations of the Peoples Civil and Religious Liberties* (1659); T.F., *Philanthropia, or A Holding Forth of Universal*

Immunitie in Exercise of Christian Religion (London, 1659). These works drew replies from anti-tolerationists; see Francis Wilde, *Legenda Lignea, with an Answer to Mr Birchleys Moderator* (London, 1653), and *Englands Settlement Mistaken* (London, 1660).

92   J[ohn] M[ilton], *A Treatise of Civil Power in Ecclesiastical Causes* (London, 1659), in Wolfe (ed.), *Complete Prose Works of Milton*, vol. 7, pp. 254–5.

93   John Milton, 'A Letter to a Friend', in Wolfe (ed.), *Complete Prose Works of Milton*, vol. 7, p. 330.

94   William Walwyn, *Tolleration Justified*, in J. R. MacMichael and B. Taft (eds), *The Writings of William Walwyn* (Athens, GA, 1989), p. 164.

95   *A Brief Confession or Declaration of Faith*, p. 10.

96   See L. Damrosch, *The Sorrows of the Quaker Jesus: James Nayler and the Puritan Crackdown on the Free Spirit* (Cambridge MA, 1996), pp. 177–228.

97   See J. T. Rutt (ed.), *The Diary of Thomas Burton*, 4 vols (London, 1828), vol. 1, pp. 24–264. For the use of Calvin, Rutherford and Cotton see p. 151; for Holland, Packer and Sprigge see pp. 78, 99–101, 166, 216–17, 247.

98   Milton, *Treatise of Civil Power*, in Wolfe (ed.), *Complete Prose Works of Milton*, vol. 7, p. 241.

99   C. Polizzotto, 'The campaign against "The Humble Proposals" of 1652', *Journal of Ecclesiastical History*, 38 (1987), 569–81; Blair Worden, 'John Milton and Oliver Cromwell', in I. Gentles, J. Morrill and B. Worden (eds), *Soldiers, Writers and Statesmen of the English Revolution* (Cambridge, 1998), pp. 243–64.

100 See, for example, Edward Barber, *The Storming and Totall Routing of Tythes* (London, 1651); *The Spirit of Persecution again Broken Loose* (London, 1655); Thomas Collier, *A Brief Answer to some of the Objections and Demurs made against the Coming in and Inhabiting of the Jews in this Common-wealth* (London, 1656); and Goodwin, *Basanistai*.

101 See, for example, Milton, *A Treatise of Civil Power*; Thomas Collier, *The Decision and Clearing of the Great Point now in Controversie about the Interest of Christ and the Civil Magistrate* (London, 1659); *The True Magistrate, or the Magistrates Duty and Power in Matters of Religion* (1659); *The Leveller, or The Principles and Maxims concerning Government and Religion which are asserted by those that are commonly called Levellers* (London, 1659).

102 Henry Stubbe, *An Essay in Defence of the Good Old Cause* (London, 1659), sigs **8v–**8r.

103 Jordan, *The Development of Religious Toleration*, vol. 4, pp. 9, 467.

104 Coffey, *Persecution and Toleration*, pp. 166–79.

105 *Toleration Disapprov'd and Condemn'd* (London, 1670).

106 Edmund Calamy, *A Defence of Moderate Non-Conformity*, 3 vols (London, 1703–5).

107 J. Bradley, 'The religious origins of radical politics in England, Scotland and Ireland, 1662–1800', in J. Bradley and D. van Kley (eds), *Religion and Politics in Enlightenment Europe* (Notre Dame, 2001), pp. 187–253.

108   See S.R.Gardiner, *History of the Great Civil War*, 4 vols (London, 1893), vol. 3, pp. 310–12.

109   John Reading, *Anabaptism Routed* (London, 1655), preface.

110   G.Lafantasie (ed.), *The Correspondence of Roger Williams*, 2 vols (Hanover, NH, 1988), vol. 1, pp. 376, 379–80.

111   Samuel Rutherford, *A Free Disputation against Pretended Liberty of Conscience tending to resolve Doubts moved by Mr. John Goodwin, John Baptist, Dr. Jer. Taylor* (London, 1649).

112   John Marshall, *John Locke: Resistance, Religion and Responsibility* (Cambridge, 1994), pp. 5–6.

113   Worden, 'Toleration and the Cromwellian Protectorate'; W.Lamont, 'Pamphleteering, the Protestant consensus and the English Revolution', in R.C.Richardson and G.M.Ridden (eds), *Freedom and the English Revolution* (Manchester, 1986), pp. 72–92; J.C.Davis, 'Religion and the struggle for freedom in the English Revolution', *Historical Journal*, 35 (1992), 507–30.

114   Bradley, 'The religious origins of radical politics'; T.Larsen, *Friends of Religious Equality: Nonconformist Politics in Mid-Victorian England* (Woodbridge, 1999).

3

The legacy of mothers and others: women's theological writing, 1640–60

Elizabeth Clarke

I

Scholars of the seventeenth century have recently become increasingly interested in the way the collapse of print censorship in England between 1640 and 1642 produced a flood of publications, many of which were theological in nature and written by godly men who during the previous decade had been denied expression by Laudian licensers.[1] However, despite the widely held belief that women were more committed to their religious practices than men, a view for which Bernard Capp has recently provided qualified support, there was no corresponding increase in theological publications by women.[2]

Cultural prescriptions against women publishing their own work had permeated very deeply into Tudor and Stuart society, and the handful of volumes published by women during the first part of the seventeenth century included few works that could be considered as 'theology'. Those that did venture into this territory were usually disguised as 'mothers' legacies' – documents whose very conditions for authorship helped to illustrate just how draconian attitudes to publication by women were. After all, the *raison d'être* of a 'mother's legacy' was the imminent death of the author as foreseen by herself, and its primary readership was ostensibly the author's children, to whom she 'privately' communicated her most precious beliefs. Nonetheless, in some cases this rationale for writing did lead to something like systematic theological reflection. Dorothy Leigh's *The mothers blessing: or, the godly counsaile of a gentle-woman* went into twenty-three editions between 1616 and 1674, and must have done much to form the widespread seventeenth-century expectation that women's religious writing should be pious and practical, more concerned with morality and spirituality than theology.[3]

A further popular example of this genre was Elizabeth Jocelin's *The mothers legacie, to her unborne childe*, written on her (accurate) expectation of dying in childbirth in 1622. It was edited by Thomas Goad, a committed Calvinist and chaplain to the Archbishop of Canterbury, George Abbot. Although he noted her other studies in theology, history and foreign languages and her 'taste and faculty in Poetry', Goad published just this one treatise by Jocelin, and probably only because it agreed with his own Calvinist beliefs.[4] Furthermore, Sylvia Brown has argued that he thought her original work too radical and edited it accordingly.[5]

Another such 'mother's legacy' (*A ladies legacie to her daughters. In three books. Composed of prayers and meditations, fitted for severall times, and upon severall occasions. As also several prayers for each day in the weeke*) was published in 1645 by Elizabeth Richardson, who was related to the Villiers family and had substantial influence at court. Its conservative packaging again denotes an apparently private document, and Richardson stresses at the start: 'I had no purpose at all, when I writ these books, for the use of my selfe and my children, to make them publicke'. Unlike other 'mothers' who left such textual testimonies, however, she was not in fact dead, but had been 'lately over perswaded by some that much desired to have [the prayers]'. It is not difficult to establish the political and religious affiliations of her supporters, as the circumstances and location of composition are explicitly spelt out in the text: 'This Booke was written at *Chelsey* in the year 1625, by E. A. at the Duke of Buckingham's house, a part whereof was lent me by the good Dutches, my most honoured lady, when the great sickness was in *London*.' This mention of the Duchess of Buckingham is enough to link Richardson's publication with others dedicated to the Duke of Buckingham's Catholic widow, all of which shared the tinge of Counter-Reformation spirituality distinctive to Henrietta Maria's court.[6]

The book's inscription asserts that the author composed the piece while she was still married to her first husband, John Ashburnham, and the extensive account of its origins was probably intended to present the writing as apolitical and to remind the reader of a time when religious culture was less polarised. Detailed study of the manuscript reveals, however, that the second part of the work was written in 1635, as the highly controversial Laudian prescriptions were taking hold in the Church.[7] Moreover, its publication in 1645 was clearly intended as an intervention in contemporary liturgical debates. The same year as it appeared, the Westminster Assembly's *A directory for the publique worship of God* became the official liturgy of the English Church in place of the Elizabethan Prayer Book and replaced the latter's set prayers with guided extempore forms.[8]

Richardson was certainly strongly opposed to these extempore prayers, declaring: 'When thou enterest into the house of God, take heed thou offerest not unto him the sacrifice of fooles, but before thou prayest, prepare thyself, thy heart and tongue.' Her volume included set prayers to be read throughout the day from waking to retiring, and also for the feasts of the Prayer Book liturgy, soon to be banned. Within its conventional packaging, therefore, Richardson's 'legacy' delivered a radically conservative political and religious message, and one highly critical of the new religious establishment.

If there remained very real cultural disincentives to the production of women's theological writings, theological reflection by women during the late sixteenth and early seventeenth centuries must nevertheless have been stimulated by the English Church's campaign to educate the population as a whole in knowledge of the Bible and sound doctrine. This was reflected in the many aids to Bible study which proliferated during these years in the shape of commentaries and concordances.[9] William Laud had discouraged the publication of such documents, raising suspicion that theological reflection by the masses was precisely what he did not want. Following his fall from power in 1641, however, the Long Parliament had commissioned its Committee for Religion to produce a new set of annotations to the Bible. When these appeared in 1645, produced by a team of mostly Presbyterian divines, their lengthy preface spelt out a narrative of proto-democratic concern for the unlearned in society. The statute of Henry VIII's reign restricting Bible-reading to the landed classes was indignantly repudiated, and it was made clear that the natural perspicuity of scripture meant that all individuals, rich and poor, learned and unlearned, men and women, were capable of correct interpretation.[10] Such a perspective emboldened many self-educated men from the lower orders not only to publish their thoughts but also to start their own sects, and a long-running controversy over the status of such 'theology' was set in train. Women with a penchant for controversy often also gravitated to the more radical sects, where their contributions were more likely to be valued.[11]

The writings of radical women have been much studied by feminist scholars, partly because their unorthodox sentiments and vehement expression seem to give them a sense of agency and purpose often missing from other women's work of the period.[12] It is difficult, however, to trace the disciplines traditionally associated with theology in the dictated 'songs' of Fifth Monarchist Anna Trapnel, or the fierce denunciations of the Quaker Hester Biddle, although, as Elaine Hobby has pointed out, many radical women did show signs of having studied the Bible systematically.[13] This article is more interested in the writings of those women who attempted to take seriously the puritan promise that they too could be interpreters of the Bible and expositors of doctrine. It will not attempt to treat these works as a unified phenomenon in which gender is the most important focus for analysis. Once the theological content of women's religious writing is given priority over their attempts to authorise it, it becomes clear that the writing practices of women during the English Revolution reflected the fragmentations of society as a whole rather than any sense of a unified female tradition. It is very rare, for example, to find evidence of one woman writer reading the work of another, although Sylvia Brown has argued that Elizabeth Jocelin had read Dorothy Leigh's work.[14] What is perhaps more interesting is the question of whether men bothered to read theological works published by women, or whether the few works that appeared represented a doomed attempt to realise a puritan vision for women that was already fatally undermined by the dominant patriarchal culture.

II

One of the first documents written by a woman in the revolutionary period was a product of the vigorous debate over religious toleration and separation from the English Church. The early 1640s saw the rapid growth of separatist congregations, whose government and discipline were conceived to be more radically biblical than the Presbyterian Church, which was itself supplanting the pre-war Church of England. The fact that the London separatist Katherine Chidley contributed to this debate was a bold step in itself, as she took it upon herself to answer a particularly authoritative intervention in the controversy by the London minister Thomas Edwards, who was to become the Presbyterians' main controversialist of the 1640s. By 1641 Chidley already had a long history of being persecuted for membership of separatist congregations. Active in a gathered church in Shrewsbury in the 1620s, she and her husband Daniel were driven out of the town at the end of the decade. They then moved to London, and in the 1630s founded an illegal separatist congregation with John Duppa and Thomas Dyer. They also met John Lilburne, and Katherine was subsequently to become active in the Leveller petitioning movement of the mid- and late 1640s.[15]

Soon after the appearance in 1641 of Edwards's *Reasons against the independant government of particular congregations: as also against the toleration of such churches to be erected in this kingdome*, Chidley issued her long refutation (*The justification of the independant churches of Christ. Being an answer to Mr. Edvvards his booke, which hee hath written against the government of Christs church, and toleration of Christs publike worship*), a work she clearly expected to be read by the

Long Parliament MPs.[16] Although in conventionally humble style she represented herself as a 'weake Instrument' and 'a poore worme', there is only one explicit reference to her gender within the eighty-one-page treatise. This was the ominous choice of a verse for the front cover, which reproduced in full the text of Judges 4: 21, describing the bloody, if godly, execution of the Canaanite general Sisera by the Kenite woman Jael.[17] It is possible that this epigraph was not even her own choice, but rather a sensationalist piece of advertising by her publisher. If so, it certainly made an impact, as Edwards mentioned her by name and linked her with Jael in the third part of his influential 1646 volume, *Gangraena* (iii, p. 170).

At the heart of Katherine Chidley's radical theology was the assumption that the gift of the Holy Spirit redressed social inequalities and rendered the poorest Christian fit to make spiritual judgements. This was in fact an orthodox doctrine of the Church of England; in his poem 'Faith' even the conservative minister George Herbert had celebrated the idea that 'A peasant may believe as much/As a great Clerk, and reach the highest stature'. But the Independents, who were taking advantage of the new freedoms of the 1640s to establish their own gathered churches, took this belief to its logical conclusion, and Chidley proudly proclaimed the right of ordinary members of congregations to elect and 'ordain' their own ministers. To Edwards's objection that such ministers might not be discerning men, she countered that they did not need to possess every spiritual gift, and that others in the spiritual body of the Church would provide discernment. She was particularly scathing about Edwards's stress on the importance of Presbyterian synods, which she declared to be unbiblical and even cursed by God, and she insisted that each congregation should only uphold what had been revealed to them directly by God.[18]

Chidley detected Edwards' fear that toleration of gathered churches would threaten the whole structure of contemporary society by undermining the power of husbands, fathers and masters, and she answered him in terms which, though primarily gendered, also referred to contemporary class distinctions:

> I pray you tell me, what power the unbeleeving husband hath over the conscience of his beleeving wife. It is true he hath authority over her in bodily and civill respects, but not to be a Lord over her conscience – and the like may be said of fathers and masters, and it is the same authority which the Soveraigne hath over all his subjects.[19]

In the light of subsequent developments, despite Chidley's assertion that the Independents 'will in all lawfull things be subject to the Kings Majesty', Edwards was right to be apprehensive about the social and political implications of the growth of Independency.[20]

Throughout her 1641 treatise, Chidley maintained an authoritative tone; her favourite refrain was 'I have told you before', a formulation which was hardly consistent with her conventional and somewhat cursory statement of women's inadequacy in writing theology, and her description of herself as a 'worme'.[21] Moreover, she was not afraid to be extremely critical of the pre-war established Church, accusing it of maintaining papist practices, and going so far as to suggest that it had been complicit in the Marian persecutions of the 1550s and had more recently provoked the unrest that led to the Bishops' War: 'Was not the sending of your *Masse-books* into *Scotland* the cause of the disturbance?' She was even prepared to make jokes. Defending the Independents against the accusation that they were 'loose in hair and apparel', she suggested that 'the haire you were offended at, might be some Periwigge, which some of them have been constrained by fear to put on, to blinde the eyes of the Bishops Blood-hounds'.[22] The source of her boldness was the sense of enfranchisement that her radical Christian reading of scripture had given her: 'wee have learnt, that the poore receive the Gospell ... [that] the liberty, power and rule should be in the whole, and not in one man, or a few'. Archbishops, bishops, deans and suffragans were dismissed as a 'rabble ... bred in the smoake of the pit', and as non-biblical officers, 'inventions of their owne'. The only officers Christ had given to the Church were biblical ones – apostles, prophets, evangelists, pastors and teachers. Chidley confidently believed that God would equip her to dispute with respected men on equal terms. At the end of *The justification* she challenged Edwards to take part in a public disputation, in which they could each choose six disputants under the rule of a neutral moderator. She clearly had every confidence that her scriptural reasoning would prevail.[23]

Edwards, of course, declined the invitation, but three years later he responded to the appearance of the tract *An Apologeticall Narration*, drawn up by leading Independents in the Westminster Assembly, by writing a second attack on several separatist men under the title *Antapologia*. Clearly frustrated at being ignored by Edwards, Chidley now re-entered the lists, publishing in early 1645 *A new-yeares-gift, or, A brief exhortation to Mr. Thomas Edwards that he may breake off his old sins in the old yeare and begin the new yeare with new fruits of love, first to God, and then to his brethren*. As well as reiterating many of the arguments of *The justification*, in this second tract Chidley joked about contemporary cultural constructions of women's writing, turning them back upon Edwards's *Antapologia*: 'finding his booke to be a *rangling – insinuating – contradictory – revengefull –* story, it appeared unto me to be a task most befitting a Woman'. The identity she chose for herself in the first sentence of this new treatise was that of the boy David, going to battle against the Philistines for want of a better champion within the Israelite ranks. Her conscious identification here was less with women as an oppressed group than with tradesmen and the poorly educated of both sexes; 'Taylors, Felt-makers, button-makers, Tent-makers, Shepherds or Ploughmen, or what honest Trade soever' are listed as the 'well-meaning Christians' who should be able to found their own gathered churches. Well aware of the biblical preference for the poor, she constantly emphasised the corresponding generosity of the Holy Spirit in endowing the ordinary Christian with theological gifts.[24] In one marginal gloss in *A new-yeares-gift*, she expressed her annoyance with the Scottish Presbyterian Samuel Rutherford, who, she claimed, had 'divers times in his book named (or rather nick-named me) instead of answering me'.[25] This may suggest that she had seen a copy of Rutherford's *The Divine Right of Church-Government and Excommunication* prior to its publication in 1646. If so, the 'nick-name' she is referring to must be Jezebel, who is mentioned along with 'false teachers' on page 9 of that tract.[26]

Katherine Chidley's writings reveal just how dramatically individual Bible-reading could affect the writing of religious radicals who had been taught by their godly ministers to trust their own interpretation of scripture. Their reception, however, also makes clear that, while a woman might be empowered by scripture to read and to write, there was no guarantee that the men in whom contemporary political and ecclesiastical power resided would take much, if any, notice of her.

III

From the opposite side of the argument, and taking a very different tack, was the fervent Presbyterian Elizabeth Warren, who between 1645 and 1649 published three theological tracts: *The old and good way vindicated* (1645); *Spiritual Thrift, or Meditations wherein humble Christians (as in a mirrour) may view the veracity of their saving graces* ... (1647); and *A warning-peece from Heaven* (1649). In her first work, *The old and good way vindicated*, Warren defended the godly Presbyterian ministry against the attacks of the separatists, whose emergence she saw as a dire calamity, and one which had provoked her against her womanly modesty to take up her pen. As Katherine Philips was also to do later, she invoked the story of Croesus's son, the dumb boy incited to speak by the immediate peril to his father. Rehearsing the *topos* of reluctance, she declares that she was asked to publish the work by her friends, an affirmation confirmed by George Jenny in a note at the end of the second edition.[27] Jenny's declaration was probably contrived to address what had clearly been a widespread opinion that the first edition had not been the work of a woman. Further proof of Warren's authorship was provided by the inclusion in the 1646 second edition of a letter she wrote to Jenny, in which she constructed herself as an exemplary woman. Dated 30 December 1645, it stated that she had not wanted to add to a second edition of her work, as she was under too much domestic stress: 'Besides my particular in the education of youth, and my ordinary businesse in governing my family, the necessity of many, especially of our Sexe, importune my care, and crave my compassion.' All these activities – education of the young, care of the family, and concern for younger women – were biblically sanctioned responsibilities for women.

In some perplexity, Warren concludes that there is nothing she can do, besides providing a sincere affirmation, to prove that she was a woman and had written the treatise herself. Several men, however, came to her aid, testifying to her exemplarity both as the author of the treatise and as a woman. No less a person than the licenser, the Presbyterian James Cranford, wrote her a testimony and an *imprimatur*: 'Having perused (not without admiration) this short, but seasonable Treatise, I could not but see fulfilled that of the Psalmist, *Out of the mouths of babes and sucklings hast thou ordained strength* ... And that of the Prophet, *Upon my hand-maids will I poure out of my spirit*.'[28] The verse from Psalm 8 was frequently invoked both by men and by women in defence of women's publications throughout the seventeenth century.[29] In her later *Spiritual Thrift*, Warren's efforts were also validated by the Presbyterian minister of Woodbridge in Suffolk, Robert Cade: 'I have lived an unworthy Minister in the same town with the Authour of this Treatise these six and twenty years, and have been a constant observer and admirer.'[30] Cade had come to the parish of St Mary, Woodbridge, in 1623. If Warren the author was the 'Ellsebeth Warren' christened there on 19 December 1617, Cade would in fact have known her for twenty-four of her thirty years.

The testimonies affixed to her work by these men claimed that Warren was no ordinary woman. Cranford's use of scripture to indicate that God could speak through anyone, including women and babies, was reinforced by other supporters who emphasised the suitability of this particular woman for receiving divine inspiration. Warren's learning was certainly untypical of her sex. Despite the 'sex-deficiency' that she conventionally pleads in her dedicatory letter, the margins of her tracts are covered, not only with biblical citations that provided scriptural authority for her ideas, but also by Latin quotations from theologians such as Chrysostom, Augustine, Bernard, Gregory, Ambrose and Calvin. Not only did she read these works in Latin and collect *sententiae*, following a commonplace-book practice that Ann Moss has described as exclusively male, she also wrote Latin and expanded on these extracts.[31] As she states in her letter in the second edition of *The old and good way vindicated*: 'the quotations indeed I collected from Authors suting the subject in their genuine sence, sometimes enlarging them'. She also justifies her 'masculine' learning in her dedication 'To the Christian Reader': 'And if any suppose me Proteus-like, to change the shape of my silent modesty, let their Christian moderation embrace this Maxime, that Grace devests Nature of no due ornament.'[32] By 1645 exemplary Presbyterian femininity seemingly did not rule out the display of knowledge of Latin.

Perhaps it helped that Elizabeth Warren, as befitted a supporter of the Presbyterian ministry, was in favour of human learning and against unqualified preachers, 'such as ascend to a higher pitch of arrogance, that ... cry down, with *Iulian*, all Christian Academies, asserting that humane learning is needlesse, and that men are qualified by immediate inspiration'.[33] *The old and good way vindicated* also included the familiar historical account of tribulations of the godly in their struggle against popery, from the halcyon days of Edward VI and Elizabeth I – 'that Heroick and prudent Princesse' – through the dark days of the Stuarts when 'the brat of Popery was almost come to birth, and our godly Ministers who should have stifled it ... were exiled and scattered into remote and distant Kingdomes, by the insulting tyranny of a Popish prelaticall Clergie', to the Presbyterian resurgence of the 1640s.[34]

There is nothing particularly gender-conscious in Warren's defence of the Presbyterian ministry, and she seems in fact to share in conventional sexist attitudes. After rehearsing arguments for equality between Christians, she goes on to rebuke those unlearned individuals whose pride led them to aspire to ordination:

> those which intrude into this mighty work, having neither due calling, nor fit abilities, for a sincere and conscientious discharge of the duty; some of such persons being merely mechanick, who leap from the limits of their lawfull station, affecting a dignity transcending their desert, and feeding like Cameleons on the aire of popular applause, *creeping into houses*, as saith the Apostle, *and holding captive poor silly women*.[35]

Unlike earlier female writers, such as Aemilia Lanyer and Anne Southwell, who had proclaimed the gender of the Church as the Bride of Christ as primarily female, Warren was prepared to accept the designation of the ordained male ministry as the Spouse of Christ, which shared in the intimate experience of the garden of the Song of Songs. From her perspective, male ministers were the 'nursing mothers' to other Christians, who 'therefore must still blesse the womb that bare us, and the paps that nourished us with that sincere milk'.[36] A second edition of *The old and good way vindicated* was published within a year. This was a rare achievement for a female author, as only four out of 130 works written by women in the 1650s were published more than once.[37]

Warren's second volume, *Spiritual Thrift* of 1647, was another work of Presbyterian learning and culture, setting out for fallen men and women how to make the most of their opportunities for sanctification, whether physical, economic or spiritual. It was arranged like a sermon on John 6: 12: 'Gather up the fragments that remaine, that nothing be lost'.[38] As in her first work, every margin is heavily annotated with Latin quotations. There is a significant change, however, in her final tract of 1649, where, in the aftermath of Charles I's execution, the apocalyptic warnings that had always lurked beneath the surface of her work took over. *A warning-peece from heaven, against the sins of the times, inciting us to fly from the vengeance to come. Or, Mournfull meditations of revealed wrath, appearing in the progresse of our sins and sorrows* was issued by the same publisher, Henry Shepherd, as her earlier work, but Elizabeth Warren was now no longer designated as 'A lover of Truth and Peace'. This was perhaps no surprise, as her argument here was vehemently anti-tolerationist and, although couched in generalities, came close to criticising those responsible for the King's execution.[39] While the front cover contained a grand engraving, the earlier testimonies by well-known men were now entirely missing. Perhaps by 1649 the writing of a woman did not need such public support to be seen as legitimate; more likely Elizabeth Warren in prophetic strain was too much for her male supporters.

IV

A third female theological writer, Mary Pope, who has often been thought of as a royalist prophet, did not feel the same need for male testimonies of support. Her 1647 tract, *A Treatise of Magistracy*, which took the form of an address to the Long Parliament, claimed an authority for herself unmediated by male hierarchies. Her only help in composition, she declared, had been God Himself and her son who had acted as her scribe.[40] The work was prefaced by twenty-four pages of dedicatory epistles; the longest of these was addressed to the King, as bishop, elder and steward of the Church, the others to the Lords and Commons, and to the Christian Reader. It is in the epistle to the reader that Pope sets out her own credentials for authorship. She has been 'an observer of the ebbings and flowings up and downe of Gods providence' over twenty years, and as a result had 'gotten understanding'. She also claims somewhat enigmatically to have acquired some position in the Church, 'God having made me a Mother in Israel'. Her main appeal, however, throughout the treatise was to the authority of her own interpretation of scripture, 'having good warrant out of Gods word' both for her message and for her right to give it as a woman. The volume is full of scriptural examples of women who had contributed to the work of God, or authoritatively spoken the words of God to their communities. In her epistle to parliament, her role model was the woman of Tekoah, who in 2 Samuel 14 spoke to David on behalf of Absalom in an attempt to secure his return from exile, a precedent she uses to call upon the MPs to bring Charles I back to London from his house-arrest at Holdenby House in Northamptonshire.

In the biblical account, although the woman of Tekoah was listened to by David, who accepted her message as the word of God, he also discerned that she had been incited to deliver her message by Joab, who had 'put the words in her mouth'. Although this might have been construed as undermining the woman of Tekoah's agency, Mary Pope positively glories in this fact, declaring that God is the one whose message she is delivering. In the epistle to the reader, she elaborates on this by claiming that the treatise was the product of co-operation between God and herself, and by declaring 'God ... forcing of me on, and as it were improving of the tallents which he has given for his glory, and serving of my generation'. At the end of the epistle to the reader, she answers the objection that her writings are nonsense with a statement of her confidence in the veracity of her own interpretation and knowledge of scripture, and her use of 'right reason'.[41]

'Nonsense' her treatise manifestly was not. On her title page she summarised the pressing contemporary religious and political concerns she was addressing, declaring:

> *the magistrate hath beene, and for ever is to be the cheife officer in the Church, out of the Church, and over the Church; and that the two Testaments hold forth. Soveraignty lieth in rule and dominion; now if soveraignty lieth in rule and dominion, I desire to ask one question in this kingdome, who is the soveraigne? Subjection lieth in duty, and obedience; rule is that which makes a king: obedience is that which constitutes a subject. Rule and dominion, I meane that which exerciseth it selfe in a pious and legitimate discipline, for the well preservation, and direction of a people; and this is that which tyeth a king to his subjects.*[42]

The context for Pope's authorship was clearly the same tradition as that to which Elizabeth Warren appealed: a Reformed theology which leant towards Presbyterianism, and which, in an echo of Warren's tract, Pope calls 'the old way and the good path', a phrase from Jeremiah 6:16. Although William Laud had used the same formulation, there is nothing Laudian about Pope's treatise, despite its evident royalism. In fact, although she does not name him explicitly, there is a strong hint that she believed the former archbishop had been allied with Antichrist.[43] The first open rebellion against God in England she equates with the Book of Sports and the collection of ship money. The sale of knighthoods and patents had also been reprehensible to God, and the Bible had not been a living presence in England during the late 1630s.[44] Apart from this hiatus, however, she asserts that in England 'Gods unerring truths have beene powerfully taught for above 100 years' and there was thus no need to break away from the national Church to form gathered churches. In her opposition to sectarianism and heresy, and in particular in her description of the problems of households divided by membership of different churches, she often sounds like Thomas Edwards. She is also particularly contemptuous of those ministers who administered Holy Communion at night in upper rooms so as to be closer to the scriptural account of the Last Supper, a practice that she declares was 'hot' in the mid-1640s when she began her treatise.[45]

Pope is nothing if not self-dramatising. In one of her appeals to Parliament, dated 27 January 1647, she announced that 'there is a child to bee brought forth, which is neither Presbyterian nor Independent', a child to whom parliament should listen.[46] This child is her prophecy, with which she is in travail at the start of her epistle to parliament, and is one that 'shall not be abortive, but shalbe brought forth in due time, and borne a goodly child'.[47] This mysterious prophecy may be her interpretation of the image of an extremely complicated candlestick in Zachariah 4:

> And now that God hath by his poore weak worthless, and unworthy hand-maid (I say) God hath by me a contemptible woman, made out the full directory which is in his Word, and Government of his Church ... all of it infolded, and comprehended, under the type of this golden Candlestick.[48]

At this point, her rational, discursive treatise becomes more characteristic of prophetic discourse. She assigns meanings to each part of the candle-stick's mechanism, employing this typology to set out her particular model of how ministry and magistracy should co-operate to the advantage of the Church. Zachariah 4: 10 also provides the source text for her warning at the end of the epistle to the reader, 'Despise not the day of small things', a clear reference to the supposed weakness of her sex. Like Katherine Chidley, however, she allies herself as a woman with other neglected classes of unlearned Protestants, and she employs the parable of the widow's mite to highlight their significance:

> Multitudes have brought their small mites to put their helping hand to contend for our Laws and Liberties, which were left unto us by our fore-fathers; and which *Magna Charta*, as I have heard, will witness, and which we are to leave as an inheritance to our childrens children, and so acciden-tally with them to contend *for the faith which was once given to the Saints, Jude 3*.[49]

Mary Pope's willingness to contribute her own 'widow's mite' in the form of her addresses to Parliament grew out of the logic of Reformed theology, with its stress on the perspicuity of scripture and the importance of every individual, whatever the handicaps of poverty, lack of education, or gender. Ironically, the same premise underlay Katherine Chidley's pamphlet, although Pope comes to a diametrically opposed conclusion about Church government. Despite her argument for the power of Christian ministry and magistracy, and support for the King as head of the Church, her tracts also display a profoundly anti-hierarchical approach to the scriptures, which allowed herself and fellow women, such as Chidley and Warren, to consider their opinions worth publishing.

Pope clearly considered that she was making a meaningful intervention in public life. Like Katherine Chidley, she wanted those who disagreed with her to respond to her treatise. She also showed herself aware of the importance of the processes of publication, and asked that someone she approved of be appointed to manage this process.[50] It is disappointing, therefore, that there is apparently no surviving trace of her petitions to Parliament. But she obviously followed developments at Westminster closely. She refers, for example, with approval to Thomas Coleman's arguments about ecclesiastical authority (even though this Presbyterian minister of St Peter's Cornhill had also spoken out against women preachers).[51] And she was clearly well known in London Presbyterian circles, as George Thomason, a potential sympathiser, supplies her full name and address at the end of his copy of her tract.

Her increasingly frantic appeals to Parliament in the run-up to the King's execution suggest that she was a name to conjure with in contemporary religious culture. Although they remain closely reasoned from scripture and rooted in immediate historical events, these final pamphlets lay claim to a greater sense of prophetic authority. On 24 January 1649, six days before the King's execution, Pope published her last rebuke to the New Model Army, the prophecy *Behold, here is a word*. In this, she reiterated both the text and message of her work published the previous month, *Heare, heare, heare, heare, a word or message from heaven*, which she clearly realised had not in fact been heard. The title page of the January pamphlet shows a supreme faith in the effectiveness of the printed prophetic word: '*Read this book imediately, and observe what God would have you doe; and doe it; and so you shall be freed suddainly out of this your bondage, through the power of God.*'[52]

V

After her failure to prevent the King's execution, Mary Pope fell silent. Perhaps she, or her sponsors, lost faith in her prophetic gift. But despite Parliament's neglect of her petitions, by the late 1640s women prophets seem to have gained some credibility. The extraordinary spiritual writing of these women prophets has been the focus of many studies in recent years, partly because of its fascinating literary texture, and partly because the words of some women, such as Elizabeth Poole, do seem to have been taken seriously by powerful men during the Interregnum.[53] Several feminist critics have attempted to explain their importance and have produced credible arguments that their femininity was actually an advantage for women uttering prophetic discourse.[54]

As stated above, however, this present article is more concerned with women who attempted that traditionally male activity of mainstream theological enquiry in a discursive, reasoned mode. During the 1650s, this phenomenon appears to have been even rarer than in the previous decade but, despite being composed in rather extraordinary verse and containing much devotional writing, one work from this decade that did contain some serious theological thinking was An Collins's *Divine Songs and Meditacions*, published in 1653. Collins has been labelled as everything from Catholic to Quaker, but her poetry actually celebrates the contemporary Independent establishment as the fulfilment of the vision of the English Reformation.[55] Moreover, in the 714-line poetic 'The Discourse' at the start of the work, she outlines her theological beliefs according to the scheme employed by the Westminster Assembly's *Large Catechism* of 1647. By discussing theological issues in almost exactly the order in which they appear in this Catechism, she engages directly with mainstream Presbyterian and Independent thought.

Collins deals in turn with the doctrines of the Trinity, the Fall, sin and its punishment, and the offices of Christ as Prophet, Priest and King.[56] She does not, however, go on to address the requirements for ecclesiastical discipline, such as the sacraments and preaching.[57] This may have been because she did not consider these issues to be within her scope as a woman, or because she was out of sympathy with the distinctly Presbyterian tone of the catechism's prescriptions in these areas. It is also perhaps significant that she declines to engage with other doctrines that were part of an earlier incarnation of puritanism, in particular predestination, the covenant with God, and perseverance.

By comparing *Divine Songs and Meditacions* with another contemporary work, *An abridgement of the whole body of divinity extracted from the learned works of that ever-famous and reverend divine, Mr.*

William Perkins, published by Thomas Nicols in 1654, one can discover what Collins owes to classic puritanism, and where she departed from it. Nicols's work shared the same basic structure and priorities as the Westminster Assembly catechism and also engaged with the subjective effect of doctrines such as justification and sanctification on the individual soul. An Collins, too, was extremely interested in this aspect of doctrine, and wrote vividly, for example, on the human experience of sanctification:

> Like as a Child new born without defect,
> A perfect man he may be sayd to be
> Because his body's perfect, in respect
> Of parts, though not in stature or degree
> Of grouth, until of perfect age he bee;
> So have the faithfull imperfections some,
> Till to a perfect age in Christ they come.[58]

Collins's 'The Discourse' also describes the Christian's combat against sin, and ends on the experience of succumbing to temptation, and being restored to grace, a topic that the summary of Perkins also highlights.[59]

Not mentioned in either the account of Perkins or the Westminster Assembly catechism was the contested topic of good works, which had traditionally been marginalised by Reformed theology. Collins, however, delivers a nuanced message on this topic, arguing for the necessity of good works, despite their inefficacy for salvation:

> Though by good works we do not gain Salvacion
> Yet these good Duties that our God requires,
> We must perform in this our conversacion,
> With all our might, endevours and desires,
> Before this short uncertain time expires,
> And at perfection must we allwaies aime,
> Though in this life we reach not to the same.[60]

This moderating doctrine had for some years also been taught from many puritan pulpits after the threat of antinomianism had raised its ugly head. The Independent theologian, William Ames, for example, had delivered a careful exposition of the importance of good works in his 1642 *The Marrow of Sacred Divinity*.[61] Collins was certainly, therefore, not attempting to be distinctive or original in her summary of doctrine. In 'The Preface', the poem which precedes 'The Discourse' in her volume, she states clearly that her intention is 'rather former works to vindicate / Than any new conception to relate'.[62] Indeed, she is extremely dismissive of anyone who 'hankers after Novelties', taking her stand in the cause of 'tru Religion', a phrase used in anti-Catholic rhetoric to describe

Reformed Protestantism.[63] Nevertheless, she carefully allows room for further revelation from God:

> Indeed I grant that sounder Judgements may
> (Directed by a greater Light) declare
> The ground of Truth more in a Gospel-way.[64]

Perhaps surprisingly, 'The Preface' contains no reference to Collins's gender. The first part of 'The Discourse', however, does make more gestures towards cultural expectation, and speaks in an explicitly female voice from stanza 1. As with many religious authors of the period, both male and female, Collins feels the need to answer the criticism that she should not have published her work, and she makes the standard defence that her poetry was written 'for my private use … alone'[65] – a stance that is something of a retreat from her bold position in 'The Preface':

> *And who esteems the favours of a Friend,*
> *So little, as in silence let them end,*
> *Nor will I therefore only keep in thought,*
> *But tell what God still for my Soule hath wrought.*[66]

'The Discourse' in fact contains in numbered stanzas four distinct reasons for publication. The first repeats the verse from Psalm 8 quoted above, so often used by women. The second quotes the parable of the talents, stressing her obligation to use the talent God has given her. The third cites possible benefits to her close family, and the fourth widens the circle of potential blessing to anyone who comes across her work, as she claims 'the image of her mind' revealed in her work will be an encouragement to spiritual growth.[67]

This, of course, was also often the stated rationale for making public a spiritual journal, as a published version could benefit others as well as to oneself. Perhaps it was this consideration that led An Collins to include in her work a potted spiritual autobiography. Frustratingly, however, as with other spiritual writings, it contains no useful historical detail by which she might be identified. We hear only of her difficult childhood, her early ignorant enjoyment of 'pleasant histories', and the subsequent spiritual delights which her knowledge of God afforded her.[68]

VI

The practice of keeping manuscript diaries seems to have blossomed from the mid-1650s, and women seem to have made particular use of this practice, as their funeral sermons often mention such journals. Edmund Calamy's 1657 sermon for Mrs Elizabeth Moore, one woman who recorded her own 'evidences for heaven' in a private journal, became a seventeenth-century bestseller and must have confirmed the idea that the manuscript journal was ideal feminine writing practice.[69] Similarly, Samuel Clarke's exemplary lives of women also often recorded excerpts from their journals as evidence of their holiness. By definition, however, all the women in Clarke's volume were already dead. In the seventeenth century, it seems, women could only safely become authors when they were no longer women.[70]

One 1658 publication, *A wise virgins lamp burning; or Gods sweet incomes of love to a gracious soul waiting for him Being the experiences of Mrs. Anne Venn*, revealed the male ideal of what female devotion should be. The tract's title offers key pieces of information that reveal how it had adopted the pattern of male-approved publication familiar from the 'mother's legacies' genre earlier in the century, Anne Venn was related to a prominent man, a republican and regicide (*'daughter to Col. John Venn, & member of the Church of Christ at Fulham'*). Her writing was originally only in manuscript, was composed in her closet, and she was already dead – *'written by her own hand, and found in her closet after her death'*. These circumstances gave the discourse maximum political effect. The self-display inherent in publication, which was so abhorred in the female sex, was avoided by the facts that the writing was doubly private – in her closet and in manuscript – and that the deceased was clearly unable to take advantage of any praise or publicity resulting from publication.

The values and conventions surrounding women's religious publications in the late 1650s, therefore, duplicated those attendant on that earlier genre of women's writing, the 'mother's legacy'. For a while, of course, some Quaker women continued to challenge these conventions in their prophetic writings. In 1662 the missionaries, Katharine Evans and Sarah Cheevers, published an account of their imprisonment and torture in Malta, and in 1667 Margaret Fell Fox produced her lively and well argued *Womens speaking justified, proved and allowed of by the Scriptures all such as speak by the spirit and power of the Lord Jesus*. The creation of the Second Morning Meeting in 1673, however, led to a new regime of censorship for prospective Quaker publications, which particularly affected such radical women.[71] Again, Lucy Hutchinson, that most theologically literate of women, did take issue with Calvin's *Institutes* in her commonplace-books, listing her objections to Book 4 in particular. She also translated part of John Owen's 1661 treatise, *Theologoumena pantodapa, sive, De natura, ortu progressu, et studio verae theologiae, libri sex*. Although translation had been an acceptable activity for women since the sixteenth century and the work was a prodigious feat of learning in terms of knowledge of Latin as well as theology, Hutchinson's work nonetheless remained in manuscript. In the early 1670s, she also composed her own systematic theological treatise but, in line with prevailing gender ideology, she wrote the work in manuscript and disguised it as a personal statement to her daughter – yet another 'mother's legacy'.[72]

Ultimately, then, the brief flowering of women's theological publication during the revolutionary years came to nothing. Although the gendered restrictions on women's publications might have encouraged the production of manuscript essays in theology, those women's manuscripts that survive still largely confine themselves to personal statements of faith, spiritual diaries, and that most deferential of female activities: the taking of sermon notes. It is difficult, therefore, to escape the conclusion that, even during the momentous, liberating years of the English Revolution, a woman's commitment to religion was judged more by her obedience to orthodoxy, than by her personal engagement with theology.

Notes

1   For details, see Arnold Hunt, 'Licensing and religious censorship in early modern England', in Andrew Hadfield (ed.), *Literature and Censorship in Renaissance England* (Basingstoke, 2001), pp. 127–46; Anthony Milton, 'Licensing, censorship and religious orthodoxy in early Stuart England', *Historical Journal*, 41 (1998), 625–51; and Elizabeth Clarke, 'The character of a non-Laudian country parson', *Review of English Studies*, 54 (2003), 479–96.

2   Bernard Capp, *When Gossips Meet: Women, Family and Neighbourhood in Early Modern England* (Oxford, 2003), p. 361.

3   This was one of the most popular publications in the seventeenth century: see Ian Green, *Print and Protestantism in Early Modern England* (Oxford, 2000), p. 637.

4   Elizabeth Jocelin, *The mothers legacie, to her unborne childe* (London, 1624), sigs a3r–v. For Goad, see Peter Lake, 'Calvinism and the English Church, 1570–1635', *Past and Present*, 114 (1987), 53.

5   Sylvia Brown, 'The approbation of Elizabeth Jocelin', *English Manuscript Studies*, 9 (2000), 129–64.

6   See Danielle Clarke, *The Politics of Early Modern Women's Writing* (Edinburgh, 2001), p. 254.

7   Victoria Burke, 'Elizabeth Ashburnham's "motherlie endeavours" in manuscript', *English Manuscript Studies*, 9 (2000), 105. The volume had certainly been recently revised and added to; one of the prayers concerned the tragic accident of the drowning of one of the Queen's maids, Anne Kirke, on 6 July 1641, an incident elegised by several poets, including Kirke's niece, Anne Killigrew. Elizabeth Richardson, *A ladies legacie to her daughters. In three books. Composed of prayers and meditations, fitted for severall times, and upon severall occasions. As also several prayers for each day*

in the weeke (London, 1645), p. 47. Sarah Poynting, 'An edition of Walter Montagu's *The Shepherds' Paradise*, Acts I–III', unpublished DPhil thesis, University of Oxford, 2000, pp. 96–7.

8 *A directory for the publique worship of God, throughout the three kingdoms of England, Scotland, and Ireland* (London, 1645), pp. 2, 38. For more details of this controversy over prayer, see Christopher Durston, 'By the book or with the spirit: the debate over liturgical prayer during the English Revolution', *Historical Research*, 79 (2006), 203.

9 There were by the 1650s, for example, several editions of Thomas Wilson's *A Christian dictionarie Opening the signification of the chiefe words dispersed generally through Holy Scriptures of the Old and New Testament, tending to increase Christian knowledge* (London, 1612). In 1622 Clement Cotton published his concordance to the New Testament, and later in the 1620s he completed his concordance to the Old Testament. The two volumes were printed together several times in the 1630s.

10 *Annotations upon all the books of the Old and New Testament* (London, 1645), sig. B3r.

11 Capp, *When Gossips Meet*, p. 358.

12 See Hilary Hinds, *God's Englishwomen: Seventeenth-Century Radical Sectarian Writing and Feminist Criticism* (Manchester, 1996).

13 Elaine Hobby, '"Discourse so unsavoury": women's published writings of the 1650s', in Isabel Grundy and Susan Wiseman (eds), *Women, Writing, History, 1640–1740* (Athens, GA, 1992), p. 25.

14 Sylvia Brown (ed.), *Women's Writing in Stuart England: the mother's legacies of Dorothy Leigh, Elizabeth Jocelin and Elizabeth Richardson* (Stroud, 1999), p. 98. Margaret Hannay has also pointed out that Elizabeth Richardson had read Mary Sidney's *A Discourse of Life and Death*, her 1592 translation of Philippe du Plessis Mornay's work, as a very early manuscript of her prayers contains her reflections on it; see Margaret Hannay, 'Elizabeth Ashburnham Richardson's Meditation on the Countess of Pembroke's *Discourse*', *English Manuscript Studies 1100–1700*, 9 (2000). The Perdita Project's on-line entry for Margaret Cunningham's manuscript autobiography points out that she quotes almost verbatim from Anne Lock's 1590 publication; see National Library of Scotland, Western MS 874, fos 363–84.

15 Katherine Gillespie, '"A hammer in her hand": the separation of church from state and the early feminist writings of Katherine Chidley', *Tulsa Studies in English Literature*, 17 (1998), 214.

16 Katherine Chidley, *The justification of the independant churches of Christ. Being an answer to Mr. Edvvards his booke, which hee hath written against the government of Christs church, and toleration of Christs publike worship; briefely declaring that the congregations of the saints ought not to have dependancie in government upon any other; or direction in worship from any other than Christ their head and law-giver* (London, 1641), sig. *4v.

17 *Ibid.*, sig. *2v, p. 80.

18 *Ibid.*, pp. 1–2, 5, 8, 9, 15.

19 *Ibid.*, pp. 25–6.

20 *Ibid.*, pp. 26, 28.

21 Hilary Hinds discusses Chidley's designation of herself as a 'poore worme' from a feminist perspective, but spends little time considering the content of the pamphlet. She argues that by describing herself thus, Chidley left Edwards 'no way to acquit himself honourably' in answering a treatise written by a woman: see *God's Englishwomen*, pp. 94–5.

22 Chidley, *The justification*, pp. 1–2, 49, 61, 64. She also employs an outrageous pun in the defence of those who fled England in the early 1630s: 'It is very probable, that they did know that the GREAT CANONS were already made, and that they were mightily charged, and overcharged, as it may appear from their shivering in pieces: but if they had held to have beene shot off, they might easily perceive, that they might beate holes in their own skins' (p. 70).

23 *Ibid.*, p. 80.

24 Katherine Chidley, *A new-yeares-gift, or, A brief exhortation to Mr. Thomas Edwards that he may breake off his old sins in the old yeare and begin the new yeare with new fruits of love, first to God, and then to his brethren* (London, 1645), sig. A2r, pp. 5, 7, 23.

25 *Ibid.*, p. 13.

26 Samuel Rutherford, *The Divine Right of Church-Government and Excommunication* (London 1646), p. 9.

27 Elizabeth Warren, The old and good way vindicated (London, 1645), sig. A3v.

28 *Ibid.*, sig. F3r–v. In the Bodleian Library, Oxford, copy of this pamphlet – Pamph. C. 75 (34) – this page of testimonies is inserted before the title page.

29 See, for example, Alice Sutcliffe, *Meditations of man's mortalitie. Or, A way to true blessednesse* (London, 1634), sig. A4v; see also the consideration of An Collins later in this article.

30 Elizabeth Warren, *Spiritual Thrift, or Meditations wherein humble Christians (as in a mirrour) may view the veracity of their saving graces …* (London, 1647), sig. B1v.

31 Ann Moss, *Printed Commonplace Books and the Structuring of Renaissance Thought* (Oxford, 1996), p. viii.

32 Warren, *The old and good way vindicated*, sigs F3r, A3v.

33 *Ibid.*, p. 16.

34 *Ibid.*, pp. 16, 31.

35 *Ibid.*, pp. 8–9.

36 *Ibid.*, sig. A3r; see also Susanne Woods (ed.), *The Poems of Aemilia Lanyer: Salve Deus Rex Judaeorum* (Oxford, 1993), p. 107; and Jean Klene (ed.), *The Southwell-Sibthorpe Commonplace Book* (Medieval and Renaissance Text Society, Tempe, AZ, 1995), p. 152.

37 Hobby, '"Discourse so Unsavoury"', pp. 20–1.

38 As in many printed sermons, each section is introduced by an abbreviated form of the sermon text.

39 Elizabeth Warren, *A warning-peece from heaven* (London, 1649), pp. 40–1.

40 Mary Pope, *A Treatise of Magistracy* (London, 1647), sig. C2v.

41 *Ibid.*, sigs C2r, C2v, C1r, C3r.

42 *Ibid.*, title-page.

43 *Ibid.*, p. 34.

44 *Ibid.*, pp. 35–6, 100.

45 *Ibid.*, pp. 4, 21; see also Thomas Edwards, *Gangraena* (London, 1646), part 2, p. 121.

46 Pope, *A Treatise of Magistracy*, sig. C3r, p. 125.

47 *Ibid.*, sig. B4r.

48 *Ibid.*, p. 59.

49 *Ibid.*, p. 117.

50 *Ibid.*, p. 131.

51 *Ibid.*, p. 125; see also, Gillespie, '"A hammer in her hand"', 216.

52 Mary Pope, *Behold, here is a word* (London, 1649), title page.

53 See Manfred Brod, 'Politics and prophecy in seventeenth-century England: the case of Elizabeth Poole', *Albion*, 31 (1999), 395–412.

54 See Diane Purkiss, 'Producing the voice, consuming the body', in Grundy and Wiseman (eds), *Women, Writing, History, 1640–1740*; and Sue Wiseman, 'Unsilent instruments and the devil's cushions', in Isobel Armstrong (ed.), *New Feminist Discourses* (London, 1992).

55 Sidney Gottlieb rehearses the various religious positions to which she has been assigned in the introduction to his edition of An Collins, *Divine Songs and Meditacions* (Medieval and Renaissance Text Society, Tempe, AZ, 1996), pp. xvii–xviii.

56 Collins, *Divine Songs and Meditacions*, pp. 15–19.

57 At this point she embarks on a discussion of the moral law and a detailed treatment of the Ten Commandments, and leaves justification and sanctification until later, whereas the Catechism has a very detailed exposition of the Ten Commandments after its description of justification and sanctification: Collins, *Divine Songs and Meditacions*, pp. 20–8; cf. *The humble advice of the Assembly of Divines now by authority of Parliament sitting at Westminster, concerning a larger catichism* (London and Edinburgh, 1647), pp. 18–43.

58 Collins, *Divine Songs and Meditacions*, p. 28.

59 Thomas Nicols, *An abridgement of the whole body of divinity extracted from the learned works of that ever-famous and reverend divine, Mr. William Perkins* (London, 1654), pp. 160–1. This is preceded by a long section on spiritual combat.

60 Collins, *Divine Songs and Meditacions*, p. 27.

61 William Ames, *The Marrow of Sacred Divinity* (London, 1642), pp. 208–13.

62 Collins, *Divine Songs and Meditacions*, p. 3.

63 *Ibid.*, pp. 5, 14.

64 *Ibid.*, p. 5. The use of hyphenated nouns formed from the word 'Gospel'

in 'The Preface', such as 'Gospel-voyce' (p. 5) confirms her affiliation to a Reformed religion which inclines to Independency.

65 *Ibid.*, p. 8.

66 *Ibid.*, p. 6.

67 *Ibid.*, p. 9.

68 *Ibid.*, pp. 10–13. See also the beginning of Elizabeth Jekyll's spiritual diary (Yale University, Beinecke Library, MS Osborn, b 221); and Ollive Cooper's diary (Dr Williams's Library, London, MS 24.49).

69 Edmund Calamy, *The Godly Mans Ark* (London, 1657), which prints his funeral sermon for Elizabeth Moore and 'Mrs. Elizabeth Moores Evidences for Heaven Collected by her self'. Ian Green identifies this as one of the bestsellers of the seventeenth century: see his *Print and Protestantism*, Appendix 1.

70 See Samuel Clarke, *A collection of the lives of ten eminent divines famous in their generations for learning, prudence, piety, and painfulness in the work of the ministry: whereunto is added the life of Gustavus Ericson, King of Sueden, who first reformed religion in that kingdome, and of some other eminent Christians* (London, 1662), pp. 433, 513. One of the women he treats is Jane Ratcliffe, and he reprints her 1640 funeral sermon, which contained extracts from her journal; see Peter Lake, 'Feminine piety and personal potency: the "emancipation" of Mrs Jane Ratcliffe', *The Seventeenth Century*, 2 (1987), 143–65.

71 See Elizabeth Clarke, 'Beyond microhistory: the use of women's manuscripts in a widening political arena', in James Daybell (ed.), *Women and Politics in Early Modern England, 1450–1700* (Aldershot, 2004), p. 212.

72 For notes on Calvin's *Institutes*, see Nottinghamshire Archives, MS DD/Hu 3, pp. 7–51. The translation of Owen and the manuscript treatise to her daughter (Northamptonshire Record Office, Fitzwilliam Misc. MS 793) were published in 1817 as *On the Principles of the Christian Religion, Addressed to her Daughter; and On Theology* (London, 1817).

PART II

Inside and outside the Revolutionary national Church

4

'The public profession of these nations': the national Church in Interregnum England

Ann Hughes

I

Throughout the 1650s, the Scottish Presbyterian Robert Baillie maintained a gloomy correspondence with old friends among the English ministry, men he had known well while serving as a Scottish representative in the Westminster Assembly in the 1640s. In his letters Baillie lamented the backsliding, failures and divisions among Presbyterians in both Scotland and England. Writing to Simeon Ashe in December 1655, he regretted that Stephen Marshall was 'a-dying: he was ever in my heart a very eminent man ... the preacher now living who ordinarily most affected my heart'. Nonetheless, Baillie insisted that 'Mr Marshall long ago lost the hearts of our Nation' and implied that he was heading for hell because of his *rapprochement* with Oliver Cromwell and his betrayal of the ideals of the Presbyterian Solemn League and Covenant of 1643. If on his deathbed Marshall could convince the Protector of the truth of the Covenant, that might be evidence his soul was in fact saved.[1]

Discussions of religious developments under the Commonwealth and Protectorate have been more concerned with the degree of liberty of conscience afforded to the population, than with the workings of the 'public profession' in the nation's parishes.[2] Most accounts of the Cromwellian Church, in particular, have agreed with Baillie on the alienation and marginalisation of genuine 'Presbyterians'. In a recent article on the 'public profession' and in particular the Cromwellian arrangements for the approval of the ministry, Jeffrey Collins characterises the Church settlement as dominated by 'magisterial Independents' and as 'the greatest administrative achievement of Oliver Cromwell's centralizing regimes'.[3]

In this chapter I, too, will argue that, despite wide disagreements over the limits of liberty of conscience and the repeated failures of Presbyterians, Independents and Baptists to reach any agreement over the 'fundamentals' of the Christian faith, in a practical day-to-day sense arrangements for the national Church in the 1650s did indeed work reasonably well. The achievements of the Protector's Church settlement did not, however, as Collins argues, depend on centralising impulses but, on the contrary, on the capacity of a flexible central regime to respond to local initiatives and campaigns. Furthermore, under Oliver Cromwell the functioning of the Church relied on sustained participation by men who on any definition should be described as Presbyterian. My use of the term Presbyterian is inevitably more flexible than Baillie's. It is not here applied only to that minority of English clergy and laity that believed in a full Presbyterian system of classes and synods as the only valid form of Church government, but more broadly to those orthodox puritans who believed in a comprehensive national Church and opposed religious toleration and the autonomy of individual congregations.

II

There was no clear path from the reforming impulses of early 1640s' parliamentarianism to the 'public profession of these nations', as defined in the Instrument of Government that established the Protectorate.[4] In the first months of the Long Parliament it was widely assumed that a 'regulated' or moderated episcopacy would be established, whereby bishops would no longer hold absolute sway in their dioceses but would govern the Church with the participation of a broader range of clergy. The Grand Remonstrance of December 1641 envisaged enforcing 'a conformity to that order which the laws enjoin according to the word of God', as well as the end of 'needless and superstitious ceremonies ... innovations ... and ... the monuments of idolatry'. However, a Presbyterian structure of parochial elderships, classes and synods was the obvious reformed alternative for a national, territorial Church. As royalism became ever more identified with the defence of episcopacy, and as Parliament became dependent on an alliance with the Presbyterian Scots embodied in the Solemn League and Covenant, an English Presbyterian Church seemed to be the likely result of a parliamentarian victory in the civil war. Charged with drawing up proposals for a reformed national Church, Parliament's Westminster Assembly of Divines was hampered both by its own divisions and by the increasing suspicion of Parliament itself, which was determined not to surrender lay control of the Church to assemblies controlled by the clergy. The 'Dissenting Brethren' in the Assembly, such as Thomas Goodwin and Philip Nye, who argued for congregational autonomy, were themselves university-educated ordained ministers, mostly orthodox Calvinists in doctrine; but their arguments for religious liberty were increasingly overshadowed in the 1640s by more dramatic claims. Sectaries in London in particular argued for complete separation of the godly from a corrupt national Church; some argued for universal redemption or denied the need for a distinct ordained ministry. By the end of the first civil war commitment to liberty of conscience and hostility to Presbyterianism and the Covenant were closely identified with Parliament's New Model Army. Consequently, the Presbyterian Church framework painfully constructed by the Assembly and watered down in any case by Parliament in a series of ordinances between 1645 and 1648, was, with the monarchy and the House of Lords, a casualty of the army-backed revolution of December 1648 and January 1649.

While the Presbyterian ordinances were not repealed, their measures for nationwide classes and assemblies were never enforced by any regime between 1649 and 1660. In some areas, such as London or Lancashire, a significant number of parishes took part in Presbyterian classes and provincial assemblies, but they were in effect volunteers; there were no mechanisms for compelling the participation of sceptics or opponents. Furthermore, as the Rump Parliament repealed all laws enjoining attendance at church, voluntary religious observance was enacted at the parish as well as the regional or national level. The religious policies of the Commonwealth or Rump regime were, however, more complex than a simple adherence to liberty of conscience or congregational independency. Within the Rump, as within puritanism more broadly, men were torn between a commitment to godly reformation and a belief in the primacy of the individual conscience. Thus, despite the open defiance of the regime by some London clerics, and even the execution of one Presbyterian minister, Christopher Love, as a royalist conspirator in August 1651, from the summer of 1649 the Rump made intermittent but serious attempts to placate the orthodox puritan or Presbyterian ministry through measures for improved clerical maintenance, attempts to define the 'fundamentals' of the faith, and legislative measures against blasphemy and adultery.[5]

The efforts of the Rump to rally orthodox opinion in the cause of godly reformation were limited by the need to conciliate an army committed to religious liberty and fearful of Presbyterian oppression. Nonetheless, the army never envisaged the disappearance of a national provision, their concern being rather to prevent compulsion. In this context, it is striking how far the religious clauses of the Instrument of Government drew on the compromise Officers' Agreement of the People of January 1649, a product of the abortive attempts at *rapprochement* with Leveller opinion.[6] Clause Thirty-five of the Instrument proclaimed:

That the Christian religion, as contained in the Scriptures, be held forth and recommended as the public profession of these nations; and that, as soon as may be, a provision, less subject to scruple and contention, and more certain than the present, be made for the encouragement and maintenance of able and painful teachers, for the instructing the people, and for discovery and confutation of error, heresy, and whatever is contrary to sound doctrine; and until such provision be made, the present maintenance shall not be taken away or impeached.

Similarly the ninth clause of the Officers' Agreement 'Concerning Religion' proclaimed 'the Christian Religion ... as the public profession in this nation', although it also asked that it should, 'by the grace of God, be reformed to the greatest purity in doctrine, worship and discipline, according to the Word of God'. The officers, too, had wanted 'able teachers' maintained 'out of a public treasury, and, we desire, not by tithes' for the instruction of the people, 'so it be not compulsive' and 'for the confutation or discovering of heresy, error, and whatsoever is contrary to sound doctrine'. Following the Officers' Agreement almost exactly, the Instrument laid down that no one was to be compelled 'by penalties or otherwise' to follow this public profession, but rather to be won over 'by sound doctrine and the example of a good conversation'. All laws against such liberty of conscience were repealed, and those who differed from the public profession were to be protected if they professed 'faith in God by Jesus Christ' and did not cause 'civil injury' to others or disturb the public peace. This liberty was not to be extended to 'Popery or Prelacy, nor to such as, under the profession of Christ, hold forth and practise licentiousness'. This last provision against licentiousness was not in the earlier Agreement.[7]

The early months of the Protectorate are a good point at which to take stock of the 'public profession' and to consider what had disappeared since 1640 and what remained. Episcopal government and in effect any national structure of Church government and discipline had now gone. There were no agreed measures for the approval or ordination of ministers and such an orthodox puritan as the Cheshire minister Adam Martindale had to approach the classes of both Lancashire and London before finding a body willing to ordain him. There was no longer any compulsion to attend the parish church. On the other hand, the basic parochial structure had endured and all research suggests that most English people still attended parochial worship rather than a gathered congregation or a sect.[8] The Commonwealth had undertaken an impressive survey of the country's parishes, the ministry and its maintenance, fulfilling a long-standing puritan aim of providing a basis for improving the status and maintenance of the clergy. It was hoped that this survey would also prompt the division of populous parishes, and the union of small, unviable ones, but little progress had been made by 1654.[9] The rights of lay people and a variety of institutions, such as university colleges, to appoint parish ministers were preserved, although Crown and Church patronage as well as that held by convicted royalists had fallen to the state. Perhaps most remarkably, the compulsory levy of tithes for the maintenance of the ministry survived the widespread disquiet of the godly and the best efforts of the radical wing of Barebone's Parliament in 1653. Here the bold certainty of the 1649 Officers' Agreement statement against tithes can be contrasted with the more hesitant or even resigned clause in the Instrument. There had been some redistribution of tithe income since the mid-1640s; 'augmentations' or additions to their income had been paid to many ministers out of tithe income from royalist compositions and confiscations and money reserved from the sale of dean and chapter lands.[10] By 1654, however, the arrangements for both authorising and paying these augmentations had become extremely tangled and uncertain.

III

Among the great legislative achievements of the early Protectorate, the measures to bring some order to the national Church deserve pride of place.[11] A crucial ordinance rationalised procedures for augmenting ministers' livings under the authority of the Trustees for the Maintenance of Ministers. Local research suggests the arrangements were successful in establishing a more certain income, perhaps to fewer ministers.[12] Cromwell also succeeded in establishing at last general procedures for approving ministers and for removing the unsatisfactory clergy who remained in post despite the sequestrations of the 1640s. Two ordinances created bodies commonly known as the 'triers' and the 'ejectors', the former a central institution for the approbation of ministers, and the latter local committees for purging the 'scandalous' and 'insufficient'. These measures were a modified version of proposals submitted to the Rump in February 1652 by John Owen and other leading Congregationalists and discussed by a committee of MPs and ministers over subsequent months. Owen, however, had suggested a committee of laymen and ministers in each county to 'examine, judge and approve' all preachers, and a central body modelled on assize procedures for the ejection of those 'Ignorant, Scandalous, Non-resident, or disturbers of the publick peace'. These ejection commissioners would have been assigned to circuits and 'go through the Nation, to enquire after, examine, judge of, and eject'.[13]

The subsequent Protectorate ordinances reversed this local and national structure envisaged by Owen. The establishment of the 'triers' (properly the Commissioners for the Approbation of Public Preachers) went very smoothly. The proposal was read twice in the council on 13 March 1654 and entrusted to a committee. This reported two days later and the final ordinance as amended by the Protector and approved by the council was issued on 20 March.[14] The verdict of both contemporaries and historians on the work of the triers has been largely positive. There is little information on ministers they rejected, although a few Anglicans as well as the maverick Independent and 'Arminian', John Goodwin, complained about their treatment. On the other hand, they approved more than 3,500 ministers before 1659, and their approbation clearly became a routine element for all ministers receiving a public maintenance.[15]

Improving the standards of the ministry had been central to puritan initiatives since the 1560s and Oliver Cromwell was predictably proud of the achievements of the triers. In his opening speech to the 1654 parliament, he argued it had been necessary to counteract the excesses of Barebone's Parliament, themselves a reaction to earlier extremes. In Barebone's, 'The axe was laid to the root of the Ministry; it was Antichristian, it was Babylonish'. Previously it had been argued 'that no man having a good testimony, having received gifts from Christ, might preach if not ordained. So now, many are on the other hand, that he who is ordained, hath a nullity or Antichristianism stamped upon his calling.' For Cromwell the creation of the triers was a flexible, broad-minded initiative that successfully steered between these two extremes. His government, he declared

> hath endeavoured to put a stop to that heady way (touched of likewise this day) of every man making himself a Minister and a preacher. It hath endeavoured to settle a way for the approbation of men of piety and ability for the discharge of that work. And I think I may say, it hath committed that work to the trust of persons, both of the Presbyterian and Independent judgments, men of as known ability, piety, and integrity, as I believe any this nation hath. And I believe also that in that care they have taken, they have laboured to approve themselves to Christ, the nation, and their own consciences.[16]

By April 1657 Cromwell had become even more convinced of the value of the triers. There had 'not been such a service to England since the Christian religion was professed in England'. In the episcopal Church, 'what pitiful certificates served to make a man a Minister! If any man could understand Latin and Greek, he was sure to be admitted.' The triers, on the other hand, valued education but only when it was combined in aspirant ministers with evidence of a 'good life and conversation' and essential signs of the 'grace of God'.[17]

Cromwell declared that the triers were 'men of known integrity and piety, orthodox men and faithful', and in 1657, as in 1654, he stressed that they included (and approved) men from a range of views from Calvinist Baptists to Presbyterians, who all came under his definition of orthodoxy. The thirty-eight triers included a few laymen among a largely clerical membership. Most of them were 'magisterial Independents' with close ties to Cromwell, such as John Owen, Joseph Caryl, Philip Nye, Sidrach Simpson, William Greenhill and William Strong; but there were also moderate, non-separatist Baptists, such as Henry Jessey, Daniel Dyke and John Tombes. Beyond their commitment to adult baptism, these last two were very conventional, and Dyke was licensed as a Presbyterian during Charles II's Declaration of Indulgence in 1672. Finally, as Cromwell had stated, there were several moderate Presbyterians among the triers, notably Thomas Manton, Obadiah Sedgewick and Anthony Tuckney.[18]

IV

At the opening of his first parliament, Cromwell also took pride in the measures taken for 'the expulsion of all those who may be judged any way unfit for this work, [or] who are scandalous'.[19] The ordinance for the ejection of scandalous ministers had proved more difficult to draft than that for the triers, probably because the council committee established to deal with it was also charged with finding a way of avoiding the 'inconvenience' of maintenance by tithes. A draft ordinance was discussed by the council on 30 May, but debate continued throughout June. On 20 June proposed amendments to the ordinance were discussed one by one and presented to the Protector, but it was only on 17 August that the measure was finally passed.[20] Modern judgements on the work of the 'ejectors' are more mixed than the verdicts on the triers. Noting that there is evidence for activity by the ejection commissions in more than two-thirds of English counties, Professor Collins has argued that they achieved rigorous control of the visible Church by the secular magistracy. Professor Durston, however, is more sceptical. He found evidence of ejectors at work in 'only a small number of counties' before the major-generals were established to quicken the pace of godly reformation in the summer of 1655. Only some fifty ministers were ejected before the summer of 1655 and, although the following twelve months saw some activity in thirty counties, there was no resultant 'wholesale purge'. During the regime of the major-generals, there were 130 ejections, equivalent to six per cent of all ministers removed between 1640 and 1660.[21]

Durston's conclusion that the impact of the major-generals' 'attempt to purge the parochial ministry was negligible' is perhaps, however, too hasty a judgement. The ejection commissions may have suffered from over-complex procedures and reluctant participation from witnesses or indeed from those nominated to serve, but other 'problems' are perhaps rather insights into the productive complexities of the 1650s public profession. The local commissions were by no means consistently supported by the Protector and councillors, who frequently reprieved ministers convicted by the ejectors – a fact which complicates the notion of centralisation.[22] After ten years of parliamentarian purges, it is impossible to be certain how many 'scandalous' or 'insufficient' ministers remained in post anyway, and so it is difficult to judge success in terms of numbers of ministers ejected, for we can never know how many 'should' have been discovered. A different perspective – looking at the ejectors rather than the ejected – suggests a more positive judgement than Durston's, but not for the reasons suggested by Collins. Certainly, in any case the ejectors were not the means through which the Protector and council subjected the Church to centralised, 'minute direction'.

The ejection ordinance appointed lay commissioners for each county with panels of ministers to assist them. An analysis of the ministers nominated in those counties where an orthodox 'Presbyterian Testimony' or manifesto against error had been drawn up in 1648 shows a striking willingness to encourage Presbyterian participation in the Protectorate Church.[23] There are, of course, many imponderables and difficulties here. There is little information on how the nominations were made, although councillors' local connections must have been important. The Shropshire commission included twenty ministers (compared with only eight for Gloucestershire and nine for Essex), a reflection no doubt of the prominence of the Shropshire man Humphrey Mackworth on the council.[24] For both Staffordshire and Warwickshire prominent ministers from all the major towns were appointed, but in other cases errors in the spelling of names and places suggest knowledge of the local situation was sketchy. A correspondent of the young MP Richard Temple reported on 5 October 1654 that the ordinance was due to become an act with additional commissioners: 'it may be your inspection therein, may doe this [Buckinghamshire] and Warwickshire a Courtesy'. This indicates some disquiet with the council's choices.[25]

Furthermore, categorising ministers on the basis of their stance in 1648 can be misleading. All eight ministerial assistants in Gloucestershire, for example, had signed the county's testimony against error, but four later 'became' Independents (or had never seen opposition to error as incompatible with Independency), and even signed the remonstrance of the radical Independent Gloucestershire churches against kingship in 1656.[26] Finally, there is so little information about which commissioners and assistants were active in the work that it must be emphasised that the nominations indicate those invited to participate, not necessarily those who took up the invitation. There is no indication, however, that 'Presbyterian' ministers were less active than Congregationalists. Wiltshire, for example, where at least half of the twelve assistants appointed to the 1654 commission were Presbyterians, saw the most ejections of all in the mid-1650s (seventeen). Here, one of their 'victims', Walter Bushnell, published a vivid, partisan account of the proceedings in his case. Those ministers most active against him were a vindictive, pipe-smoking Adoniram Byfield and Humphrey Chambers, respectively one of the scribes and one of Wiltshire's representatives in Westminster Assembly.[27]

Notwithstanding all the caveats and difficulties, the prominence of Presbyterians among the ejectors' assistants in London and the thirteen counties subjected to analysis is remarkable.[28] The proportion ranged from a minimum of a third in the West Riding of Yorkshire and Essex, to 100 per cent in Warwickshire.[29] Ten out of the twelve nominations in Cheshire had signed the *Attestation* against error; one was a younger man, and the twelfth was the prominent Congregationalist Samuel Eaton, who was himself drawing closer to Cheshire and Lancashire Presbyterians in the face of Quaker assaults. Nine out of ten Lancashire assistants had signed the county's *Harmonious Consent*, and several, such as Edward Gee and Richard Hollingworth, had been active polemicists against Independency in the 1640s. Some others, such as Charles Herle and John Angier, were more conciliatory Presbyterians, but Michael Briscoe was the lone Independent. Well known Independents, such as Philip Nye, Matthew Barker and Joseph Caryl, were predictably included among the nineteen assistants appointed in London, while prominent Presbyterians such as Calamy and Ashe were missing. Six of the nineteen here, including Lazarus Seaman, Samuel Clarke and Arthur Jackson, had, however, signed the 1647 *Testimony*. Most remarkably, the London assistants included two men imprisoned for complicity in the Love plot, Jackson and a younger man, Roger Drake, as well as the very moderate Presbyterian Richard Vines. The Norfolk assistants made up a characteristic Cromwellian panel. Eleven of the twenty-one men were probably Presbyterians, while the list was headed by the friendly enemies, the two town preachers of Yarmouth, the veteran Independent William Bridge and the Presbyterian John Brinsley, who had been briefly suspended for refusing the Engagement.

Dissatisfaction with the commitment of some of the commissions prompted additions of both laymen and ministers in 1656 and 1657. It is hard to discern any specific character to the clerical additions but they do not seem to be aimed at diluting Presbyterian influence. No ministers were added to the Cheshire commission, already predominantly Presbyterian, while at least eight of the thirteen men added in Warwickshire were

Presbyterians or conformists. In London, eminent men from both 'camps' were among the fourteen additions: Calamy, Manton, Bates and another Love plotter, William Jenkyn, from the Presbyterians; Greenhill, Carter and Cockayne from the Independents. Perhaps the aim was balance. Six of the eight Gloucestershire additions were Presbyterian, while five out of seven men added in Devon were Congregationalists. In both cases this could be seen as counteracting the existing bias of the assistants.[30]

V

The breadth of opinion represented among both the triers and the ejectors is matched by other aspects of the Church in the 1650s. Broad participation was made possible by the Protector's own attitudes and the complex image he projected, as well as by the Presbyterians' own willingness to serve. From the 1640s until his death, Oliver Cromwell professed a commitment to liberty of conscience, combined always with a generous definition of religious orthodoxy, within which Presbyterianism was usually high-lighted.[31] Speaking to his first parliament on 12 September 1654, he insisted that liberty of conscience was a fundamental of the Instrument of Government:

> Every sect saith, Oh! give me liberty. But give him it, and to his power he will not yield it to anybody else ... All the money of this nation would not have tempted men to fight upon such an account as they have engaged, if they had not had hopes of liberty, better than they had from Episcopacy, or than would have been afforded them from a Scottish Presbytery, or an English either, *if it had made such steps or been as sharp and rigid as it threatened when it was first set up*.[32]

A report on his address to the mayor, aldermen and common council of London, three days later had him denouncing '1. the violent Cavalier, 2. the rigid Presbyterian, 3. the dangerous Anabaptist'.[33] More flexible Presbyterians and moderate Baptists clearly, however fell within the Cromwell's definition of orthodoxy. When his first parliament sought to limit liberty of conscience, he regretted the MPs had not made

> such good and wholesome provisions for the good of the people of these nations, for the settling of such matters in things of religion as would have upheld and given countenance to a Godly Ministry, and yet would have given a just liberty to Godly men of different judgements, men of the same faith with them that you call the Orthodox Ministry in England, as it is well known the Independents are, and many under the form of Baptism, who are sound in the Faith, only may perhaps be different in judgment in some lesser matters.[34]

On the other hand, in his opening speech to his second parliament, he criticised Independents who reviled Baptists as unsound, as well as Baptists who attacked Presbyterians:

> as I would not be willing to see the day on which England shall be in the power of the Presbytery to impose upon the conscience of others that profess faith in Christ, so I will not endure any reproach to them ... I have had boxes and rebukes on one hand and on the other, some envying me for Presbytery, others as an in-letter to all the sects and heresies in the nation.

He also welcomed the support he had received from Presbyterians, expressed in 'petitions, and acknowledgements, and professions from whole counties'.[35] Similarly, his secretary, John Thurloe, praised Presbyterians in a letter to George Monck in Scotland, in which he expressed his exasperation with the Fifth Monarchists: 'The Presbyterian speakes as well of the Kingdome of Christe as these men, and many of them as holy, and I am sure much more knowing even in spirituall things.'[36]

Cromwell's flexibility enabled him to gain the approval of men of varying views, all of whom could construct a Protector to their own liking. In April 1654 *Mercurius Politicus* printed an address to the Protector from Coventry, which praised his rescue of 'Religion, Magistracy, Ministry, Laws and Liberties' from 'the violation of prophane and irregular pens and tongues', and another from York, which more even-handedly thanked him for doing 'great and wonderfull things ... in delivering us from the eminent and pressing dangers on the right hand and on the left'.[37] Some two years later, a far from 'Humble Remonstrance of divers Justices of the Peace, Ministers of the Gospel Churches of Christ and other wel-affected persons' in Gloucestershire warned Cromwell against the 'spirit of vanity, slumber and lukewarmnes' seizing on the people of God and called on him to make 'a tender and serious review' of all the army's 'Remonstrances, Solemne engagements and vowes made to the Almighty in the day of their Straits'.[38] The implications of this were rather different from Coventry's defence of ministry and magistracy.

Cromwell's willingness to enter discussions with those who disagreed with him (and with each other) gave opportunities to Presbyterians as well as Gloucestershire zealots anxious to overthrow 'Antichrist's kingdom'. It should also be stressed that Presbyterians, whose hopes for overall Church reform had by the mid-1650s been comprehensively defeated, had very little choice but to participate in the bodies established under the Protectorate if they were to have any influence on the 'public profession'. As Simeon Ashe ruefully replied to Robert Baillie's proposal that new treatises on Church discipline be printed, the works were too long for any stationer to publish, 'that controversie lyeth dead among us'. He added, however, that on a local level 'Through God's mercy, many act presbyteriallie in London, and in many counties, both in reference to ordination and admission to the sacrament, notwithstanding of discouragements.'[39]

This overall failure in principle, balanced by real opportunities in practice, can be illustrated at all levels of the Protectorate's public profession. At the top, as we have shown, Presbyterians were represented among the triers, while at the most basic level Presbyterian ministers were continually active providing testimonials for those seeking approbation. Ashe himself provided testimonials for eminent Londoners, such as Richard Vines and William Jenkyn, as well as provincial ministers, such as Thomas White in Kent and Samuel Fisher in Cheshire. These examples also reveal the broad tolerance (or indifference) of the triers in accepting testimonials and approving appointments. Fisher, for example, who was presented by the Presbyterian politician, Sir George Booth, had refused the Engagement and been examined in 1650 over his opposition to the Commonwealth, and Jenkyn had been heavily involved in the Love plot. Other Love plotters were among those providing testimonials for White (Roger Drake and Thomas Watson) and Vines (James Nalton). The more cautious Edmund Calamy acted with Ashe in all four examples but his name is also found testifying to the godliness of the noted Stepney Congregationalist William Greenhill.[40]

Local connections often overrode differing views on Church government and indeed on the Protector's Church settlement. When William Sparrow was formally presented to the vicarage of Halstead in Essex by the Protector in May 1654 (he had been there in fact since 1650), those providing him with a testimony included the local godly gentleman, Richard Harlackenden, and two well known ministers, the Congregationalist John Stalham and the unaligned Ralph Josselin. A few weeks later Josselin 'preacht for Mr Sparrow at Halsted, who was sent for to preach before the Protector', but the two men often disagreed. When the ejection commissioners began their work in Essex in February 1656, Josselin commented: 'Mr Sparrow preacht, he commended and encouraged the commissioners. For my part I saw no beauty in the day, neither do I joy to see ministers put under the lay power.'[41]

VI

The Protector's personal contact with Sparrow is emblematic of the industry he and his advisers devoted to the public profession. A significant proportion of the council's business was with the Church. On 16 July 1657, for example, sixteen augmentations were approved by the council with the Protector present; and on 27 August twenty-five orders for the union of small parishes were agreed.[42] But this conscientious activity was by no means an indication of centralising impulses. On the contrary, whether by accident or design, the Protectorate had established frameworks which gave full play to initiatives from below. All early modern governments had limited capacity for sustained supervision of local affairs and opportunities for local mobilisation of resources and action were especially facilitated within Church structures where older arrangements had been dismantled and new ones remained uncertain. The importance of productive exploitation of the frameworks established under the Protectorate can be demonstrated through examining Church patronage, augmentation of ministers' livings, and the settlement of ecclesiastical disputes.

As Collins has stressed, Cromwell had immense religious patronage, amounting to as many as forty per cent of all of the triers' presentations. As Protector he had inherited the Crown's patronage as well as the right to fill livings left vacant for six months and the patronage surrendered by royalists. His position as Chancellor of Oxford University gave him control of further livings.[43] But Cromwell's patronage was exercised with respect for local people and most often on petition rather than through central control. In November 1653, he thanked Henry Weston for his 'favour' in approving the formal presentation of one Mr Draper to a living in his gift following the death of the sequestered incumbent. The Protector had recommended Draper because he was 'very able and honest, well approved of by most of the good ministers thereabout, and much desired by the honest people who are in a religious association in those parts'.[44] Writing to Richard Baxter in April 1654, a Kentish man reported how the parishioners of Maidstone had applied to the Protector as the patron of their living on the death of their eminent puritan minister, Thomas Wilson. They had received 'a very favourable reception' and 'a liberty to spy out a man fit for them'.[45]

Similarly, much of the council's work on ministers' maintenance involved rubber-stamping detailed proposals from the communities concerned. It was as amenable to the complex proposals from Manchester for the support of the town's Presbyterian clergy as it was to the petition from Norfolk in support of the Congregationalist, Christopher Amiraut.[46] Local petitioners were adept at presenting their case in terms designed to appeal to the godly councillors. In 1654 twenty-one men from Mansfield in Nottinghamshire asked that they agree to the grant of three separate sums (£94 in total) to their new minister, John Firth, 'a man of most gracious qualifications and spiritual abilities' who had been presented to the living by the Protector. He had left a previous living of £200 per annum to take up the post in Mansfield, where 'the common enemy of mankind, taking occasion thereby, hath poisoned the spirits of very many with that erroneous spirit of quaking, whereby the interest of Satan hath increased more and more in the said town'. The council predictably approved this detailed and well-judged request.[47]

Finally, the council revealed a breadth of sympathies in dealing with religious disputes. It frequently intervened to moderate the proceedings of the over-zealous Berkshire commissioners for scandalous ministers. These commissioners were very active at an early stage, energetically prosecuting the heretical mystic John Pordage in the autumn of 1654 at a time when proceedings were suspended in other counties because of doubts of the legitimacy of the ordinance once Parliament had sought to revise it. Pordage was first summoned on 18 September, and finally ejected after several meetings on 8 December. On his own account, seven ministers and six laymen were active in his prosecution.[48] Pordage was surely a legitimate target, but others were more questionable. John Owen complained to Thurloe in March 1655 that 'some few men of mean quality and condition, rash, heady, enemys of tiths' were 'casting out on slight and trivial pretence very worthy men'.[49] The council intervened several times during 1656 and 1657 on behalf of Thomas Fitch of Sutton Courtenay who had complained of harassment, and the additional Berkshire ministerial assistants appointed in October 1657 were notably moderate men. Two well-connected Congregationalists were among the ten new appointments, but at least another five were Presbyterians, two of whom conformed in 1662.[50]

An extended dispute over the living of Whitchurch in Shropshire saw Cromwell and the council defending Thomas Porter, a man denounced as 'a factious and rigid Presbiterian, praying and preaching not only against the Engagement, but allso against the present government, and a sower of sedition and discord in the parish'. Porter had held Whitchurch for some years but early in 1654 the patron, the second Earl of Bridgewater, presented Dr Nicholas Barnard to the living. Both Bridgewater and Barnard had Anglican-royalist affiliations, but Bridgewater sought to protect his position as patron by appealing to the Protector's avowed hostility to rigid Presbyterianism. Detailed charges were drawn up against Porter with witnesses testifying he had sought to dissuade his parishioners from taking the Engagement, declaring it 'to be damnation to them that tooke itt' and condemning those who were 'for saveing of there selfe and estates to breake the solemne league & covenant'. He refused to observe the regime's fast and thanksgiving days, and kept instead days of 'his owne appoyntment, wherein he usually prayed for his brethren the Scots prosperitye'. Porter, it was also alleged, had sent money and clothes to the Scots' army despite being well known as a 'covetous close handed man, seldome or never giveinge anything to the poore'. In a funeral sermon preached about a year after the battle of Worcester, he spoke of the 'Emperor' Saladin, who after all his victories had only a sheet to show for it, adding: 'I belive its more then ye high flowen att Saincts' had gained from their victory. Cromwell nonetheless wrote in typical conciliatory fashion to Bridgewater that, despite the 'very good report' he had of Porter, 'Yet it is with this cleernesse that I shall leave yor L^{opp} most free to exercise yor owne libertie, assuring yor L^{opp} that if you shall intend the reall good of the people in your choyce, a person answering that wilbe equally acceptable to mee, as Mr Porter'.[51] Despite the evidence presented by Bridgewater, Porter continued at Whitchurch until 1662 and was one of the ministers appointed to assist the Shropshire ejection commissioners in August 1654.

On other occasions, however, the council did rule against Presbyterians. When Zachary Crofton, the minister of St Botolph Aldgate in London, sought to bar the fiery Fifth Monarchist preacher John Simpson from lecturing there, he found himself under examination by the London ejectors and subject to pressure from the council. Crofton was characteristically indignant that he should be denounced while those 'men that have openly enveighed against the Lord Protestor, as Tyrant, Great man at White-hall, and provoked against him an Ehuds dagger' were protected. Simpson had indeed preached against the Protectorate, denouncing the triers and ejectors as limbs of Antichrist. Nonetheless, in August 1657 a heavyweight group from the long-suffering council, including Charles Fleetwood, Philip Skippon and Richard Cromwell, was sent to urge Crofton to allow Simpson access to his pulpit.[52]

VII

This account of a regime offering opportunities for lobbying and participation to men of widely differing views is of course a partial narrative. A focus on the set-piece confrontations in Oliver's parliaments, or on the repeated failures to reach agreements on the fundamentals of the faith, suggests a more pessimistic verdict on the public profession of the 1650s. In the first protectoral parliament attempts were made to revise the whole religious settlement embodied in Cromwell's ordinances. There were tense disagreements over the proper limits to liberty of conscience, highlighted in the attack on the Socinian John Biddle, and attempts to enumerate heresies to be outlawed and to restrict public maintenance to those who accepted the public profession. David Smith has argued that the debates in this parliament revealed the unbridgeable cleavage within parliamentarian puritanism over liberty of conscience and godly reformation.[53] The issues reappeared in 1656 and 1657 in Cromwell's second parliament with the assault on the Quaker James Nayler and the more restrictive religious clauses of the Humble Petition and Advice. Similarly, Baptists, Independents, and Presbyterians – Cromwell's orthodox grouping – could never agree on a basic confession of faith. John Owen's 1652 proposals were defeated by the determined lobbying of Baptists and others who regarded them as too limited. At the end of Oliver's Protectorate, his Presbyterian chaplain, John Howe, regretted to Richard Baxter that moves towards unity had been sabotaged by 'so steady a resolution to measure all indeavours of this kind by their subservience to the advantage of one partie' so that 'the worke here [is] hopelessly laid aside'.[54]

But this is precisely the point. Set-piece debates in Parliament or moves to reach agreement in principle did indeed encourage intransigence, as Baptists, Independents and Presbyterians sought to maximise their own 'party's' advantage. In these circumstances the hesitations or contradictions in Oliver Cromwell's stance, offering conflicting hopes of overall success, could be a disadvantage. Failure to agree in principle, however, never prevented renewed efforts to achieve unity, and never halted practical cooperation over Church affairs. The correspondence of the idiosyncratic Presbyterian Richard Baxter demonstrates continual attempts to achieve some unity of the godly, among whom Baxter and many of his associates counted moderate episopalians. As Robert Abbott, a veteran moderate puritan, wrote to Baxter in 1650, 'yet am I for Timothies presbytery which I conceive to be a Regulated Episcopacy, and so I think are you'. In March 1652 Baxter urged Thomas Hill, Master of Trinity College, Cambridge, to mobilise petitions for accommodation, canvassing episcopalians as well as Independents and Presbyterians. Throughout the 1650s Baxter proposed that committees of moderate men from all parties be established to focus on points of agreement (especially doctrine) and achieve compromise on divisive issues (such as Church government). Baxter always argued for the inclusion of episcopalians and claimed he would exclude only Seekers and papists from discussion. Even Anabaptists and Arminians were not beyond the pale.[55] Baxter's attempts to achieve unity around particular principles never succeeded, but his working associations of ministers, pioneered in Worcestershire in the autumn of 1652, found imitators in Hampshire, Dorset, Wiltshire, Somerset, Sussex, Gloucestershire, Cumberland and Westmoreland.[56]

Furthermore, Baxter's correspondence reveals over and over again warm if sometimes difficult relationships among men who, even while they differed on how the episcopal Church should be replaced, shared a common, complex background in puritanism before the civil war. In July 1650 Robert Abbott explained to Baxter why he had left his living of Cranbrook in Kent after many years. He had been 'wearied from thence by 1000 of my Godly people who were suddenly perverted in the begin-ning of these bloudy times'. As he expanded three months later: 'some fell to be Brownistes, some to be Independents, some to be Anabaptists, some to be Antinomians, and some to be High Walkers above all ordinances: but except thease 2 latter, I count them all pious persons, saving the presumption of theire leaders who had beene my best catechumeni.'[57] The references to 'my people' and 'pious people' suggest how it was possible for theological debate, pastoral relationships and practical support (such as provision of testimonials) to be exchanged among men of differing views. Although stubborn adherence to contrasting positions sabotaged a common confession of faith, or a formal agreement among the godly, in other contexts disagreement was seen as normal and productive. The Coventry Presbyterian John Bryan wrote to Baxter in June 1657 thanking him for the gift of '2 most precious treatises'. He went on to state that, 'although in some things my judgment differs somewhat from yours', he was so pleased by 'the beames of by-light which dart into my mind and the candor I find in the writer towards dissenting brethren, that I rejoice to see my opinions which I have long hugd, brought to the barr & arraigned & condemned'.[58]

Many discussions of the Interregnum Church establish such strict criteria for success that the inevitable conclusion is that it was a failure. While by the most extreme standards of godly reformation there was no general transformation of English people's religious understanding and behaviour, it is insufficiently recognised that a commitment to godly rule was as much part of the self-definition of the 1650s regimes as a realistic programme. Equally, if there was no generally agreed replacement for the episcopal Church, a more nuanced analysis suggests that for much of the 1650s and especially during Oliver's Protectorate the public profession worked well in practice.[59] A very broad range of puritans, including the most 'rigid' of Presbyterians, acquired better maintenance and enlarged preaching opportunities. They could participate freely in the structures established for the approval of the public ministry, and through lobbying and petition they could exert significant control over local patronage and ecclesiastical resources. The flexibility and openness of the religious poli-cies of Protector and council created a system that could be energised from below through manipulating rhetorics designed to appeal to Oliver and his associates. As the parishioners of Maidstone, Mansfield and Whitchurch discovered, the public profession established in 1654 was one that could easily be moulded to local aspirations.

Notes

A version of this chapter was presented at the January 2004 colloquium organised by the History of Parliament Trust to mark the 350th anniversary of the founding of the Protectorate. I am most grateful for the comments and suggestions made on that occasion.

1 David Laing (ed.), *The Letters and Journals of Robert Baillie AM*, 4 vols (Edinburgh, 1841–42), vol. 3, pp. 302–3.

2 Blair Worden, 'Toleration and the Cromwellian Protectorate', in W. J. Sheils (ed.), *Persecution and Toleration*, Studies in Church History, 21 (Oxford, 1984), pp. 199–233; J. C. Davis, 'Cromwell's religion', in John Morrill (ed.), *Oliver Cromwell and the English Revolution* (London, 1990), pp. 181–208; Barry Coward, *Oliver Cromwell* (London, 1991). See also John Coffey's contribution to this volume.

3 Jeffrey R. Collins, 'The Church settlement of Oliver Cromwell', *History*, 87 (2002), 18–40.

4 For a recent survey of developments, see Ann Hughes, 'Religion, 1640–1650', in Barry Coward (ed.), *A Companion to Stuart Britain* (Oxford, 2003), pp. 350–73.

5 Blair Worden, *The Rump Parliament, 1648–1653* (Cambridge, 1974), pp. 207, 233–5, 243–7.

6 This seems to me to be a more important context for the Protectorate religious compromise than the parliamentary expedients of the early 1640s cited by Collins (p. 34). It is worth noting that the Army/Independent 'Heads of the Proposals' of August 1647 had nothing to say about a public profession but concentrated on removing the coercive power of bishops and establishing liberty of conscience, including liberty to refuse the Solemn League and Covenant. It hoped also for 'some remedy' for the 'present unequal troublesome and contentious' maintenance of the ministry by tithes; see S. R. Gardiner (ed.), *Constitutional Documents of the Puritan Revolution* (Oxford, 1962 edn), pp. 321, 324.

7 *Ibid.*, p. 416, compared with pp. 369–70.

8 For an eloquent demonstration of this, see John Morrill, 'The Church in England, 1646–9', in John Morrill (ed.), *Reactions to the English Civil War, 1642–1649* (London, 1982), pp. 89–114, reprinted in John Morrill, *The Nature of the English Revolution* (Harlow, 1993).

9 The Commonwealth Survey, however, laid the basis for the achievements of the Protectorate. British Library, Lansdowne MS 459, described by Collins (p. 33) as 'a surviving register of church livings that was supposedly used by the Ejectors', is in fact extracts from the 1650 parochial survey in selected counties. See Jane Houston, *A Catalogue of Ecclesiastical Records of the Commonwealth, 1643–1660 in the Lambeth Palace Library* (Farnborough, 1968), p. 198.

10 For a fuller account of these complex arrangements, see Rosemary O'Day

and Ann Hughes, 'Augmentation and amalgamation: was there a system-atic approach to the reform of parochial finance, 1640–60?', in Rosemary O'Day and Felicity Heal (eds), *Princes and Paupers in the English Church, 1500–1800* (Leicester, 1981), pp. 167–93.

11 Ivan Roots, 'Cromwell's ordinances: the early legislation of the Protectorate', in G. E. Aylmer (ed.), *The Interregnum: the Quest for Settlement* (London, 1972), pp. 143–64.

12 For Derbyshire and Warwickshire, see O'Day and Hughes, 'Augmentation and amalgamation'. Alex Craven's important forthcoming Manchester PhD will clarify developments in Lancashire.

13 Collins, 'Church settlement', pp. 24–7; *The Humble Proposals of Mr Owen, Mr Thomas Goodwin, Mr Nye, Mr Sympson and other Ministers* (London, 1652), pp. 3–4.

14 *Calendar of State Papers Domestic* [hereafter *CSPD*], 1654, pp. 27, 33, 40.

15 For the figure, see Collins, 'Church settlement', p. 30. Martin Winstone, 'The Church in Cromwellian England: Initiatives for reform of the ministry during the Interregnum', unpublished M.Litt. thesis, University of Oxford, 1996, is the fullest account. Richard Temple of Stowe is a well documented example of a patron helping his ministers to obtain the necessary approval. On 1 March 1659, following his presentation of a new minister to Stowe, he asked the triers 'to performe and fulfill all and every those matters which belonge to yor office': Huntington Library, Temple MSS, Manorial Documents, Box 5. He had earlier arranged an approbation for Richard Mansell of Burton Dassett, Warwickshire: Box 14, 2168, 20 December 1654.

16 W. C. Abbott (ed.), *The Writings and Speeches of Oliver Cromwell*, 4 vols (Cambridge, MA, and London, 1937–47), vol. 3, pp. 437, 440.

17 Abbott (ed.), *Writings and Speeches*, vol. 4, pp. 495–6 (part of a speech on the offer of the crown, 21 April 1657). Cf. the passage in Cromwell's opening speech to his second parliament in September 1656, 'neither Mr Parson nor Doctor in the University have satisfied those that have made their Approbations'; *Ibid.*, vol. 4, p. 273.

18 Abbott (ed.), *Writings and Speeches*, vol. 4, p. 495. For the names of the triers, see C. H. Firth and R. S. Rait (eds), *Acts and Ordinances of the Interregnum*, 3 vols (London, 1911), vol. 2, p. 856. Additional information on the Triers and other ministers is taken from the *Dictionary of National Biography* [hereafter *DNB*] and, where relevant, from A. G. Matthews, *Calamy Revised* (Oxford, 1934). For Dyke, see Matthews, *Calamy Revised*, p. 176.

19 Abbott (ed.), *Writings and Speeches*, vol. 3, p. 440.

20 *CSPD, 1654*, pp. 146, 190, 220, 308. I am grateful to Peter Gaunt for advice on the council debates.

21 Collins, 'Church settlement', pp. 23, 30, 40; Christopher Durston, *Cromwell's Major-Generals: Godly Government during the English Revolution* (Manchester, 2001), pp. 158–66.

22 *Ibid.*, p. 166. See, for example, the case of the eminent moderate puritan Nehemiah Rogers in Essex who was allowed to continue preaching in

October 1656; *CSPD, 1656–7*, p. 127. For other examples, see *ibid.*, p. 231, and *CSPD, 1657–8*, pp. 49, 375. The Protector and council did not even fully enforce their order preventing ejected ministers using the Book of Common Prayer, or acting as chaplains and tutors in private houses.

23 For the Testimonies of 1648, prompted by a London denunciation of error, heresy, blasphemy and schism, see Ann Hughes, *Gangraena and the Struggle for the English Revolution* (Oxford, 2004), pp. 373–8. Lists of signatories are included in Matthews, *Calamy Revised*, pp. 553–8.

24 I owe this point to Dr Gaunt.

25 Huntington Library, Temple Manuscripts, Box 14, item 1000.

26 Additional information has thus been taken from Matthews, *Calamy Revised*, and *DNB*.

27 Durston, *Cromwell's Major-Generals*, p. 182, n. 43; Walter Bushnell, *A Narrative of the Proceedings of the Commissioners ...* (London, 1660). I owe this reference to Durston's comprehensive study.

28 The counties discussed are Cheshire, Devon, Essex, Gloucestershire, Lancashire, Norfolk, Northamptonshire, Shropshire, Somerset, Stafford-shire, Warwickshire, Wiltshire and the West Riding of Yorkshire.

29 Apart from the counties discussed in the text, I judge that two-thirds of the assistants in Devon, Shropshire, Somerset and Staffordshire, and about half of those in Gloucestershire and Northamptonshire, were Presbyterians.

30 For the additions, see The National Archives, Public Record Office [here-after TNA: PRO], Protectoral Council Order Books, SP 25/78, p. 241 (Warwickshire, 24 Oct. 1657); SP 25/78, p. 231 (London, 22 Oct. 1657); SP 25/78, p. 239 (Devon, 24 Oct. 1657); and SP 25/78, p. 240 (Gloucestershire, 24 Oct. 1657).

31 For useful, contrasting accounts of Cromwell's religion, see the references in note 3 above and Derek Hirst, 'The Lord Protector', in Morrill (ed.), *Oliver Cromwell and the English Revolution*.

32 Abbott (ed.), *Writings and Speeches*, vol. 3, p. 459, italics mine.

33 *Ibid.*, vol. 3, p. 466.

34 *Ibid.*, vol. 3, p. 586; Cromwell's closing speech, 22 Jan. 1654/5.

35 *Ibid.*, vol. 4, p. 272; Cromwell's speech to parliament, 17 Sept. 1656.

36 *Ibid.*, vol. 3, p. 620; Jan. 1655.

37 *Mercurius Politicus*, 30 March–6 April 1654, pp. 3384, 3387.

38 Bodleian Library, Oxford, Rawlinson MS A39, no. 528. I owe this reference to Durston, *Cromwell's Major-generals*.

39 Laing (ed.), *Letters and Journals of Robert Baillie*, vol. 3, pp. 306–7.

40 Lambeth Palace Library, MS Comm III/3; Register of Admissions to Livings by the triers, including the names of those giving testimonials; pp. 101 (Fisher), 108 (White), 138 (Greenhill), 233 (Jenkyn), 245 (Vines).

41 For the testimonial, see *ibid.*, p. 61; Alan Macfarlane (ed.), *The Diary of Ralph Josselin, 1616–1683* (Oxford, 1976), pp. 327, 362–3. Josselin was himself added to the Essex assistants in December 1657; see TNA: PRO, SP 25/78, p. 334.

42 *CSPD, 1657–8*, pp. 28–9, 82; selected from many similar examples.

43 Collins, 'Church settlement', p. 31.

44 Abbott (ed.), *Writings and Speeches*, vol. 3, pp. 120–1.

45 N. H. Keeble and Geoffrey F. Nuttall (eds), *Calendar of the Correspondence of Richard Baxter*, 2 vols (Oxford, 1991), vol. 1, pp. 136–7.

46 *CSPD, 1654*, pp. 263, 312, 177. See also, among many other examples, Bideford and Topsham in Devon, and Yarmouth on the Isle of Wight; *ibid.*, pp. 125, 263, 312.

47 *Ibid.*, p. 250.

48 John Pordage, *Innocencie Appearing Through the Dark Mists of Pretended Guilt* (London, 1655), pp. 1, 95–6, 103–4. For the suspension of proceedings in Buckinghamshire, see William Hart to Richard Temple, 7 Oct. 1654, Huntington Library, Temple MSS, Box 14, item 1001.

49 Thomas Birch (ed.), *A Collection of the State Papers of John Thurloe Esq.*, 7 vols (London, 1742), vol. 3, p. 281. Owen was especially worried about attacks on Edward Pocock, the eminent oriental scholar, who was not in the end ejected.

50 Abbott (ed.), *Writings and Speeches*, vol. 4, pp. 181–2; *CSPD, 1657–8*, pp. 150–1, 230; TNA: PRO, SP 25/78, p. 239. The Congregationalists were John Batchelor, the press licenser, and John Oxenbridge of Eton. The Presbyterians included William Gough of Inkpen, who had refused to accept sequestered livings in the 1640s and continued to attend his parish church after ejection. He was licensed as a Presbyterian in 1672: Matthews, *Calamy Revised*, p. 230.

51 This account of the Whitchurch dispute is taken from Huntington Library, Ellesmere MSS, facsimiles 8044, 8046–7, 8538–42, 8044, Cromwell to Bridgewater, 9 May 1654, 8045; Bridgewater to Cromwell, 28 June; and 8539–40, articles of evidence against Porter sent up to the Council by Bridgewater are quoted. The council established a committee to discuss the matter on 26 Apr. 1654; *CSPD, 1654*, p. 119.

52 Zachary Crofton, *Malice Against Ministry Manifested* (London, 1657), p. 27. For Simpson's view of the Protectorate, see David Loewenstein, *Representing Revolution in Milton and His Contemporaries* (Cambridge, 2001), p. 147. For the council's interventions, see *CSPD, 1657–8*, pp. 50, 62. For the Protector's typical willingness to meet with Simpson despite his fiery preaching in December 1654, see Abbott (ed.), *Writings and Speeches*, vol. 3, p 546.

53 David L. Smith, 'Oliver Cromwell, the first protectorate parliament and religious reform', in J. P. Parry and Stephen Taylor (eds), *Parliament and the Church, 1529–1960* (Edinburgh, 2000); *Commons Journal*, vol. 7, pp. 370, 377, 387, 398–401, 412. Collins, 'Church settlement', pp 28–9, has a more favourable view of the parliament. I think the import of complex, tactical votes is difficult to assess.

54 C. Polizzotto, 'The campaign against the Humble Proposals of 1652', *Journal of Ecclesiastical History*, 38 (1987); Keeble and Nuttall (eds), *Calendar of Baxter Correspondence*, vol. 1, pp. 308–9, John Howe to Richard Baxter, May 1658.

55 Keeble and Nuttall (eds), *Calendar of Baxter Correspondence*, vol. 1, pp. 74–7, 89, 93, 187, 224. Baxter regretted that Howe did not believe it practical to include episcopalians in unity discussions in 1658: *ibid.*, pp. 302–3.

56 *Ibid.*, vol. 1, pp. 94–5, 105–7, 219.

57 *Ibid.*, vol. 1, pp. 58, 61.

58 *Ibid.*, vol. 1, p. 257.

59 For an account stressing the advantages as well as the problems for the godly in the 1650s, see Ann Hughes, 'The frustrations of the godly', in John Morrill (ed.), *Revolution and Restoration: England in the 1650s* (London, 1992), pp. 70–90.

5

A ministry of the gospel: the Presbyterians during the English Revolution

Elliot Vernon

I

In April 1650 Nehemiah Wallington, the turner and stalwart Presbyterian ruling elder of the parish of St Leonard Eastcheap began timidly to write a letter of disapprobation to Matthew Barker, the Congregationalist preacher who had recently replaced the venerable Presbyterian Henry Roborough as the minister of the parish. Wallington bemoaned the fact that Barker's preaching had made 'the way to heaven [appear] easier than it is' for the flock of St Leonard's. His error, Wallington counselled, was to tell parishioners that all they had to do was to 'give consent to Christ and the match is made'. Wallington requested that Barker should instead denounce his fellow parishioners for 'Contempt of the Gospel, the breach of protestations and Covenants' and should advocate 'Mortification' of the flesh as the 'few ... despised Presbyterians' do.[1]

Although Wallington favoured Presbyterian ministers, modern historians have rarely acknowledged or taken seriously the Presbyterians' experiment with the further reformation of the Church of England during the English Revolution. John Morrill has even described the orthodox godly clergy's attempts as 'negative' and 'sterile'.[2] The historiographical roots of such conclusions lie with William Shaw, the towering Victorian scholar of Interregnum ecclesiastical history. Shaw wrote in 1900 of the 'impotence of presbytery', arguing that the Presbyterians' failure was due to 'the indifference, or dislike, of the great bulk of the laity' and the 'triumph of the Army [which] struck a death blow at the Presbyterian discipline'.[3] Shaw followed A. H. Drysdale's 1889 study, which had argued that the failure of civil war and Interregnum Presbyterianism could be ascribed to its obsession with ecclesiological controversy. Drysdale claimed that this was pursued to the neglect of the pastoral functions of the ministry and concluded that 'the Presbyterian ministers were very greatly to blame for not striving to exercise their whole pastoral functions and discipline'.[4]

This essay seeks to re-examine this long historiographical orthodoxy, and to reinforce some recent work by historians which has invited us to rethink our perceptions of civil war and Interregnum Presbyterianism. While noting that the period was a time of high frustration for the godly, Ann Hughes has argued that the Presbyterians never gave up their hope for national and local reformation.[5] Likewise, Eamon Duffy has contextualised the long history of the English Reformation in terms of a general reforming mission to awaken mere, formal Christians and create 'a godly people out of a nation of conformists'.[6] Duffy has asserted that 'If one had to identify the one central preoccupation of godly ministers in Stuart England, it would be the urgent necessity of saving the multitude' and 'the task of *awakening* the sinner to his need for grace and conversion'.[7] Set in this context, rather than that of political failure, the Presbyterianism of the revolutionary period can be seen as part of the ongoing English puritan ambition to refashion the parishes of the Church of England into reforming institutions where 'heart-religion', rather than cold, formalist profession, would predominate.

II

Although both an emasculated 'primitive' episcopacy and Congregationalism were mooted as possible alternative official or state Church structures in the early days of the civil war, the Solemn League and Covenant of 1643 and the intellectual dominance of the Presbyterian clergy in the Westminster Assembly of Divines ensured that the Assembly would propose a Presbyterian settlement. The common law Erastianism of many members of the Long Parliament also meant, however, that the *iure divino* pretensions of the clericalist Presbyterians would not find fruit in the English Church of the revolutionary period. Instead, the structure of English Presbyterianism was developed in an unsatisfactory and ramshackle fashion through various acts and ordinances that came into force between 1645 and 1648.

The authority and powers of the English Presbyterian settlement were detailed through these acts and ordinances. Each parish was to elect a congregational eldership consisting of the minister and between two and six laymen. The eldership was to examine the congregation and exclude sinful and scandalous parishioners. Individual congregations were to be grouped together into a classis consisting of at least seven parishes, and classical presbyteries would meet in monthly sessions to supervise the parochial elderships. The classis was not to make decisions unless it had a quorum of eight ruling elders and four ministers. This imbalance between laity and clergy was a deliberate decision by Parliament aimed at reducing the threat of clerical domination. Once a quorum was present, however, any decisions of the classis were to be binding upon its constituent congregations.[8]

Under this statutory scheme, the classical presbyteries were to have a tripartite function: to settle ministers and elders in vacant or errant congregations; to ordain ministers; and to act as local ecclesiastical courts of review and appeal over congregational presbyteries.[9] Where we have extant minute books of classical presbyteries in operation, it is apparent that the second of these functions – the ordination of ministers – was taken very seriously, with ordinations taking place only after the presentation of degrees and references. The ordinands were also required to satisfy the classis of their godliness and preaching ability through disputation. Once appointed, ministers were subject to continuing supervision. An example of a classis exercising its reviewing or judicial function against one of its own ministers is shown from the minutes of the Wirksworth classis in Derbyshire. On 20 April 1652 complaint was made that John Wiersdale, the minister of Bradley, had been administering Holy Communion to parishioners excluded from a neighbouring congregation in Wirksworth, 'not only to the offence of the minister and godlie people there but also to the hindrance of Reformacion'. Wiersdale had also allegedly censured parishioners for holding private prayer meetings. The classis ordered that he attend and give reasons for his actions. On 18 May he appeared and 'did ingenuouslie confesse and acknowledge that the charges were true'. The classis accepted his apology and ordered that Peter Watkinson of Kirk Ireton 'in a brotherlie manner … earnestlie exhort him according to his promise to act more carefully and regularly'.[10]

Above the classis in the hierarchy was the provincial synod or assembly. In theory, these provincial assemblies were intended to be the highest rung of Presbyterian government. They were to have powers equivalent to local episcopal courts and were to be the last ecclesiastical courts of appeal before matters went to a parliamentary committee. The provincial assemblies shared the same powers as the classical presbyteries and were also 'to judge and determine controversies of faith, and cases of conscience according to the Word'.[11] Each was to meet every six months and was to consist of a minimum of thirty-six members drawn from subordinate classical presbyteries.[12]

As might be expected, the statutes which instituted this disciplinary structure were deeply unpopular with the clericalist Presbyterian ministry which, through the Westminster Assembly, had originally presented to Parliament a model based on the Church of Scotland. In November 1645 London's Presbyterian ministers signed a petition to the city's common council complaining that parliament's statutes 'take no notice at all of any intrinsecall power in the ... [presbytery] derived unto them from Christ'. Instead, Parliament had given parish presbyteries an authority that was only 'of politicall constitution and meerly to be derived from the Civil Magistrate'.[13] But by June 1646 the London ministers had realised that the unwavering nature of parliamentary Erastianism and the decline of Scottish influence meant that they were unlikely to achieve a more clericalist settlement, and they conceded that even this watered down Presbyterian discipline would have no prospect of succeeding unless they co-operated with Parliament's scheme. As a result, they published a pamphlet stating their commitment to Parliament's Erastian statutes, in the hope that the future would offer further opportunities to reform the Church.[14] Their public decision to cooperate with Parliament's structure was a signal to other ministers in the localities to begin the work of constructing Presbyterianism government.

The imposition of Presbyterian discipline made most headway in Lancashire and London, the only two regions that definitely formed provincial assemblies. In Lancashire seven out of nine classical presbyteries met regularly, while in London eight out of twelve classes were formed in the 1640s and two more were added in the mid-1650s. It is also possible that Devon formed a province.[15] In other counties, the system was far less stable, with only a few isolated classical presbyteries being set up: Somerset had four out of nine potential classical presbyteries operational; the West Riding of Yorkshire appears to have had three or four classes; and Northumberland, Hampshire and Derbyshire had two operational classes. Many counties had only one active classis, which may well have represented the influence of local godly patrons. In Surrey only the Reigate classis operated, while in Warwickshire only the Kenilworth classis met and ordained ministers. Shaw concluded that the sole ordaining classis in Essex was Ongar, and in Lincolnshire, Folkingham.[16] It is clear from this that the statutory Presbyterian Church was a stillborn entity. The decline of Scottish influence in England, the bad blood between Parliament and the clergy, and the rise of the New Model Army meant that Presbyterianism lacked the magisterial support necessary to implement the discipline. Despite their laments, however, the ministers and elders who found themselves in control of England's 'lame Erastian' Presbyterianism did all they could to put the discipline into practice.

The degree of success achieved by the Presbyterian evangelical mission depended on the commitment of Presbyterian pastors and lay elders

in those parishes where their government was operative. As a result of
the seizure of power in 1649 by an army committed to a wide measure
of religious toleration, despite their official status as ministers of the
'national' Church under the acts of the 1640s, the Presbyterian clergy
soon effectively found themselves in the same voluntary situation as the
separatists and Congregationalists. Unlike the separatists and radical
Independents, however, they remained committed to the conception of a
national Church containing both saints and sinners, and their belief that
they should labour to preach the gospel to a mixed body of Christians, and
not just the visible saints, was at the root of the Presbyterian project. As the
heirs to the Jacobean and Caroline puritan movement, the Presbyterians
of the revolutionary era were agreed that true reformation meant moving
beyond merely formal religious duties to the enlivening of the individual
conscience and, unlike the anti-formalists who argued that prescribed
Church structures 'shut up' Christ, they saw ecclesiastical discipline as a
vehicle for awakening sleepy Christians to divine grace.[17]

This position was outlined in a 1646 debate concerning the nature of
reformation between the anti-formalist William Dell and Christopher
Love, then Presbyterian minister of St Agnes and St Anne Aldersgate
London.[18] Dell had preached that Reformation was 'the *taking away* and
destroying of the body of sin, out of the faithful and elect by the presence and operation of the righteousnesse of God, dwelling in their hearts
by faith'.[19] The concomitants of this were that 'A carnall Reformation is
not suitable to a spiritual kingdom' and that the civil magistrate should
not make laws for conformity to a national Church, as his sole duty was
to encourage preachers to carry on the work of heart-reformation.[20] To
Love and his fellow Presbyterians this was a prescription for civil and
spiritual anarchy and represented a threat to the souls of unconverted
sinners. Love argued that a Presbyterian national Church was the divinely
warranted formula for the 'most peace, union, and brotherly love' in
Christian society.[21] The purpose of formal Church government was to
win souls and to nurture their growth, as well as to protect them from
soul-damning errors.[22] Dell's anti-formalism was perceived as one such
error, and Love argued that the reformation of sinful hearts was the
result of God's grace acting, through the mediation of Jesus Christ, on
the members of His Church.[23]

III

For the Presbyterians the principal arena for edification was the parish
church. Despite the arguments of some scholars who have suggested that
the increasing social status of parish ministers was alienating them from

their congregations, parish sources show that many vestries were still demanding a preaching ministry.[24] The London vestry of St Lawrence Jewry, for example, which elected Christopher Love as its minister in March 1649, asked in return for his stipend that he preach twice on the sabbath and once on fast days.[25] At St Christopher-le-Stocks in London, James Cranford was obliged to preach twice on the sabbath and at the monthly preparation sermon before the Lord's Supper. In addition, he was paid an extra £20 per annum to provide the parish with morning prayer.[26]

The Presbyterians were determined to make preaching the keynote of parochial discipline. In January 1648 the First London Classis drew up a constitution for the better promotion of 'knowledge and godlines' in its precinct. It ordered that the parish elderships ensure that the minister guided 'all in his flock' and that 'people ... have prophesyings once a week'. Furthermore, to oversee the work of reformation in the parish, the classis moderator was regularly to be given accounts of the work of the parish ministry. Likewise, between November 1648 and February 1649, the Lancashire Provincial Assembly worked out a programme of preaching and catechising for its ministers to follow.[27] It also published a pamphlet exhorting all 'governors of families ... to see to the godly ordering of their households; to observe constantly and to bring all under their charge unto family duties of religion'.[28]

Proper observance of the sabbath was another major concern of the Presbyterians. The parliamentary ordinance of April 1644 'for the better observation of the Lord's Day' ordered all magistrates and parish officials to seek out and punish sabbath-breakers.[29] The parochial elderships took this order to heart and made great efforts to impose sabbatarian discipline on their parishes. The Lancashire Provincial Assembly declared that 'Sittinge and drinkeinge unnecessarily in an alehouse or taverne on the Lord's day shall bee censurable' by excommunication.[30] In London, a scurrilous Independent tract of July 1647 warned that the Presbyterian lay elders would soon stop visiting taverns on the sabbath and instead do so on weekdays to convince people of the Independents' treason.[31] It suggests that Londoners were very familiar with Presbyterian elders engaging in Sunday tavern raids, a fact which the minute book of the Fourth Classis confirms. In December 1646 the Fourth Classis thanked John Mold, a ruling elder of St George Botolph Lane, 'for procuring justice to be done on certaine profaners of the Sabbath by Taverne hunting'.[32] The sanctifying of the sabbath was essential to the Presbyterians' attempt to instil the life of piety into the parish church. Ultimately, Presbyterian ministers hoped that the strict observance of religious duties each Sunday might lead to an inward conversion and prepare their parishioners for the intense experience of receiving the 'great seal' of the covenant of grace: the sacrament of the Lord's Supper.

The Presbyterians' missionary aims extended, however, beyond Sunday duties to more rigorous attempts to awaken the sleepy souls in the parish pews. One of the London Presbyterians' strategies for bringing the whole parish to the Word was the morning exercise. This event was an adaptation of the familiar combination lecture.[33] It consisted of a month-long series of short lectures held in a single parish. They would begin at seven every morning and each day a different preacher would expound a biblical text and a single doctrine for half an hour. After this the parish congregation would join with the preacher in prayer for a further half an hour before the working day began. The intention behind this hour-long exercise was to provide godly edification without being a 'prejudice' to civil affairs.[34] At the end of the month-long series of lectures the whole parish would join together for a day of fasting, and it is possible that this was crowned by the celebration of Holy Communion.[35] Although related to the pre-revolutionary combination lecture, the morning exercises differed in that they were short devotions that focused a congregation or area on one religious theme for a designated short period. Like the 'holy fairs' of Scotland and America, they combined elements of evangelistic outreach and catechetical instruction, and also exploited the public fascination with famous preachers.[36] By bringing these factors together, the Presbyterian ministers engaged with their parishioners and struggled to sanctify and deepen their spiritual lives.

The morning exercise emerged as a result of Parliament's defeat at Leicester in May 1645, but soon became a regular event.[37] John Price, a member of John Goodwin's gathered congregation, made the association between the morning exercise and Presbyterians most explicitly, commenting that they were 'pleased to call them the Ark of God in their frequent removals month after month from place to place'. According to Price, however, the exercises were 'a judgement rather than a mercy', and were characterised by 'ranchor, frowardnesse and distemper'.[38] His criticisms sparked an anonymous defender to claim they were nothing more than a form of evangelical outreach, that aimed 'to discover the evils, and errours of the times impartially, that Gods people may be humbled for them and avoid them', as well as to 'keep up the life and power of godlinesse in the hearts of the hearers'.[39] Another Presbyterian, Thomas Case, commented favourably on the spiritual refreshment that a monthly morning exercise could provide, noting: 'In times of feares many that have come trembling and dismayed with evil tidings, have [been] dismist with comfort and encouragment'. Some, Case asserted, 'have drawn their first spiritual breath in this aire, others have been preserved and secured'.[40] The morning exercises seem to have been popular events in the worship of the godly citizens of the capital. In a sermon to prepare his parishioners for the exercise, Case exhorted 'let the zeal and forwardnesse of other places provoke you' for 'how is this Morning Exercise sued for and begg'd for by Ministers and their well-affected people'.[41] As another indication of their popularity, an anonymous defender talked of the 'thousands of godly persons in and about this City' who rise all year long 'that by attending ... they may finde him who their soul loveth'.[42]

IV

Derek Hirst has argued that in the 1640s 'many of the godly clergy had concentrated their efforts on the pulpit and the press, at the price of neglecting the minimum task of catechizing the young'. The result was that the 1650s saw a failing puritan ministry 'clutch' at catechising as a response to the perception that they had failed in their pastoral roles.[43] This perception needs modifying. We must always guard ourselves against accepting unquestioningly the puritan rhetoric of complaint; it was a constant refrain of evangelical Protestantism throughout the early modern period and was as much a trope as a description of reality.[44] Ian Green's magisterial study of catechising has demonstrated that during the seventeenth century catechising was a ubiquitous and uncontroversial feature of English religious life, which by 1642 had become 'a ladder joining the clerical and lay elite ... with the rest of the population'.[45] If reasons are to be sought as to why the Presbyterian clergy promoted catechising with renewed effort after 1640, we should look to the pastoral and evangelical concerns that we are discussing throughout this chapter. The new emphasis on catechising that emerged in the polemics of the Presbyterians was dictated, as we shall see, by the placement of the Lord's Supper at the centre of the converted Christian life.

A parliamentary ordinance of 20 October 1645 had laid down the minimum standard of knowledge necessary for a person to come to the Lord's Supper, and catechising provided the means of supplying the doctrinal fundamentals to those who were unchurched by their ignorance. The catechisms that followed Parliament's ordinance were designed to assist the parishioner to master enough of the fundamental material to claim a right to the Lord's Supper. Zachary Crofton, the minister of St Botolph without Aldgate, London, taught his parishioners that 'catechizing is the way to ... knowledge in rudiments of Religion', and was therefore 'an absolute duty incumbent on every man'.[46] The Presbyterian ministers were also resolute that if people wished to come to the Lord's Table they must have the self-knowledge to examine their spiritual condition; they therefore hoped that catechising would go beyond the basics of faith and provide the knowledge necessary for spiritual self-examination. The ministers reasoned that if parishioners had the knowledge to examine their consciences, they would become awakened to their sins and feel the need to seek God for the internal reformation of their lives. The London Provincial Assembly asserted in its *Exhortation to Catechizing* that the aim of catechising was 'to advance, the glory of God's grace, to staine the pride of *man's nature*; to make the saints walke much the more comfortably ... [and] to damne up that cursed fountaine of self conceit, whence daily issue so many impure streames'.[47] In this context, catechising cannot be viewed solely as a last ditch effort to reform ignorant parishioners; it was also an integral part of the ministry's evangelical efforts within the parish. In exhorting their ministerial colleagues to catechise, the London Provincial Assembly described the truths of Christianity as appearing as 'but a worthless shell' that 'secretly incloseth the invaluable pearl'. The London ministers went on to assert: 'To open the shell is the Catechists task'.[48]

It is not therefore surprising to find both the Lancashire and the London provincial assemblies directed the policy of catechising as a cornerstone of the Presbyterians' evangelising drive in the parishes. The publication of the Westminster Assembly's *Shorter Catechism* in September 1648 saw both provincial assemblies make a concerted effort to encourage congregational presbyteries to engage in the practice. In November 1648 the Lancashire Provincial Assembly ordered 'That the ministers and ruling elders are to labour according to their places to bring all their people to the knowledge of the Christian faith and religion' and recommended the use of the *Shorter Catechism*.[49] Parish records show that the provincial assemblies' orders had some effect. The vestry minutes of St Christopher-le-Stocks for 2 February 1649, for example, record that James Cranford 'did proffer and desire to catechise those younge people of the parish', and that 'the vestrey did willingly and thanckfully accept of and doe promise to send their children accordingly'.[50]

If catechising was a predominant feature of Presbyterian pastoral effort throughout the 1640s, why did the 1650s witness such a great deal of complaint literature from both Presbyterian ministers and other orthodox godly clergy? Eamon Duffy and Patrick Collinson have both equated the puritan attack on profane culture with an attack on youth culture, and it was of course the young who were the main object of catechising.[51] It takes no great leap of imagination to conclude that apprentices, servants and children found catechising an unwelcome chore ordered by their superiors, and that in an ecclesiastical environment that lacked the sanctions of Church courts there was consequent resistance to it. In 1655 the London

Provincial Assembly, still campaigning to establish regular catechising, argued that 'the *general aversness* of *young ones* from ... catechizing, is not the least argument of its *singular usefulnesse*. The more unwilling they are ... the more reason we have to presse them to it.'[52] Catechising probably remained patchy in Interregnum Lancashire too, for in 1657 the First Lancashire Classis was still ordering all ministers in its area to catechise the families of their parishes.[53]

Resistance to catechising was not, however, a new phenomenon of the 1650s, and this argument in itself does not fully explain why the orthodox clergy perceived their campaign as a rearguard battle. The abundance of Presbyterian rhetoric of complaint about spiritual declension is more likely the result of the magisterial vacuum regarding Church polity at the political centre and the concomitant of toleration for religious heterodoxy. The publication in particular of the Socinian *Racovian Catechism* and the views of John Biddle can be seen, from the perspective of the Presbyterians, as an invitation to bewail the spiritual condition of the young.[54] During 1655 and 1656 the ministers of the Wirksworth classis mooted every point of doctrinal contention with the Socinians in readiness to combat the influence of the *Racovian Catechism*.[55] The orthodox godly clergy often chose to use the theme of the seduction of the young by sectaries as a trope in their complaints. Zachary Crofton grumbled that 'the youth of this age through want of catechizing, are captivated with Heresies and Schism'.[56] When they reflected upon the spread of heterodoxy in their public testimonies, the Presbyterian ministers declared that its cause was the failure of godly ministers and householders to catechise.[57] In 1655 the London Province argued that the heresies of the age 'did at first spring meerly from ignorance' and that 'Had there beene more Catechizing, there would have beene lesse Apostasie. Had it not beene for want of seasonable instructions, we had not seene so many licentious insurrections, against the sacred truths, and ordinances of God.'[58]

The Presbyterians' complaints about the neglect of catechising have to be balanced against their efforts to instil it as a regular practice in the parishioner's spiritual life. Although it cannot be doubted that catechising was resisted by many – especially the young – the rhetoric of neglect also betrays their strong evangelical drive in the parishes. The regular directives from the provincial assemblies and classical presbyteries to the parish ministry demonstrate that the Presbyterians were united in their desire to provide the young and ignorant with the fundamentals of knowledge that seventeenth-century Reformed theology demanded. The campaign for catechising must therefore be seen as one part of the Presbyterians' evangelical policy. Along with the regular provisions of preaching and the insistence on sabbath duties, it was a key element of their campaign to create a structure for religious experience that would awaken 'mere' Christian parishioners to a lively faith and lead them to seek God and the salvation of their souls.

V

In addition to preaching and catechising, at the centre of the Presbyterians' effort to further their evangelical project in the Church was their vision of the sacrament of the Lord's Supper as the goal and central privilege of the converted saint. Historians from Shaw to Hirst have argued that they were guilty of such extreme rigorism that they were prepared to suspend Holy Communion altogether rather than allow the Lord's Supper to be contaminated by unworthy partakers, the readily available examples of Ralph Josselin and Richard Baxter being cited to prove this assertion. But this accusation that the Presbyterian clergy were pastorally negligent needs to be countered by arguments that the Interregnum saw the development of a new and pious sacramentalism.[59] Their efforts were guided by the intention to make the parish church a vehicle for the reformation of the laity, and innovations concerning the Lord's Supper have to be set in this context.

Presbyterians argued that the sacrament was the seal of the covenant of grace and was ordained by Christ to confirm the faith of his professing disciples. Most of them held that, while it could further the sanctification of the justified believer, it had no power to convert the unfaithful or unregenerate. Thus, far from being a celebratory event that the whole parish community could share in, it was to be reserved for those who had already awoken to the life of faith.[60] In his spiritual diary, Nehemiah Wallington gives us a practical summary of how this doctrine affected a Presbyterian communicant, noting:

> Hee that lives by faith, he lives in the use of the ordinances; he cannot pray, heare, read, nor receive the Sacrament without faith ... [However,] a carnall man he finds no relish in them but put these ordinances to a man that hath faith and he will prize them.[61]

The effect of this doctrine was that the Presbyterian ministry stressed the need for religious preparation before coming to the Lord's Table. This was in accordance with St Paul's injunction to the Corinthians (1 Corinthians 11: 28) that 'every one is to examine himself, lest he eat judgement to himself, not discerning the Lord's Supper'. Thomas Bedford, the minister of St Martin's Outwich in London, described this Pauline judgement as 'an irrevocable sentence of wrath, to be poured upon the man'. The only way to avoid it was 'by preparation of the soul for a worthy partaking'. The Lancashire Provincial Assembly stated: 'The Temple of God ... is holy;

the Lord's Supper is an holy thing ... The prohibition of Christ is definite: "Give not that which is holy unto the dogs".'[62] It counselled its ministers to seek its advice to prevent both the 'boundless administration' and the 'non-administration' of the Lord's Supper in their area.[63]

The Presbyterians insisted that the token for entry to the Lord's Supper was the knowledge to fulfil the necessary level of introspection required by 1 Corinthians 11: 28. Roger Drake, the minister of St Peter Westcheap and a moderator of the London Provincial Assembly, commented that 'there can be no faith without knowledge'. He added, however, that although those unable to examine their spiritual health were to be denied entry, the ministry was 'willing to take pains with them, by instruction to fit them for the Sacrament in the future'.[64] Richard Vines noted that this was 'a Doctrine of hard digestion' as 'the generality of people in this land ... are not prepared'.[65] Religion to them was 'but an ancient custome, or tradition received from father to son' and so 'hard wedges [were needed to] cleave hard knots'.[66] The ministers of both Presbyterian provinces seem indeed to have concentrated their pastoral efforts upon hammering such hard wedges into their parishioners. We have already noted preaching, catechising and, in London, the morning exercises. Alongside these mechanisms there also seems to have been a fashion for catechetical sermons to prepare parishioners for the Lord's Table. The eucharistic treatises of Presbyterians such as Richard Vines, Francis Roberts and Thomas Bedford all began life as long series of preparation sermons preached to their flocks.[67] It was hoped that the effect of this preparation would be that the Christian would receive spiritual comfort not just in the intense experience of receiving communion but also in their daily lives. For Nehemiah Wallington at least, preparation and sacramental piety seems to have had the desired effect, for in his spiritual diary he wrote:

> [Now you can see] the fruit of the Sacrament, in that God's Holy Spirit moves me now to set on holy duties with holy preparation. As to prepare and seat my self for the Lords day as all the week, so the night before to leave the world about five or six a clock and betake my self to read and pray with my family, thus to remember the Lords day before it come. You little think the profit and benefit that is to be had in so doing: how one duty sets us for another.[68]

The stress on the Christian life being a regular cycle of self-humiliating preparation punctuated by an intense and sanctifying communion with the divine at the Lord's Table takes us to the heart of the Presbyterians' evangelical ambitions for the Church. Recognising that the English people were but partly reformed and that, if they did not actually sleep in their pews, they slept in their faith, Presbyterians saw their discipline, and particularly suspension from the Lord's Supper, as the principal instrument to correct this problem. Indeed, as Patrick Collinson has noted, following the discrediting of auricular confession after the Reformation, discipline was the only means the godly clergy had of turning the parishes into vehicles of evangelisation.[69]

The issue of admission, especially the requirement that would-be communicants should appear before the whole eldership, was one of the most unpopular features of the Presbyterian system. In Thomas Cawton's London parish of St Bartholomew-by-the-Exchange, the vestry expressed open defiance over this issue. On 27 August 1649 the vestry recorded 'the p[ar]ish greevances especially through want of the sackrament [of] the Lords Supper'. Cawton was 'desired to administer the ... [Lord's Supper] wthout [the parishioners] coming before the Elders', and asked to 'deliver the Sackariment to all his p[ar]ish [and] to begit [them to] love one wth an other'.[70] Likewise, John Wiersdale of Bradley in the Wirksworth classis in Derbyshire, who, as we saw above, was accused of administering the sacrament to those excluded in neighbouring parishes, defended himself by arguing that he had been 'importuned by his people' to administer the sacrament and had acceded to their request, 'being destitute of Congregational elders'. This decision, he claimed, had caused those excluded by the elderships of other parishes in the classis to flock to his church to receive.[71]

That there was a large reduction in the numbers admitted to the Lord's Supper can be discerned from the churchwardens' accounts of St Lawrence Jewry, London. Throughout the 1640s and early 1650s, the St Lawrence vestry was mainly Presbyterian; after the sequestration of Thomas Crane in September 1643, the parish fell under the successive ministries of Anthony Burges, Christopher Love and Richard Vines.[72] Using the purchase of communion wine as a rough (though admittedly imperfect) guide to the number of communicants, we can begin to measure the number of parishioners admitted to the Lord's Supper under the Presbyterian discipline. The table at Appendix 1 details the expenditure on communion wine during the period 1640–55 (see below, p. 132). It reveals that the pre-war figure of over £12 per annum dropped dramatically to a low point of around £3 10s after the introduction of Presbyterian discipline in the period from 1645 to 1647. This may indicate that Anthony Burges and his parochial elders were denying the sacrament of the Lord's Supper to as many as three-quarters of their parishioners. Access to the Lord's Table continued to be regulated throughout 1647 and 1648, for the churchwardens' accounts note the purchase of a book to record which parishioners were permitted to receive communion.[73] As the figures for the period from 1647 to 1650 show, the effect of this move seems to have been to stabilise the level of communicants, as expenditure on communion bread and wine remained just over a quarter of the 1640–41 figure.

Appendix 1 further suggests that as the civil war progressed and ecclesiastical discipline broke down, progressively fewer communicants came forward to the Lord's Table. It would appear that in the period from 1640 to 1645 half the parish had voluntarily absented themselves from Holy Communion, with much of this loss occurring under the ministry of Thomas Crane. We can only speculate as to the reasons, but wartime disruption, apathy and irreligion, the collapse of the Church courts, sectarianism and dislike of the minister (either Crane or Burges) may all have contributed to the absence of so many parishioners. The gradual rise in expenditure on communion bread and wine between 1647 and 1655, however, hints that the Presbyterian ministers and parish elders were not happy to let so many members of their congregation neglect the Lord's Supper, and that the massive drop in admissions to Holy Communion remained a concern of the vestry throughout the revolutionary years. On his election in March 1649, Christopher Love was asked 'To admit all of his parish to that table that desire it, and are not knowne to be either grosly scandalous, or notoriously knowne to be of ill and scandalous life'.[74] Three months later, however, he was simply 'desired for to administer the sacrament'.[75] Despite these appeals from his vestry, the figures for Love's brief ministry suggest that he admitted around the same number of communicants as his predecessor, Burges.

Under the ministry of Richard Vines in the mid-1650s, the expenditure on communion bread and wine again rose to the 1643 levels. The parish records for Vines' ministry hint that there had been resistance to the parochial presbytery by many of the parishioners under the previous Presbyterian ministers. On 22 February 1654 the 'major part of the Parishioners' met with Vines and, after 'severall debates concerning the Elders', agreed that 'the housekeepers and theire wives, now inhabitants of this p[ar]ish should be admitted to the Sacrament of the Lord's Supper of whose lives there appeare noe scandalls, provided, that they should give accompt of theire knowledge to Mr Vines and the Elders to sitt with Mr Vines'.[76]

Perhaps the most telling example of the alliance between the vestry leadership and the parochial presbytery is to be found in the parish of St Mary Aldermanbury in London. On 16 February 1648 a vestry of forty of the most substantial parishioners met and heard 'certaine grievances of some particular persons of our parish in relation to them not being admitted to the Ordinance of the Lord's Supper'.[77] It is possible that the problem of non-admission had led to a refusal to pay tithes, as the yearly income from this source had dropped in 1647 from its usual figure of around £95 to only about £23.[78] Such a shortfall meant that the parish was unable to pay the wages of the minister and the parish clerk. The parish was not, however, willing to compromise by abandoning the presbytery. The vestry pronounced that in matters of discipline 'the parishioners shall and will give ... [the elders] all incourignment and assistance' and that the 'Minister and Elders ... appeared ... to have done that which was justifiable and commendable in these places'. Interestingly, the vestry noted that since 13 December 1646 'two hundred and upward' of the parish 'had bene Admitted to the Sacrament by the Eldership'.[79] To resolve the problem, a parish committee consisting of the most important members of the vestry alongside the eldership was convened to meet with the aggrieved.[80] This appears to have been successful, for the churchwardens' accounts for 1648 record that the problem of tithe refusal had been settled.[81]

Once again, therefore, the issue of suspension from the Lord's Supper has to be seen within the nexus of the Presbyterians' pastoral and practical theology.[82] The London Province proclaimed in its *Vindication*: 'The externall Government and Discipline of Christ ... is absolutely necessary to the well being of a Church'.[83] Roger Drake clarified this point further in respect to the Lords' Supper. The Church, Drake wrote, 'must proceed by the rule of visibility, and cannot admit any till he be visibly converted'.[84] The 'proper end' of the eldership's examination was therefore not to exclude but to provide 'preparation of all sorts for the Sacrament'.[85] Drake was optimistic that 'a few months' of Presbyterian discipline could rescue even the 'meanest' from their soul-damning ignorance.[86] The Lancashire Provincial Assembly meanwhile asserted that any blame for the problems caused by exclusion lay not with Presbyterian discipline but with the would-be communicants, arguing 'that no person of age, that names himself by the name of Christ, would ordinarily absent or wretchedly deprive himself thereof, but that he labour for knowledge to enable him to examine himself for faith'.[87]

Some Presbyterian ministers, however, seem to have been all too aware of the potentially divisive results of sacramental exclusion and to have tried to conciliate those who objected to it. In one of his sermons at St Lawrence Jewry in the mid-1650s, Richard Vines admitted to his parishioners: 'I professe my hearty sorrow for the rents and discontents which have ensued [from examination by the eldership]'.[88] He went on, however, to remind them that the Presbyterian discipline was not without precedent, and that even under episcopacy admission to the sacrament had been conditional on the learning of the catechism.[89] He also pointed out that all the eldership required to be satisfied of potential communicants' suitability was their profession that they could examine themselves in line with the apostolic injunction of the Pauline epistle to the Corinthians.[90]

Unlike separatism, Presbyterian theory and practice did not admit of the luxury of the Church being solely a covenanted gathering of the saints; indeed the Presbyterians were insistent that the visible Church would remain a mixed body until Armageddon.[91] Thomas Bakewell, a baker and ruling elder of the London parish of St Bride Fleet Street, asserted this point in a controversy with some Independents in 1650. The national Church of England was, Bakewell declared, 'a true Church' for 'we have the word of God truely taught, and the Sacraments truly administered'.[92] Furthermore, he argued, unlike separatist congregations, Presbyterian parishes honoured the covenantal promise of baptism. Although, as we have seen, the profane would be denied the Lord's Supper until they showed signs of conversion, all baptised parishioners were nonetheless 'admitted into the Universall Visible Church'.[93] In a similar light, the Lancashire Provincial Assembly specifically prohibited its ministers from refusing to baptise the children of those 'parents lyinge under the imputation of ignorance or scandall'.[94]

Professor Collinson has suggested that in the pre-revolutionary Church the solution to the problem of the mixed body was semi-separatism.[95] The Presbyterians' sacramental practice provided an evangelical twist to this semi-separatist logic. By setting a symbolic bar to the Lord's Table in the course of divine service, they turned Holy Communion into an intensely symbolic centre. Leigh Eric Schmidt has seen a similar pattern in the evangelical drives of the Scottish communion fairs, where participation in Holy Communion 'held out the promise of greater mutuality and community'.[96] The symbolic boundary to the Lord's Table in the revolutionary Presbyterian communion created, to borrow Collinson's phrase, 'concentric circles of religious intensity' which pious parishioners could cross as they progressed in their life of faith.[97] For most Presbyterian ministers during the English Revolution this was the true aim of their pastoral efforts. Richard Vines told his parishioners that the Lord's Supper was 'an inner ordinance' that 'appertains to them that are Disciples already'. In the early Church it was 'the utmost end' of the *catechumeni* and the *lapsi* 'for which they waited a long attendance to be admitted to this communion, and then properly be called fideles'.[98] This demonstrates most clearly how the Presbyterians wrote the Reformed theology of salvation into their experiment with Church government, and more importantly how their pastoral and practical actions throughout the Interregnum were informed by the evangelical mission for the reformation of their parishioners' lives.

VI

The Presbyterian Church structure of the 1640s was meant to be the replacement for a discredited episcopacy and a further step in England's long Reformation. Events and politics conspired, however, to make the Presbyterian polity far more limited in scope than the national Church envisioned by the Solemn League and Covenant. English Presbyterianism of the revolutionary period was born from the ultimately unhappy alliance between an Erastian English Parliament and the clericalist imperialism of the Scots. As a movement, it was doubly unlucky in that the Anglo-Scottish alliance crumbled in the first years of its existence and that the New Model Army became the *de facto* power dominating English politics throughout the 1650s. William Shaw's damning assessment of Presbyterianism's impotence in the face of the army's victory in the political sphere cannot be seriously challenged. But his verdict that it failed in its evangelical mission can be questioned, as it ignores the fact that it was a structure that arose just as much out of the conviction and voluntarism of the moderate English puritan ministry and laity as from the machinations and fortunes of Anglo-Scottish politics. Nor is A.H.Drysdale's criticism that the Presbyterians were too involved in high polemic and failed to focus on their pastoral and evangelical functions sustained by a close scrutiny of the evidence. The English Presbyterian clergy were first and foremost 'ministers of the gospel'. Their polemical tracts were written as weapons in the battles they were waging against 'parish Anglican', Congregationalist and sectarian opponents for the hearts and minds of the English people. They were only one tool used in a continuing quest to provide an authoritative Church structure that would continue the work of reformation in England, which had been interrupted since the accession of James I.

The surviving records of the parish, classical and provincial presbyteries show that, whatever their degree of success, the English Presbyterians laboured endlessly in their mission to provide a godly ministry to their flocks. At the heart of this attempt to use Church government as a means of awakening the masses to the Holy Spirit was the celebration of the sacrament of the Lord's Supper. In the Presbyterian conception, admission to the Lord's Supper was a spiritual goal for the converted parishioner to aim at, not a simple ritual of communal cohesion. That the issue of exclusion caused controversy and dispute was inevitable, as it represented an attempt to bring the semi-separatist logic of Jacobean and Caroline conformist puritanism into the very fabric of the life of the Church. Given the political and religious fluidity of the period, the fact that the Presbyterian system failed to establish itself as the national Church of the revolutionary era is not surprising. What analysis of the surviving evidence does show, however, is that for all the rhetoric of decline and failure, both at the time and in modern historiography, the English Presbyterians laboured, often heroically, to use the parochial Church structure as a mechanism for the further reformation of English people. The real measure of the success of their missionary activity during the English Revolution was the major contribution it made to the resilience and vibrancy of Restoration non-conformity.

Appendix: annual expenditure on communion wine at St Lawrence Jewry, London, c. 1640–55

Date	Minister	Expenditure		
1640–41	Thomas Crane	£12	3s	10d
1642–43		£9	3s	0d
1643–44		£7	10s	0d
1644–45	Anthony Burges	£6	10s	0d
1645–46		£3	10s	0d
1646–47		£3	9s	10d
1647–48		£4	18s	0d
1649–50	Christopher Love	£4	16s	0d
1654–55	Richard Vines	£7	10s	0d

Source: based on figures in Guildhall Library, London, MS 2593/2, St Lawrence Jewry, churchwardens' accounts, fols 8, 44, 65, 88, 109, 125, 145, 179, 192.

Notes

1 British Library [hereafter BL], Sloane MS 922, fols 169v, 170r–v.
2 John Morrill, 'The Church in England, 1642–1649', in John Morrill, *The Nature of the English Revolution* (Harlow, 1993), p. 174.
3 William A. Shaw, *A History of the English Church during the Civil War and the Commonwealth*, 2 vols (London, 1900), vol. 2, pp. 100, 136.
4 A. H. Drysdale, *The History of the Presbyterians in England: The Rise, Decline and Revival* (London, 1889), p. 349.
5 Ann Hughes, 'The frustrations of the godly', in John Morrill (ed.), *Revolution and Restoration: England in the 1650s* (London, 1992), pp. 70–90.
6 Eamon Duffy, 'The long Reformation: Catholicism, Protestantism and the multitude', in N. Tyacke (ed.), *England's Long Reformation, 1500–1800* (London, 1998) pp. 41–2.
7 Eamon Duffy, 'The godly and the multitude in Stuart England', *The Seventeenth Century*, 1 (1986), 34–5.

8   C. H. Firth and R. S. Rait (eds), *Acts and Ordinances of the Interregnum*, 3 vols (London, 1911), vol. 1, p. 1196.

9   *Ibid.*, vol. 1, pp. 753–4, 1062–3, 1195, 1199.

10 J. Charles Cox (ed.), 'Minute Book of the Wirksworth Classis, 1651–1658', *Journal of the Derbyshire Archaeological and Natural History Society*, 2 (1880), 155–8.

11 Firth and Rait (eds), *Acts and Ordinances*, vol. 1, pp. 1197, 1204.

12 *Ibid.*, vol. 1, pp. 1196–7.

13 Corporation of London Record Office, Journal of Common Council, 40, fol. 152.

14 [The Ministers of the Gospel in the Province of London], *Certaine Considerations and Cautions agreed upon by the Ministers of London* (London, 1646).

15 Cox (ed.), 'Wirksworth Classis', p. 141.

16 Shaw, *History of the English Church*, vol. 2, pp. 24ff.

17 J. C. Davis, 'Against formality: one aspect of the English Revolution', *Transactions of the Royal Historical Society*, 6th Series, 3 (1993), 269, 275, 277–9.

18 Love was elected minister of St Agnes and St Anne in late 1644. He seems to have taken up his position around 13 May 1645. See Guildhall Library, London [hereafter GL], MS 587/1, St Agnes and St Anne Aldersgate churchwardens' accounts, fols 60v, 65r–v.

19 William Dell, *Right Reformation: or the Reformation of the Church of the New Testament represented in Gospel Light* (London, 1646), pp. 4–5.

20 *Ibid.*, pp. 6, 26, 28.

21 Christopher Love, *Short and Plaine Animadversions* (London, 1646), pp. 8, 25.

22 *Ibid.*, p. 11.

23 *Ibid.*, p. 13.

24 Barbara Donegan, 'Puritan ministers and laymen: professional claims and social constraints in seventeenth-century England', *Huntington Library Quarterly*, 47 (1984), 90, 92–3, 99; Rosemary O'Day, 'Immanuel Bourne: a defence of the ministerial order', *Journal of Ecclesiastical History*, 27 (1976), 106.

25 GL, MS 2590/1, St Lawrence Jewry, vestry minutes, fols 382–3.

26 Edwin Freshfield (ed.), *The Vestry Minutes of St Christopher-le-Stocks* (London, 1886), p. 35.

27 Dr Williams's Library, London [hereafter DWL], MS 201.12, typescript of the MS 'Records of the London Provincial Assembly', pp. 21, 23; W. A. Shaw, *Material for an Account of the Provincial Synod of the County of Lancaster* (Manchester, 1890), pp. 33–4.

28 [The Lancashire Provincial Assembly], *A Solemn Exhortation made … within this Province of Lancaster* (London, 1649); for a comparable exhortation in London, see also 'Records of the London Provincial Assembly', p. 21.

29 Firth and Rait (eds), *Acts and Ordinances*, vol. 1, pp. 420–2. For more

details of sabbath observance, see Christopher Durston's contribution to this volume.

30 Shaw, *Provincial Synod of the County of Lancaster*, p. 35.

31 *The Lamentation of the Ruling Lay Elder* (London, 1647), pp. 1–4.

32 Charles E. Surman (ed.), *The Register Booke of the Fourth Classis in the Province of London 1646–1659*, Harleian Society Publications, 82–3 (1952–3), p. 6.

33 Patrick Collinson, 'Lectures by combination: structures and characteristics of church life in seventeenth-century England', in Collinson, *Godly People: Essays on English Protestantism and Puritanism* (London 1983), pp. 467–98.

34 Thomas Case, *The Morning Exercise ... Preached at Giles in the Fields, During the Moneth of May 1655* (London, 1655), p. 14.

35 *Ibid.*, pp. 101–12; 'Records of the London Provincial Assembly', p. 80.

36 Leigh Eric Schmidt, *Holy Fairs: Scottish Communions and American Revivals in the Early Modern Period* (Princeton, 1989). See also Patrick Collinson, 'Elizabethan and Jacobean puritanism as forms of popular religious culture', in Christopher Durston and Jacqueline Eales (eds), *The Culture of English Puritanism, 1500–1700* (Basingstoke, 1996), pp. 47–50.

37 'Records of the London Provincial Assembly', p. 18.

38 John Price, *The Pulpit Incendiary* (London, 1648), p. 2.

39 [Anon.], *The Pulpit Incendiary Anatomised or a Vindication of Sion Colledge and the Morning Exercises* (London, 1648), p. 8.

40 Case, *The Morning Exercise*, p. 26.

41 *Ibid.*, p. 22.

42 *The Pulpit Incendiary Anatomised*, pp. 3–4.

43 Derek Hirst, 'The failure of godly rule in the English Republic', *Past and Present*, 132 (1991), 33–66.

44 Patrick Collinson, *The Religion of Protestants: the Church in English Society 1559–1625* (Oxford, 1982), pp. 199–200.

45 Ian Green, '"For children in yeeres and children in understanding": the emergence of the English catechism under Elizabeth and the early Stuarts', *Journal of Ecclesiastical History*, 37 (1986), 424; see also Ian Green, *The Christian's ABC: Catechisms and Catechising in England, c.1530–1740* (Oxford, 1996).

46 Zachary Crofton, *Catechizing God's Ordinance* (London, 1656), sig. A2v.

47 [The London Provincial Assembly], *An Exhortation to Catechizing* (London, 1655), p. 15.

48 *Ibid.*, p. 6.

49 Shaw, *Provincial Synod of the County of Lancaster*, p. 32. The London province ordered the same: see 'Records of the London Provincial Assembly', p. 36.

50 Freshfield, *Vestry Minutes of St Christopher-le-Stocks*, p. 39.

51 Duffy, 'The long Reformation', p. 37; Collinson, *The Religion of Protestants*, pp. 139–40, 224–30.

52 *An Exhortation to Catechizing*, p. 9.

53 [Issac Allen], *Excommunicato Excommunicate, or a Censure of the Presbyterian Censures and Proceedings in the Classis at Manchester* (London, 1658), p. 2.

54 *Ibid.*, p. 8.

55 Cox (ed.), 'Wirksworth Classis', pp. 184–200.

56 Crofton, *Catechizing God's Ordinance*, sig. A4v.

57 *An Exhortation to Catechizing*, pp. 11, 13.

58 *Ibid.*, pp. 5–6.

59 See Margaret Spufford., 'The importance of the Lord's Supper to seventeenth-century dissenters', *Journal of the United Reformed Church History Society*, 5 (1993), 67; and E. Brooks Holifield, *The Covenant-Sealed: The Development of Puritan Sacramental Theology in Old and New England, 1570–1720* (New Haven, CT, and London, 1974), pp. 126, 133.

60 Holifield, *The Covenant-Sealed*, chap. 4, *passim*; [the London Provincial Assembly], *A Vindication of the Presbyterial Government and Ministry* (London, 1650), p. 61; [Roger Drake?], *A Vindication of Two Serious Questions* (London, 1646), pp. 14, 23.

61 BL, Additional MS 40883, fols 178v–179.

62 Thomas Bedford, *Some Sacramental Instructions* (London, 1649), p. 152; [The Lancashire Provincial Assembly], *An Exhortation directed to the elders of the Several congregations within the Province of Lancaster* (London, 1655), pp. 5–6.

63 *Ibid.*, p. 9.

64 Roger Drake, *A Boundary to the Holy Mount, or A Barre against Free Admission to the Lord's Supper* (London, 1653), p. 33.

65 Richard Vines, *A Treatise of the Institution, Right Administration and Receiving of the Sacrament of the Lord's Supper in XX Sermons at St Lawrence Jury, London* (London, 1657), pp. 152, 335.

66 *Ibid.*, pp. 152, 335.

67 *Ibid.*; see also Francis Roberts, *A Communicant Instructed, or Practical Directions for Worthy Receiving of the Lord's Supper* (London, 1651).

68 BL, Additional MS 40883, fol. 21v (author's punctuation).

69 Patrick Collinson, 'Shepherds, sheepdogs, and hirelings: the pastoral ministry in post-Reformation England', in W. J. Sheils and Diana Wood (eds), *The Ministry: Lay and Clerical*, Studies in Church History, 26 (1989), pp. 216–19.

70 GL, MS 4384/1, St Bartholomew-by-the-Exchange, vestry minutes, fol. 99. The ruling elders at St Bartholomew's were among some of the most engaged 'political' Presbyterians in city politics; they included Col. Samuel Harsnett, Capt. John Jones, Capt. Richard Venner and Stephen White.

71 Cox (ed.), 'Wirksworth Classis', p. 157.

72 GL, MS 2590/1, St Lawrence Jewry, vestry minutes, fol. 341.

73 GL, MS 2593/2, St Lawrence Jewry, churchwardens' accounts, fol. 151.

74 GL, MS 2590/1, St Lawrence Jewry, vestry minutes, fol. 383.

75 *Ibid.*, fol. 390.

76 *Ibid.*, fol. 431. It is noteworthy that the vestry ordered that the entire parish enter into a covenant to accept Vines as the minister: see fols 432–7.

77 GL, MS 3570/2, St Mary the Virgin, Aldermanbury, vestry minutes, fol. 58v.

78 GL, MS 3556/2, St Mary the Virgin, Aldermanbury, churchwardens' accounts, unfoliated; compare accounts for 1647 with those for 1639–40 and 1640–41.

79 The ruling elders at Aldermanbury included Walter Boothby, Ninion Butcher and William Smart.

80 GL, MS 3570/2, St Mary the Virgin, Aldermanbury, vestry minutes, fol. 58v. Tai Liu notes that Aldermanbury had 103 houses in 1638; based on a calculation of four adults per house, the parish elders had admitted just under half of the parish. See Tai Liu, *Puritan London: A Study of Religion and Society in the City Parishes* (London, 1986), p. 218.

81 GL, MS 3556/2, St Mary the Virgin, Aldermanbury, churchwardens' accounts, unfoliated; see accounts for 1648.

82 Holifield, *The Covenant-Sealed*, p. 73.

83 [The London Provincial Assembly], *A Vindication of the Presbyterial Government*, p. 1.

84 Drake, *A Boundary to the Holy Mount*, sig. A3v.

85 *Ibid.*, p. 58.

86 *Ibid.*, p. 58.

87 [The Lancashire Provincial Assembly] *A Solemn Exhortation made ... within this Province of Lancaster* (London, 1649).

88 Vines, *A Treatise of the Institution, Right Administration and Receiving of the Sacrament of the Lord's Supper*, p. 370.

89 *Ibid.*, p. 372.

90 *Ibid.*, p. 375.

91 Wilfred W. Biggs, 'The controversy concerning free admission to the Lord's Supper, 1652–1660', *Transactions of the Congregational History Society*, 16 (1949–51), 187.

92 Thomas Bakewell, *A Brief Answer to Objections of all Sorts, against Presbyterian Churches and Government* (London, 1650), p. 6.

93 *Ibid.*, p. 11

94 Shaw, *Provincial Synod of the County of Lancaster*, p. 35.

95 Patrick Collinson, 'The cohabitation of the faithful and the unfaithful', in O. P. Grell, J. I. Israel and N. Tyacke (eds), *From Persecution to Toleration: the Glorious Revolution and Religion in England* (Oxford, 1991), pp. 58–65.

96 Schmidt, *Holy Fairs*, pp. 217–18.

97 Collinson, 'Elizabethan and Jacobean puritanism as forms of popular religious culture', p. 54.

98 Vines, *A Treatise of the Institution, Right Administration and Receiving of the Sacrament of the Lord's Supper*, p. 141.

6

English Catholics at war and peace

William Sheils

I

The importance of anti-popery in contributing to English identity during the decades leading up to the civil wars has been well chronicled.[1] It operated at both the popular and elite levels and in counties as distant as Cheshire and Essex, manifesting itself not only in sermon literature but also in more popular graphic art, where visual representations of the papist often accompanied a scurrilous text, as in the case of the 1641 broadside *Rome brought to Bed in England*, itself a reworking of Samuel Ward's 1621 engraving *Double Deliverance*.[2] During the 1630s the presence of Catholic priests in London in the foreign embassies and at the royal court in the household of Henrietta Maria aroused suspicion about the religious policies of Charles I and William Laud, particularly among those Protestant gentry committed to Calvinist reform, and these fears were not allayed by the King's policy towards the Scottish Kirk after 1638.[3] The activities of Catholics in Ireland were also a cause of great concern to the leading opponents of Crown policy, and suspicions about royal intentions hampered attempts to send an army to deal with problems there.[4] When the unsettled state of Ireland flared into insurrection in October 1641, producing atrocities such as the massacre of Protestants at Portadown, popular fear of Catholicism was greatly accentuated, and the details were exploited by the King's opponents to undermine public trust in Charles.

Throughout the summer of 1642, both in fast sermons before Parliament and from parochial pulpits throughout England, events in Ireland were construed as both a judgement on the nation's recent failure to keep its covenant with God and as a warning about what the future might hold if royal policy was not amended. It is undoubtedly true that, in the febrile atmosphere of 1641–42, fear of popery was a critical factor in preparing the opponents of the King to think the unthinkable and to take up arms against him in defence of Protestantism and the ancient privileges of the people.[5] This was especially true in the north, where the Reformation had been slow to take root and where large numbers of Catholic land-owners still exercised significant social power. When Protestant refugees from Ireland arrived in Yorkshire in January 1642, rumours began to circulate about the intentions of local Catholic gentlemen, and popular anti-Catholicism played a significant part in persuading the middling sort of the region to raise the trained bands in support of Parliament. When hostilities began in August 1642, the King initially attempted to distance himself from any association with Catholics by forbidding them to serve in his army, but by the end of September he had changed his mind and had commanded the Earl of Newcastle to accept recruits into his northern army 'without examining their consciences (more than their loyalty to me)'.[6]

The anti-popery of the decades leading up to the civil wars and Catholic protestations of loyalty to the Crown in the years immediately after the Restoration of 1660 combined to establish a tradition which closely identi-fied the cause of English Catholics with that of the monarchy and which until recently was frequently deployed by both Catholics and Protestants for contemporary political or ideological purposes.[7] The impact of the civil war fighting and the subsequent abolition of the monarchy upon English Catholics is therefore an issue of central importance to our understanding of the revolutionary period, and involves several lines of investigation: firstly the political choices made by Catholics during hostilities; secondly their reaction to government policy and its impact on relations with their Protestant neighbours in the localities; thirdly their negotiations with the varying regimes which followed the execution of Charles, and especially those which some of the clerical leadership maintained with Cromwell; and finally, the impact which these years had on the ways in which Catholics perceived themselves and their religion in a period of rapid religious and political change and experimentation.

II

Given the extent to which Parliament employed the rhetoric of crypto-popery and Catholic scheming at court in the run up to the civil war, we may begin by examining the extent to which those fears were justified. Did English Catholics represent 'an army in waiting' ready to rally to the royalist cause? The question of military action is both the most obvious and the most contentious issue at stake. The work of Keith Lindley has set out to challenge the traditional view – based both on parliamentary propaganda on the eve of war and on Catholic claims to loyalty to the Crown following the Restoration – that Catholics flocked to the King's army. From a study of recruitment in six counties in the early years of the war he concluded that nowhere 'did Catholics form more than a minority of the Royalist army'. These findings were the more significant in that his sample included the counties of Yorkshire and Lancashire, where Catholic landowning families were still numerous. Building on the earlier work of John Aveling for Yorkshire, Lindley demonstrated that in his counties only a minority of the landed Catholic families had members who fought on the King's side, and that, while they were very unlikely to side with Parliament at this stage, most Catholics preferred to remain aloof from hostilities.[8]

Lindley's view was subsequently challenged by Peter Newman, who posed the question in a rather different form. From a study of 1,600 men who held field and regimental command in royalist armies not only in the early stages of the war but throughout the period 1642–60, he asked not how many Catholic gentlemen rallied to the royal cause, but what proportion of royalist officers were Catholic. Newman identified 250 (or 15.6 per cent) of the officers in his study as Catholic, and on this basis suggested that the outbreak of hostilities brought many Catholic individuals into public affairs for the first time, producing a new class of men whose emergence could fuel parliamentarian and Protestant fears. Less than one-sixth of the Catholic field officers had any experience of public office prior to 1642, though an exception has to be made in the case of Sir Edward Waldegrave who had been knighted in 1607 and had served on several local commissions thereafter; despite being in his seventies at the onset of the war he commanded in the field and was commended for his actions. Newman's figures demonstrate that Roman Catholic gentry did rally to the King's cause in sufficient numbers to make them a significant element within his armies, but also that in no county did they represent a majority of the known Catholic landowners, with the exception of Lancashire, or of the royalist officers in arms.[9]

In Worcestershire, a royalist county with a high proportion of Roman Catholic gentry families such as the Talbots, Sheldons and Habingtons, and where rumours of popish plotting had circulated in 1641, the evidence suggests that, notwithstanding the fact that the city of Worcester was a major centre of military activity from 1642 until its capture by Parliament in July 1646, the majority of Catholics resident in the county remained neutral. This did not preclude, however, close organisation and commitment from those who did fight, and it was the Catholics among the defenders of besieged Worcester who were most anxious to continue resistance in 1646. This commitment may have owed as much to events consequent on war as to an initial identification with Charles's cause, for Catholics in the county seem to have suffered particularly heavily from plundering soldiers, as the account of one of the most active royalists, William Sheldon of Beoley, testifies. In 1653 he wrote as follows:

> in September 1643 my house at Weston in Warwickshire was ransacked and my cattle and goods taken away by soldiers, to a great value. That in December following my house at Beoley in Worcestershire was burned to the ground and all my cattle and goods there plundered by the soldiers ... I and my wife were forced for our safety to go to the city of Worcester, and, after a short stay there, removed to a small farmhouse in the parish of Clifton on Teme ... until all our goods were also taken away by soldiers and the house threatened to be burned.

As an early recruit to Charles's cause who was identified by Parliament as one of its principal opponents in the county, Sheldon's experiences may not have been typical. It has been suggested, however, that similar depredations may have accounted for the recruitment to the royalist side of the Earl of Shrewsbury and William Habington in 1651.[10] Even in Worcestershire, however, there were many who remained aloof. The Throckmorton family, whose Catholic credentials went back into Elizabeth's reign when members of the family had been involved in plots and conspiracies against the state, remained resolutely neutral despite the fact that their main residence at Coughton in Warwickshire was occupied and extensively damaged by a parliamentary garrison in 1644.[11] The evidence from as Catholic a county as Worcestershire indicates that the majority of Catholic families preferred to remain neutral, even though many of them suffered more severely than their Protestant neighbours from military action against their property.

While Catholics represented a very small minority within the overall leadership of the King's armies, their participation was subject to wide regional variations. Not surprisingly, among the officers it was lowest in those puritan heartlands of the southern Midlands and East Anglia, where recruitment in general to the royalist cause was also low. In these counties fewer than 10 per cent of officers were Catholic, a figure which suggests that in those parts of the country where they had been most quickly and effectively removed from local political office, Catholics did not seek to take advantage of the confused environment of the 1640s to reassert their claims. Although some exceptions to this pattern can be found, such as the Bedingfield family of Oxburgh in Norfolk, the response of most Catholics in these years provides compelling evidence of the success of both governments and the godly from the 1580s onwards in gradually depoliticising their Catholic subjects, while simultaneously keeping their

Roman Catholicism at the forefront of political debate.[12] A fresh, ironic twist had been given to this story during the Personal Rule in the 1630s, when the financial needs of the Crown had led to stricter enforcement of recusancy fines, increasing income from that source threefold and thereby alienating some of those who might otherwise have been predisposed to the royalist cause.[13]

In contrast, royalist activism was most pronounced in those areas of the country where the Catholic presence had been both numerically and politically strongest in the early seventeenth century. In Staffordshire 30 per cent of all field officers were Catholic, in Northumberland 39.5 per cent, and in Durham 48 per cent. In the religiously polarised county of Lancashire, where there were heavy concentrations of both puritan magistrates and Catholic gentry, religion seems to have been a key factor in decision making; 60 per cent of royalist officers here were Catholic and most of them joined the army in the very early stages of the war. Nor did their wartime experiences diminish significantly their contribution to the royalist cause: despite the loss of 15 officers – two-fifths of the total – through death between 1642 and 1658, a list of Lancashire royalists holding commissions from the exiled Prince Charles in 1658 identifies about 40 per cent of them as Catholic.[14]

The evidence then suggests that Lindley's conclusions about Catholic military participation require some modification. While most Catholic gentry, like their Protestant neighbours, chose to remain aloof from involvement if they could, they were represented more heavily among the royalist officers in arms than the size of the community might suggest. That level of representation was subject to wide regional variations which, in many respects, reflected the progress of the Reformation in the provinces over the previous century. As such, it is impossible to describe their support for Charles in the language of contemporary parliamentary propaganda as a 'rush to arms' by an excluded minority keen to regain its power, however effectively that interpretation was deployed at the time. This was no attempted coup masked in the language of loyalty, but the predictable response of Catholic aristocrats and gentry, faced with a crisis of authority, in those parts of the country where their social power still retained some link with local political structures, and where regional authority had been shared with prerogative institutions, such as the Council in the North and its equivalent in the Marches.[15] These were the counties where Charles was most successful in raising support from the Protestant gentry also, and it may be that, as in Cumberland and Westmoreland, the decision of individual Catholics about whether to take arms or not was influenced not so much by their religion but by the prevalence of royalism among their Protestant neighbours. Comparison of the figures for Lancashire, where members of over half the Catholic families (132 out of 226) bore arms for the King, and those of East Anglia, where only six families out of 34 in Suffolk and eleven out of 29 in Norfolk did so, suggests that royalist activism among Catholic gentry was strongest in those areas where they had been most tenacious in clinging on to some semblance of political power, and at its weakest among those families who had been most effectively excluded from local government in the previous two generations.[16]

III

The plundering of Catholic property by parliamentary forces in Worcestershire has already been noted as having had some influence in activating otherwise hesitant gentlemen to support the Crown, and relations between Catholics and their neighbours at all social levels were particularly fraught in those regions which saw extensive military engagement, such as the west country and the clothing districts of the West Riding.[17] Even without plunder, the wear and tear on property caused by the billeting and victualling of armies can be seen in the household accounts of substantial Catholic families such as the Salvins of Croxdale in County Durham, or the Meynells of the North Riding, whose estate at Kilvington was near to the main route to Scotland and thus saw the full force of troop movements, though Thomas, the head of the family, and his eldest son seem to have remained aloof from active engagement.[18] Furthermore, where Parliament held sway, as in Gloucestershire from 1644, government policy increased the financial burdens on Catholics.[19] But while there is no doubt that relations between Catholic gentry and their neighbours were sharpened by the experience of war, it is not clear how much this was due to political rather than to religious allegiance. At the popular level the rhetoric of anti-popery continued to be deployed by Parliament, and legislation against Catholics was stiffened by ordinance in 1643 when instructions on fining were issued to county committees. All royalists were to suffer sequestration of goods and estates, while papists, whether royalist or not, were to have the existing statutes enforced rigorously. The definition of those who came under the act was extended to include not only convicted recusants, but anyone who had attended mass since the outbreak of war, had harboured a known papist in his house, or had failed to take the Oath of Abjuration. In addition, double taxation was retained for Catholics, and their dependants would only be eligible to receive the remittance of one-fifth of the estate income for their support if it was agreed that the children of the family were brought up as Protestants. County committees were enjoined to implement this regime, which, in formal terms, weighed heavily on Catholics.[20]

The system was introduced to the North Riding of Yorkshire following the royalist defeat at Marston Moor in 1644 and the establishment of a county committee in 1645. But in a region with such a pervasive Catholic presence it is not surprising that some of the committee's members had close links with recusants and attempted to mitigate its impact. They included the secretary of the sequestration committee, Ralph Rymer, who in 1653 acted as one of the executors to the will of the devout Catholic John Metcalfe, and who was praised for his cooperation by Thomas Meynell, who suffered sequestration for his religion. Other office-holders also had close family connections: after military service with Parliament, Edward Saltmarsh settled in the county and served on the committee, but he was later to marry a Catholic wife, to help her family to evade sequestration, and later to become a Catholic himself with two sons as priests. An even more spectacular case was John Rushworth, secretary to both Fairfax and Cromwell, who at great personal expense acted as an agent for delinquent Catholic families, repurchased their estates in his own name, and used his connections with Catholic merchants in London to help them to secure loans.

In such a county, Catholic gentry were likely to find sympathetic support even among the office-holders. But there were two categories of Catholic – those who had fought and those who had not – and they were subject to differing laws. Among the former, whose lands were to be confiscated and sold, were the Frankes of Knighton and the Pudseys of Hackforth, families already in financial difficulties at the start of the war and for whom the exactions of the 1650s were to prove the last straw. More common was the experience of the Cholmleys of Brandsby, who despite confiscation continued to farm their lands throughout the 1650s and to recover ownership after 1660, or of Thomas Tankard of Brampton, whose estates at Brampton, Roecliffe, Givendale and Boroughbridge were sold, leaving him with only a small cottage in Wensleydale, for which he was forced to compound. Despite all this and chiefly through the good offices of Rushworth, he had regained possession of most of his estate by 1662.

Among the non-combatant Yorkshire Catholics was the Meynell family of North Kilvington, whose surviving papers allow close analysis of their fortunes at this time. In 1644–45 their land was sequestrated at an annual value of £400 and let by the state to tenant farmers, who were to pay Thomas £142 a year in lieu of his third share. He was, however, presented with a bill for £300 for arrears of recusancy composition, which remained unpaid in 1648. By that date the government was finding it difficult to secure sufficient farmers to exploit the confiscated lands and Meynell was allowed to farm his own property for £250 a year, though forbidden to cut down woodland which remained the preserve of the state. This prohibition was subsequently withdrawn for an increased rent, and in

1654, while the policy of sequestration was under review by Cromwell, the Meynells through their steward attempted to reduce the charges on the property. Failing this, they then challenged the original conviction for recusancy on technical grounds and won the case. More importantly, before they could be reconvicted, the family conveyed the estate to trustees who included some Protestant neighbours, and so escaped the full financial penalties of the law. Their case was not untypical. With the tacit approval of their neighbours, most North Riding Catholics survived the financial exactions of these years, and only nine landowning families out of a total of around seventy were obliged to sell up; of these, six remained in the county in reduced circumstances.

Evidence of persecution other than financial is also sparse in the North Riding. Only four priests were arrested between 1645 and 1660, all at the instigation of soldiers and not the local bench, and none of them was executed. Occasionally Catholics were presented at quarter sessions; two women were warned not to teach, a few alehouses were closed down, and there was one seizure of popish vestments in 1656 from the very public chapel of Lord Eure in Malton. The temper of the county can also be gauged from relations between the two branches of the Fairfax family: that of the parliamentary general Sir Thomas at Denton in the West Riding, and that of his Catholic cousins at Gilling. The general, whose former steward was clerk of the peace in the North Riding, was guardian to the young Gilling viscount who, despite being a firm and open Catholic, was never prosecuted. Both families shared an interest in their common ancestry, which led to scholarly exchange, and in 1660 it was at the Gilling house that a secret meeting was called by the general to plan Monck's arrival in England.[21]

It was one thing to be a Catholic landowner in a county such as the North Riding, but the experience here needs to be compared with that of their co-religionists in counties where puritanism was deeply rooted. Staffordshire was a divided county with a significant Catholic presence, but one which had also been the focus of popular anti-papal scares from the time of the Irish rising of 1641.[22] It was under parliamentary control from an early stage of the war and the county committee was vigorous in enforcing financial demands against Catholics in the years following 1643. An overhaul of the committee after the second civil war did not change this policy, and in 1650–51 the financial difficulties of the government led to a rigorous imposition of fines and to significant increases in the rents paid by recusants farming their own estates; Thomas Petre's rent was raised from £170 in 1650 to £200 in 1651, and that of Lady Gertrude Aston from £173 to £318. Some mitigation was provided by the change from annual rents to leases for years – usually seven – which allowed Catholics to plan their finances better, but the cost of their religion remained severe for the more substantial gentry. Walter Astley, who had been paying £30 a year to the Crown in 1640, was paying £110 annually to Parliament in 1652, and Peter Gifford's forfeitures rose from £140 to £783 between the same dates. In all, the revenues derived from Catholics in the county rose from £927 paid by 87 individuals in 1640, to £4,467 paid by 54 individuals in 1650–52.

The squeeze was clearly focused on the larger landowners. Although some families, such as the Biddulphs of Biddulph, had relations on the county committee who could mitigate the charges, the thoroughness with which the policy was pursued in the county had more than a merely financial impact on the Catholic gentry. Richard Astley of Patshulland and Humphrey Gifford of Water Eaton – each the heir of a prominent recusant family – took the Oath of Abjuration and converted to Anglicanism after the Restoration. Despite some moderation of the policy following Cromwell's appointment as Lord Protector in 1653, the Catholics of Staffordshire did not enjoy the same degree of support or collusion from their Protestant neighbours as had been shown to their Yorkshire coreligionists, and they survived the years between 1640 and 1660 in a 'state bordering on exhaustion', reduced substantially in both numbers and social importance.[23]

Elsewhere, the later years of the Interregnum saw a more rigorous enforcement of legislation against Catholics under an act of 1657 that allowed for the confiscation of two-thirds of all papist property. Following this legislation, 639 Catholics were reported to the authorities in Hampshire and a further 222 names were returned to the Exchequer from the neighbouring county of West Sussex, where the Browne family, viscounts Montague, stood at the apex of an extensive Catholic network.[24] Here the gentry sustained a Catholic presence among the people similar to that in parts of the North Riding of Yorkshire, and in some parishes papists accounted for up to 40 per cent of the population. The gentry supported each other through loans and securities and, like Sir Garret Kempe of Slindon, created a network of contacts in London and on the continent for the maintenance and support of their children. Here, however, the likeness ended. In this southern coastal county, close to the continent and with strongly puritan urban communities such as that at Rye, the most recent historian of Sussex has concluded that 'the political crisis of the 1640s brought out the full force of their [the gentry's] deeply emotional loathing of the Catholic faith and its adherents'.[25]

That conclusion suggests that relations between Catholics and Protestants in the localities were sharpened by the divisions of war, and that anti-Catholicism became an increasingly important factor within local politics. But while local authorities did often follow the lead of Parliament in the vigorous implementation of legislation, their campaigns were generally short-lived and, although revealing of fundamental attitudes, did not exactly reflect the normal pattern of relations between neighbours. Once hostilities ceased, there were relatively few examples of predatory assaults on Catholic property, and when these did take place they usually concerned families that had been active in the royalist cause. Even here the evidence remains ambivalent; in Cornwall, Nicholas Borlace of St Erme, who had been a colonel in the royalist army, successfully appealed to Cromwell to have his estate rent reduced against the wishes of the county committee, one of whose members, John Jago, had driven the colonel's wife and children from their home in revenge for an earlier eviction he had suffered at Borlace's hands during the war. Not only did Borlace win his case, he also secured his rents from the copyhold tenants through the Committee for Compounding. In this instance the central authorities upheld the law against the wishes of the local committee, to the benefit of a prominent Catholic and royalist, while in another the local committee found it impossible to proceed against Sir John Arundell of Lanherne as, due to 'his faire demeanour to his tenants', it was unable to produce evidence of his delinquency.[26]

While some Catholic royalist activists could find refuge in the law and in their local reputation, this was not guaranteed. In Norfolk the Bedingfield family of Oxburgh provided four soldiers for the King. One of them was wounded in the siege of Lincoln, gaoled for two years and then went into exile, where he was joined by another brother. Their moated family house suffered heavy damage during the wars, and the extensive family estate in Norfolk was sequestrated following the exclusion of the head of the family, Sir Henry, from the general pardon of 1647 and his subsequent imprisonment in the Tower. Both the Norfolk and Suffolk estates were sold, the latter to the Society for the Propagation of the Gospel in New England which retained ownership after 1660. Under the later Stuarts the family regained most of their Norfolk properties, though only after sustaining losses of around £45,000 during the revolutionary period.[27]

For some Catholic royalists, exile – or flight as they would have seen it – was another response to the experience of defeat. In the case of the Bedingfields, an oil painting of the later seventeenth century, which depicts the escape from England of the royalist officer Henry and shows him and his family sheltering under the protective cloak of Our Lady's Mantle, still adorns the walls of their Oxburgh house. Indeed, it was the experience gained by Catholics in smuggling clergy in and out of the country which assisted Prince Charles's escape after the battle of Worcester in 1651. The court that grew up around the exiled Prince in Paris and Flanders contained several prominent Catholics, but was beset by faction, poor finances, and disagreement over policy. While it was important for Charles to distance himself from the many prominent Catholics in his entourage, and especially from his mother, the Catholic seminary college at Douai and the English religious houses on the continent provided important channels of communication both to royalists in England and to the continental powers who supplied the Prince with funds.[28] At the centre of these contacts was Mary Knatchbull, Abbess of the Benedictine Convent in Ghent. Providing Charles with shelter and with funds, she was at the heart of the royalist intelligence system, and was in regular correspondence on political matters with Edward Hyde and others. Her contacts in England convinced her that the best hope for a restoration of the monarchy lay in a comprehensive religious settlement on Protestant lines, which offered space to her co-religionists but did not subvert the religious developments of the previous two decades. No doubt many of the exiled royalists, Catholic or otherwise, continued to engage in conspiracy, but among the more significant of them the politics of belligerence had been replaced by that of accommodation and even by the hope of toleration.[29]

IV

So far we have assessed the practical consequences for the laity of military defeat, sequestration and exile, but these experiences also led to reconsideration by both parties of the relationship between Roman Catholics and the state. Discussions began as early as 1647 following the end of the first civil war when Sir Thomas Fairfax, in his design to restore Charles I to the throne on the New Model Army's terms, entered into discussions with leading Catholic peers, gentry and clergy, including Henry More, the Jesuit provincial, the superiors of the other religious orders, and three secular priests representing the chapter, about the possibility of some toleration for Catholics in return for their support of the proposal. The meetings were partly at the initiative of the Catholics themselves, who based their arguments for toleration not only as previously on a promise of their loyalty, but also on freedom of conscience. In return for a settlement with the King incorporating the repeal of the recusancy laws, Catholics would be allowed private but not public worship; they would also remain excluded from office and would be required to deny that papal claims to a deposing power and to political authority over English Catholics were articles of faith.[30] The possibility thus proposed, of Catholics acquiring a status similar to that of Protestant dissenters within a pluralist religious settlement, marked a significant new departure from debates preceding the civil war about the Oath of Allegiance.

Although nothing came of these discussions, their breakdown produced an even more radical proposal. The source of this new scheme was Paris, where two English secular clergy looked to Gallican ideas of churchmanship as a model for a national Catholic Church loyal to the regime and with some independence from the papacy in matters of jurisdiction and organisation. The author of the scheme was Henry Holden, professor of theology at Arras College, and his associate was the philosopher priest, Thomas White, also known as Blacklo, who in 1655 published *The Grounds of Obedience and Government*, recommending acceptance of Cromwell's title. Their scheme stated that Parliament should issue an oath of allegiance to all English Catholics, under pain of banishment, and then establish up to six bishops in England with limited diocesan jurisdiction. Ideally these men would be appointed by the pope, but if he refused to act they could be consecrated in Ireland or France, and the papacy would not be able either to remove or instruct them without the consent of the government. To enforce episcopal authority over clergy and laity, all missionaries with papal faculties would be required to take an oath of obedience to the diocesans, thereby diminishing the authority of the Jesuits.[31]

Unsurprisingly, these proposals divided the Catholic clergy and failed to attract much support in either England or Rome. From the early 1650s, however, under the vigorous leadership of a civil war convert, John Sergeant, who acted as their secretary from 1653, the Blackloists, as they came to be called, gained control of the English chapter. Under Sergeant's direction the secular clergy adopted a policy of accommodation to the Cromwellian regime where possible, and worked to ensure that, if the pope was not going to appoint bishops to govern the English Catholic community, neither would he be able to impose any other form of authority, and especially not one involving the Jesuits.[32] Nor was coexistence sought only by the Catholics, for, as John Coffey's earlier contribution to this volume reveals, the period was one in which the idea of toleration was voiced both outside and within the governing circles. Radicals such as the Leveller, Richard Overton, had raised the possibility of toleration for Catholics as early as 1645, and it remained the Leveller position until 1648 at least. Others, like the former New England cleric Roger Williams, argued the case in almost Lockean terms, stressing the futility of trying to coerce conscience through law or punishment.[33] In addition to these radical voices, at the head of the regime Oliver Cromwell, whether for pragmatic reasons or from a deeply held belief, advocated, if not complete toleration, then liberty of conscience for his Catholic subjects. This was to be a restricted freedom in which priests were permitted to exercise a pastoral ministry, but not to proselytise.

For the likes of Blacklo and his associates among the secular clergy this was enough to justify loyalty. Cromwell's own openness to Catholic aristocrats such as Lords Brudenell and Arundell, and to the enigmatic philosopher Kenelm Digby, his restoration of the Irish and colonial properties of Lord Baltimore in Maryland, and his refusal to forbid attendance at mass in the chapel of the Venetian embassy, reinforced their confidence in him.[34] These actions can, of course, be interpreted as an essentially pragmatic recognition of the need to retain the support of influential Catholics at home and abroad, but his protest at the execution of the Jesuit John Southworth in June 1654 represented more than this. Southworth had been condemned to death before, and in 1630 had had his sentence commuted to banishment, an order which he had ignored. He remained active in London in the 1630s and went underground during the war years, emerging again in the early 1650s when he was working from the house of the Spanish ambassador. Arrested in 1654, probably in the wake of the discovery of an assassination plot against Cromwell, he was hanged, drawn and quartered at Tyburn, the only priest to be executed under the Protectorate. His speech from the scaffold, requesting that 'Catholics, being free-born subjects, should enjoy that liberty [of conscience] as others do as long as they live obedient subjects to the Lord Protector and the laws of the nation', reflected the sentiments of the seculars and many of his lay co-religionists, and may have been shared by Cromwell, who arranged for his dismembered body to be sewn up and transferred to Douai for burial.[35]

Southworth's case was exceptional, but the very fact that it was an exception, reveals how far the politico-religious debate had shifted during the war years. At the outbreak of the civil war Cromwell had been an almost archetypal godly gentleman fired by a hatred of popery. By the mid-1650s, while he remained firmly committed to godly reformation, he was also suspicious of organised, institutional religion and, like the Blackloists, the Levellers and other radical groups such as the Quakers, had come to an understanding of the relationship between the state and the religion of the individual which recognised, in varying degrees, the claims of liberty of conscience. Within that recognition there was room for negotiation, and protagonists on both sides took advantage of that space to try to create a *modus vivendi* that, unlike previous attempts, was rooted in the realm of ideas as well as in the practicalities of co-existence. The debate was cut short by Cromwell's death before it had got very far, but in the course of the 1650s both Catholics and Protestants had begun to imagine the previously unimaginable – the terms under which Catholics might organise and practise their religion openly within a Protestant state and without interference from the papacy.

While in the longer perspective the ideas of Holden and his associates were to have important consequences, in the short term the restoration of monarchy eclipsed their outlook, and heralded instead a return to a form of court Catholicism once more located about the person of Henrietta Maria. This recalled the circumstances of the 1630s and was again to arouse suspicions in Parliament, even though this was now an Anglican rather than a puritan assembly. In this transformed post-1660 environment the Jesuits and the leaders of the other Catholic religious orders saw an opportunity to restore their influence over court and metropolitan Catholicism. Chief among them was the aristocratic Dominican Philip Howard, shortly to be made a cardinal, who reinvigorated the Roman connections of English Catholicism, displacing the Blackloists who were now tainted by their association with the Cromwellian regime.[36]

V

The work of Alison Shell and Brian Cummings has recently brought attention to the contribution of recusant writers to English culture following the Reformation, alerting us to the importance of the contemplative and confessional as against the polemical and political, though each drew on the other. The upheavals of the revolutionary years of the mid-seventeenth century did not produce major works from Catholic intellectuals, but just as the experience of war and revolution opened up political possibilities, so it encouraged Catholics to reflect on the spiritual lessons to be drawn from their situation. Imprisonment and exile had long been commonplaces of Catholic identity and central to its rhetoric of suffering, and when Sir Henry Bedingfield found himself imprisoned in the Tower for two years for his support of the King during the first civil war, he sought the consolation of his religion. He composed a meditation on the Passion, couched in conventional terms and dedicated to his wife, as well as several other prayers, including a series of 'Aspirations of a Devout Soul'. These spoke to his immediate circumstances, as follows:

> 8. Jesus, in honor of your life, humble on earth, I accept with a willing heart all humiliations which shall happen to me, though repugnant to myself.

> 9. O Jesus, I renounce all the repugnances which I have to suffer, and to beare humiliations, I accept them, though never so contrary to my sense, to unite myself to your holy will to the eande that, whatsoever is in me refractory to what they enjoine, may be a subiect to my conforming myself to them and submitting me to you.[37]

Such words, written by a soldier, reflect a quietist resignation in the face of suffering that was at odds with the active espousal of military action by him and his sons during the wars. Perhaps we should not make too much of such conventionally toned prison writings, but by suggesting that, in conforming to rather than resisting the demands of his persecutors, he might also be serving his Saviour, Bedingfield interiorised his experience in ways similar to many of his fellow Catholic gentry.

A similar emphasis on contemplative prayer can be found in the writings of the idiosyncratic Benedictine, Augustine Baker, who had died on the eve of the war but whose writings had been circulating in manuscript within clerical circles since the 1620s. Baker had tried his vocation with the Benedictine community at Padua but had returned to England in 1606. Resident in the Worcestershire home of Sir Nicholas Fortescue, he began to experiment with contemplative devotion, reading widely in the Spanish mystics. The life of prayer and the responsiveness of the individual to the workings of the Spirit formed the basis of his theology, and in the 1620s he translated or copied for the Benedictine convent at Cambrai where he was spiritual director some of the central texts of the medieval English mystical tradition, including those of Richard Rolle and Julian of Norwich. He also composed a number of treatises and sermons of his own which circulated in manuscript and his views on the workings of the Spirit on the individual conscience aroused suspicions of illuminism among the more orthodox.[38] In this respect, if not in others, Baker's views anticipated those of the radical sectaries, such as the Quakers and Baptists, who believed in the primacy of the Spirit over the Law in governing behaviour.[39]

It is not surprising therefore to find that in 1657 Baker's works were brought together and published as *Sancta Sophia*, nor that the editor was another Benedictine, Serenus Cressy. Cressy's career drew together many strands in the religious life of the period: as a Hookerian intellectual he had been a member of the Great Tew circle in the 1630s and had received ecclesiastical preferment before converting to Catholicism in 1646. During his noviciate in 1648, at the same time as Bedingfield was writing in the Tower, Cressy composed a 'Treatise on the Passion', and on his profession he took a name alluding to his commitment to peace. He subsequently studied at Paris under Henry Holden, where he absorbed the political views of the Blackloists, writing on the Oath of Allegiance in 1661. In addition to editing Baker's works, he later published translations of two English medieval mystical works, Walter Hilton's *Scale of Perfection* and the *Revelations of Divine Love* of Julian of Norwich.[40]

VI

It would be foolish to suggest that the career of Cressy was representative. Similarly, to characterise the trajectory of Catholicism in this period as one of moving from a belligerent royalism in 1642 to contemplative devotion in 1658 would be to ignore the variety of experiences which English

Catholics endured in these years. Conspiracy against the Cromwellian regime continued to involve Catholics, though, like Lord Bellasis within the Sealed Knot or the Lancashire Catholic gentry at the time of Booth's rising, they were usually marginalised by their Protestant accomplices who were anxious to distance themselves from any taint of popery. In 1656 Charles Stuart recruited a small army in Flanders, drawn from Irishmen previously in the service of the French Crown and a steady flow of disaffected English, including some Catholics. Neither its composition nor its organisation, however, troubled the Cromwellian agents there and any projected plans for invasion were dogged by poor organisation and indecision.[41] Notwithstanding their active support for the Crown during the civil wars of the 1640s, the great majority of Catholic royalists did not engage in conspiracy thereafter, nor were they encouraged to. This owed something to the sensitivities of Protestant conspirators, but rather more to the views and circumstances of their fellow Catholics, many of whom had accommodated themselves to the regime.

We have seen that in general Charles I's army included a larger proportion of Catholic gentlemen than was to be found in the landowning population as a whole, but that active royalism was subject to wide regional variation. The decision to fight or not probably owed more to the political temper of the locality than to the religious allegiance of individual Catholics and, Lancashire excepted, even in those areas of pronounced royalist support the majority of their gentry co-religionists preferred to remain aloof from military engagement, if not politically neutral. Even among supporters of monarchy activism was a minority choice and conspiracy even more so. The policies of Charles I in the 1630s had contributed to this, but the treatment of Catholics under the successive regimes after 1649, whether pragmatic or principled, consolidated it. Catholics undoubtedly suffered severe financial penalties through fines and sequestration but, as we have seen, most families managed to hang on to their estates, albeit at some cost and in diminished circumstances. Those for whom this period did result in financial ruin, such as the Sayers of Worsall in the North Riding or the Fleetwoods of Calwich in Staffordshire, had usually already been in difficult circumstances at the start of the wars.[42]

A more significant factor in the decline in the numbers of Catholic landowning families was defection, or conversion, to Protestantism. How far this was the result of government policy and how much it owed to individual conviction or the climate of religious experimentation in these years is difficult to ascertain, but a number of former recusants took the Oath of Abjuration, to become at first church-papists and later in some cases conforming Anglicans within the Restoration Church. Among them were some spectacular cases, such as that of Lord Bellasis's nephew, Lord

Fauconberg, who became an officer in the Protector's guard and married Cromwell's daughter.[43] While it was undoubtedly the case that Catholic landowners were reduced in number and wealth during the revolutionary years, this trend was part of a long process of attrition that had started before 1640. Despite the evidence from Staffordshire cited above, the middle decades of the seventeenth century did not witness a marked acceleration in that process. As for the 'people' who have not figured greatly in this account so far, it is difficult to generalise about them with confidence, since they are largely missing from the records, only appearing briefly before godly magistrates for minor offences. The overall impression is that in places such as West Sussex, Lancashire and the North Riding, where Catholics can be found in substantial numbers before 1640, they re-emerged as vigorous communities in the post-Restoration period. This was equally true of London, which probably housed the largest population of non-gentry Catholics outside the Lancashire heartlands, and which was the setting for significant popular anti-Catholic and anti-Irish demonstrations in the early years of the civil war. Despite this, the metropolitan Catholic community survived, recovered and eventually flourished alongside the courtly Catholicism of the Restoration.[44]

Those strategies for survival which the Catholic community had been developing since 1559 served it well during these years, but in some ways this is the less interesting part of the story, for the Interregnum brought opportunities as well as difficulties. Catholics shared in the religious ferment and excitement of these years, and the emergence of the political programme of the Blackloists, with its emphasis on toleration and liberty of conscience, and its Gallican model of churchmanship, marked a significant intellectual break from previous attempts to locate English Catholics within a Protestant state, while the publication of the works of Augustine Baker, represented a renewed engagement with the contemplative tradition within English Catholicism. That these developments were cut short in 1660, when the restoration of the monarchy brought for many Catholics a return to a more traditional politics located around the monarchy and the papacy, should not obscure their longer term significance.[45] Both developments prefigured the quietist and tolerationist values of the Catholic Enlightenment and the Cisalpine movement of the later eighteenth century, thereby contributing to an important aspect of the English Catholic tradition.[46] Thus, while the tumultuous years between 1642 and 1660 were undoubtedly ones of suffering and endurance for English Catholics, it should not be forgotten that, in common with the experience of other religious groups, they were also ones of enquiry, experiment and possibility.

Notes

1 R. Clifton, 'Fear of popery', in Conrad Russell (ed.), *The Origins of the English Civil War* (Basingstoke, 1973), pp. 144–67; Peter Lake, 'Antipopery: the structure of a prejudice', in Richard Cust and Ann Hughes (eds), *Conflict in Early Stuart England: Studies in Religion and Politics, 1603–1642* (London, 1989), pp. 72–106.

2 William Hunt, *The Puritan Moment: the Coming of Revolution in an English County* (Cambridge, MA, 1983), pp. 293–4; H. Pierce, 'Unseemly Pictures: Political Satire and Graphic Art in England, 1600–1640', unpublished PhD thesis, University of York, 2004, esp. chapters 2 and 5; Ian Gentles, 'The iconography of revolution', in Ian Gentles, John Morrill and Blair Worden (eds), *Soldiers, Writers and Statesmen in the English Revolution* (Cambridge, 1998), pp. 97–8, 106.

3 Caroline Hibbard, *Charles I and the Popish Plot* (Chapel Hill, NC, 1983); Conrad Russell, *The Fall of the British Monarchies, 1637–1642* (Oxford, 1991), pp. 27–131; Kevin Sharpe, *The Personal Rule of Charles I* (New Haven, CT, and London, 1992), pp. 769–825.

4 Russell, *British Monarchies*, pp. 414–21.

5 H. R. Trevor-Roper, 'The Fast Sermons of the Long Parliament', in H. R. Trevor-Roper (ed.), *Religion, Reformation and Social Change* (London, 1967), pp. 294–344; W. J. Sheils, 'Provincial preaching on the eve of the civil war: some West Riding fast sermons', in Peter Roberts and Anthony Fletcher (eds), *Religion, Culture, and Society in Early Modern Britain* (Cambridge, 1994), pp. 302–5.

6 Andrew Hopper, '"The Popish Army of the North": anti-Catholicism and parliamentarian allegiance in civil war Yorkshire, 1642–46', *Recusant History*, 25 (2000–1), 12–28; quotation at p. 17.

7 J. C. H. Aveling, *Northern Catholics: the Catholic Recusants of the North Riding of Yorkshire, 1558–1790* (London, 1966), p. 323; J. C. H. Aveling, *The Handle and the Axe* (London, 1976), pp. 353–8.

8 Keith Lindley, 'The part played by Catholics', in R. B. Manning (ed.), *Politics, Religion and the Civil War* (London, 1973), pp. 126–76; B. G. Blackwood, *The Lancashire Gentry and the Great Rebellion* (Manchester, 1978), pp. 39–45, 65; Aveling, *Northern Catholics*, pp. 301–9.

9 P. R. Newman, 'Roman Catholic royalists: papist commanders under Charles I and Charles II', *Recusant History*, 15 (1979–81), 396–405.

10 C. D. Gilbert, 'The Catholics in Worcestershire, 1642–1651', *Recusant History*, 20 (1990–91), 336–57; P. Styles, 'The city of Worcester during the civil wars', in R. C. Richardson (ed.), *The English Civil Wars: Local Aspects* (Stroud, 1997), pp. 186–238.

11 Gilbert, 'Catholics in Worcestershire', 345; Ann Hughes, *Politics, Society and Civil War in Warwickshire, 1620–1660* (Cambridge, 1987), pp. 209, 258.

12 Newman, 'Roman Catholic royalists', 404; *Oxford Dictionary of National Biography* [hereafter *ODNB*], *sub* Bedingfield family.

13 Sharpe, *Personal Rule*, pp. 302–3.

14 Newman, 'Roman Catholic royalists', 403–4; Blackwood, *Lancashire Gentry*, p. 65.

15 J. R. Phillips, *Memoirs of the Civil War in Wales and the Marches*, 2 vols (London, 1874); J. T. Cliffe, *The Yorkshire Gentry from the Reformation to the Civil War* (London, 1969), pp. 188–209, 243.

16 B. G. Blackwood, 'Parties and issues in the civil war in Lancashire and East Anglia', in Richardson, *English Civil Wars*, pp. 278–80; C. B. Phillips, 'The royalist north: the Cumberland and Westmorland gentry, 1642–60', in Richardson, *English Civil Wars*, pp. 239–60, esp. p. 243.

17 Hopper, '"The popish army of the north"', pp. 17–24; David Underdown, *Revel, Riot and Rebellion: Popular Politics and Culture in England, 1603–1660* (Oxford, 1985), pp. 165, 217–18.

18 Aveling, *Northern Catholics*, pp. 302, 309.

19 A. Warmington, *Civil War, Interregnum and Restoration in Gloucestershire, 1640–1672* (Woodbridge, 1997), pp. 39–40.

20 Aveling, *Handle and Axe*, pp. 170–1.

21 Aveling, *Northern Catholics*, pp. 304–18; J. C. H. Aveling (ed.), 'The Meynell Papers', *Miscellanea*, Catholic Record Society, 56 (1964), 76–112.

22 I. Atherton and M. Cooksby, 'Staffordshire and the Irish revolt of 1641', *Staffordshire Studies*, 13 (2001), 55–78.

23 T. S. Smith, 'The persecution of Staffordshire Roman Catholic recusants, 1625–1660', *Journal of Ecclesiastical History*, 30 (1979), 327–51.

24 A. M. Coleby, *Central Government and the Localities: Hampshire, 1649–1689* (Cambridge, 1987), p. 61; Anthony Fletcher, *A County Community in Peace and War: Sussex 1600–1660* (London, 1975), pp. 96–7.

25 Fletcher, *County Community*, pp. 98–101, 104, 111–13; W. J. Sheils, 'Catholics and their neighbours in a rural community: Egton chapelry, 1590–1780', *Northern History*, 34 (1998), 117–43.

26 M. Coate, *Cornwall in the Great Civil War and Interregnum, 1642–1660* (Truro, 1963), pp. 263–5.

27 J. H. Pollen (ed.), 'The Bedingfield papers', in *Miscellanea VI*, Catholic Record Society, 22 (1909), 1–177; the painting is illustrated on the frontispiece.

28 John Miller, *Charles II* (London, 1991), pp. 8–16; Aveling, *Handle and Axe*, p. 176.

29 Caroline Bowden, 'The abbess and Mrs Brown: Lady Mary Knatchbull and royalist politics in Flanders in the late 1650s', *Recusant History*, 24 (1998–99), 288–308; C. Walker, 'Prayer, patronage and political conspiracy: English nuns and the Restoration', *Historical Journal*, 43 (2000), 1–23.

30 K. J. Lindley, 'The lay Catholics of England in the reign of Charles I', *Journal of Ecclesiastical History*, 22 (1971), 219–21; T. H. Clancy, 'The Jesuits and the Independents', *Archivum Societatis Jesu*, 40 (1971), 67–89.

31 A. F. Allison, 'An English Gallican: Henry Holden (1596/7–1662), Part One', *Recusant History*, 22 (1994–95), 319–49; John Bossy, *The English Catholic Community, 1570–1850* (London, 1975), pp. 62–8; *ODNB*,

sub Henry Holden and Thomas White. For their links to Hobbes see
J.R.Collins, 'Thomas Hobbes and the Blackloist conspiracy of 1649',
Historical Journal, 45 (2002), 305–31, esp. pp. 310–23.

32 Bossy, *Catholic Community*, pp. 68–9.

33 Norah Carlin, 'Toleration for Catholics in the puritan revolution', in
O.P.Grell and R.Scribner (eds), *Tolerance and Intolerance in the European
Reformation* (Cambridge, 1996), pp. 216–30.

34 Blair Worden, 'Toleration and the Cromwellian protectorate', in W.J.Sheils
(ed.), *Persecution and Toleration*, Studies in Church History, 21 (1984),
pp. 199–233; J.C.Davis, 'Cromwell's religion', in J.S.Morrill (ed.), *Oliver
Cromwell and the English Revolution* (London, 1990), pp. 181–208.

35 E.E.Reynolds, *John Southworth, Priest and Martyr* (London, 1962);
ODNB, sub John Southworth.

36 Aveling, *Handle and Axe*, pp. 180–6; John Miller, *Popery and Politics in
the Reign of Charles II* (Cambridge, 1973), pp. 33–50.

37 Alison Shell, *Catholicism, Controversy and the English Literary
Imagination, 1558–1660* (Cambridge, 1999), pp. 146–68, esp. pp. 163–4;
Brian Cummings, *The Literary Culture of the Reformation: Grammar
and Grace* (Oxford, 2002), pp. 328–64; Pollen (ed.), 'Bedingfield Papers',
p. 13.

38 J.McCann and H.Connolly (eds), *Memorials of Father Augustine Baker
and other Documents relating to the English Benedictines*, Catholic Record
Society, 28 (1933); *ODNB, sub* David Baker.

39 J.F.McGregor and B.Reay (eds), *Radical Religion in the English Revolution*
(Oxford, 1984), pp. 57–68, 147–9.

40 For the intellectual roots of Cressy's work, see A.Brown, 'Anglo-Irish
Gallicanism, c.1635–c.1685', unpublished PhD thesis, University of
Cambridge (2004); *ODNB, sub* Hugh Paulinus Cressy.

41 David Underdown, *Royalist Conspiracy in England, 1649–1660* (New
Haven, CT, 1960), pp. 94, 275.

42 Aveling, *Northern Catholics*, p. 310; Smith, 'Staffordshire Roman Catholics',
349.

43 Aveling, *Handle and Axe*, p. 177.

44 B.G.Blackwood, 'Plebeian Catholics in the 1640s and 1650s', *Recusant
History*, 18 (1986–87), 42–58; essays by M.Gandy (London) and
M.Wanklyn (Madeley, Staffs.), in Marie B.Rowlands (ed.), *Catholics of
Parish and Town, 1558–1778*, Catholic Record Society, monograph series, 5
(1999), pp. 153–78, 210–36; Sheils, 'Catholics and their neighbours', 120–4;
Michael Mullett, '"A receptacle for papists and an Assilum": Catholicism
and disorder in late seventeenth-century Wigan', *Catholic Historical
Review*, 73 (1987), 390–408; S.J.Loomie, 'London's Spanish chapel before
and after the civil war', *Recusant History*, 18 (1987), 402–10.

45 Miller, *Popery and Politics*, pp. 3–50. How far recusancy was subse-
quently linked to the Stuart cause is a matter for debate; Bossy in *Catholic
Community* and Aveling in *Handle and Axe* see it as marginal, whereas
P.K.Monod, *Jacobitism and the English People, 1688–1788* (Cambridge,

1989), pp. 132–8, suggests that it had a continuing hold on the northern gentry, at least until the failure of the '15.

46 Eamon Duffy, 'Ecclesiastical democracy detected', *Recusant History*, 10 (1969–70), 193–209, 309–31; 13 (1975–76), 123–48; T.W. Blanning, 'The Enlightenment in Catholic Germany', in R. Porter and M. Teich (eds), *The Enlightenment in National Context* (Cambridge, 1981), pp. 178–95; N. Davidson, 'Toleration in Enlightenment Italy', in O. P. Grell and R. Porter (eds), *Toleration in Enlightenment Europe* (Cambridge, 2000), pp. 230–49; Mark Goldie, 'The Scottish Catholic Enlightenment', *Journal of British Studies*, 30 (1991), 20–62.

7

Suffering and surviving: the civil wars, the Commonwealth and the formation of 'Anglicanism', 1642–60[1]

Judith Maltby

I

> Between 1640 and 1642 the Church of England collapsed, its leaders reviled and discredited, its structures paralysed, its practices if not yet proscribed, at least inhibited. In the years that followed, yet worse was to befall it. And yet in every year of its persecution after 1646, new shoots sprang up out of the fallen timber: bereft of episcopal leadership, lacking any power of coercion, its observances illegal, anglicanism thrived. As memories of the 1630s faded and were overlaid by the tyrannies of the 1640s ... the deeper rhythms of the Kalendar and the ingrained perfections of Cranmer's liturgies bound a growing majority together.[2]

Professor John Morrill, quoted above, has rightly identified a set of historiographical contradictions about the Stuart Church in a series of important articles.[3] Historians have until recently paid little attention to the positive and popular elements of conformity to the national Church of England in the period before the civil war. The lack of interest in conformity has led to a seventeenth-century version of the old Whig view of the late medieval Church: the Church of England is presented as a complacent, corrupt and clericalist institution, 'ripe' – as the English Church in the sixteenth century was 'ripe' – to be purified by reformers. However, if this was the case, how does one account for the durable commitment to the Prayer Book demonstrated during the 1640s and 1650s and the widespread – but not universal – support for the 'return' of the Church of England in 1660?

'In April 1660, three weeks before the Declaration of Breda and proc-lamation of Charles II, Easter, a forbidden festival, was celebrated in most parish churches up and down the country. If the collapse of the old Church had presaged the downfall of the monarchy, it was to be the Church's survival which would herald the Restoration.'[4] These are remarkable claims about a Church whose pre-1642 historiography was dominated until recently by widespread acceptance of the critiques of the godly.[5] We can now speak, however, of a set of religious attitudes, practices and beliefs which found authenticity, comfort and renewal in conformity to the official and lawful forms of the Christian religion as offered by the Church of England. As civil war descended on the English portion of the British Isles, one could also speak of a religious tradition which was firm in its loyalty to the Church of England, expressed principally in support for the liturgy and episcopacy, but unhappy about the Laudian innovations of the 1630s. This tradition found a voice in a series of petitions in support of episcopacy and liturgy to the Long Parliament in the months leading up to the outbreak of the civil war. Although it is reasonable to assume that the tribulations of the middle of the century created marriages of convenience between Laudians and Prayer Book Protestants – indeed redrew some boundaries between these groups – it would be a mistake to see the views under examination in this essay as evidence of the 'popularity' of Laudianism before the civil war. As Professor Robert Ashton has rightly remarked, in the late 1640s 'Royalism was in fact a far more common Anglican characteristic than ritualism'. Placing the early Stuart Church within a longer-term perspective on the events of the turbulent middle decades of the seventeenth century troubles some historiographical waters and raises some important questions about the popular life of the Church of England on either side of 1642.[6]

What to call the set of religious convictions explored in this essay is more than a problem of semantics or an excuse for pedantry. Terms such as 'Prayer Book Protestants', 'Church of England loyalists' and 'followers of the "Old Church"', however long-winded, are to be preferred to the term 'Anglicans'. To single out Prayer Book loyalists as '*the* Anglicans' before the Restoration begs enormous scholarly and historical questions, as it treats the emerging multi-denominational character of English Christianity after 1660 as a foregone conclusion.[7] Further, it implies 'ownership' of a Church by particular groups within it and 'unchurches' sets of individuals who were as much a part of the *ecclesia anglicana* as those retrospectively canonised as the 'true Anglicans' by, as Diarmaid MacCulloch has so rightly warned us, the highly successful revisionists of the Oxford Movement.[8]

If we may now accept the existence of English Christians before 1642 whose religious identities and loyalties were formed and became *in*formed by conformity to the established Church of England yet who can properly be distinguished from Laudian sympathisers, a simple but important question emerges. What happened to that set of religious convictions in the face of a parliamentary and puritan onslaught? In the 1640s the Long Parliament embarked on a series of pieces of legislation which achieved far more than the taking away of the Church of England's historic privileges and the placing of it on an equal footing with its emerging competitors in the religious marketplace. Its aim was not disestablishment but rather the proscription and suppression of what were for many the Church of England's most defining and best-loved features.[9] To call the suppression of the Church of England systematic would imply greater consensus and coherence among parliamentarians, even among moderate Presbyterians, than is likely. The attack on the Church of England managed to be both haphazard and thorough. While recent criticisms that too much coherence has been ascribed to pre-1642 Prayer Book Protestantism need to be taken seriously, it is nonetheless striking to note the specific and carefully chosen targets of the contemporary parliamentary reformers: the Prayer Book, its festive calendar, and episcopal polity.[10]

II

The theological case against the Book of Common Prayer centred on more than concerns about its residual popery. To some more precise Protestants, the very idea of a *set* form of liturgy was unacceptable, though this was not a view held in any sense by all we might categorise as 'puritan'. The parliamentary reformers of the 1640s were faced with a problem not shared by the Tudor architects of the Church of England. Though he was aware of many errors in the medieval rites that the Prayer Book had replaced, Thomas Cranmer saw positive good in set forms of liturgy. One of the objectives of Common Prayer, after all, was to provide uniformity of practice throughout the country. The group of divines and others brought together as the Westminster Assembly by parliamentary ordinance in 1643 was divided on this very notion of 'set' and 'free' prayer. To some of the moderate Presbyterian view, their original intention was to reform, not suppress, the Book of Common Prayer. To more radical Protestants, however, any notion of set forms of public prayer smacked too much of incantation rather than of intercession. In the end, the result owed much to the Scottish presence and influence in the Assembly.[11]

A Directory for the Public Worship of God was first authorised for use in 1645 and was largely what it proclaimed itself to be – not a liturgy but a set of *directions* for the conduct of public worship in England.[12] Given the abuse heaped upon the authorised liturgy for decades by the godly, the *Directory*'s 'Preface' was surprisingly civil and even respectful of the landfalls that the Prayer Book represented on the larger journey to a properly reformed Church. 'The Preface' maintained that the Book of Common Prayer was without a doubt an improvement on the 'Vain, Erroneous, Superstitious and Idolatrous' worship of the medieval Church and had 'occasioned many Godly and Learned men to rejoyce much in the Book of Common-Prayer at time set forth; Because the Masse, and the rest of the Latine-Service being removed, the Publique Worship was celebrated in our own Tongue'.[13]

But, however useful in the early days of the Reformation, the Prayer Book had proved itself to be at odds with many other Reformed Churches, full of popish ceremonies, and a stumbling block to otherwise honest Christians who could not in conscience conform to it. The sheer familiarity of the Prayer Book turned it into something 'no better than an Idol by many Ignorant and Superstituous people, who pleasing themselves in their presence at that Service, and their Lip-labour in bearing a part in it, have thereby hardened themselves in their ignorance and carelesnesse of saving knowledge and true piety'.[14] The *Directory*'s authors denied that they were motivated by a 'love [of] Novelty', or that their work represented any 'intention to disparage our first Reformers', who, 'The Preface' maintained, would if they were still alive of course be on the side of further reform. Engaging in a difficult balancing act, they acknowledged that the Edwardian Reformers were 'Excellent Instruments raised by God to begin the purging and building of His House, and desire they may be had of us and posterity in everlasting Remembrance, with thankfulnesse and honour'. But that was then, this was now, and providence called for 'further Reformation'.[15]

To those more familiar with the Prayer Book, the *Directory* reads like a set of stage directions without the speaking parts. E. C. Ratcliff notes that it needs to be seen as a compromise between moderates and radicals in the Westminster Assembly; nonetheless it was largely a victory for the latter for, as he also notes, it was 'not so much a prayer book as a rubric book'.[16] It provided the minister with guidance on what he should say at various services but almost never provided the actual words. Significant exceptions to this general rule include the words to be used at the precise moment of baptism, which are firmly trinitarian, and the marriage vows.[17] Nonetheless, the use of godparents in baptism and the ring in marriage – both prohibited practices in the *Directory* – appear to have been wide-spread.[18]

We await a major study of the English *Directory*, but it appears not to have been a best seller. There is little evidence in churchwardens' accounts for its purchase across a geographically diverse set of counties.[19] There must have been considerable confusion in the localities, however, as in 1648 six clergymen in Cambridgeshire were indicted for 'refusing to administer the sacrament but according to the Directory'.[20] Simply, the *Directory* appears not to have met the fundamental needs of many English Christians. Sir Henry Turner, the Speaker of the House of Commons, when introducing the Uniformity Bill in 1662, spoke for many when he attacked the suppression of the Book of Common Prayer and its replacement by the *Directory*. He remarked that the Prayer Book was 'decried as superstitious, and in lieu thereof nothing, or worse than nothing was introduced'.[21] It has been noted that, in the post-Reformation Church, one of the attractive things about the Prayer Book to the laity was that it curtailed overly enthusiastic clergy from endlessly chopping and changing the church service as the fancy took them.[22]

To many Prayer Book Protestants the *Directory* must have looked like the worst of all possible worlds, in that it prohibited many popular rituals of the reformed English rite while at the same time giving ministers far too much liberty in their verbal expression. The Prayer Book may have smacked of popery to some, but the *Directory* was itself intensely clerical. Apart from psalm singing, the active participation of the laity in the service was virtually eliminated. Even the Lord's Prayer, if it was to be included, was to be said by the minister alone.[23] The 'sacred dialogue' between clergy and people – the disparaged 'lip-labour' of ordinary men and women that marked conformist worship – was firmly rejected.[24] In the interests of freeing the Holy Spirit, the laity were now not to be spared the full blast – in Richard Hooker's cutting phrase – of those 'voluntary dictates' proceeding from a clergyman's 'extemporal wit'.[25] No wonder Sir Henry Turner saw the *Directory* as 'worse than nothing'.

III

Despite the prolonged attack over several generations by elements within the established Church, the Book of Common Prayer proved harder to sink than might have been expected from the puritan critiques of it. Evidence for the liturgy's buoyancy abounds and, despite its prohibited status, some English Christians continued to use it for worship. Further, the Prayer Book provided more than a framework for the hour or two spent inside a church building for public worship or a structure for household use and the solitary prayer of individuals. Through Morning and Evening Prayer it gave shape to the day, though one suspects that, apart from a few exceptions, Cranmer's intention that the offices become the daily prayer of all the people of God rather than simply of a monastic and clerical elite was never realised.[26] The Prayer Book helped to mark immense and universal moments in the life cycle, such as birth and death, and Common

Prayer also structured and shaped the year, providing days and seasons of solemnity and celebration. Although one may see it as a very impoverished cousin to the riches of the fifteenth-century world portrayed in *The Stripping of the Altars*, the Prayer Book nonetheless provided over thirty saints' days and other festivals of the Christian year based on the life of Christ.[27] Yet another popish remnant in the eyes of some, these holy days were banned shortly after the book which had authorised their use.[28]

Thereafter, provision of Prayer Book rites in the revolutionary period was, at best, episodic. The layman John Evelyn failed in 1652 to find any services at all on Christmas Day, though at other times he succeeded in finding churches in London itself which used the banned Prayer Book.[29] On another Christmas Day, in 1657, he and other devotees of the Prayer Book were intimidated by parliamentary troopers. He recorded in his famous diary:

> I went with my wife &c: to Lond: to celebrate Christmas day … Sermon Ended, as [the minister] was giving us the holy Sacrament, The Chapell was surrounded with Souldiers: All the Communicants and Assembly surpriz'd & kept Prisoners by them … [They] examined me, why contrarie to an Ordinance made that none should any longer observe the superstitious time of the Nativity (so esteem'd by them) I durst offend, & particularly be at Common prayers, which they told me was but the Masse in English.

Evelyn and his fellow communicants then proceeded to make their Christmas communion under testing circumstances.

> These wretched miscreants, held their muskets against us as we came up to receive the Sacred Elements, as if they would have shot us at the Altar, but yet suffering us to finish the Office of Communion, as perhaps [it was] not in their Instructions what they should do in case they found us in that Action.[30]

Coolness in the face of armed troopers was sometimes required of the clergy as well. According to his contemporary biographer, John Hackett (later Bishop of Coventry and Lichfield in 1661) calmly continued to read divine service even when a parliamentary soldier of the Earl of Essex had a pistol pointed at him. Hackett and another future bishop, George Bull (consecrated Bishop of St David's in 1705), each committed to memory the funeral service and the baptismal services respectively so that they would appear to be praying extempore. The ruse worked, as this account of a funeral of a prominent puritan conducted by Hackett at the end of the Interregnum illustrates:

> there being a great concourse of men of the same fanatical principles [as the deceased], when the company heard all delivered by him [Hackett] without

book, and, with free readiness, and profound gravity ... they were strangely surprised and affected, professing that they had never heard a more suitable exhortation, or a more edifying exercise even from the very best and most precious men of their own persuasion!

The assembled godly were aghast when Hackett revealed to them that not one syllable had been his own and how 'all was taken word for word out of the very office ordained for that purpose in the poor contemptible Book of Common Prayer'.[31] Examples of such Prayer Book use can be multiplied from around the country.[32]

The attack on the festivals of the Christian year was perhaps one of the parliamentary government's greatest misreadings of the religious sensibilities of many English people.[33] Indeed, it has been recently noted that the Prayer Book calendar was popular not only in England but also among the seventeenth-century colonists of Virginia – providing not only a system for dating letters but even for attending Church.[34] It is worth remembering in the current discussions about secularism that there was a debate in the seventeenth century as well over how 'religious' a festival Christmas was. Richard Baxter was clear that the observance of Christmas had no place in a properly reformed Church. In a sermon preached in 1657 he remarked 'Tomorrow ... is the day called Christmass day, and many days called Holy days do follow it ... There is no proof that ever I saw ... that the Church observed any of these days, of many hundred years after Christ.'[35]

Yet to many contemporaries, clergy and laity alike, the government's continued observance of national 'feast days' such as Armada Day or the discovery of the Gunpowder Plot, contained a bitter irony.[36] The laywoman, Elizabeth Newell, presented a theological critique of this state of affairs in a series of poems she collected in honour of the banned feast of Christmas from 1655 into the 1660s. The following poem purports to be written for Christmas Day 1658:

> What! the messias born, and shall a day
> Bethought to much expensiveness to pay
> To that memorial; shall an Anniversie
> Be kept with ostentation to rehearse
> A mortal princes birth-day, or defeat
> An Eighty Eight, or powder plots defeat [?]
>
> ... And shall we venture to exterminate
> And starve at once the memory and date
> Of Christ incarnate, where in such a store
> Of joy to mortals lay, as never before
> The sun beheld, a Treasury of Bliss,
> The birth day of the world as well as his.

To Elizabeth Newell, her opponents lacked any proper understanding of Christology, or indeed of the relationship of the incarnation to salvation: 'Ingrateful Man; It was for only thee/And for thy Restitution, that he/Did stoop to wear thy raggs ... was content/Thus to affirme thy nature'.[37] It should be noted how *theologically* informed and not simply 'spiritual' are the poems she collected.

Discussion of the tribulations of John Evelyn, John Hackett, Elizabeth Newell and other members of the gentry and clergy could, however, give the impression that adherence to the Prayer Book was a preoccupation only of the better sort and religious professionals. On the contrary, it has been shown that fidelity to the liturgy was also to be found further down the social ladder, and that Newell's preservation of theologically sophisticated verse gives expression to views held more widely across the social spectrum. In March 1648, violence erupted in Blandford in Dorset when a group of locals rescued a minister who had been arrested for using the proscribed liturgy.[38] Support for the Prayer Book was an element in the complex set of component parts that made up the popular uprisings by the Clubmen Associations in counties like Dorset and Wiltshire.[39] In 1647 indignation turned to violence in Canterbury when local people resisted the Kent Committee's attempt to suppress Christmas celebrations. The few shopkeepers who did open on Christmas Day were attacked by a mob. Significantly, the law-breaking soon took on political as well as theological overtones, as the crowd 'were soon shouting royalist slogans, "crying up King Charles, and crying down the Parliament", assaulting Roundheads, and consuming the free beer offered by citizens who set up holly-bushes at their doors.'[40] David Underdown has also noted evidence of continued celebration of Christmas in the 1650s in Cornwall and Devon. He maintains that where Christmas was, royalism was likely to be present as well.[41] It must be remembered that the Prayer Book was 'common prayer' – a 'levelling text' – which provided some common culture across social and gender divisions. Even illiteracy did not close one off from the culture of the Prayer Book. While to its hotter protestant critics the familiarity of the Prayer Book was its fatal flaw, turning it into an 'idol', to its adherents its familiarity was its greatest aid to devotion.

Prayer Book loyalism was to be found not only cutting across social and educational divisions but crossing an ocean as well. Thousands of miles to the west, without benefit of bishops or ecclesiastical courts, conformity to the Prayer Book appears to have been widespread in the lay-dominated Church of colonial Virginia. The mid-seventeenth-century Virginian Church managed to be a broad Church, its lay leaders winking at puritan infractions as adeptly as any moderate Jacobean bishop. Indeed it would appear that the general 'external' – and significantly non-

Christian and 'savage' – threat to the colonists provided by America's first inhabitants made many of the theological disputes of the mother Church seem somewhat arcane. Only in the 1640s, after the threat from the indigenous population was reduced, did the Virginian authorities turn to suppressing groups that would not use the Prayer Book, and then generally only moving against the most radical forms of nonconformity. In 1649, the Norfolk county authorities banished to Maryland a group of individuals who would not conform to the Prayer Book – the same book which had been banned several years before in England. They seem to have taken particular delight in sending such godly zealots to a colony renowned for its popery. Eventually even Oliver Cromwell had to strike a deal with the Virginians. Following a visit by his commissioners in the early 1650s, the colonists were given a general amnesty and permission to use the banned Prayer Book for another year, provided the prayers for the King and royal family were omitted. In fact, it is likely they simply continued to use the old liturgy throughout the rest of the Interregnum – a speculation strengthened by the 'Cavalier' clergy who took up livings in Virginia in the 1650s.[42] It is intriguing to speculate further that a Book of Common Prayer, shorn of its royalist references, provided a precedent in the late 1780s as the new Episcopal Church revised its Prayer Book to remain distinctively Anglican yet thoroughly republican.[43]

In his diary, John Evelyn provides numerous examples of both the use of the Book of Common Prayer and widespread observance of the holy days of the Prayer Book calendar. But at certain times government zeal was such that the Evelyn family, as others, had to make do with the private use of the Prayer Book at home.[44]

> *1 Jan* [1653]: I set a part in preparation for the B: *Sacrament*, which the next day *Mr. Owen* administered to me & all my family in *Says-Court*, preaching on: 6: John 32. 33. shewing the exceeding benefits of our B: Saviours taking our nature upon him.[45]

The minister in question, Richard Owen, also conducted other important rites for the household, baptising the Evelyn children and churching their mother at home according the Prayer Book.[46] Alongside such explicit acts of dissent as Christmas Communion, there developed among Church of England loyalists an inward and quietist spirituality focused on the home and the interior religious life.[47]

It is tempting to see the domestication and 'privatising' of Prayer Book Protestantism in this period as a parallel to the experiences of recusants under Elizabeth and the early Stuarts. If there were no Church of England equivalents of the Jesuits, there were plenty of obstructive and uncooperative clergy and laity. As with Roman Catholicism, the customs of the

'Old Church' often survived in the household, sponsored by gentry who had the social standing to reduce their personal risk and the finances to support sympathetic clergy. Women too emerge as important actors in the maintenance of proscribed observances kept alive in the domestic sphere. It is surely right not to see Roman Catholicism as 'hermetically sealed' in post-Reformation English society.[48] Yet there is a sense as well that this particular comparison can be overdone.[49] Overall, nothing gives the sense of a widely held view among Church of England loyalists that they saw themselves as a 'continuing' or 'true' Church in struggle with a 'false' one. The mindset appears – especially as one moves to less public (and polemical) reflections on the state of the Christian faith in England – of *the* Church under the influence of a misguided or even wicked leadership. For example, take Evelyn's account of attending his own parish church in 1653:

> 30 [January, 1653]. At our own *Parish Church*, a Stranger preached on I *Apoc.* 5.6 describing the greate benefits don us by our B: Lord: Note, that there was now & then, an honest orthodox man gotten into the Pulpet, and though the present *Incumbent* were somewhat Independent; yet he ordinarily preachd sound doctrine, & was a peaceable man, which was an extraordinary felicity in this age.[50]

These are not the reflections of a Christian who has 'unchurched' his theological and ecclesiological antagonists. However deep in error the mainstream Protestant opponents of the Church of England might be, it was in a sense a family quarrel, whereas the Church of Rome was seen as outside the household. It is always worth remembering, of course, that most violence is precisely domestic violence. The influence of the religious upheavals of the middle of the century on Protestant ecclesiology deserves much more scholarly attention, as does a consideration of these events on England's Roman Catholic community.[51]

IV

Elizabeth Newell, John Evelyn and John Hackett are examples of individuals who negotiated to some extent with the new religious order. Others did not. Figures are not certain but between two and three thousand clergy were ejected from their livings during this period by agencies such as Parliament's Committee for Plundered Ministers. Such figures could represent an ejection rate as high as 25 per cent, although there was considerable regional and local variation as the initiative passed from Westminster to the localities, and the figure is mitigated by the hundreds of clergy who achieved preferment to another parish after ejection. Clergy

lost their livings or other forms of preferment for a variety of offences
including royalism, the use of the Prayer Book, failure to preach, moral
offences or simply over-frequenting the alehouse – or some fascinating
combination of all these 'crimes'.[52] Although this does not diminish the
ferocity with which roughly one thousand clergy were ejected at the
Restoration for their failure to conform to a new Act of Uniformity, it does
put it in some perspective, and indeed goes part of the way not to justify
such actions but to make them understandable. Professor Ivan Roots's
assessment of the political settlement of 1660 is apposite for the Church
as well: 'there was only a smear of blood at the Restoration, but a whole
streak of meanness'.[53]

V

One of the striking things about the survival of features of the 'Old
Church' in this period is the lack of leadership provided by members of
the episcopate. Outlawed practices, such as the use of the Prayer Book or
the observation of holy days, survived in large part owing to the courage
of clergy and laity, not to any overt leadership provided by the bishops.
In fact, the bishops in England ignored repeated requests from the exiled
court in the 1650s to consecrate more of their order to make up for diminishing numbers.[54] That said, they did not completely disappear from the
scene. By 1650, only a third of English and Welsh sees were vacant, and a
third of the bench at the start of the civil war survived to be restored to
their privileges at the Restoration.[55]

And if bishops provided little public leadership to their flocks during
this time of trouble, they did respond to requests for secret ordinations. It is noteworthy as well that the individual bishops who defied the
parliamentary and Interregnum government were not theologically mono-
chrome. Among those active in this way were Robert Skinner of Oxford
(translated to Worcester in 1663), Brian Duppa of Salisbury (translated
to Winchester in 1660), Henry King of Chichester, Joseph Hall of Exeter
(translated to Norwich in 1641), Ralph Brownrigg of Exeter and Thomas
Morton of Durham. Hall, Brownrigg and Morton in particular could
hardly be described as 'Laudians'.[56] Yet even Robert Skinner of Oxford,
who was sequestered by Parliament at one point and who can be comfortably located towards the Laudian end of the spectrum, was later given
a licence to preach in the 1650s.[57] The romanticised portrait of bishops
languishing with the King abroad or reduced to poverty at home appears
to be more the stuff of Anglican hagiography than history.

A number of younger clergy (we do not know how many) often with
no first-hand experience of episcopal government, sought out a second

ordination from the hands of these 'redundant' bishops. It was, in truth, a sort of 'top-up' view of ordination, as these younger men appear to have continued to serve in the Interregnum Church. Such evidence again argues against the notion of the Church of England as a kind of 'recusant' or 'underground' Church. What motivated them to seek such episcopal alternatives was presumably a variety of factors including a search for stability in a period of uncertainty and change in many areas of English life. Jeremy Taylor dryly observed of these youngsters that 'never had the excellency of episcopal government been so obvious ... as now that it was lacking'.[58]

VI

In what ways did individuals make sense of – and construct a theology of – what was to them a catastrophic religious experience? The Warwickshire clergyman Christopher Harvey, like others, used the imagery of the Exile. His popular collection of religious verse written in imitation of George Herbert's *The Temple* was significantly entitled *The Synagogue*. For the Jews of the Babylonian captivity and later of the Diaspora who were denied access to the Temple – the place of sacrifice and access to God – synagogues became a way of remaining faithful in the face of the ungodly. Harvey stayed in his benefice from his institution in 1639 until his death in 1663, and in that sense qualifies as a 'survivor' not a 'sufferer'. He nonetheless had a strong sense of living in a state of internal exile.[59] By the third edition of *The Synagogue*, published in 1657, he had become in the words of the one admirer of his verse, a prophetic voice reminding his readers not to forget 'Israel' in the midst of ungodliness.

> Sir,
> While I read your lines, methinks I spie
> Churches, and churchmen, and the old hierarchie:
> What potent charms are these! you have the knack
> To make men young again, and fetch back time.
> ...
>
> The mid-space shrunk to nothing; manners, men,
> And times, and all look just as they did then;
> Rubbish and ruin's vanisht, everywhere
> Order and comliness afresh appear.
> What cannot poets do? They change with ease
> The face of things, and lead us as they please.
> Yet here's no fiction neither: we may see
> The poet, prophet; his verse, historie.[60]

Prayer Book Protestants attempted to make sense of their suffering Church in time-honoured ways: as identification with the sufferings of Christ, or as divine judgement for sin. In a fascinating set of correspondence with a puritan friend called Lang, the Sussex gentleman John Martin rejected the view that the degraded state of the Church of England in the 1650s was in any sense a sign of judgement on its liturgy or polity. In 1656 he wrote:

> For my owne part, I cannot be of your mind, who judge our Church Forsaken of the Lord, because Afflicted by men; when I consider, that Our Saviour himselfe was a man of Sorrowes, & therefore will never be angry with His Spouse, when she is made like Him. I am rather confirm'd we are the True members of Christ our Head, because there are so many in combination, that endeavour our Extirpation.[61]

Nothing, not even the 'wild extravigancies' of his own side, maintained the Sussex layman, would drive him 'out of the Good Old Way'.[62] Biblical paradigms of Hebrew exile or identification with the redemptive sufferings of Christ helped some to make sense of the apparent collapse of their religious tradition.

Inevitably given the Christian psyche, however, some saw the miseries of the 1640s and 1650s as divine punishment. As an earlier generation had interpreted the persecutions of Mary I as divine disapproval of the half-heartedness of the Edwardian Reformation, so too the destruction of the Church of England by the Long Parliament was seen by subsequent Protestants as an expression of divine wrath for past errors and sins.[63] But while the religious drivers were the same, one might reflect, the conclusions were strikingly different. The Norfolk gentleman Clement Spelman (1598–1679) raised these very issues in a draft letter written at the Restoration to the new Bishop of Durham, John Cosin. Spelman related to Cosin that, while part of the royalist garrison at Oxford in 1646, he had republished with an extensive introduction by himself a tract in defending tithes by his father, Sir Henry Spelman (1564?–1641).[64] Having read this Spelman tract, Charles I asked to see Clement and 'afterwards said when god pleased to restore him, hee would restore his impropriacions to the church', a resolution, reflected Spelman, 'befitting so pyous a prince'.[65]

But monarchial devotion was not the overarching theme of Clement Spelman's letter to the new bishop. Spelman embarked on a fascinating theological and historical analysis for England's and the Church of England's ills over the past two decades. Cataloguing the long dynastic troubles of the Tudors and early Stuarts, he blamed the woes firmly on the seizure of Church property by the Crown. While he expressed no hint of remorse over the destruction of the monastic life, he concluded that this unjustified misappropriation of Church property was a great sin:

> for gods punishment never exceed[s] the offence, and since the punishment was nationall I must beleeve the sinne soe too, and I know noe nationall sinne in England but that of Sacrilidge committed as a Law by act of parliament, whereto everyone is Cosentinge eyther actually by himselfe or implicitively by his Representative in parliament.[66]

That the destruction of the Church of England, with its liturgy and festivals, and unrest of the years of civil war were God's wake-up call to the new Restoration regime, Spelman was in no doubt:

> And when wee observe gods method in our punishment, wee have reason to believe that, that Sacriledge drue on us this punishment, for the same order the King & Kingdome tooke to Robb god and the Church, the same methode god observes to punish the King and Nation.

Constructing an eerie symmetry, Spelman notes that, as Henry VIII used Parliament, sitting in St Stephen's Chapel, to rob the Church, so God, to punish both king and nation, used Parliament, again sitting in St Stephen's Chapel, to pass an act to dissolve the monarchy: an eye for an eye, or a dissolution for a dissolution.

> The Kinge makes use of a Crumwell to Dissolve the Monastryes, and god of a Crumwell borne in a dissolved Monastrye to punish the Kinge, thus our punishment sprang from our Sinnes.

This relentless divine punishment for sacrilege, in the mind of Spelman, pursued Charles I to his last sacramental act:

> King Henry 8 had taken all the Challices from the Alters of the Dissolved Monasterys and the parliament and Crumwell seise all the Kings plate soe that the day before that his Majestie dyed hee was necesitated to send to the Taverne at Charing-Cross to borrow a Cup wherein to receive his last Communion at St James a disolved hospitall his prison, whence the next daye his Majestie goes to Whitehall the place of his murder first a Religious house one of the 40ty dissolved, and given to Cardinall Wosley by him built for the ArchBp of Yorke, but againe torne from the Church by King Henry 8: and made his Court.

Spelman went on to suggest that funds could be annexed to impoverished dioceses such as Chester and Peterborough (significantly both cathedral churches were former monastic houses) to help 'expiate a Continued Sacrildge'. A devout layman, he urged the new bishop to encourage Charles II to 'religiously pay what his father piously promised to the Church' an act which would make Cosin a 'Nathan to our David'.[67] Sadly, there is no reply among Cosin's papers at Durham.

VII

This raises another emerging theme which can only be touched on here: the real ambivalence towards the monarchy and the Supreme Governorship of the Church of England. We are familiar with the 'cult' of Charles I, a king far more impressive and useful to his co-religionists in death than he ever was in life. John Spurr has written powerfully of the psychological effect of the execution of the King on the nation, an effect shared by Laudians, puritans and those in between.

> To many this was not simply the nadir of a cause, but the beginning of the end: God had removed the English Josiah, and the ruin of Judah herself could only be a matter of time ... The anniversary of the regicide and the expiation of the nation's guilt now became central motifs in the prayers of intercession used by the 'mourners in Sion'.[68]

Ironically, given the suppression of the Church calendar and the Prayer Book by parliament, Charles's martyrdom created a new 'holy day' and a market for new liturgies. In the royal chapel in Paris, John Cosin adapted the daily offices of the Book of Common Prayer to provide a service to be used every Tuesday – the day of Charles's execution. Morning and Evening Prayer began with the verse: 'Enter not into judgement with thy servants O Lord, for no flesh is righteous in thy sight', and instead of the more upbeat *Venite*, Psalm 121 ('I will lift up mine eyes') was to be used. The portion of the psalms appointed to be read antiphonally reveals a sense of desolation. The readings from scripture appointed to be used also matched the sombre mood: for Morning Prayer, Genesis 28:10–end (God's promise to Jacob in a dream to be with him) and Luke 21:1–21 (the foretelling by Christ of the sufferings of his followers and the destruction of Jerusalem); and for Evening Prayer, 2 Chronicles 20:1–21 (the prophet Jahaziel tells the people of Judah that God is with them in the face of a much larger enemy), and 1 Peter 2 (identification with Christ as the rejected stone and a call to accept the proper political and social order). The psalm appointed was, appropriately, Psalm 130, *De Profundis*, 'Out of the deep'. The responses were redrafted to emphasise the need for divine protection and intervention to secure the restoration of Charles II in the future. Additional material for Holy Communion reflected these concerns as well.[69]

There was, nonetheless, a striking undercurrent of unease and discontent among Church of England loyalists about Charles himself and, more significantly, about basing claims for the authenticity of the established

Church on arguments around the Supreme Governorship. In the 1647 edition of *The Synagogue*, Harvey included poems extolling every Church officer of the now defunct Church of England from the parish sexton to the bishop. But in his construction, the top of the ecclesiastical totem-pole was the bishop; there is no poem called 'The Supreme Governor'. In fact, Harvey contrasted unfavourably the precious metals of the communion plate with the gold of a royal crown:

> Never was gold or silver gracèd thus
> Before:
> To bring this Body and this Blood to us
> Is more
> Then to crown kings.

As I have commented elsewhere, it is very tempting indeed to see this as a veiled, though rather thinly veiled, criticism of Charles's Supreme Governorship. Harvey continues:

> A King unto Whose Cross all kings must vail
> Their crowns
> . . .
> Whose frowns and smiles
> . . .
> doom them either unto weal or woe.
> A King Whose will is justice, and Whose word
> Is pow'r
> And wisdom both; a King, Whom to afford
> An hour
> Of service truly
> Perform'd and duly,
> Is to bespeak eternity of bliss'.[70]

Even Cosin's customised Prayer Book appointed the first Collect at Morning Prayer to be one for the Church, not for the sovereign: 'Lord, we beseech thee, let thy continuall pity cleanse and defend thy Church: and because it cannot continue in safety without thy succour, preserve it evermore by thy help and goodness, through Jesus Christ our Lord.'[71] This prayer had also appeared in the Prayer Books before the civil war and was in fact to become the Collect for Trinity 16 in the 1662 Book of Common Prayer. But in 1662, as in this post-regicide rite, the word 'Church' replaced the more 'godly' term 'congregation'.[72] For many Church of England loyalists the Stuarts were at best a mixed blessing.[73]

VIII

The period of England's, to date, brief experiment with religious localism and republicanism saw the suppression of the Book of Common Prayer, of episcopal polity and (perhaps most unpopular of all) of the traditional ritual year. The experiences of these suppressions helped *to form* an 'Anglican' identity, though even in this period it is a problematic word to use with any degree of historical and scholarly integrity. We must always remember that it was little used by contemporaries. In many ways, 'episcopalian' is a better term, though ironically the fact that this is so is due more to lay and clerical faithfulness than to episcopal leadership. What we observe in the 1640s and 1650s is the hardening of certain religious traditions *within* the larger Church of England existing before the civil war, and their emergence as *the* Church of England. The formation of this religious identity was greatly aided by the retrospective spin-doctors of the Restoration Church of England, the biographer Izaak Walton being both the most notable and most engaging of them. It is Walton, not Richard Hooker, who in many ways deserves the title of 'the Inventor of Anglicanism'.[74] As John Morrill, has remarked: 'religious commitment is best observed in periods of persecution'.[75] Before the civil war, religious identities invested in the liturgy, the calendar and episcopacy formed a flexible and considerable strand *within* the larger national Church. In Cromwell's England, it was the suppression not of the monarchy but of these same key components of a religious tradition that helped paradoxically to create a self-conscious 'Anglicanism'.

Notes

1 This chapter is a slightly revised version of my essay of the same title which appeared in Stephen Platten (ed.), *Anglicanism and the Western Christian Tradition: Continuity, Change and the Search for Communion* (Norwich, 2003). An earlier version has also appeared as '"The Good Old Way": prayer book Protestantism in the 1640s and 1650s', and was first given as an Ecclesiastical History Society Plenary Lecture for 2000–1. That lecture was subsequently published in R. N. Swanson (ed.), *The Church and the Book*, Studies in Church History, 38 (Woodbridge, 2004). I am grateful to Elizabeth Clarke, Christopher Durston, Arnold Hunt, Elizabeth Macfarlane and Alison Shell for their comments.

2 John Morrill, 'The attack on the Church of England in the Long Parliament', in John Morrill, *The Nature of the English Revolution* (London, 1993), p. 89.

3 The religious context of the English Civil War' (1984); 'The attack on the Church of England in the Long Parliament' (1984); 'The Church in

England, 1642–1649' (1982): all reprinted in Morrill, *Nature of the English Revolution*. See also the introduction to that volume, 'Introduction: England's wars of religion'. There are useful discussions of the Church of England in the 1640 and 1650s in John Spurr, *The Restoration Church of England, 1646–1689* (New Haven, CT, 1991), chapter 1, and Robert Ashton, *Counter-Revolution: The Second Civil War and Its Origins, 1646–8* (New Haven, CT, 1994), chapter 7. The most thorough treatment in print of the Church of England in this period, however, remains W. A. Shaw, *A History of the English Church During the Civil Wars and under the Commonwealth, 1640–1660*, 2 vols (London, 1900).

4 Morrill, 'Attack on the Church of England', pp. 89–90.

5 For a historiographical critique, see Judith Maltby, *Prayer Book and People in Elizabethan and Early Stuart England* (Cambridge, 1998), pp. 1–19. The work of Professor David Underdown is also critical to our concerns. Perhaps more than any other historian, Underdown has uncovered the *popular* elements of conservative or traditional politics in the 1640s and 1650s and has alerted us to the existence of considerable attachment to the 'Old Church', the Prayer Book and Church festivals. See David Underdown, *Revel, Riot and Rebellion: Popular Politics and Culture in England 1603–1660* (Oxford, 1987), esp. chapters 5, 8, 9, 10.

6 Ashton, *Counter-Revolution*, p. 230, though see later for caution about the shades of royalism among Church of England loyalists. Maltby, *Prayer Book and People*, chapter 3; Judith Maltby, 'Petitions for episcopacy and the Book of Common Prayer, 1641–1642', in Stephen Taylor (ed.), *From Cranmer to Davidson: A Church of England Miscellany*, 7 (Woodbridge, 2000), pp. 105–67; David Underdown, *A Freeborn People: Politics and the Nation in Seventeenth-Century England* (Oxford, 1996), pp. 56–7. Cf. Christopher Haigh, 'The Church of England, the Catholics and the people', in Peter Marshall (ed.), *The Impact of the English Reformation, 1500–1640* (London, 1997), pp. 253–4; Alexandra Walsham, 'The parochial roots of Laudianism revisited: Catholics, Anti-Calvinists and "Parish Anglicans" in early Stuart England', *Journal of Ecclesiastical History*, 49 (1998), 620–51.

7 By the end of the eighteenth century, the range of religious options available created, despite the existence of two established Churches in Britain, a pluralism more akin to the new United States than to much of the rest of Europe: James Obelkevich, 'Religion', in F. M. L. Thompson (ed.), *The Cambridge Social History of Britain, 1750–1950* (Cambridge, 1990), p. 311 and *passim*.

8 Diarmaid MacCulloch, 'The myth of the English Reformation', *Journal of British Studies*, 30 (1991), 1–19. See also Maltby, *Prayer Book and People*, pp. 233–7; Peter Lake and Michael Questier, 'Introduction', in Peter Lake and Michael Questier (eds), *Conformity and Orthodoxy in the English Church, c.1560–1660* (Woodbridge, 2000), p. xix. For the use of the word 'Anglican' in this period, see for example Christopher Haigh, *English Reformations: Religion, Politics and Society under the Tudors* (Oxford,

1993); Walsham, 'Parochial roots'; Morrill, 'Church in England'; and Ashton, *Counter-Revolution.*

9 Morrill, 'Church in England', pp. 149–54; Shaw, *English Church,* vol. 1, pp. 337–57; Paul Hardacre, *The Royalists during the Puritan Revolution* (The Hague, 1956), pp. 39–44; C. H. Firth and R. S. Rait (eds), *Acts and Ordinances of the Interregnum, 1642–1660,* 3 vols (London, 1911), vol. 1, pp. 582, 607.

10 Lake and Questier, 'Introduction', pp. xv–xvi. Cf. Marshall, *Impact of the English Reformation,* pp. 232–3.

11 Horton Davis, *The Worship of the English Puritans* (Glasgow, 1948), pp. 98–114. For a detailed discussion of the formation of the *Directory,* see Bryan Spinks, *Freedom or Order? The Eucharistic Liturgy in English Congregationalism, 1645–1980* (Allison Park, PA, 1984), pp. 14–15, 31–51. I am grateful to Professor Spinks for his assistance. Peter King, 'The reasons for the abolition of the Book of Common Prayer in 1645', *Journal of Ecclesiastical History,* 21 (1970), 335–7; Shaw, *English Church,* vol. 1, pp. 337–49.

12 Morrill, 'Church in England', pp. 152–3; Shaw, *English Church,* vol. 1, pp. 353–4.

13 *A Directory for the Public Worship of God, Throughout the Three Kingdoms of England, Scotland and Ireland* (London, 1645), pp. 1–2.

14 *Ibid.,* p. 4.

15 *Ibid.,* p. 6. Petitions defending the Prayer Book early in the Long Parliament made much use of the honoured status of the Edwardian bishops and martyrs who had championed it: Maltby, *Prayer Book and People,* chapter 3; Maltby, 'Petitions', pp. 113–67.

16 E. C. Ratcliff, 'Puritan alternatives to the Prayer Book: the *Directory* and Richard Baxter's *Reformed Liturgy*', in Michael Ramsey (ed.), *The English Prayer Book, 1549–1662* (London, 1963), p. 64; Davis, *Worship,* pp. 127–42; Spinks, *Freedom or Order?,* pp. 31–6.

17 *Directory* pp. 45, 62–3. Ironically it paraphrases the Prayer Book in several places. For example in the directions for baptism, the minister is reminded that those baptised are 'bound to fight against the Devill, the World and the Flesh' – a paraphrase of the Book of Common Prayer: *Directory,* p. 42, and see also pp. 49–50.

18 David Cressy, *Birth, Marriage and Death: Ritual, Religion, and the Life-Cycle in Tudor and Stuart England* (Oxford, 1997), pp. 153, 347.

19 Based on my survey of extant Cheshire churchwarden accounts; Morrill, 'Church in England', pp. 152–3, 156, 164–7; Linda York, '"In Dens and Caves": the Survival of Anglicanism during the Rule of the Saints, 1640–1660', unpublished PhD thesis, Auburn University, 1999, pp. 100–1; Underdown, *Revel, Riot and Rebellion,* pp. 255–6; Cressy, *Birth, Marriage and Death,* p. 175; King, 'Reasons for abolition', 337; Ashton, *Counter-Revolution,* pp. 230–1.

20 Morrill, 'Church in England', p. 168.

21 *Journal of the House of Lords,* vol. 11, p. 470, cited in Ratcliff, 'Puritan alternatives', p. 56.

22 Maltby, *Prayer Book and People*, pp. 44–5.

23 Ratcliff, 'Puritan alternatives', p. 72.

24 Parishoners took offence when clergy did not allow them to make the authorised responses in the Prayer Book: Maltby, *Prayer Book and People*, pp. 40–4.

25 From Book V.xxv.4 of Richard Hooker, *Of the Laws of Ecclesiastical Polity*, in W. Speed Hill (ed.), *The Works of Richard Hooker*, 7 vols (Cambridge, MA, 1977), vol. 2, p. 116.

26 See George Guiver, *Company of Voices: Daily Prayer and the People of God* (London, 1988), pp. 115–26.

27 However impoverished the Protestant liturgy was compared with its late medieval counterpart, Eamon Duffy has admitted that 'Cranmer's sombrely magnificent prose, read week by week, entered and possessed their minds, and became the fabric of their prayer, the utterance of their most solemn and vulnerable moments': Eamon Duffy, *The Stripping of the Altars: Traditional Religion in England, 1400–1580* (New Haven, CT, 1992), p. 593.

28 On 8 June 1647 the Long Parliament abolished church festivals, though the *Directory* had already ordered their extinction: Firth and Rait (eds), *Acts and Ordinances*, vol. 1, pp. 954, 607. A further proclamation against the observance of Christmas was issued on 24 December 1652: R. S. Steele (ed.), *A Bibliography of Royal Proclamations of the Tudor and Stuart Sovereigns 1485–1714*, 2 vols (Oxford, 1910), vol. 1, p. 360 (no. 2981).

29 '*Christmas day* no sermon anywhere, so observed it at home, the next day we went to *Lewisham*, where was an honest divine preach'd on 21 *Matt:* 9 celebrating the Incarnation, for on the day before, no Churches were permitted to meet &c; to that horrid passe were they come.' (E. S. de Beer (ed.), *The Diary of John Evelyn*, 6 vols (Oxford, 1955), vol. 3, pp. 78–9).

30 *Ibid.*, vol. 3, pp. 203–4.

31 Thomas Plume, *An Account of the Life and Death of the Right Reverend Father in God, John Hackett, Late Lord Bishop of Lichfield and Coventry*, ed. Mackenzie M. C. Walcott (London, 1865), pp. 64–6. The incident dates from just after the Restoration, but illustrates the point. John Evelyn was able to give his mother-in-law a traditional Prayer Book funeral in 1652: see Cressy, *Birth, Marriage and Death*, p. 416.

32 Morrill, 'Church in England', pp. 164–8; Spurr, *Restoration Church*, pp. 16–17; Ashton, *Counter-Revolution*, pp. 230–4, 247, 259–61.

33 Ashton, *Counter-Revolution*, pp. 238–41.

34 Virginians modified the Prayer Book calendar as well to take into account the different rhythms of the colony's agriculture and of its premier crop, tobacco. Local events led to the development of additional days along the lines of Armada Day or the Fifth of November, such as the designation of 22 March as a day of thanksgiving for the deliverance of the colony from an Indian massacre in the 1620s. The Assembly ordered that day 'be yeerly Solemnized as [a] holydaye'. Edward L. Bond, 'Religion in Seventeenth-Century Anglican Virginia: Myth, Persuasion, and the Creation of an American Identity', unpublished PhD thesis, Louisiana State

University, 1995, pp. 188–95. For more on colonial 'Anglicanism', see below, pp. 165–6.

35 Cited in Geoffrey Nuttall, *Richard Baxter* (London, 1965), p. 54. Baxter did defend the keeping of Easter Day, as the evidence was much stronger for its observation by the earliest Christians and commended the celebration of the Lord's Supper on that day: Nuttall, *Baxter*, p. 55.

36 Evelyn, *Diary*, vol. 3, pp. 47–8, 144, 235, for Gunpowder Plot celebrations in the 1650s; Ronald Hutton, *The Rise and Fall of Merry England: the Ritual Year 1400–1700* (Oxford, 1994), pp. 212, 221–2.

37 New Haven, Beinecke Library, Osborn MS b.49, Elizabeth Newell, 'Collection of devotional verse, *c.*1655–1668', pp. 12–13. I am grateful to Elizabeth Clarke for bringing this manuscript to my attention and for other helpful discussions concerning Newell.

38 Underdown, *Revel, Riot and Rebellion*, p. 230. See also King, 'Reasons for abolition', 338–9; John Morrill and John Walter, 'Order and disorder in the English Revolution', in Richard Cust and Ann Hughes (eds), *The English Civil War* (London, 1997), p. 315. For wide-spread support for the Prayer Book across social divisions in the pre civil-war period, see Maltby, *Prayer Book and People*, pp. 80–1, 181–227.

39 Underdown, *Revel, Riot and Rebellion*, pp. 156–9, 180, 226, 255; David Underdown, 'The chalk and the cheese: contrasts among English Clubmen', in Cust and Hughes (eds), *English Civil War*, p. 295.

40 Underdown, *Revel, Riot and Rebellion*, p. 260.

41 *Ibid.*, pp. 256–63, 267.

42 Conformity to the Prayer Book was also enforced in Barbados during the 1650s: Larry Gragg, 'The pious and the profane: the religious life of early Barbados planters', *The Historian*, 62 (2000), 269–70, 271–2, 275–77. Between 1637 and 1660, nearly thirty ministers migrated to the island: Gragg, 'Pious and profane', 268, but cf. 281–2.

43 Bond, 'Religion in seventeenth-century Anglican Virginia', pp. 186–222; George MacLaren Brydon, *Virginia's Mother Church and the Political Conditions under which it Grew*, 2 vols (Richmond, VA, 1947–52), vol. 1, pp. 122–3, 129–31. I am grateful to Professor Robert Prichard for this reference and for the possible connection made to the development of Anglicanism in America in the late eighteenth century.

44 Evelyn, *Diary*, vol. 3, pp. 203–4, see also vol. 3, pp. 97–8, 144, 225.

45 *Ibid.*, vol. 3, p. 79.

46 *Ibid.*, vol. 3, pp. 75, 76, 89, 90, 147, 195. For home churchings see Cressy, *Birth, Marriage and Death*, p. 225; David Cressy, 'Purification, thanksgiving and the churching of women in post-Reformation England', *Past and Present*, 141 (1993), 140–1.

47 Spurr, *Restoration Church*, pp. 21–2.

48 Walsham, 'Parochial roots', 651.

49 Cf. Claire Cross, 'The Church in England, 1646–1660', in G. E. Aylmer (ed.), *The Interregnum: the Quest for Settlement, 1646–1660* (London, 1974), p. 114.

50 The incumbent in Evelyn's description was Thomas Malory who was deprived in 1661: Evelyn, *Diary*, vol. 3, pp. 80–1, 81 n. 5.

51 These are some of the very issues being addressed in this collection of essays.

52 Cross, 'Church in England', pp. 110–14; Susan Doran and Christopher Durston, *Princes, Pastors and People: the Church and Religion in England 1529–1689* (London, 1991), pp. 154–7; Anne Laurance, '"This sad and deplorable condition": an account of the sufferings of northern clergy families in the 1640s and 1650s', in Diana Wood (ed.), *Life and Thought in the Northern Church c.1100–1700* (Woodbridge, 1999), pp. 465–7. Professor Green estimates around 2,780 clergy were deprived: Ian Green, 'The persecution of "scandalous" and "malignant" parish clergy during the English civil war', *English Historical Review*, 94 (1979), 508. See also Clive Holmes (ed.), *The Suffolk Committees for Scandalous Ministers 1644–1646*, Suffolk Records Society, 13 (1970), pp. 10–14, 18–20. Holmes notes that charges of 'popish innovation' were more common than accusations of dissent from Calvinist orthodoxy: Holmes, *Suffolk*, p. 19. J. W. F. Hill, 'Royalist clergy of Lincolnshire', *Lincolnshire Architectural and Archaeological Society, Reports and Papers*, 40 (1935), 34–127.

53 Ivan Roots, *The Great Rebellion, 1642–1660* (London, 1966), p. 261.

54 Ronald Hutton, *The British Republic, 1649–1660* (London, 1990), pp. 91–2, 97; Cross, 'Church in England', pp. 110–14.

55 Nigel Yates, Robert Hume and Paul Hastings (eds), *Religion and Society in Kent, 1640–1914* (Woodbridge, 1994), pp. 5–6.

56 Cross, 'Church in England', p. 113; W. J. Sheils, *Restoration Exhibit Books and the Northern Clergy, 1662–1664*, Borthwick Texts and Calendars: Records of the Northern Province, 13 (1987), pp. i–xvi. A number of Irish bishops were active in England in this way as well.

57 *Oxford Dictionary of National Biography*, sub Robert Skinner.

58 Spurr, *Restoration Church*, pp. 141–3; Jeremy Taylor paraphrased by Spurr, *Restoration Church*, p. 142; Cross, 'Church in England', pp. 110–14; Hutton, *British Republic*, pp. 91–2; Doran and Durston, *Princes, Pastors and People*, pp. 156–7. For examples of episcopal ordinations in the 1650s, see Evelyn, *Diary*, vol. 3, pp. 8–9 (in Paris), 172, 172 n. 1. For the question of what should replace ordination by bishops in England, see Shaw, *English Church*, vol. 1, pp. 243, 320–37.

59 Judith Maltby, 'From *Temple* to *Synagogue*: "old" conformity in the 1640s–1650s and the case of Christopher Harvey', in Lake and Questier, *Conformity and Orthodoxy* (eds), pp. 94–103, 114–16.

60 Christopher Harvey, *The Complete Poems of Christopher Harvey*, ed. A. B. Grosart (The Fuller Worthies' Library, privately printed, 1874), pp. 88–9. The poem was reportedly written in 1654(/5?). See Maltby, '*Temple* to *Synagogue*', pp. 114–15, 120.

61 Folger Shakespeare Library, 'The Letterbook of John Martin', MS V.a.454, p. 18.

62 *Ibid.*, p. 18. I am grateful to Mr David Cleggett, the archivist of Leeds Castle

Foundation, and Miss Yeandle, the archivist of the Folger Shakespeare Library, for their assistance with this manuscript.

63 See the oration of John Hales to Elizabeth I in 1559 in John Foxe, *Acts and Monuments* (London, 1576), pp. 2005–7. See also, Catherine Davis, '"Poor persecuted little flock": Edwardian Protestant concepts of the Church', in Peter Lake and Maria Dowling (eds), *Protestantism and the National Church in Sixteenth-Century England* (London, 1987), pp. 78, 81, 94–5. I am grateful to Tom Freeman for these references. For the attempts by English radicals to make sense of their defeat in 1660, see Christopher Hill, *The Experience of Defeat: Milton and some Contemporaries* (New York, 1984).

64 This is likely to be Henry Spelman's *De non tenerandis ecclesis* (first edition, 1613). Clement's letter is almost certainly to John Cosin and dated *c*.1660–62; Durham University Archives, Cosin LB 1b, no. 94. See also 'Clement Spelman' and 'Sir Henry Spelman' in the *Oxford Dictionary of National Biography*.

65 Durham University Archives, Cosin LB 1b, no. 94.

66 *Ibid.* Clement was very much his father's spiritual and intellectual heir. Sir Henry's extensive treatment of his theme in *The History and Fate of Sacrilege* was not published until 1698. He provided a gazetteer of former monastic lands in Norfolk and catalogued a variety of terrible fates which had befallen the families that turned church property to secular uses: Henry Spelman, *The History and Fate of Sacrilege* (London, 1698), pp. 243–82; Alexandra Walsham, *Providence in Early Modern England* (Oxford, 1999), pp. 109–10.

67 Durham University Archives, Cosin LB 1b, no. 94. This remarkable description of Charles's last hours is not mentioned in the classic account by C. V. Wedgwood, *The Trial of Charles I* (London, 1964), pp. 177–82.

68 Spurr, *Restoration Church*, pp. 20–1; Maltby, '*Temple* to *Synagogue*', p. 115.

69 Durham University Archives, Cosin Library B.IV.4, *A Forme of Prayer, used in the King's Chapel upon Tuesdayes, in these Times of Trouble and Distresse* (Paris?, 1649).

70 Harvey, *Poems*, pp. 26–7; Maltby, '*Temple* to *Synagogue*', p. 115.

71 Durham University Archives, Cosin Library, B.IV.4.

72 F. E. Brightman, *The English Rite: Being a Synopsis of the Sources and Revisions of the Book of Common Prayer*, 2 vols (London, 1921), vol. 2, pp. 516–17; Marion J. Hatchett, *Commentary on the American Prayer Book* (San Francisco, 1995), p. 190.

73 For a discussion of earlier ambivalence towards the royal supremacy, see Davis, 'Edwardian Protestant concepts', pp. 78–9.

74 See Jessica Martin's excellent *Walton's Lives: Conformist Commemorations and the Rise of Biography* (Oxford, 2001); Peter Lake, *Anglicans and Puritans? Presbyterian and Conformist Thought from Whitgift to Hooker* (London, 1988), pp. 225–30; and Maltby, *Prayer Book and People*, pp. 235–7.

75 Morrill, 'Church in England', p. 150.

8

Freedom to form: the development of Baptist movements during the English Revolution

Mark Bell

I

Like many religious terms from the early modern period, 'Baptists' was first a term of derision and only later a mark of honour. In the first half the seventeenth century the term most frequently used to describe these radical Christians was 'Anabaptists' – one deliberately chosen to conjure up the horrors of the continental Anabaptist kingdom at Munster in the 1530s. The Baptists, however, never willingly accepted the term and worked for most of the seventeenth century to dissociate themselves from the anarchism and violence of Munster. Instead of Anabaptists, they preferred phrases such as 'the group of baptised believers meeting at' before finally, late in the century, settling upon 'Baptist'. Yet such a synopsis might give the false impression that there ever was a single monolithic Baptist movement. While there were a number of linked Baptist movements, bearing some family resemblance to each other, the different circles of believers were nevertheless distinct. One of the twentieth century's best expositors of Baptist beliefs has described modern American Baptists as existing under one name but many faces.[1] This was in fact always the case throughout Baptist history, even from the earliest times.

This exploration of early English Baptists will be divided into three parts. First an effort will be made to identify those elements of theology common across the various movements. Second an overview of the main divisions among early seventeenth-century Baptists will be given. Finally the essay will look at the Baptists' political activity during the revolutionary period, and in particular their relationship with the democratic secularism of the Levellers and the theocratic millennialism of the Fifth Monarchists. As we will discover, many of the structures of early English Baptist theology were established before the mid-century revolutionary explosion, but it was only during that time of turmoil, when new ideas regarding the nature and legitimacy of the national Church were called into question, that there was the freedom for the early Baptist movements to form. The English Revolution was the breakout moment for English Baptists. With the episcopal courts frozen, the Baptists were able to emerge as an important and permanent part of the British political and theological landscape to far reaching effect. They debated and developed a distinct theology, tested and adopted a unique Church structure and inter-Church organisation, and gathered sufficient adherents to survive repeated subsequent bouts of state repression. Indeed, it is possible to say that without the mid-century revolution the English Baptist movements of the seventeenth century would have looked strikingly different, had they emerged at all.

II

The fact that the Baptists were never a monolithic movement does not preclude some discussion of 'Baptist' theological beliefs in terms of the ideas that would have been shared, though not exclusively, by the different Baptist movements. The most distinctive mark of the early English Baptists was the practice of believers' baptism. Unable to find any scriptural support for infant baptism, the Baptists rejected this practice as a papal innovation, viewing it as part of the Antichristian pall that had obscured true doctrine. Proper baptism required that the believer be capable of professing for him or herself faith in Christ and personal salvation. By aligning their practice with biblical standards, the Baptists were taking a theologically radical position that cut across many prevailing ideas with regard to Christian unity, for if children were not to be baptised the universality of the Church was denied. Most early modern Christians viewed baptism less as a sign of faith and more as a rite of entry into the Church and by extension society. As Baptists on the other hand required belief before baptism, it was irrational to baptise infants. They thus put forward a radically individual theology, in which baptism did not convey salvation, but was rather a proclamation of it. It was not impossible that other Christians were also saved, but, not having been baptised as adults, they were lacking in the proper ordinances of the true Church. Believers' baptism was a radical departure, in that it emphasised individual autonomy and faith and flouted ideas of a universal Church. But for Baptists it was a departure that was essential for the restoration of the true Church.

A related belief common to Baptists was that the national Church of England was not a true Church, and that Christians must therefore separate from it and seek communion with other true believers. The Baptist congregation, therefore, was made up of voluntary members. Each individual made a conscious choice to join and all members – all men anyway – enjoyed an equal status in a democratic Church structure.[2] Having abandoned hope that the 'but half-reformed' national Church could be sufficiently rectified, Baptist congregations aimed to separate themselves completely from its impurities, and all Baptists were thus 'separatists'. Once outside the national Church, their intent was to recover true worship and doctrine from the papal and Antichristian shroud which had covered it. This recovery did not require either a national Church or historical continuity with other independent Churches. Rather, in the spirit of where two or more are gathered together, the authority of the individual congregation was sufficient to endow the Church with legitimacy.

But early English Baptist theology was Independency with an important distinction. The classic Independent congregation existed on the basis of a congregational covenant, which in a sense meant that each congregation was an independent Church. Baptists on the other hand saw themselves as in fellowship with other baptised believers who shared their theology. Thus, despite a strong respect for congregational autonomy, the different Baptist movements did regard each other as part of the same family of Christians. By the 1650s both of the predominant branches of English Baptists (General and Particular) had developed the regular practice of holding joint congregational meetings under the structure of associations, or, as they most frequently referred to them, 'general meetings', where representatives from individual congregations came together for theological discussion and mutual support. During the English Revolution, Baptists could without theological contradiction even aspire to a national Baptist association. Despite their inability to actualise this aspiration, Interregnum Baptists therefore *looked* more like a modern denomination than other contemporary loose circles of congregations.

The Baptists' reliance on the absence of infant baptism from the Bible as support for their rejection of the practice demonstrates a hermeneutic that was to characterise them throughout the seventeenth century. The Bible was not only a sufficient source for divine wisdom; it was for them the only such source. It alone could act as an antidote to the sickness of Catholic innovation and impurity, and provide a litmus test for re-establishing God's Church. If the Bible described a sacrament or ordinance, then it was to be practised precisely in the way it revealed. If it did not, such rites had to be rejected. Unlike the leaders of the Elizabethan Church, Baptists leaders viewed few things as 'indifferent' to salvation. Their strict biblicism was to be the main source of their disputes both with other Protestants and with each other.

Purity was another central Baptist concern, though not so much a theological doctrine as an impulse that determined doctrine. God, in an act of infinite mercy, was calling His people out of impurity and into sanctification. This was an act reserved for the end of time and was not to be taken lightly or pursued half-heartedly. Thus the need for complete purity was a major concern, particularly for the 'hotter' sort of Baptists. Even for universalists, such as the General Baptist Edmund Chillenden, who rejected predestination in favour of the possibility that all human-kind might be saved, this concern with purity was a guiding aspect of his theology. He explained that the Baptists were 'a holy people called out of the world ... they being begotten again, purged, and cleansed from all uncleanness and unholiness, made pure by the washing of water [and] by the Word ... and they may not suffer any unclean or unholy person to come in and be of fellowship with them.'[3] Chillenden's comment reflected not only the idea that believers' baptism marked a clear separation from an unclean Church, but also that the new pristine Church could not tolerate any impurity.[4] It is nevertheless notable that the strong emphasis on purity of belief and practice which dominates public Baptist polemic and private congregational records may have been more breached than observed; for the most common problems which plagued early Baptist congregations concerned members either attending their parish churches or questioning the inerrancy of the Bible.[5]

Baptist movements during the seventeenth century were also charac-terised by a sense of apocalyptic urgency, and the belief that they were living through 'the last days' was a prominent theme of Baptist writing and preaching. In 'these latter days' the truth of Christianity was being re-revealed and the struggle between good and evil was coming to a climax. The Baptists saw themselves as important characters in this final act. Their insistence that the smallest points of doctrine be followed with the utmost precision was a result of their belief that the re-establishment of the true Church and the casting out of all that was impure were neces-sary parts of the last days. Believers' baptism, the forming of independent churches, and the re-establishment of true doctrine were integral parts of this millennial project. Indeed, as I have argued elsewhere, the way in which these apocalyptic visions were actualised is the key to explaining the development of the Baptists during the revolutionary period.[6]

Related to this strong apocalyptic impulse was an equally strong anti-Catholicism, which marked Baptist movements both during the English Revolution and for decades thereafter. For Baptists, the Roman Catholic Church had usurped the rightful place of Christ as the head of the Church, and as such had revealed itself as the Antichrist. Its doctrines and their adherents were therefore not merely misguided but literally diabolical. It was essential therefore that anything redolent of Catholicism be purged from belief and practice. This anti-Catholicism must be borne in mind when viewing the Baptists as forerunners of modern toleration theory. Some modern Baptists lay claim to an important legacy as innovators in the idea of religious tolerance. While this claim is occasionally overblown, it was certainly a central Baptist principle that the magistrate should have no authority over the Church and that state religious persecution was invalid. Catholics, however, were not merely enemies of true faith, but also of civil order, and as such it was never doubted that the sword of the magistrate should be brought down promptly upon them.

Additionally, the Baptists always held the belief that they were obliged to testify on behalf of the truth, and that as a result it was appropriate for them to try to influence governments. They certainly never believed that other variants of Christianity were in any way as equally 'true' as theirs and should be tolerated on that basis. Rather they held that the state should be fundamentally separate from the Church and should not therefore discipline the godly. The combining of the sword of the state with the sword of the Gospel was a clear sign of Antichristian popery. Nor was this outlook limited to the question of persecution, but it applied also to other areas such as the payment of tithes and the licensing of preachers. Such beliefs, however, were continuously in tension with the biblical injunction of obedience to the civil powers and the magistrate's duty to punish sin and irreligion, and Baptists debated the extent of their civil duties throughout the seventeenth century.[7]

These central aspects of seventeenth-century Baptist theology were hammered out at an early stage in the small clandestine and exiled gathered churches of the late Elizabethan and early Stuart period. They were refined after they became the subject of open debate at the start of the 1640s, and once established they were to guide Baptist development throughout the turbulent years of enthusiasm and despair that followed.

III

Like many nascent religious movements, the early Baptists were plagued by a number of ostensibly trivial theological squabbles that were in large measure the result of their strong drive for purity and its accompanying apocalyptic expectations. Indeed, at times there seemed to be more controversy among so-called Baptists than between them and other denominations. This was particularly true in the late 1650s when the triangular debates between General, Particular and Seventh-Day Baptists began in earnest. The numerous theological conflicts and differences which affected the early Baptists included disputes over biblical translation and tithes, and the controversy over the laying on of hands. They are manifestations of the Baptists' fervent belief that they needed to get doctrine exactly right if they were to recover the lost truth of the Gospel, rescue it from the Babylonian whoredom of Rome, and thus re-establish Christ's rule on earth. The minute details of these controversies are beyond the scope of this chapter, but for our purposes the Baptists can be divided into three broad camps: the General, the Particular, and the Seventh-Day Baptists. While these groups were clearly distinguished by significant theological differences, they were not as stringent or mutually exclusive as the modern historian might wish.[8]

The General Baptists are generally considered to be the first of the English Baptists and trace their origins back to John Smyth. Smyth was born in the mid-1500s and by the early seventeenth century was already being censured for his unlicensed preaching. By 1606 he had moved from being a critic of the Church of England to becoming a separatist in charge of a small covenanted congregation. To avoid persecution, he took his congregation to Holland, where he concluded not only that his own baptism into the Church of England was insufficient, but also that the baptism of infants had no biblical basis.[9] Seeking a new baptism but deciding that no pre-existing Church could provide him with one, he first baptised himself and then other members of his congregation, a move considered so radical that it even disturbed some of the other English exiled religious communities in Holland. Determined to follow Christ rather than fashion, Smyth and his congregation continued to seek out true doctrine, and soon came to reject both predestination and original sin. Their soteriology thus became 'general', since they believed that salvation was generally available to all. By 1607, then, the first English General Baptists in exile in Holland had already adopted many of the central theological principles of the movement.

Yet Smyth did not believe it best for his new Church to exist in complete isolation. By 1610 he had applied for his congregation to join a local group of Dutch Mennonites with whom they had come into contact. While he and his followers had certainly been susceptible to the theology of Anabaptism before their interaction with these Mennonites, until that point it seems to have had only a very limited influence upon them, and for this reason Smyth's self-baptism is seen as more separatist than Anabaptist in inspiration. By 1610, however, Smyth had become sufficiently convinced of the errors of infant baptism, of the validity of believers' baptism, and of a number of other Mennonite theological principles that he felt comfortable joining these descendants of the early sixteenth-century continental Anabaptists.[10] But his effort to merge his congregation with the Mennonites met with resistance on both sides, and one prominent member of Smyth's congregation in particular, Thomas Helwys, objected to the move on the grounds that it would invalidate apostolic succession. In so doing he was not so much rejecting the Dutch Anabaptists as refuting the idea that the English congregation was illegitimate in its own right. Helwys and eight members of the Smyth congregation subsequently separated from Smyth to form their own congregation, which in 1612 returned to England. That same year Smyth died and his remaining congregation was afterwards integrated into the Mennonites.

Helwys's congregation continued to worship in secret in England, and by 1640 several other General Baptist congregations had emerged. New leadership was provided by evangelists and preachers, such as Thomas Lambe, leader of one of the most important London congregations in the 1640s, and Henry Denne, leader of the well-known congregation at Fenstanton in Cambridgeshire. Like Smyth and Helwys before them, Lambe and Denne were highly critical of Calvinist predestinarian principles and advocated instead a theology of general redemption. This position placed the General Baptists in direct opposition to the prevailing Calvinist consensus of the 1640s and 1650s, but their democratic structure and message of universal salvation held real appeal for some of the urban and rural 'middling sort' of mid-seventeenth-century England.

The Calvinist counterparts to the General Baptists first appeared in the 1630s as a development within London semi-separatism. These Calvinist Baptists are usually referred to as 'Particular Baptists', since they believed that Christ had died only for the elect. The precise origins of the Particular Baptists are unclear, but probably date back to the early 1600s and the congregation founded by Henry Jacob. Jacob was a semi-separatist, in that, while he did not see the Church of England as a true Church, he drew back from the radical step of full separation or denunciation. Despite this compromise stance, Jacob endured continual persecution and eventually left England for Virginia. Parts of his congregation, however, remained in existence, and in 1630 a serious argument broke out within the group after one of the members had their child baptised at the parish church. In the fall-out from the argument, a small group under the leadership of John Duppa left, and in 1633 Samuel Eaton, who had received a 'further baptism', led off another splinter group. Both the Duppa and Eaton congregations should probably be labelled as radical separatists rather than Baptists, in that they rejected the baptism of the Church of England on the specific grounds that it was a false Church rather than from a general belief that all infant baptism was invalid and should be replaced by believers' baptism.[11] Eaton had probably received his 'further baptism' from one Jonathan Spilsbury, a humble London button-maker. By 1638 half a dozen members of the Jacob remnant, 'being convinced that Baptism was not for infants, but professed believers, joined Mr. Jonathan Spilsbury', and thus on the eve of the drastic religious upheaval of the 1640s, a clear Calvinist Baptist congregation under the leadership of Spilsbury already existed in the capital.[12]

While both the Particular and General Baptists existed before 1640, the final group under discussion emerged only after the calling of the Long Parliament. The Seventh-Day Baptists were referred to as such because of their belief that Saturday, the seventh day of the week, was the true sabbath and should be observed as such. For them, moving the sabbath from Sunday to Saturday was an important part of restoring the true Church. While congregations of Seventh-Day Baptists did not begin appearing until the 1650s, some of their principles had been expressed a generation earlier by John Traske, who in the early 1600s became convinced that many aspects of the old Jewish law were still binding on contemporary Christians. In 1616 he was arrested for expressing a number of heretical views, including the idea that the true sabbath was on Saturday; he subsequently, however, recanted many of his positions and upon release joined the remnant of the Jacob congregation. The first clearly recognisable Seventh-Day Baptist congregation in England – the London Mill Yard Congregation led by Peter Chamberlen – only appeared a generation later in the early 1650s. Thereafter, the Seventh-Day Baptists proved a considerable irritant to the General and Particular Baptists, winning away many of their members during the late 1650s. Less eager than their General and Particular counterparts to establish a clear organisational structure and win acceptance from the broader society, the Seventh-Day Baptists struggled to survive the difficulties of the Restoration period, though they later evolved into Seventh-Day Adventism.

These brief descriptions, intended to highlight the diversity of early Baptist thinking and history, cannot fully do justice to the subtle and complex nature of Baptist thought during the English Revolution. In addition, there was one other type of Baptist movement that had considerable influence. This was made up of Baptists who, while they adhered to believers' baptism and the other central theological tenets of the movement, refused to deny communion to those who had not yet undergone believers' baptism, and who were, as a result, largely shunned by their General and Particular brethren. There were nonetheless a significant number of such 'open communion', or 'Independent' Baptist congregations – the best-known being those of John Bunyan and Henry Jessey – and they attracted some of the best known Baptist preachers.[13] The London Jessey congregation, which contained much of the remnant of the original Jacob congregation, continued to have significant influence on London sectarianism into the late seventeenth century.

IV

As part of their obligation to witness against the Beast, the Baptists were eager to participate in both the theological and political debates of their time, and as the 1640s began they found that they had unprecedented opportunity to disseminate their beliefs. The primary tools they employed were public preaching and the cheap London press. The Baptists frequently preached to open-air audiences in London and did not refrain from commenting on the politics of the day. They would pray for the release of political prisoners and preach about current injustices. They were also successful military preachers and chaplains, and a number of them exercised a significant influence over the parliamentarian soldiery. In the 1650s the Baptists also set up funds to support evangelists working in the dark corners of the kingdom, remote areas where they believed the government had failed to bring true preaching.

Additionally, with the collapse of censorship that accompanied the meeting of the Long Parliament, the London press was soon flooded with Baptist printed works. Baptists utilised the press primarily to engage in theological disputes and as a means of clarifying their positions to the public. But as part of the spirit of the time, they also took the opportunity to expound their views on political topics. For the Baptists, of course, any such distinction would have been a false one, as their theology and politics were so intricately connected it would have been senseless to try to differentiate between them. The most important Baptist publications were their Confessions. The first Baptist Confession of Faith, the work of seven London Particular Baptist congregations, appeared in 1644. It is notable that, in contrast to the leaders of London Independency and Presbyterianism, not one of the signatories of this important document had received any formal theological training. The aim of the Confession was twofold. On the one hand the Particular Baptists wanted to differentiate themselves from the General Baptists on the issue of predestination and to make clear that they were firmly within the Calvinist consensus. At the same time, they also wanted to disavow any relationship with continental Anabaptism. Furthermore, at a time when the world appeared to be being 'turned upside down', many were accusing the early Baptists of being anarchists who did not acknowledge or respect any form of civil government. This point was firmly refuted in the Confession and emphasised in subsequent revisions. This first Confession thus had a distinctly political purpose. It was an attempt to convince the prevailing powers that the Baptists were not radical anarchists, but merely wanted to practise their beliefs in peace. It argued that Christ's kingdom on earth was a spiritual kingdom, not a material one, that 'a civil magistracy is an ordinance of God set up by God ... and that in all lawful things commanded by them subjection ought to be given by us'. It also acknowledged that the supreme temporal power in England was 'the King and Parliament freely chosen by the kingdom'. The writers therefore were careful to emphasise that they were bound to obey all laws and render unto Caesar that which was Caesar's.[14] Confessions continued to fulfill an important role for the Baptists in the late 1640s and 1650s, and to offer opportunities for the movements to explain their respective positions to the general public as well as to each other.

Undoubtedly, however, during the mid- and late 1640s the political education of most Baptists came in the ranks of the New Model Army. Many Baptists held the godly belief that the parliamentary army was an instrument of God – a mighty and righteous hammer which would set the kingdom right and smash the forces of Antichrist. As a result they were very concerned with the direction of military affairs, even if not actively enlisted. Like many other contemporaries, they looked to determine providence in each victory and setback, and did not censor themselves when reaching their conclusions. Numerous Baptists also joined the parliamentarian army both as soldiers and chaplains, and found that the openness of the regular camp-fire conversations clarified their ideas and sharpened their wits. Baptist enlistment reached such heights that some commentators expressed concern that there were 'swarms of Anabaptists in our armies'.[15] Tolerance seems to have flowed from the top of the military hierarchy, in that, as well as pragmatically recognising that he needed all the support he could find, Oliver Cromwell demonstrated considerable empathy for the earnestness of Baptist beliefs. In a revealing letter in which he addressed concerns about the theology of one Baptist lieutenant, Cromwell wrote: 'the State, in choosing men to serve them, takes no notice of their opinions, if they be willing to faithfully serve ... that satisfies'. On another occasion, when it was mentioned that a different Baptist officer preached better than he fought, he quickly retorted: 'Truly I think that he that prays and preaches best will fight best.'[16] Many Baptists did indeed prove both able fighters and preachers throughout the wars.[17] Once among the ranks, either as soldiers or preachers, they were quick to spread their views and their anti-academic individualistic message found a ready audience in this new segment of the 'middling sort'. But soldiers were not their only converts, for as they moved across the kingdoms they also established gathered Baptist Churches within the communities near their encampments.

One of the most notable cases of the preaching and free discussion of radical ideas within the parliamentarian army concerned Paul Hobson, a prominent Particular Baptist who, along with another army captain, was arrested in the summer of 1645 for illicit preaching. Although an unlicensed layman, Hobson would allegedly preach wherever he could find a pulpit; according to the hostile Presbyterian, Thomas Edwards, 'where ever he came he would preach publicly in the churches, where he could get pulpits, and [also] privately to the soldiers'.[18] He escaped serious punishment, however, through the support of Cromwell, who on other occasions also offered his protection to a number of similar firebrand Baptists, such as William Packer, who fell foul of their military superiors.[19] Cromwell's advocacy of these men revealed the fine line he continually had to walk between toleration and social order, particularly as, in a classic case of perception being a more powerful political force than fact, conservative polemicists such as Edwards, who were appalled by the extremism of men like Hobson and Packer, were having a much greater impact on public opinion than the actual activities of the Baptists themselves.[20]

The English Revolution then provided the Baptists with the opportunity to express their views openly, to gain converts, and, primarily through their involvement with the army, to begin to exert some political pressure. These experiences and a growing sense of a common identity and fledgling organisational structure changed the movements, and throughout the revolutionary period there was a tension between those elements within them that desired an aggressive ongoing pursuit of the millennium and those that urged moderation and consolidation of the progress already made. Two crises in particular demonstrate how the events of the period helped shape the emerging denominations and define their relationship with the state. The first was in rise of the Leveller movement in the mid-1640s, and the second the advent of the Fifth Monarchists in the 1650s.

V

While many of their more conservative puritan contemporaries shared the Baptists' belief that the civil war was a fight between the forces of good and evil and that the New Model Army was a divine instrument, they did not share their hope that it would establish religious toleration. This hope was, however, shared by the Levellers, a radical political movement which originated in London around 1645 and advocated a number of reforms, including widening the franchise, throwing open enclosed lands, abolishing the monarchy and establishing the equality of men under the law. It is reasonable to presume that the bases for the Leveller's egalitarian ideas, particularly their emphasis on universal equality and accountability before God, derived in part from General Baptist theology, and the Levellers also shared the Baptists' desire for religious liberty and the removal of tithes.[21]

Numerous personal affinities also brought the Baptist and Leveller movements together. The three most prominent Leveller leaders, John Lilburne, William Walwyn and Richard Overton, were close to the London Baptist congregations, which as a result played a vital role in the organisation of the Levellers' programmes and campaigns. In the early days of the movement John Lilburne 'received the support of the Baptists led by his old friend William Kiffin', who had been his fellow apprentice. William Walwyn also had a history of associating with Baptists. Amid the negative press that the Baptists were receiving in the early and mid-1640s, in 1644 Walwyn published *The Compassionate Samaritane*, in which he defended 'Brownists and Anabaptists'. Although by his own admission he was 'no separatist', he empathised with the Baptists and could testify to 'the innocency of their intentions and honesty of their lives'. They were not Anabaptists, but rather honest Christians.[22] The other leading Leveller, Richard Overton, had particularly close relations with the General Baptists, and it seems certain that at some point in his life he was a member of a General Baptist congregation, though the official status of his membership during the 1640s is unclear.[23] Thomas Lambe's London congregation served as a hub for Overton's political activities and served as a place where the latest Leveller petitions could be read and those in agreement could sign up. General Baptists also played a central role in the distribution of Leveller literature, and there are numerous reports of Baptist leaders and itinerant evangelists being apprehended while carrying Leveller manifestos.[24] But while common goals, mutual enemies and shared military experiences allowed Baptists and Levellers to cooperate in the mid-1640s, their alliance was always unstable, and though their agendas frequently overlapped they were never identical.[25] The Levellers, for example, went one step beyond the Baptists by rejecting godly rule and advancing the legitimacy of the 'secular' state on the basis of rationality as opposed to divine grace. Ultimately this opened up a gap between Baptists and Levellers which proved too great to bridge.

The problems this difference of outlook created for the Baptist–Leveller relationship can be gauged from a sermon preached by the Baptist evangelist Thomas Collier to a group of soldiers at Putney in 1647. It was later published under the title *A Discovery of the New Creation*, and, as far as Christopher Hill was concerned, it contained most of the major points of the Leveller programme.[26] Collier informed his auditors that a new day had truly come for England, and that the soldiers' success against the King, religious freedom and the Levellers' proposed reforms were all blended without distinction in a beam of radiance reflecting the New Jerusalem. He explained that in 'this new creation there is not only new heavens, but a new earth', which would soon see a number of radical changes, including 'the execution of righteousness, justice and mercy, without respect of persons ... to undo every yoke'. Both spiritual and temporal oppression would be eradicated, and the new earth would be without 'spiritual oppressions in matters of conscience'. In addition to the spiritual oppression of religious persecution, a list of 'temporal oppressions' were to be removed; these included the 'tyrannical and oppressing laws, and courts of justice' and tithes. Collier concluded this section of his sermon by declaring: 'whatsoever bears but the face of oppression in it, let it be removed ... It is the great design of God at present to exalt righteousness, and certainly God calls for it at your hands'.

But while these envisioned reforms were indeed consistent with the Leveller agenda, they only represented half of the Baptists' vision. For Collier went on to explain that alongside the new earth was a new heaven, and before the new earth could be formed Christ was to establish a 'glorious kingdom ... the kingdom of heaven that is in the Saints ... Where God is manifesting himself, there is his and the Saints' kingdom.' Reforms were to come about not through new laws based on rationality and natural rights, but by 'the abundance of light' that would accompany Christ's coming. The unity and equality the Levellers envisioned was only conceivable to the Baptists in terms of a 'godly rule', and they thus missed the point of the Levellers' programme. Collier explained that it was:

> only the glorious light of this new creation that will put an end to these divisions amongst Christians. It is not magisterial power ... but that one Spirit of light and truth that must bring the Saints into this unity ... And the truth is that nothing else will be able to put an end to these divisions but this spiritual dispensation, this new creation of God ... and this is and shall be the glory of this heaven, unity and peace amongst Saints.[27]

For Collier then, as for many other Baptists, the promise of future political transformation was closely connected to the millennium. The full realisation of the reforms the Levellers sought would come about as part of an eschatological transformation, not as part of a 'secular' order free from godly rule. The Baptists' sympathy for the Levellers was thus grounded in the former movement's eschatology, and this had three implications. First, as the threat of a compulsive Presbyterian settlement faded the Baptists were less inclined to support the Levellers. Second, as they realised that the Levellers' proposals were not grounded in shared concerns, their affinity for the secular movement subsided. Finally, as the more conservative Baptist leaders began to adopt a less radical eschatology in order to consolidate the gains already achieved, those aspects of the Leveller agenda which Baptists had supported in an effort radically to reform society became less attractive.

Once the victory of Independency was secured by the New Model Army at the end of the 1640s, the Particular Baptists broke their ties with the Levellers, as their conservative leaders were now confident that they could pursue their goals without them. On the last Sunday of March 1649, Leveller supporters came to the gatherings of the Particular Baptists in London in their usual fashion hoping to gain the congregations' support for their latest petition. But some of the congregations were not persuaded; indeed, three days later Daniel Axtell, a member of Kiffin's London Particular Baptist congregation, arrested the Leveller leader Richard Overton. Lilburne and Walwyn soon joined him in the Tower. When Baptists visited them there, rather than being sympathetic, they requested that they desist from their critiques of the new military government. Surprised by this apparent betrayal, the Leveller leaders refused to mitigate their positions.

Lilburne, Overton and Walwyn were even more stunned by the Particular Baptists' subsequent actions. The following Sunday, the Particular Baptist leaders presented to their congregations their own petition, denouncing the one previously put forward by the Levellers. This new petition demonstrated their continued effort to define themselves in contrast to Anabaptists. They noted 'how through the injustice of historians, or the headiness of some unruly men formerly in Germany called Anabaptists, our righteous profession heretofore hath been and now may be made odious, as if it were the fountain and source of all disobedience'. Now, however, they defined themselves in stark contrast to the Levellers too, and in so doing by implication conflated them with Anabaptist anarchy and defined themselves as the antithesis of such beliefs. Although it was common knowledge that Baptist congregations served as a Leveller support network, the new Baptist petition assured the authorities that 'our meetings are not at all to intermeddle with the orderings or altering civil government'. After circulation among the London Particular Baptists it was presented to the Rump Parliament, and the MPs subsequently responded that 'for … Christians walking answerable to such professions as in this petition you make, they do assure you of liberty and protection'.[28]

The degree to which the two movements had been intertwined is demonstrated by the depth of the Levellers' sense of betrayal. Lilburne struggled to explain what had made 'the preachers in the Anabaptist congregations so mad at us'. Having fought for their 'liberties' and 'never put a provocation upon them that I know of', he could not understand why they had turned on him. Walwyn, who as we have seen had been one of the earliest defenders of the Baptists, considered the petition 'an ill requital for our faithful adherence unto them in the worst of times, and by whose endeavors under God they attained that freedom that they now enjoy'. Overton meanwhile was certain that 'the generality of the [Baptist] people dissented from their petition against us', and claimed that 'they had scarce ten in some congregations to sign it, in some not above two or three, in some none'.[29]

Not long after the Particular Baptists had effectively cut their ties with the Levellers, the London book collector George Thomason picked up another Baptist text critical of the movement. On 24 May 1649, he acquired a copy of *The Levellers Designe Discovered* by the well-known General Baptist leader Henry Denne. Earlier in May, Denne helped to orchestrate an army mutiny at Salisbury, and he was subsequently apprehended, tried and sentenced to death following Cromwell's defeat of the army Levellers at Burford in Oxfordshire. He was, however, miraculously pardoned at the last moment while another three leaders of the mutiny were executed. While not certain, it is plausible that Denne's pardon was in exchange for his denunciation of the Levellers. In the tract he clearly distanced himself from the Leveller agenda and urged unity and obedience among the soldiers. To any who might object to this on the grounds that there were still 'oppressions and ... grievances of the people' to be addressed, he responded that it was best now to wait and be thankful for what had been achieved without pressing for further changes. Indeed he declared that he was thankful his uprising had failed, commenting: 'I do admire the great providence of God, who withheld them from turning things upside down.'[30] This new denunciation by a leading General Baptist sounded the death knell for the Levellers' relationship with the Baptist movements. Both Particular and General Baptists had shown the Leveller leaders that they could no longer depend on their support and organisation. The fellow travellers parted ways, but while the Leveller movement was left stranded and quickly faded away, the Baptists survived.

VI

For the London Baptist leadership the Levellers had been a sharp rock upon which their efforts to convince their contemporaries that they were not anarchical Anabaptists might well have been dashed. As a result of narrowly avoiding this pitfall, they were better ready to meet the next significant challenge which came in the form of the Fifth Monarchists. Fifth Monarchism was the last and most pronounced manifestation of the intense millenarian radicalism unleashed by the Reformation. The movement took its name from the belief that the fifth monarchy of King Jesus – the rule of Christ and his saints on earth – was imminent, and developed as a response to waning apocalypticism. The general apocalypticism that had pervaded English Protestantism in the 1640s had crested with the execution of Charles I but then began to fade in the 1650s. Those who clung to it now formed a distinct movement and saw themselves as God's faithful remnant in a hostile world. Many of them, such as the Baptist James Troppe, saw Charles I's execution as the final preparation for the fifth monarchy of King Jesus, and believed it was time to establish 'Christ's monarchical and personal reign upon earth over all the kingdoms of the world'. In the event, such expectations went unfulfilled. The calling of Barebone's Parliament in 1653 was a major step in the right direction, but it lasted only six months before being wound up by the army regime. In the aftermath of its dismissal many Fifth Monarchists were deeply disappointed and began to express their intense frustration and anger at the government's thwarting of their ends and the consequent delaying of Christ's return.[31]

While the Fifth Monarchists drew some recruits from Presbyterianism, the bulk of their followers were Independents and Baptists, and, although it is difficult to state this with certainty, there is some evidence to suggest that a majority of them accepted the central Baptist practice of believers' baptism.[32] But if the Baptist and Fifth Monarchist movements overlapped in the early 1650s, the establishment of the Protectorate forced them to differentiate themselves from each other. For when Barebone's Parliament collapsed and surrendered its powers to Cromwell, the 'hotter' Fifth Monarchist saints were outraged, while the majority of Baptists drew back from directly opposing the Protectorate. As a result, individuals were forced to choose between obedience and opposition; almost overnight the faithful divided and entire congregations were transformed.

Like the Levellers before them, the Fifth Monarchists needed the support of the gathered congregations if they were to be effective, and as a result they made a concerted effort to recruit members of these churches to join them in their opposition to the Cromwellian Protectorate. Unlike the Levellers, however, they were unable at any stage to mobilise sufficient support from the Baptists. By the mid-1650s, the Baptists had developed an emerging denominational identity, a core of leaders and an organisational system, all of which combined to help them distance themselves from Fifth Monarchism. Nevertheless, the Fifth Monarchists' numerous efforts to recruit the Baptists demonstrate how closely related the movements were, and the effort Baptist leaders had to exert to resist their advances is a further testimony to the two sects' inherent connection.

In 1654 the Fifth Monarchists issued a declaration to coincide with the beginning of the first protectoral parliament. In addition to mounting a violent attack on the government, in the hope of convincing borderline Baptists and Independents to join their cause the declaration contained a forceful denunciation of the apostasy of the godly, stating 'Oh, did we ever think to see so many hopeful Instruments in the Army, Churches, and elsewhere, to be so fully gorged with the flesh of Kings, Captains, and Nobles ... so as to sit with ease and comply with Antichrist, the World, Worldly Church and Clergy?'[33] It was signed by 150 supporters, including a number of prominent Baptists, a fact which suggested that an alliance between the Baptists and the Fifth Monarchists had already been established.

But once it appeared in London, the Baptist leaders acted swiftly to distance themselves from it and to inoculate their congregations against further charges of anarchy. They insisted that names had been forged or placed in a way which suggested that entire congregations had given their support, when only individual members had done so. Led by William Kiffin, they threw themselves into an effort to limit the damage. They visited various congregations and issued letters denouncing the Fifth Monarchists.[34] They also coordinated a show of support for the Protectorate, gathering declarations of loyalty from throughout the realm and declaring, 'We profess our subjection to your highness and most honorable Council, as the happy powers ordained of God.'[35] As a result the prospect of a full alliance between Baptists and Fifth Monarchists slipped away.

By the late 1650s the Fifth Monarchy movement had begun to decline. Effective government persecution and the failure to win substantial support from other sectarian congregations had weakened the initial momentum generated by the outrage at the establishment of the Protectorate. But as the movement faltered, some members were driven to even more radical extremes. By the beginning of 1657 Thomas Venner was contemplating a final revolution and, though not a Baptist himself, was looking to Baptist congregations to support his plans. Some were indeed receptive to his tactics, but believed that his timing was wrong, in that his proposed action was premature according to their interpretation of the eleventh chapter of the Book of Revelation. This stated that the 'holy City' shall be 'tread under foot, two and forty months' and only then would the reign of Christ begin. Since the Protectorate was seen as the little horn referred to in the biblical text, its time would end on 16 June 1657, not in April as Venner planned. The Baptists therefore refused to sign up.[36] This proved a fortunate decision, as government spies got wind of the uprising before it even started. Over two dozen men along with significant stores of ammunition were seized and Venner was captured and placed in the Tower, though he managed to secure his release before the Restoration.[37] The publicity surrounding this abortive uprising insured that few borderline Baptists were willing to associate with the Fifth Monarchists. Nevertheless, the Fifth Monarchists remained persistent to the end and continued to look to the Baptists as their natural allies in the war against Antichrist. Indeed, government reports from the period record that at a large Baptist meeting in Dorchester in Dorset in 1658 one group wanted to hold a vote about whether or not they should join with the Fifth Monarchists, before the London leadership quashed the idea.[38]

The restoration of the monarchy was a serious blow to those who held out hope for godly rule. Even before Charles II was back on the throne the authorities began mopping up Fifth Monarchists, and once he had returned most of the remaining leadership was imprisoned. Ironically, Thomas Venner, the one man who should certainly have been kept behind bars, remained at liberty. Gathering together a group fuelled by their desperation and rapidly fading millennial dreams, he dared to make one last attempt to install King Jesus. After publishing in 1661 their revolutionary manifesto, *A Door of Hope*, Venner and his fellow saints revised their old plan of attack, pouring into London, crying 'King Jesus, and the heads upon the gate'. While they fought with tenacity, their small force was quickly defeated. Venner and his troops were promptly executed and their heads put on display as a warning that the new regime would not tolerate such religious extremes. In the aftermath of Venner's rising, the Baptists again went into print distancing themselves from the Fifth Monarchists and pointing out that those who had attacked London largely believed in infant baptism and had not been members of Baptist congregations. But their defence fell on deaf ears. The uprising was seen by many as a second Munster and reinforced the belief that religious zealots such as the Baptists were antithetical to civil order. Numerous innocent Baptists were arrested, their internment marking the start of a dark and difficult time for the movements, as religious persecution rapidly replaced the quasi-toleration of the revolutionary years.[39]

It was not surprising that the Baptists suffered persecution following the Restoration, for even during the Interregnum their views had been seen as deeply heretical by the vast majority of the nation. What is perhaps a surprise is that they survived, when many other sects that had blossomed during the revolution disappeared. The survival of the Baptists was a result of reaching a moderated theology and politics combined with a sense of fellowship with other believers and an organisational structure that could continue to guide the development of their movement. As the major Baptist denominations reached some level of accommodation with mainstream society, the zealous millenarians migrated towards the newer Baptist expression, the Seventh-Day Baptists, who welcomed chiliast refugees from the Baptists and Independents to such an extent that they were frequently confused with the Fifth Monarchists in subsequent years.[40] The mainstream Baptist movements also sustained serious membership losses at the hands of the Quakers, who in many ways rediscovered the freedom and democratic nature of the earliest Baptist congregations. The 1660s saw a retreat into a world of sectarian in-fighting for the Particular and General Baptists, who became preoccupied by debating with Quakers and Seventh-Day believers. After 1662 sectaries were able to merge with dissenters to form a considerable body of religious thinkers and believers in opposition to the Anglican Church. But Baptist identity was not dulled by the journey into dissent. Their distinctive influence remained, and their arguments for democracy and toleration were subsequently to have a major impact upon both the British Isles and the new British colonies.

VII

It is hard to determine just how many 'Baptists' there were in England on the eve of the Restoration. Not only is it difficult to define a 'Baptist', there are few sources which can provide an accurate estimate of their numbers, though one historian has speculated that there may have been as many as 25,000 Baptists of all persuasions by 1660.[41] Whatever the exact total, their impact extended far beyond their numbers. Peering into a 1640s London meeting of 'baptised believers' or listening in on the preaching of an army minister 'falsely called Anabaptist', we gain a perspective on a Church dissolved and a new culture in the making. The Elizabethan settlement, with its Catholic appearance and hierarchical theology, had vanished. What remained was a Protestant theological core inherited from the first Reformation, but refined in the fires of the second. In the absence of bishops and bells, there was instead an immediate plea for reform, an urgent augury of the divine will, and a priesthood of – if not quite all – at least far more believers. By navigating between the radical democracy of the Levellers and the radical theocracy of the Fifth Monarchists, the leadership of the Particular and General Baptists had set a course that ensured the survival of their congregations and meant that their movements would become permanent fixtures on the British religious and political landscape. The English Revolution had allowed Baptists the freedom to form, blossom and establish the foundations of a denomination that would have a major impact on the religious make-up of the modern world.

Notes

1   Samuel S. Hill, *One Name but Several Faces* (Athens, GA, 1996).
2   While Baptist congregations were egalitarian, with regard to gender their approach was tempered by social norms, in that women appear to have been second class members, although they may have enjoyed greater freedoms in some Baptist congregations than they did in the broader society. See

B.R.White, *The English Baptists of the Seventeenth Century* (London, 1996), chapter 4, and Keith Thomas, 'Women and the civil war sects', *Past and Present*, 13 (1958), 42–62.

3 Edmund Chillenden, *Nathans Parable* (London, 1655), p. 8.

4 The importance of 'purity' for religion is well known. For an effort at tracing the importance of this concept in political revolutions, see Barrington Moore's provocative but limited thoughts on the subject in *Moral Purity and Persecution* (Princeton, 2000).

5 E.B.Underhill (ed.), Records of the Churches of Christ, Gathered at Fenstanton, Warboys, and Hexham. 1644–1720 (London, 1854); B.R.White (ed.), *Association Records of the Particular Baptists of England, Wales, and Ireland to 1660* (London, 1971–74).

6 See Mark R.Bell, *Apocalypse How: Baptist Movements during the English Revolution* (Macon, 2000).

7 For more details see John Coffey's earlier contribution to this volume.

8 For the details of these debates, see White, *English Baptists*; White, *Association Records*; and Bell, *Apocalypse How*.

9 Bell, *Apocalypse How*, p. 35.

10 *Ibid.*, p. 37 n. 12.

11 *Ibid.*, pp. 59–60.

12 *Ibid.*, p. 61.

13 B.R.White, 'Open and closed membership among English and Welsh Baptists', *Baptist Quarterly*, 24 (1971–72); for Bunyan, see Richard Greaves, *Glimpses of Glory* (Stanford, CA, 2002).

14 William J.Lumpkin (ed.), *Baptist Confession of Faith* (Valley Forge, PA, 1969), pp. 156–71.

15 A. S. P. Woodhouse (ed.), *Puritanism and Liberty* (London, 1938), p. 388.

16 W.C.Abbott (ed.), *The Writings and Speeches of Oliver Cromwell*, 4 vols (Cambridge, MA, 1937–47), vol. 1, pp. 277–8; vol. 2, p. 378.

17 Unlike the pacifist Anabaptists, the English Baptists had few reservations about war: see White, *English Baptists*, p. 53.

18 Thomas Edwards, *Gangraena*, part I (London, 1646), p. 33.

19 For Packer, see Christopher Durston, *Cromwell's Major-Generals: Godly Government during the English Revolution* (Manchester, 2001), pp. 50–1.

20 Bell, *Apocalypse How*, pp. 64, 90–5; J. F. McGregor, 'The Baptists: fount of all heresy', in J. F. McGregor and B. Reay (eds), *Radical Religion in the English Revolution* (Oxford, 1984), pp. 23–64; Michael Mullett, 'Radical sects and dissenting churches, 1600–1750', in Sheridan Gilley and W. J. Sheils (eds), *A History of Religion in Britain* (Oxford, 1994), p. 196. For Edwards, see now also Ann Hughes, *Gangraena and the Struggle for the English Revolution* (Oxford, 2004).

21 See Bell, *Apocalypse How*, chapter 6.

22 *A Biographical Dictionary of British Radicals*, vol. 2, p. 95; David Wooton (ed.), *Divine Right and Democracy* (New York, 1986), pp. 248–9; William Haller (ed.) *The Leveller Tracts 1647–1653* (New York, 1944), p. 354.

23 Richard Overton is often identified as a General Baptist; see, for example,

William Haller, *Liberty and Reformation in the Puritan Revolution* (New York, 1955), pp. 175–8; and C. Burrage, *Early English Dissenters* (Cambridge, 1912), vol. 2, pp. 216–18. For Overton's Baptist views, see also Iwan Russel-Jones, 'The Relationship between Theology and Politics in the Writings of John Lilburne, Richard Overton and William Walwyn', unpublished DPhil thesis, University of Oxford, 1987, pp. 87–90; and Marie Gimelfarb-Brack, *Liberté, Egalité, Fraternité, Justice! la vie et l'oeuvre de Richard Overton, Niveleur* (Berne, 1979).

24 Edwards, *Gangraena*, part II (London, 1646), pp. 17–18.

25 A similar case exists for the Levellers' relationship with other gathered Churches; see Murray Tolmie, *The Triumph of the Saints* (Cambridge, 1977), and Russel-Jones, 'The Relationship between Theology and Politics'.

26 Christopher Hill, *The World Turned Upside Down* (London, 1972), p. 59.

27 Thomas Collier, *A Discovery of the New Creation* (London, 1647), pp. 3–40; reprinted in Woodhouse (ed.), *Puritanism and Liberty*, pp. 390–6.

28 *The Humble Petition and Representation of Several Churches of God in London, Commonly (though Falsly) called Anabaptists* (London, 1649), pp. 4–8.

29 Haller (ed.), *Leveller Tracts*, pp. 213, 228–30, 374; William Walwyn, *The Foundation of Slaunder Discovered* (London, 1649), p. 19.

30 S. R. Gardiner, *The History of the Commonwealth and Protectorate, 1649–1656*, 4 vols (London, 1903), vol. 1, pp. 53–4; Henry Denne, *The Levellers Designe Discovered* (London, 1649), pp. 6, 8.

31 For the Troppe quotation, see W. T. Whitley, 'Seventh Day Baptists in England', *Baptist Quarterly*, 12 (1946–48), 252.

32 For the debate on this issue, see Bell, *Apocalypse How*, p. 167 n. 5.

33 *A Declaration of Several of the Churches of Christ* (London, 1654), pp. 1, 4, 6 (misnumbered as 4), 8–10, 17, 19.

34 Samuel Richardson, *Apology for the Present Government and Governour* (London, 1654), p. 14; J. Nickolls (ed.), *Original Letters and Papers of State* (London, 1743), pp. 159–60.

35 Quoted in A. C. Underwood, *A History of the English Baptists* (London, 1947), p. 84.

36 Champlin Burrage, 'The fifth monarchy insurrections', *English Historical Review*, 25 (1910), 723–4, 728–9, 732, 736.

37 *Ibid.*, pp. 726, 738–9; Louise F. Brown, *The Political Activities of the Baptists and Fifth Monarchy Men in England during the Interregnum* (Washington, DC, 1912), p. 113.

38 For the details of the event, see Bell, *Apocalypse How*, pp. 196–7.

39 Burrage, 'Fifth monarchy insurrections', 739–44; B. S. Capp, *The Fifth Monarchy Men* (London, 1972), p. 199; *The Humble Apology of some commonly called Anabaptists* (London, 1661), p. 8.

40 Bell, *Apocalypse How*, chapters 10 and 11.

41 McGregor, 'The Baptists', p. 33.

PART III

Local impacts of religious revolution

'Preaching and sitting still on Sundays': the Lord's Day during the English Revolution

Christopher Durston

I

The men and women who lived through the twenty years of revolution in England between 1640 and 1660 experienced just over one thousand Sundays, and throughout these dramatic and turbulent years the question of how they should observe these religious first days of the week remained highly contentious. The revolutionary years saw the continuation of a long-standing theological controversy over the origins and nature of the Lord's Day that had been raging for more than half a century. They also witnessed the concerted efforts of a succession of godly regimes to impose upon the people their particularly austere vision of the way Sunday should be observed. This essay will begin by filling in the pre-1640 background and then consider the contemporary debates and governmental initiatives over Sunday observance, before attempting to discover how, in the midst of revolution, the English people behaved on this most frequent and visible expression of their collective religious experience.

II

Controversy over the origins, nature and observance of the Lord's Day had existed for many years before 1640. Elizabethan and early Stuart divines had debated a number of contested issues surrounding the day: whether it was instituted at the beginning of time or later by Moses; whether the fourth commandment – 'Remember the sabbath day and keep it holy. Six days shalt thou labour and do all thy work, but the seventh day is the sabbath of the Lord thy God' – was a perpetual moral law which applied to Christians as well as Jews; whether the day was more appropriately labelled 'Sunday', 'the Lord's Day' or 'the Christian sabbath'; and whether it should be taken as starting at nightfall or midnight on Saturday, or dawn on Sunday. During the early seventeenth century a few radical 'Judaising Christians', like John Traske, Theophilus Brabourne and their followers, had even begun to observe a Saturday sabbath, on the grounds that the early Church had been wrong to replace the Jewish sabbath on the last day of the week with the Christian Lord's Day on the first.

The most controversial question in this debate preceding the civil war, however, was how the population should spend those parts of Sunday which were not taken up by Church services, and in particular whether it was necessary to devote the whole of this time to private and family religious exercises and to shun all secular forms of relaxation and leisure. For religious conservatives and many of those in the mainstream of orthodox Protestant opinion, indulgence in 'harmless' recreations and leisure pursuits after attendance at divine worship was an acceptable, even advisable, way to pass what was for most people their one day in the week free from work. But from the last quarter of the sixteenth century onwards, many of those within the puritan wing of the established Church had begun to espouse a very different, sabbatarian approach to Sunday observance, and to argue instead that whole of the day should be given over to an uninterrupted cycle of public and private devotional exercises and charitable works. For these puritans, Sunday was 'the Christian sabbath' or, as they often put it, the 'market-day of the soul'. After preparing for it carefully on Saturday evening, they devoted the whole of the day to a round of Church attendance, prayer, Bible-reading, mediation, discussion of sermons and relief of the sick and poor, and they regarded participation in any other, non-religious activities as scandalous and deeply offensive to God.[1]

As a result of initiatives by the first two Stuart kings, during the twenty-five years which preceded the civil war these sabbatarian puritans found themselves locked in an increasingly bitter battle with the ecclesiastical and secular authorities. In 1618, in response to an order by an assize judge in Lancashire banning dancing and music on Sundays, James I issued a 'Book of Sports', which gave official backing to participation in recreations on that day, so long as they were 'without impediment or neglect of divine service'. Among the pursuits specifically sanctioned by the Book were both mixed-sex and morris dancing, may-games, strenuous sports and church-ales – or wakes – on feast days. Although some bishops tried to minimise its impact, puritans were outraged by the Book of Sports, and during the last years of James's reign some of them attempted unsuccessfully to force the King to retract it and agree instead to the sabbatarian bills they promoted in the 1621 and 1624 parliaments.

Charles I's accession in 1625 was followed by the rapid rise to power within the Church of the fiercely anti-puritan Laudian faction, and in 1633 on the advice of his Archbishop of Canterbury, William Laud, Charles reissued his father's Book of Sports and ordered every minister in the country to publicise it in his parish church. Both Charles and Laud were deeply suspicious of puritan religiosity and determined that Sunday should be seen as a feast day and an appropriate time for celebrations such as church ales. A number of puritan clergy were deprived for opposing the reissued book, and throughout the remainder of the 1630s all theological works advocating the puritan approach to Sunday observance were banned. The alternative anti-sabbatarian view, meanwhile, was vigorously promoted in works such as John Pocklington's *Sunday No Sabbath* and Peter Heylyn's *The History of the Sabbath*, both of which claimed that the fourth commandment had been abrogated by Christ. When the London puritan minister, George Walker, preached a sermon against the Book of Sports in 1638, in which rather unadvisedly he seems to have compared Charles and Henrietta Maria to the Old Testament idolaters Ahab and Jezebel, he was hauled before the privy council, deprived of his living and imprisoned for six months.[2] As a result of the Caroline government's endorsement of Sunday recreations and proscription of sabbatarian beliefs, as Kenneth Parker has commented, by 1640 'attitudes towards sabbath recreations were indeed one of the clearest means of determining religious and political allegiances'.[3]

III

Given this context, it is not surprising that the months that followed the meeting of the Long Parliament in November 1640 saw the publication of a spate of tracts in which the puritan vision of Sunday was strongly reasserted. As the 1640s progressed and press censorship broke down, the arguments in these sabbatarian tracts were in turn challenged by other authors, with the result that, as John Ley put it, the sabbath became 'a ball betwixt two Rackets ... bandied this way and that by mutuall contradiction, not onely between the godly and the profane (which is no newes) but amongst many of those who are in no mean accompt in the Church of God'.[4]

During the course of 1641, a clutch of major sabbatarian tracts was published in England. Broadly similar in content, they shared three main themes: fierce criticism of Charles and Laud's policy towards Sunday observance; trenchant reiteration of the puritan view that the fourth commandment remained morally binding and required the whole of Sunday to be devoted to religious and charitable works; and detailed discussion of precisely which activities were and were not acceptable on that day. In *The Sabbath's Sanctification*, the Blackfriars minister, William Gouge, declared that those who had opposed the puritan Sunday had 'put a knife to the throat of religion', and in his *Vindiciae Sabbathi* George Abbot, the nephew of the Jacobean archbishop, declared that 'the plot of the times has been against the power of Godlines, which could never be pulled down whilest the Sabbath stood upright'.[5] Richard Bernard, the rector of Batcombe in Somerset, meanwhile, argued in his *Threefold Treatise of the Sabbath* that 'prophanation of the Lord's Day' was 'not the least cause of the evills and calamities of our age'.[6] For John Ley, the minister of Great Budworth in Cheshire, the Christian sabbath was 'the training day of Military Discipline, by which the church of Christ is unto the Synagogue of Satan … terrible as an Army with Banners'; and for George Walker, who could now express his sabbatarian beliefs without fear of punishment, it was the 'strong hedge and fence of true Religion'.[7] Hamon L'Estrange declared that it was 'divinely instituted, immutable and totally to be sanctified'.[8]

All these authors were in agreement that ungodly activities such as 'foolish talking and jesting', 'idle words', 'corrupt communication', 'toying wantonnesse', 'lasciviousness in words, song or gesture', 'banquettings' and 'revellings' were totally inappropriate on the sabbath.[9] Several also gave their opinions on other, less clear-cut grey areas with regard to what was acceptable practice. Gouge pointed out that ministers and churchwardens were exempt from the prohibition against working, and argued that those living at a distance from their local church could travel to services by boat or coach. He also made clear that it was acceptable to help neighbours in distress on Sundays, for instance by helping to put out fires.[10] Richard Bernard similarly counselled that simple food could be prepared, that physicians could be summoned for the sick, and that walking in gardens or fields to take the air was acceptable.[11] George Walker even found 'cheerefull feasting' acceptable, on the grounds that this would prompt individuals to worship God with 'thankfulnes of heart'. At the same time, however, he roundly denounced both Roman Catholics who had turned Sunday into 'a day of liberty' and radical Anabaptists who 'esteeme and observe no day at all'.[12]

In addition to these works of theology, the early months of the Long Parliament also saw the appearance of *Mercy Triumphing over Judgement, or a Warning for Sabbath-breakers*, by one Thomas Jones of Hereford. In this doggerel verse pamphlet, Jones recounted how he had been punished for his persistent sabbath-breaking, and in particular for spending much of Whit Sunday of 1624 in his local alehouse, by being struck dumb for four years following a fall from his horse. Eventually restored to his senses in

1628, he had vowed to observe the sabbath assiduously. As he explained in his text:

> Though I did once prophane His day of rest
> Henceforth I hope t'observe his Sabbath blest
> For on that day within his sacred Booke
> My heart and soul for profit there shall looke
> His grace and favour I have found againe
> He with his blessings doth my life sustaine.

Having drawn out this sabbatarian message, Jones concluded by presenting his readers with a prayer for repentant sabbath-breakers.[13]

Within five years of the appearance of these works, the Long Parliament had emerged victorious from its civil war against Charles I, and by the second half of the 1640s the ideas advanced in them had become the official policy of England's new godly rulers. Between 1645 and the late 1650s the new sabbatarian orthodoxy continued to be endorsed by a succession of often weighty theological tomes. The most notable of the twenty or so works published during these years were Daniel Cawdrey and Herbert Palmer's *Sabbatum Redivivum or the Christian Sabbath Vindicated*, Thomas Shepard's *Theses Sabbaticae or the Doctrine of the Sabbath*, and Philip Goodwin's *Dies Dominicus Redivivus or the Lord's Day Enlivened*. These titles defended the Christian sabbath not only against the defeated Laudians, but also from the now much more serious challenge from a growing number of religious radicals, who were denying that the fourth commandment remained morally binding, and rejecting what they saw as the stultifying rigidities of the new establishment in favour of more anti-formal and spiritually liberating expressions of religious belief and practice.

The first part of Cawdrey and Palmer's *Sabbatum Redivivum* was published on May Day 1645, and the remaining three sections appeared in late 1651 after Palmer's death. One of the most detailed and elaborate defences of the puritan sabbath ever published, this Stakhanovite work was not aimed at the casual bedtime reader, nor was it to feature in the mid-seventeenth-century bestseller lists. The first section alone ran to nearly 400 pages and the following three to around another 700. In 1652 Cawdrey himself admitted that the first instalment had been 'too big, or to dear for many stomacks to venture on, which made the stationers hitherto afraid to undertake the impression of the rest'.[14] In 1645 the authors described the sabbath as 'the Compendium or Continent of all Religion', and claimed that 'publique toleration of the profanation of that day' was the chief cause of the calamitous civil war which the country was then experiencing. By 1652 the main focus of their anger was the Anabaptists 'who cry down the sabbbath, either as Antichristian or ceremonial', and the radical preachers who 'with swelling words of vanity everywhere cry down tithes to save men's purses; and sabbaths to please men's fancies'. In opposition to these libertarians, they vigorously reasserted the core Calvinist doctrines that the Christian sabbath had been divinely instituted at the beginning of time and required abstinence from all labour and all forms of sport and recreation.[15]

1649 saw the publication of *Theses Sabbaticae or the Doctrine of the Sabbath* by the New England pastor, Thomas Shepard. In a sub-section of the work entitled 'The Sanctification of the Sabbath', he, too, deplored what he saw as the growing tendency among 'a loose and wanton genera-tion' of radical sectaries to view 'outward forms and observation of daies to be too coarse and too low and mean a work for their ennobled spirits'. Shepard's support for the sabbath was uncompromising, and he was even prepared to consider the introduction of the death penalty for 'presump-tuous sabbath-breakers'. John Cotton's original laws for Shepard's native Massachusetts Bay Colony had in fact made sabbath profanation a capital offence, although this punishment had later been reduced. Another distinctive element of New England practice advocated in the work was the custom of accounting the sabbath from sunset on Saturday to sunset on Sunday.[16]

In his *Dies Dominicus Redivivus*, published in 1654, Philip Goodwin reiterated the view that the sabbath was 'the compendium and epitome of the whole picture of piety', and the 'Fort-Royal of Religion'. He, too, claimed that the sabbath was now endangered as much by 'such who pretend unto the highest pitch of sanctitie' as by 'the Atheistically wicked', declaring dramatically that 'as the blessed body of Christ was cruci-fied between the theeves, so the blessed day of Christ is now crucifying between loose sectaries and prophane sinners'. He also made a passionate appeal to the county justices of the peace to take a firmer line against 'sabbath-sins', and in particular against those who spent the day drinking in alehouses, 'the suburbs and seminaries of Hell'. Protecting the sabbath was, he argued, the 'main end' of the magistracy, which should constitute 'a wall of fire for this day's defence'.[17]

But, while the puritan sabbath found plenty of literary supporters during the 1640s and 1650s, it was also frequently attacked in works penned by those to the right and left of the post-war Calvinist middle-ground. One writer from the conservative end of the Protestant spectrum who challenged the new sabbatarianism was the Laudian Bishop of Derry, John Bramhall. Bramhall's *The Controversies about the Sabbath and the Lord's Day* was probably written in the early 1640s but, perhaps because no printer was the prepared to associate himself with its by then unfashionable views, was not published until after the Restoration. Bramhall cast doubt on the argument that the sabbath was instituted by divine law, asserting instead that Sunday observance was not scriptural but validated by 'perpetual practice and the tradition of the Catholic church'. He also argued that Christians were not obliged to keep as strict a sabbath as the Jews, and that it was sufficient merely to put aside some time for worship conducted 'with gravity and decency'. He then goaded his puritan adversaries by arguing:

> most of those controversies which we have about the Lord's Day, for the lawfulness or unlawfulness of this or that labour or this or that recreation, do depend upon humane [human] law, which doth vary according to divers exigencies of times and places ... But this is the humour of the times to serve up every petty controversie to a fundamental point of religion, whereupon salvation and damnation doth depend.[18]

It was not until nearly a decade later that such anti-sabbatarian ideas finally began to see the light of day in revolutionary England, and then – perhaps because the nation had by now experienced several hundred strict puritan Sundays – they were to prove quite popular. At the beginning of 1650, the amateur Gloucestershire theologian Edward Fisher published his *A Christian Caveat to the Old and New Sabbatarians*, in which he stated that the sabbath had been observed by the early Church not as a legal requirement but as *adiaphora*, that its members had made no clear distinction between Sunday and other days of the week, and that 'the Lord's Day is appointed for us to rejoyce on'. Fisher also provocatively declared that 'the observation of the Lord's Day hath no precept, no practice throughout the scriptures and consequently is no day appointed by God, Christ or his Apostles to be kept holy'.[19] According to one of his sabbatarian critics, over the next few years Fisher's tract sold in the region of 6,000 copies.[20]

Another conservative author who challenged the sabbatarian orthodoxy of post-civil war England was the influential divine Jeremy Taylor. Unlike Cawdrey and Palmer's *magnum opus*, Taylor's *Rules and Exercises for Holy Living*, published in 1650, *was* destined to become one of the best-sellers of its day. While conceding that Sunday ought to be a day kept free of work and predominantly religious in character, Taylor insisted that 'the Lord's Day, being the remembrance of a great blessing, must be a day of joy, festivity, spiritual rejoicing and thanksgiving'. He argued that, while all unlawful or scandalous activities were to be avoided, the people should preserve their 'Christian liberty' and not suffer themselves to be 'entangled with a yoke of bondage', and he went on to suggest that 'even a good action may become a snare to us if we make it an occasion of scruple ...

binding loads upon the conscience not with the bands of God, but of men and of fancy, or of opinion or of tyranny'.[21]

The puritan Sunday also came under attack during these years from writers from the other, radical end of the Protestant spectrum. As early as 1643, the future Leveller William Walwyn had complained in his tract *The Power of Love* that 'men are not pleased except salvation be proved to be very difficult to bee obtained, it must still depend either on our beleeving, or doing, or repenting, or selfe-deniall, or sabbath-keeping, or something or other, or else man is not pleased'.[22] Six years later in 1649, Gerrard Winstanley argued in his tract *Truth Lifting Up its Head Against Scandals* that a strict observance of the first day was not warranted by the New Testament and that keeping it was 'not a forced business but a voluntary act of love'.[23] The same year he and William Everard began to dig up St George's Hill in Surrey on a Sunday. In his later tract *The Law of Freedom in a Platform*, he advocated that one day each week should be kept as a day of rest, but did not specify that it should be Sunday and argued that to foster 'fellowship in friendly love', people should spend it discussing history, current events and other educational themes.[24]

In early 1650 the former New Model Army chaplain William Dell published anonymously *The Doctrine of the Sabbath*. Addressed to the members of the Rump Parliament who were then discussing the sabbatarian bill which would became law that April, he cited a number of authorities in support of the view that the Jewish sabbath was a ceremonial rather than a moral practice which did not apply to contemporary Christians. He argued that the Christian sabbath was 'something more and else then the world commonly doth esteem it', and warned the Rumpers to 'take heed that they do not impose Jewish superstition on the common-wealth under the pretence of Gospel Reformation'.[25] The following year the prominent London Independent William Parker published an attack on the proceedings of the Westminster Assembly of Divines under the title *The Late Assembly of Divines' Confession of Faith Examined*. He accused its members of having been preoccupied with outward forms to the neglect of the interior, spiritual side of religion, and even claimed that strict adherence to sabbath regulations was 'some kinde of superstition and idolatry' and thus a sin against the second commandment. Rather than 'forbearing the works of our lawful calling one day in seven', he argued, Christians would be better advised 'abstaining and resting ... from our own wicked thoughts, words and works all the dayes of our life'.[26]

Another famous radical who opposed the rigid application of sabbath laws was the poet John Milton. In his *Colasterium*, published in 1645, Milton commented that 'it is not the formal duty of worship, or the sitting still, that keeps the holy rest of sabbath; but whosoever doth most according to charity, whether he work or not, hee breaks the holy rest of sabbath least'.[27] Later, in his unpublished *De Doctrina Christiana*, he argued that the sabbath of the Jews was 'peculiar to themselves' and had been inaugurated for 'the express purpose of distinguishing them from other nations'. According to Milton 'those who live under the Gospel are emancipated from the ordinance of the law in general' and 'least of all can they be considered as bound by that of the sabbath'. Finding no New Testament injunction for the keeping of a strict sabbath, he argued that the sanctification of the day should be 'spiritual and evangelical, not bodily and legal' and a 'voluntary, not a constrained observance, lest we should merely substitute one Egyptian bondage for another; for the spirit cannot be forced'.[28]

The later 1650s also saw the appearance of a number of works that, in the pre-war tradition of Traske and Brabourne, rejected Sunday observance in favour of the keeping of a Saturday sabbath. In 1657, Thomas Tillam published *The Seventh Day Sabbath Sought Out and Celebrated*, and the same year John Spittlehouse and William Saller advocated the Saturday sabbath in *An Appeal to the Conscience ... Touching the Sabbath Day*. These works in turn were answered by the Quaker George Fox's *An Answer to Thomas Tillam's Book*, and by Jeremiah Ives's *Saturday No Sabbath*.[29]

IV

While these and other writers remained preoccupied with their theological in-fighting, the MPs of the Long Parliament were busy imposing a set of strict sabbath regulations upon the nation. In September 1641, they resolved that 'the Lord's Day should be duly observed and sanctified; that all dancing, or sports either before or after divine service be forborne and restrained; and that the preaching of God's word be promoted in the afternoon'.[30] In February 1643 they proclaimed the keeping of a national fast day as an act of expiation for 'the wicked profanation of the Lord's Day by sports and Gamings, formerly encouraged even by authoritie', and three months later, they it instructed that all remaining copies of the Book of Sports were to be destroyed.[31]

These measures were a prelude to the first major piece of sabbatarian legislation, which was passed in April 1644. The act, which was steered through Parliament by the influential Herefordshire puritan Sir Robert Harley, stipulated that the sabbath should be sanctified by the exercise of 'piety and true religion, publickly and privately'. Everyone, including wandering beggars and vagabonds, was required to attend church and all commercial activity was banned, as was all other work and all travel 'without reasonable cause'. No-one was to participate in or attend any gatherings for wrestling, shooting, bowls, bell-ringing, masques, wakes, church-ales, or dancing, and all maypoles were to be destroyed. Stiff financial penalties were imposed for breaches of the act and the use of informers was encouraged, the proceeds of the fines being split between the informants and the poor. In order, however, to avoid 'judaizing scruples', the act pointed out that meat could be cooked in private houses and sold 'in a moderate way' in inns and victualling houses, and that milk could also be sold in the morning and evening.[32] At godly Cratfield in Suffolk the parish not only obtained a copy of the act but also framed it and hung it in the church.[33]

Later that year the members of the Westminster Assembly of Divines, who had been charged by Parliament with the task of devising a new liturgy to replace the Book of Common Prayer, held their own debate on Sunday observance. After agreeing that the most appropriate title for the day was the compromise formula 'the Lord's Day, the Christian sabbath', they found themselves at odds about whether to allow 'sober feasting' and whether to condemn worldly thoughts as well as discourses. After some discussion, they rejected the minority view that legislation which concerned itself with people's thoughts was both over-scrupulous and unenforceable and went ahead with the prohibition on secular thinking. They also stipulated that the preparation of food should not keep servants from their Sunday observance. In January 1645, the fruit of their labours, the *Directory for Public Worship*, declared that 'the whole day was to be spent in public worship, reading of scripture, meditation, repetition of sermons, catechising, conferences for prayer, the singing of psalms, visiting the sick and relieving the poor, and such like duties of piety, charity and mercy, accounting the sabbath a delight'.[34]

In October 1645 and August 1648 ordinances were passed barring known sabbath-profaners from receiving communion, and in March 1648 Parliament began to give a second reading to a new sabbatarian bill. The renewal of the civil war and the subsequent political crisis which culminated in the regicide delayed its passage into law, but in April 1650 the Rump finally passed this second act, which extended the 1644 regulations and increased both the powers of local officials to police the act and the penalties for those who transgressed it. No traveller was now to be received at any inn after midnight on Saturday or to leave before 1 a.m. on Monday, no legal writs were to be served or executed, and no-one was to use a boat, horse or coach, except for travel to church. While licensed inns and alehouses could still open at times when church services were not taking place, anyone found singing, dancing or tippling in them was to suffer a heavy fine. The responsibility for enforcing the act was laid squarely at the door of local JPs, constables and churchwardens, who were liable to heavy fines if they defaulted in their duties.[35] The following month the Rump ordered that every parish was to obtain its own copy of the new act.[36]

At the beginning of 1657 a third sabbatarian bill was introduced into Cromwell's second protectoral parliament by the godly MP for Exeter, Thomas Bampfield.[37] It received its first reading in early January, but was then delayed by other more pressing business and was only taken up again in the final days of the sitting. On 20 June 1657 the House spent six hours discussing the proposed new legislation, the debate clearly revealing the tensions and divisions between the moderate and hard-line supporters of the Cromwellian regime.[38] One member argued that the existing measures were already too strict, and complained that the day after the 1650 act had become law his boat had been impounded after he had travelled by river to a service at Somerset House. The lawyers Sir John Glynn and Bulstrode Whitelocke both objected to a proposal to give local officials the power to enter forcibly any private houses where they suspected the sabbath was being profaned, Whitelocke declaring: 'I would not have the people of England enslaved.' Others, however, argued that the move was essential because 'now a-days the greatest disorders were in private houses, by sending thither for drink, drinking in alehouses being both more penal and suspicious'. To deny the authorities powers of entry, they claimed, would 'give liberty for private houses to be as profane as they please'. After a division the clause was accepted by 53 votes to 30.

A second issue which occupied a great deal of the MPs' attentions was whether it was acceptable to sit outside one's house or to walk in fields or churchyards on the sabbath, activities which the earlier acts had allowed. Several members argued that it was important that the population should have some means of enjoying fresh air, and one argued that a ban would be unenforceable as those accused of 'profane and idle sitting' could simply claim they had been meditating on God. William Lenthall commented that 'in some parts of the city unless people have liberty to sit at doors, you deprive them of most of the air they have all week', and Edward Whalley pointed out that some of his Nottingham constituents who lived in the city's caves had a particular need to take the air. Others spoke in favour of a ban; one claimed that if the clause was removed the whole bill might as well be laid aside, and another declared that if it were not included 'there may be profaneness by sitting under some eminent tree in a village, or an arbour, or Gray's Inn Walks'. In the event, this attempt to impose a major new restriction on Sunday activities was narrowly defeated by 37 to 35 votes.

The bill became law on 26 June 1657. After repeating the earlier

injunctions against travel, tippling and sports, it went on to list some of the
work activities which were banned; these included grinding corn, washing
clothes, collecting loans or taxes, melting tallow, burning turf or earth,
and engaging in the trades of butcher, grocer, barber or shoemaker. All
'unnecessary' walking in churchyards during the time of divine service was
also made illegal, and those caught 'vainly and prophanely walking' were
to be fined ten shillings. Because bargemen and other travellers along rivers
that formed part of county boundaries had in the past escaped conviction
as a result of jurisdictional confusion, the act now empowered the JPs of
either bordering county to prosecute them. It concluded by stating that 'for
the better execution of the powers aforesaid', constables, churchwardens
and overseers of the poor could now 'demand entrance into any dwelling
house or other place whatsoever suspected by them to harbor, entertain
or suffer to be any persons prophaning the Lord's Day'.[39] Parishes were
required to purchase a copy of this new act and over the next few months
a great many did so.

V

The impact of these acts was largely dependent on how they were interpreted and enforced by the government's representatives in the localities,
the intensity of local enforcement varying according to both the size of
the godly faction on the county bench and the outlook and reliability of
the constables and churchwardens on whose presentments they relied.
While central government never gained complete control over the local
magistracy, by the late 1640s most counties did contain a fair sprinkling
of puritan JPs who were more than willing to prosecute profaners, and as
a result between 1646 and 1660 there was a steady stream of convictions
at quarter sessions for sabbath-breaking. Edmund Hopwood, a puritan
justice of the peace from south Lancashire, convicted ten individuals for
breaches of the sabbath during 1656, and some of the villagers of Durston
in Somerset were punished for the same offence by their godly local JP,
Edward Ceeley.[40] In the Essex town of Braintree in 1646 the municipal
authorities considered erecting a railing across a local highway to prevent
Sunday travelling.[41]

One of the most zealous local prosecutors was the godly merchant
Robert Beake, who served as a JP in Warwickshire and Mayor of
Coventry in 1655 and 1656. Beake set a number of men in the stocks for
travelling on Sunday and imprisoned three Quakers in a cage for this
offence. When another traveller claimed he had been journeying to hear a
sermon because one was not available in his local church, Beake insisted
he prove this. In December 1655 he arrested a servant who had come to

Coventry from Warwick to buy torches for the funeral of his mistress's son, only releasing him after consulting with several ministers who assured him the journey was a 'work of mercy'. In early March 1656 he posted soldiers on the roads around Coventry to catch illegal Sunday travellers. He also prosecuted several townspeople for grinding corn, cutting hair and tippling in alehouses, and he took action against a local alehouse-keeper who had locked up several churchwardens after they had come to search his premises.[42]

In many other communities, where local power was not monopolised by godly zealots like Beake, the legislation was not enforced with such enthusiasm, but across the country as a whole the embargoes on work, travel and leisure activities seem to have been widely observed. Foreigners resident in the country during the 1650s were certainly struck by the distinctive character of the English Sunday. The Venetian ambassador commented in 1652 that 'the day is generally observed here with extraordinary piety and respect'. Six years later his successor confirmed this impression, remarking in March 1658 that 'the day is held in extreme veneration by the people', and in June that 'this people spends that day in church as the only festival they observe, and any kind of recreation is forbidden'.[43] The following year, a Frenchman visiting London reported that 'the religion of England is preaching and sitting still on Sundays'.[44]

This foreign testimony is confirmed by other domestic evidence. The Presbyterian Richard Baxter claimed that at Kidderminster in Worcestershire, where he was minister during the late 1640s and 1650s, 'on the Lord's Day there was no disorder to be seen in the streets, but you might hear a hundred families singing psalms and repeating sermons as you passed through the streets'. If true, this was in direct contrast to the situation before the civil war in his native Shropshire village, where his father's attempts to lead family scripture readings on Sundays had regularly been disturbed by the noise made by those singing and dancing around a nearby maypole.[45] That the sabbath was occasionally profaned by some of the inhabitants of the West Riding of Yorkshire during the late 1650s is revealed by the diary of a local JP from Woodkirk, John Pickering. On the basis of evidence supplied by informers, Pickering convicted around twenty men and women during the two-year period between September 1656 and August 1658 for travelling, working or tippling in alehouses on the sabbath, eight of them for offences committed one Sunday in late October 1657. The fact, however, that during the same period his informers brought him evidence that led to the conviction of nearly three times as many individuals for profane swearing may suggest that, while not unknown, sabbath-breaking was not especially widespread in this part of Yorkshire.[46] This impression is confirmed by some modern scholarship.

In his study of attempts to bring about a reformation of manners in Essex and Lancashire, Keith Wrightson found that the 1640s and 1650s saw relatively few presentments and convictions for sabbath-breaking and that, even if few people embraced 'active godliness', most of the population of these two counties seem to have at least abstained from work and avoided open profaneness on Sundays.[47]

Contemporary diary evidence also reveals that some individuals took their sabbath duties very seriously. Although, as we have seen, Bulstrode Whitelocke later opposed some of the more extreme elements of the 1657 act, he nonetheless gave over his Sundays to 'a serious and close study of divinity'. He regularly took notes during the morning sermons in his local church and spent the afternoons repeating and discussing them within his family.[48] When he visited Lutheran Sweden on a diplomatic mission in 1654 he was shocked at the laxity with which Sunday was observed there.[49] Nor was sabbatarianism restricted to the godly. The conservative supporter of the old pre-war Church, John Evelyn, regularly supplemented what was for him the meagre fare on offer in his local parish church at Deptford in Kent with private communion services and family catechising in his own home. He also made frequent trips to London to attend Book of Common Prayer services on major-feast days, travelling up on Saturdays to avoid prosecution for sabbath-breaking.[50]

If for the laity Sunday was a day free of labour, for many of the clergy it was one of prolonged and onerous activity. Ralph Josselin, the godly minister of Earls Colne in Essex, 'expounded the word' in his parish church on nearly every Sunday during the 1640s and 1650s, and when he missed one Sunday in 1659, as a result of travelling to Oxfordshire to visit a dying friend, he asked God's pardon for his 'work of mercy'. He normally preached twice, occasionally three times, and usually for several hours at a stretch. In March 1647 he began a systematic exposition of scripture, preaching weekly on each of the books of the Bible in turn. Not surprisingly, he found these sabbath exertions extremely taxing. He frequently commented in his diary that he felt under-prepared for his sabbath duties, struggled to summon up enthusiasm for his subject matter, and was left disappointed by his performance. During the second half of the 1650s he also became very worried that his Sunday worship might be disrupted by itinerant Quaker missionaries. The degree of stress that these exertions caused is revealed by the fact that on several occasions in 1656 he experienced classic anxiety dreams during Saturday night. In one of these, he dreamed he was officiating at a service improperly dressed and unable to conduct the liturgy properly; his own Bible had inexplicably disappeared and been replaced by an unfamiliar book, and he struggled to lead the congregation in the singing of the metrical psalms.[51]

VI

But, if observance of the sabbath regulations was widespread, it was by no means universal. Some breaking of the rules was sanctioned – indeed even committed – by the authorities themselves. On 8 August 1641, the House of Commons itself sat for the first time ever on a Sunday to pass a resolution requesting Charles I to delay a journey to Scotland planned for the next day. After concluding their business, they drew up a declaration justifying their breach of the sabbath and warned other, inferior organisations not to seek to follow their example.[52] Thereafter, exigencies of war and national defence led to regular transgression of the sabbath regulations. The first major battle of the civil war at Edgehill was fought on a Sunday afternoon in late October 1642, and the following year those helping to strengthen London's fortifications were permitted to work on the sabbath.[53] In July 1648 those delivering provisions to the parliamentary besiegers of Colchester were allowed to ignore the prohibitions on Sunday travel.[54] During the 1650s, both the republican council of state and Cromwell's protectoral council held meetings on Sundays during periods of crisis, such as the 1651 invasion by Charles Stuart and the Dutch War.[55] In February 1652 a naval engagement with the Dutch occurred on a Sunday, and in 1653 and 1654 those responsible for repairing ships and provisioning the fleet also worked on that day.[56] In the autumn of 1655 some of the county commissioners assisting the major-generals met on Sunday to assess their royalist neighbours for the decimation tax, and government post-riders were allowed to travel on Sundays.[57] Cromwell's first protectoral parliament also met for its initial session on Sunday 3 September 1654. This date was chosen because it was the anniversary of Cromwell's famous victories at Dunbar and Worcester, but some of the MPs were nonetheless unhappy; before they listened to Cromwell's welcoming speech they openly expressed their concern at this official flouting of the sabbath regulations.[58]

And if, as has been argued, many English men and women did nominally and outwardly adhere to the sabbath regulations, significant numbers of them remained grudging and sporadic in their observances, especially after the removal in 1650 of the legal requirement to attend Sunday services in the parish church. On numerous occasions between 1646 and 1660 Ralph Josselin recorded in his diary his deep disappointment at his parishioners' lack of enthusiasm for Sunday worship. In March 1647 he remarked that his congregation had grown 'very thinne' and had 'litle care of his [God's] worship', and the following September he commented that 'the people, especially [the] poore of both sexes and men are exceeding carles of the sabbath'. The next year he repeated that people were 'regardles and careles of the worship of God', and in 1653 he complained: 'oh how deadly and drowsily doe people here [hear]'. In February 1656 he wrote that 'persons in this corner much withdraw from the word', and at the end of that year he exclaimed: 'oh how dead our hearts are under ordinances'. When he heard of the passing of the 1657 sabbath act, he expressed the hope that God would 'doe good by it', but two years later in 1659 he was forced to concede that the sabbath was still 'a day most woefully slighted, especially by youth'.[59] While dissatisfaction with the religious standards of the laity was the constant refrain of early modern clergymen, Josselin's comments would seem to provide clear evidence that those individuals who found the duties of the Interregnum puritan sabbath spiritually uplifting and invigorating were never more than a small minority.

A sizeable minority was more flagrant in its sabbath-breaking. Throughout the Interregnum, the laws were flouted all over the country by those who worked, engaged in sports and other recreations, or spent most of the day drinking. This reality was frequently acknowledged by the authorities themselves. In March 1656 the JPs of London, Westminster and Middlesex complained that the sabbath was 'very much prophaned and the observation thereof very much neglected' by tradesmen who continued to sell their produce and by those who spent the day in alehouses; and a few months later Sir John Glynn declared at the Worcestershire assizes that he wished there was 'noe need of any lawe but that the spiritt of God in their hearts could make them conscientiously observe that day, but that doth not doe, neither can the labour of the minister prevaile, but the sword of the magistrate must come in'.[60] The following year the preamble to the 1657 sabbath act stated that it was 'found by daily experience that the first day of the week ... is frequently neglected and prophaned to the dishonour of Christ'.[61] In April 1654 the Mayor of Berwick asked the government to increase the fines for Sunday labouring, as many of the local salmon fishermen continued to work on that day and risked the ten shillings' fine because they could make far more than that when they sold their catch.[62] In March 1656, London's major-general, Sir John Barkstead, seized a number of horses which were being exercised by their grooms in the capital on the sabbath and made their owners pay ten shillings for their release.[63]

Throughout the late 1640s and 1650s, too, many Londoners gathered at Moorfields to the east of the city on Sundays to watch or take part in sports. In the spring of 1648, the Lord Mayor provoked a full-scale riot after he sent his watchmen to disperse the 'loose fellows' who gathered there every week to drink, engage in sports and commit 'other disorders'.[64] Four years later in 1652, after being informed that cudgel fights were still being staged there every week, the council of state sent its own investigator to find out who was involved. It was unable, however, to suppress these gatherings, which were still occurring on the eve of the Restoration, when Samuel Pepys was among the crowds that flocked there.[65] The cleric William Bushnell, meanwhile, admitted to the Cromwellian ejectors in 1656 that regular Sunday stowball matches were held at Box in Wiltshire during the early 1650s, and that the participants included 'gentlemen as of good a rank and repute as were most in the neighbouring parts'.[66]

Less energetic profaners either took themselves off to their local alehouse for the day or stayed at home and got drunk. The Quaker leader George Fox was well aware that many people spent much of what he pointedly always referred to as 'the First Day' in their local alehouse, and on occasions followed them there in an attempt to convert them.[67] In February 1655 the Mayor of Harwich informed the council that the lack of a preacher in his town had led to profaneness, tippling and gaming, and the same year the Norfolk justices heard evidence that an innkeeper from Swannington allowed servants to tipple in his house on Sundays 'and there spend there moneys to the great dishonour of the glory of God and the hurt and p'judice of there masters'.[68] At the Somerset assizes at Chard in the summer of 1656, the grand jury complained that the sabbath was commonly profaned in that county 'by frequent resort of ill disposed persons to innes and alehouses on that day'; and around the same time the Hampshire justices were informed that in their county it was becoming common to hold all-night parties in private houses on Saturdays, and that those who attended them were frequently 'soe distempered' by Sunday morning that they were 'altogether unfitt for the duties of that day'.[69] In October 1656, a number of men from Bollington in Cheshire were indicted at their local quarter sessions for resorting every Sunday to an alehouse and returning home drunk to 'abuse their wives, terrify their children and trouble their neighbours, nothinge at all matteringe the breach of the lawes both of God and man'.[70]

VII

Despite such frequent transgressions, the puritans who ruled England between 1645 and 1660 did achieve some measure of success in forcing their subjects to observe Sundays in the manner they believed their God required. The fact that even on the eve of the Restoration the sabbath regulations were still in force is revealed by the early pages of Samuel Pepys's famous diary. On Sunday 12 February 1660 Pepys, who was of course nobody's puritan, spent two hours with some friends in an increasingly desperate and ultimately vain search for an alehouse where they could have a lunchtime drink, before returning home to record in his diary, 'but not finding any open, we darst not knock'. Four months later, however, following Charles II's return, he and his drinking companions had the choice of most of London's inns and taverns, and could now travel between them on the barges of the Thames watermen, who were once again operating openly on Sundays.[71]

The greater freedom in London after Charles II's return was replicated elsewhere in the country. According to Anthony Wood, in Restoration Oxford the townspeople were once more able to congregate in the streets during service time, sit on benches and gossip, walk or ride in the fields, and drink in taverns and alehouses – activities which had been 'accounted damnable' before 1660.[72] As we have seen, Ralph Josselin had frequently expressed his disappointment at his parishioners' lack of commitment to Sunday worship during the 1650s, but after the King's return he was to become even more despondent about the growth of open profanity. In August 1660 he recorded in his diary that 'people wonderfully neglect the sabbath', and a year later that 'God's holy day is most men's vain day'. In December 1661 he wrote that the sabbath was 'sadly neglected, profanes wonderfully abounding', and in April 1662 that 'the Lord's Day is most sadly prophaned in all places'. After the penal laws requiring church attendance were reinstated in 1663, Josselin noted that 'divers of the ruder sort of people' had started turning up at church again, and commented ruefully that 'the statute of paying 1 shilling when absent from divine service is more then the feare of god's command'. But if his parishioners were now once more attending church on Sundays, they were no longer even pretending to perform any other religious duties and, as he confirmed in the summer of 1664, the puritan 'holy day of rest' had by now become 'the sport and pleasure day of the generall rout of the people'.[73]

Although the nation had been obliged to conform outwardly to the sabbath laws introduced during the 1640s and 1650s, the campaigns of the godly regimes of those years to change hearts and minds and to persuade the people to embrace sabbatarianism with real enthusiasm had fallen on a great many deaf ears. Most English men and women seem to have retained a preference for a less spiritually intense Sunday, one in which divine worship could be combined with opportunities either to relax or to observe or participate in a range of traditional pursuits. Thus, while the godly campaign to impose the puritan Sunday upon the English people was in the short term relatively successful, it was only achieved at the high cost of alienating the people from their rulers and promoting a widespread desire for a return to the less stringent religious culture of the pre-war period.

Notes

1 See Kenneth L. Parker, *The English Sabbath: A Study of Doctrine and Discipline from the Reformation to the Civil War* (Cambridge, 1988), and David S. Katz, *Sabbath and Sectarianism in Seventeenth-Century England* (Leiden and New York, 1988).

2 George Walker, *The Doctrine of the Holy Weekly Sabbath* (London, 1641), epistle dedicatory; *Calendar of State Papers, Domestic* [hereafter *CSPD*], *1638–9*, pp. 98, 231, 431, 533; *CSPD, 1639*, pp. 99, 31, 70; *CSPD, 1640–1*, p. 277.

3 Parker, *English Sabbath*, p. 214.

4 John Ley, *Sunday a Sabbath* (London, 1641), epistle dedicatory.

5 William Gouge, *The Sabbath's Sanctification* (London, 1641), epistle dedicatory; George Abbot, *Vindiciae Sabbathi* (London, 1641), epistle dedicatory.

6 Richard Bernard, *A Threefold Treatise of the Sabbath* (London, 1641), p. 177.

7 Ley, *Sunday a Sabbath*, epistle dedicatory; and Walker, *Doctrine of the Holy Weekly Sabbath*, epistle dedicatory.

8 Hamon L'Estrange, *God's Sabbath Before the Law ... and Under The Gospel* (Cambridge, 1641), epistle dedicatory.

9 The list is from Bernard, *A Threefold Treatise of the Sabbath*, pp. 224–5.

10 Gouge, *The Sabbath's Sanctification*, p. 11.

11 Bernard, *A Threefold Treatise of the Sabbath*, pp. 78–9.

12 Walker, *Doctrine of the Holy Weekly Sabbath*, pp. 139–40, 161.

13 Thomas Jones, *Mercy Triumphing over Judgement, or a Warning for Sabbath-breakers* (London, 1640).

14 Daniel Cawdrey and Herbert Palmer, *Sabbatum Redivivum or the Christian Sabbath Vindicated* (London, 1645 and 1651), part 2, epistle to reader.

15 *Ibid.*, part 1, epistle to reader; part 2, epistle to reader, and p. 136.

16 Thomas Shepard, *Theses Sabbaticae or the Doctrine of the Sabbath* (London, 1649), part 4, pp. 35, 50.

17 Philip Goodwin, *Dies Dominicus Redivivus or the Lord's Day Enlivened* (London 1654), epistle dedicatory; epistle to reader; pp. 132, 150.

18 John Bramhall, *The Controversies about the Sabbath and the Lord's Day*, in John Bramhall, *The Works of the Most Reverend Father in God John Bramhall D.D.* (Dublin 1677), pp. 916–31; the quotation is p. 931.

19 Edward Fisher, *A Christian Caveat to the Old and New Sabbatarians* (London, 1650), pp. 7–17; the quotation is p. 17. For more details of Fisher's writings, see my article 'Edward Fisher and the defence of Elizabethan Protestantism during the English Revolution', *Journal of Ecclesiastical History*, 56 (2005).

20 John Collinges, *Responsoria ad Erratica Piscatoris, or a Caveat for Old and New Prophaneness* (London, 1653), advertisement to reader.

21 Jeremy Taylor, *The Rules and Exercises of Holy Living*, in C. Page Eden (ed.), *The Whole Works of the Right Reverend Jeremy Taylor D.D.*, 10 vols (London, 1849), vol. 3, pp. 172–4.

22 William Walwyn, *The Power of Love* (London, 1643), in Jack R. McMichael and Barbara Taft (eds), *The Writings of William Walwyn* (Athens, GA, and London, 1989), p. 91.

23 Gerrard Winstanley, *Truth Lifting Up its Head Against Scandals* (London, 1649), p. 72.

24 Gerrard Winstanley, *The Law of Freedom in a Platform* (London, 1652), in Christopher Hill (ed.), *Winstanley: 'The Law of Freedom' and Other Writings* (Cambridge, 1983), pp. 345–7.

25 William Dell, *The Doctrine of the Sabbath* (London, 1650), pp. 2–8.

26 William Parker, *The Late Assembly of Divines' Confession of Faith Examined* (London, 1651), pp. 235–46.

27 John Milton, *Colasterium* (London, 1645), in F. A. Patterson *et al.* (eds), *The Works of John Milton*, 18 vols (New York, 1931–40), vol. 4, p. 264.

28 John Milton, *De Doctrina Christiana*, in Patterson *et al.* (eds), *Works of John Milton*, vol. 17, pp. 171–91.

29 For more details, see Katz, *Sabbath and Sectarianism*, pp. 22–47.

30 Parker, *English Sabbath*, p. 218.

31 C. H. Firth and R. S. Rait (eds), *Acts and Ordinances of the Interregnum*, 3 vols (London, 1911), vol. 1, p. 81; Parker, *English Sabbath*, p. 218.

32 Firth and Rait (eds), *Acts and Ordinances*, vol. 1, pp. 420–2; *Commons Journal*, vol. 3, pp. 440–1, 447.

33 L. A. Botelho (ed.), *Churchwardens' Accounts of Cratfield, 1640–1660*, Suffolk Records Society, 42 (1999), 60.

34 'A Journal of the Assembly of Divines kept by John Lightfoot', printed in Richard Cox, *The Literature of the Sabbath Question*, 2 vols (Edinburgh, 1865), vol. 1, pp. 229–30; Firth and Rait (eds), *Acts and Ordinances*, vol. 1, pp. 598–9.

35 *Ibid.*, vol. 1, pp. 791, 1206; vol. 2, pp. 383–7.

36 *CSPD, 1650*, p. 164.

37 J. T. Rutt (ed.), *The Diary of Thomas Burton Esq.*, 4 vols (London, 1828), vol. 1, pp. 295, 310.

38 Rutt (ed.), *Diary of Thomas Burton*, vol. 2, pp. 260–2.

39 Firth and Rait (eds), *Acts and Ordinances*, vol. 2, pp. 1162–70.

40 Derek Hirst, 'The failure of godly rule in the English Republic', *Past and Present*, 132 (1991), 56, 59.

41 K. E. Wrightson, 'The Puritan Reformation of Manners with Special Reference to the Counties of Lancashire and Essex, 1640–1660', unpublished PhD thesis, University of Cambridge, 1973, p. 178.

42 Levi Fox (ed.), 'The diary of Robert Beake, Mayor of Coventry, 1655–1656', *Dugdale Society Miscellany*, Dugdale Society, 31 (1977), 114–36.

43 *Calendar of State Papers, Venetian* [hereafter *CSPV*], *1647–1652*, p. 245; *CSPV, 1657–1659*, pp. 179, 217.

44 Quoted in Katz, *Sabbath and Sectarianism*, p. xi.

45 M. Sylvester (ed.), *Reliquiae Baxterianae* (London, 1696) pp. 2, 83–4.

46 'The justice's notebook of Captain John Pickering, 1656–60', *Miscellanies*, Thoresby Society, 11 (1904), 69–100; 15 (1909), 71–80.

47 Wrightson, 'Puritan Reformation of Manners', pp. 212–13.

48 Ruth Spalding (ed.), *The Diary of Bulstrode Whitelocke, 1605–1675* (Oxford, 1990), pp. 177–8, 266, 279–80.

49 *Ibid.*, pp. 318, 387–8.

50 E. S. de Beer (ed.), *The Diary of John Evelyn*, 6 vols (Oxford, 1955), vol. 2, p. 252; vol. 3, *passim*.

51 Alan Macfarlane (ed.), *The Diary of Ralph Josselin, 1616–1683* (London, 1976), *passim*, but esp. pp. 297–8, 364, 379–80, 382, 442, 450.

52 *Commons' Journal*, vol. 1, pp. 245–6.

53 *CSPV, 1642–3*, p. 256.

54 Macfarlane (ed.), *Diary of Ralph Josselin*, pp. 129–30.

55 *CSPD, 1651*, p. 362; *CSPD, 1651–2*, pp. 254, 303, 328, 346, 368, 377, 400; *CSPD, 1652–3*, pp. 10, 237; *CSPV, 1657–9*, p. 179.

56 *CSPD, 1652–3*, pp. 180, 212–13; *CSPD, 1653–4*, p. 447; *CSPD, 1654*, p. 147.

57 Bodleian Library, Rawlinson MS A32, fols 647–50; *CSPD, 1655*, p. 22.

58 Spalding (ed.), *Diary of Bulstrode Whitelocke*, p. 394; W. C. Abbott (ed.), *The Writings and Speeches of Oliver Cromwell*, 4 vols (Cambridge, MA, 1937–47), vol. 3, pp. 431–2.

59 Macfarlane (ed.), *Diary of Ralph Josselin*, pp. 93, 98, 104, 136, 152, 208, 298, 346, 363, 376, 386, 406, 454.

60 British Library, Thomason Tracts, E.1065.6; Bodleian Library, Rawlinson MS, C182, fols 101–2.

61 Firth and Rait (eds), *Acts and Ordinances*, vol. 2, pp. 1162–70.

62 *CSPD, 1654*, pp. 103–4.

63 Bodleian Library, Carte MS 131, fols 179–80.

64 Robert Ashton, *Counter-Revolution: The Second Civil War and its Origins* (New Haven, CT, and London, 1994), pp. 234–41.

65 *CSPD, 1652*, pp. 303–16; Robert Latham and William Matthews (eds), *The Diary of Samuel Pepys*, 12 vols (London, 1970), vol. 1, pp. 53–4.

66 Walter Bushnell, *A Narrative of the Proceedings of the Commissioners appointed by Oliver Cromwell for the Ejecting of Scandalous and Ignorant Ministers in the Case of Walter Bushnell, Clerk* (London, 1660), p. 60.

67 John L. Nickalls (ed.), *The Journal of George Fox* (London, 1952), p. 112.

68 *CSPD, 1655*, p. 46; D. E. Howell James (ed.), *Norfolk Quarter Sessions Order Book*, Norfolk Record Society, 26 (1955), p. 81.

69 J. S. Cockburn (ed.), *Somerset Assizes Orders, 1640–1659*, Somerset Record Society, 71 (1971), pp. 46–7; Hampshire Record Office, Q1/3, p. 292.

70 J. H. E. Bennett and J. C. Dewhurst (eds), *Quarter Sessions Records … for the County Palatine of Chester, 1559–1760*, Record Society of Lancashire and Cheshire, 94 (1940), pp. 165–6.

71 Latham and Matthews (eds), *Diary of Samuel Pepys*, vol. 1, pp. 53–4, 201, 206.

72 A. Clark (ed.), *The Life and Times of Anthony Wood, Volume 1*, Oxford Historical Society, 19 (1891), 359.

73 Macfarlane (ed.), *Diary of Ralph Josselin*, pp. 467, 481, 485, 489, 500, 509.

10

'So many sects and schisms': religious diversity in Revolutionary Kent, 1640–60

Jacqueline Eales

I

At the end of 1641 Henry Oxinden of Deane described the existence in Kent of 'so many sects and schisms'. A future member of the parliamentarian county committee in Kent, Oxinden catalogued these groups as separatists, puritans and conformists. He complained most strongly about the conformists, who he said supported a pompous clergy as well as the dignity and the authority of the bishops. Oxinden did not support any of these 'sects', but aligned himself firmly with the reform of episcopacy outlined in Lord Saye and Sele's speech of 24 May 1641 to the House of Lords calling for the removal of the civil powers of the bishops.[1]

Religious belief was one of the most important ideologies contributing both to the outbreak of civil war in 1642 and to the subsequent political splintering. Kent provides a uniquely rich case study of the significance of religious belief in the period, for no other county offers such diversity combined with such detailed documentation. Between 1640 and 1660 it is possible to find every shade of Protestant religious dissent in Kent from Presbyterians to followers of the self-proclaimed prophet Ludowicke Muggleton.[2] Royalists in Kent, meanwhile, continued to support the established Church even after 1645 when The Long Parliament substituted the *Directory for Public Worship* for the Book of Common Prayer, closely followed by the abolition of episcopacy the next year. Similarly, Kent's small Catholic population also maintained its faith in the face of the renewed political pressures of the period. Leading royalist and Catholic families were subject to the seizure of arms in 1642 and the sequestration of their estates from 1643 onwards. The 1650s also saw renewed restrictions and penalties imposed on both these groups as the Commonwealth and Protectorate governments struggled to maintain political security in the face of widespread opposition to their rule. This included a ban on standing or voting in the elections to the two protectoral parliaments of 1654 and 1656.[3]

Some areas of the county had experience of religious nonconformity reaching back into the early sixteenth century. Before the Reformation, Kent had developed a strong tradition of Lollard dissent in several Wealden parishes, such as Cranbrook, as well as in a number of towns, including Maidstone, Ashford and Canterbury. A significant number of the Marian Protestant martyrs had also come from Kent and their deaths in Canterbury, Maidstone and Rochester in the 1550s were long remembered in the county. In Elizabeth I's reign there is evidence of the spread of both moderate puritanism within parish hierarchies and of separatist activity. The transmission of nonconformist religious beliefs has been associated by some historians with the cloth industry and its trade routes into Kent.[4] It also relied, however, on a number of other factors which will be further explored below.

Parliament's administrative control of Kent from August 1642 onwards encouraged a significant spread of religious and political radicalism in the county; Kent was a stronghold for the General Baptists in the 1640s, while the Quakers claimed many local converts in the 1650s.[5] Such congregations which formed outside the constraints of a national Church were seen by their adherents as more egalitarian than the episcopal and Presbyterian Churches. In 1646 the Independent preacher John Saltmarsh, rector of Brasted in Kent, summed up the impact that membership of the Independent gathered churches had on their congregations when he wrote that 'the interest of the people in Christ's kingdom is not only an interest of compliance and obedience and submission, but of consultation, of debating, counselling, prophesying, voting'.[6] Saltmarsh's words epitomised the religious and political freedoms that characterised the English revolution in the 1640s and 1650s.

These freedoms are exemplified by the spiritual quest of Luke Howard. A conformist in the mid-1630s when he was apprenticed to a Dover shoemaker, his master's involvement with local separatists introduced him to the London Independent congregation in Coleman Street led by John Goodwin. In 1644 Howard was among the first in Kent to accept adult baptism at the hands of the Particular Baptist leader, William Kiffin. He later rejected Kiffin's belief in predestination and followed the General Baptists, but then, after rejecting the act of baptism itself, he fell into 'a seeking state again'. His use of the word 'seeking' is significant as it denotes the rejection of all forms of organised worship. Howard eventually converted to Quakerism in 1655 in response to the first of the Quaker missions into Kent led by John Stubbs and William Caton, and he played a significant role in Quaker circles until his death in 1699.[7]

Samuel Fisher was another prominent Quaker convert in Kent whose 'pilgrim's progress' resembled Howard's. Fisher had been ordained into the established Church and had served as a chaplain to Sir Arthur Hesilrige. In 1643 he was appointed by Parliament as lecturer in the Kent parish of Lydd and later became vicar there. He resigned this living when he became a General Baptist, and in 1653 published a tract against infant baptism, *Baby-Baptism Meer Babism*. In 1655 Fisher held a series of meetings with the Quakers on their first missions into Kent, which resulted in his conversion. He was an active disputant and in July 1649 had debated the lawfulness of infant baptism with a group of Presbyterian ministers at Ashford. In April 1659 he and several other Quakers engaged in three disputes with the Presbyterian minister, Thomas Danson, at Sandwich. Such public religious debates were a distinctive feature of the civil-war period, and were sometimes attended by large numbers of local ministers and laity. The Ashford meeting, for example, was said to have lasted for six hours and to have attracted 3,000 auditors who listened with 'so much devotion without any interruption'.[8] It was common for all of the protagonists to claim victory in demonstrating religious truth against their opponents' errors and blasphemies. Given the variety of different religious opinions in Kent, it is no surprise that a considerable amount of religious debate emanated from the county not only in such public meetings, but also in print throughout the period.

Studies of counties during the civil war have traditionally focused on the political allegiance of the gentry and their local administrative roles, but by using religion as an alternative organising theme it is possible to integrate groups other than the gentry into the analysis. Such an investigation reveals that religious and political debate were closely connected at county level and that religious disputes galvanised all sectors of provincial society. By the end of the 1630s the religious policies of the Personal Rule had created considerable disquiet in many Kent parishes. In particular the altar policy instigated in 1633 by the new Archbishop of Canterbury, William Laud, was widely interpreted as a return to pre-Reformation and Roman Catholic practices. In the winter of 1640–41 the link between the newly railed altars and Catholic 'superstition' was explicitly made by the laity in a number of parishes across Kent, including Dartford near London, Horsmonden in the Weald, and Sturry near Canterbury. A group of parishioners from the Wealden parish of Rolvenden complained, for example, that their vicar, Thomas Higginson, had set up an altar 'in the most superstitious way he could' and had opposed the parish over the altar 'all that he might'.[9]

Concerns about this and other Laudian 'innovations', including the renewed emphasis on both church decoration and ceremonialism, merged in the early 1640s with longer term puritan demands for church reform in Kent and elsewhere. In the winter of 1640–41 some 2,500 inhabitants of the Kentish Weald signed the London 'Root and Branch' petition calling for the total abolition of episcopacy. This was a demand that can be traced back to the early days of the Elizabethan puritan movement, when radicals argued that there was no argument for the divine right of bishops and that the office should be expunged from the reformed Church along with all other unwarranted Catholic usage. To the Crown, however, this was a dangerous argument that could be extended to the case for the divine right of kings – hence James I's famous dictum 'No bishop, no king'. After some discussion with the promoters of the petition, Sir Edward Dering, one of the MPs for Kent, presented a revised version of it to the House of Commons calling only for the abrogation of the bishops' 'hierarchical power', rather than for complete abolition of their function.[10]

In the spring of 1642 as many as six thousand men signed a pro-parliamentarian petition from Kent calling for comprehensive religious reform to be undertaken with the advice of an assembly of divines. This petition was subscribed in Canterbury, Rochester, Maidstone, Ashford, Dartford, Hever and the Cinque Ports, as well as in other areas of the county. Its circulation marked a major fracturing of political and religious opinion in Kent and it is possible to identify the nucleus of a parliamentarian party in the county among the petitioners, as those men who were most committed to Church reform and in particular to the abolition of bishops would also prove to be those most committed to the parliamentarian cause after 1642.[11]

The investigation of religious opinion can also facilitate our under-standing of the central role played by the provincial clergy in both shaping and reflecting lay attitudes during the civil war and Interregnum. In 1640, as members of the established Church, the clergy discussed a range of religious reforms in terms of national rather then local policies, and the pulpit provided them with a ready made forum for spreading their views to a variety of congregations. Before the outbreak of the civil war, royalist sermons were to be heard in the two Kent cathedrals at Rochester and Canterbury, as well as at the county assizes at Maidstone. But once the war had started the royalist clergy were gradually silenced and replaced by parliamentarian ministers, who urged resistance to the King in sermons preached before the House of Commons at Westminster and the Kent county committee at Knole. Parish preaching could also be highly political and as a result there was a high turnover of parochial clergy during the civil war period.[12] In Kent some royalist and conformist clerics withdrew voluntarily when the county fell under parliamentarian control at the start of the war. Others were forcibly replaced by Presbyterian or Independent clergy in the succession of parliamentarian purges that took place over the next fifteen years. The importance that the civil authorities placed on the political support of the clergy is reflected in the very high level of clerical ejections in Kent. Alan Everitt has calculated that, out of a total of 450 livings, 233 Kent benefices and canonries were either sequestrated or forcibly vacated between 1642 and 1660.[13]

The interdependence of religion and politics in the early modern period and the fact that opposition to the established Church could pose a direct challenge to the authority of the King is shown by the prosecution in 1642 of Francis Cornwell, curate of a parish near Maidstone. Cornwell was accused of sedition for stating publicly in June 1641 that 'if the king enjoined the book of common prayer or any other testimonies or discipline that were not expressly delivered in God's words, we ought not to obey him'. He was found guilty at the winter assizes in 1642 and sentenced to a year's imprisonment. After his release, he published a tract against infant baptism in 1644, and the same year he was one of 119 Baptists who signed a church covenant at Smarden.[14] In early January 1649 Cornwell and a number of his fellow Baptists signed a petition from Kent calling for the trial and execution of the King that attracted 1,135 signatures from radical groups in the county.[15] Although by no means an inevitable process, Cornwell's trajectory from rejecting both the authority of the Prayer Book and infant baptism to supporting the regicide is a clear example of the religious and political radicalisation that many people experienced in the 1640s and 1650s. Many other critics of the Church in 1640 and 1641 who were not prepared to accept radical reforms of either state or Church and who felt compelled to support the Crown when war broke out became royalists, while some religious opponents of Charles I accepted the war but baulked at the execution of the King.

II

While religious diversity in mid-seventeenth-century Kent was encouraged by the upheavals of the civil war years, its roots lay in the Reformation period when Kent acquired a national reputation as a centre of religious radicalism. Kent was a county where a 'fast reformation' had undoubtedly taken place in the mid-sixteenth century. The pre-existence of Lollardy in Kent had helped to ease the acceptance of the official Reformation in the 1530s and 1540s. The energies of reforming archbishops, such as Thomas Cranmer, were also a unique contributing factor, since the metropolitan see of Canterbury was seen as a model for other dioceses to follow.

Geography also played a major role, as it was easier for regimes centred at Whitehall and Westminster to enforce religious change in counties closest to the capital. Kent's proximity to London allowed radical religious ideas to infiltrate the county from the metropolis, while contact with the nearby continent encouraged reformed religious ideas to travel along established trade routes. During Elizabeth I's reign, French and Dutch Protestant traders and refugees also set up their own congregations in key economic centres in Kent, such as Canterbury, Maidstone and Sandwich, where they provided models of godly reform.

As a result of these various factors, the enthusiasm for Protestantism in some Kent parishes and pulpits outstripped the expectations of the authorities and by the early seventeenth century strong pockets of nonconformity existed in Kentish parishes near London, in the Weald, and in the major towns and ports including Maidstone, Ashford, Canterbury, Sandwich and Dover. The Wealden parishes tended to be large with scattered populations, where local elites and officials found it difficult to police nonconformist activities. Similarly, urban centres offered conventiclers a certain degree of anonymity.[16] Kent thus offers a striking contrast to more conservative and economically less developed counties in the west, the midlands and the north, such as Cornwall, Herefordshire and Lancashire, where the Reformation was accepted more slowly and where, in some cases, a significant Catholic population survived into the mid-seventeenth century. These were also the areas where there was strong royalist support and where parliamentarianism was more muted than in Kent.[17]

While Kent's religious history bears some similarities to neighbouring counties, such as Essex, Sussex and Suffolk, it also has some unique features which must be taken into account.[18] In the 1630s religious radicalism in Kent was undoubtedly strengthened by the county's direct experience of the Laudian innovations, which were promoted both in the cathedrals and in some parish churches. Kent was the only English county to contain two dioceses, and in the opening stages of the civil war the county's two cathedrals at Rochester and Canterbury were influential centres of support for the Crown and Laudianism. By the mid-1640s, however, the cathedral clergy had been sequestrated and replaced by 'well affected ... and orthodox' ministers who supported the parliamentarian cause.[19] Fears about Laudianism were also reinforced in Kent in the 1630s and early 1640s by the contentious attempt in 1634 to force the independent French and Dutch Protestant stranger congregations in the county to conform to the practices of the English Church.[20] Like London and Norwich, where there were similar large foreign congregations, Kent experienced a local example of the wider Caroline policy of creating religious uniformity in the three kingdoms. During his treason trial in 1644, Laud was accused of suppressing these foreign congregations in order to create discord between the English Church and the continental reformed churches and to give 'papists' the advantage in the 'overthrow, and extirpation of both'.[21]

The belief that Laud was party to a 'popish plot' to ensnare the King and undermine Church and state was widely held by parliament's supporters and was based on the powerful tradition of anti-Catholic polemic that had grown up in England since the Reformation.[22] But anti-Catholicism within Kent should also be read against local experiences. The martyrologist, John Foxe, recorded the burning of forty-one Marian martyrs in Canterbury – a figure that was only exceeded by the forty-six who died in London – and a further eleven martyrs died at Rochester and Maidstone.[23] Such an intense level of religious persecution contributed to the emergence of radical and popular support for the Reformation in Kent both during and after Mary's reign, and left an enduring legacy of local anti-Catholicism that continued to be an active force throughout the civil war period and beyond.

Anti-Catholicism was thus a significant theme in many of the petitions to Parliament from Kent in the early 1640s. In January 1641, for example, Sir Edward Dering received a petition from Canterbury which complained about the tyrannical government of the Archbishop and the cathedral clergy. The petitioners made a clear connection between the altar policy and Catholic practice by emphasising that the new altar in the cathedral was 'dressed after the Romish fashion' with a cloth. The petition was promoted by, among others, Richard Culmer, the curate of nearby Harbledown.[24] During the 1630s Culmer had suffered deprivation from the ministry for over three years for refusing to read the Book of Sports, and in the 1640s he would be one of the leading Presbyterian supporters of Parliament in east Kent. In 1644, in his book *Cathedral News from Canterbury*, he argued that the cathedral clergy had promoted both Laudianism and royal absolutism in their sermons and had attacked Presbyterianism as rebellion against royal government. Culmer also charted the resistance to the 'cathedralists' mounted by the godly townsmen when, in a highly charged act of popular iconoclasm, the new cathedral font was vandalised and the figures of Christ, the Holy Spirit in the form of a dove, and the twelve apostles were removed.[25] The attack took place on Candlemas – 2 February 1642 – the celebration of the purification of the Virgin Mary. Thus, as John Walter has persuasively argued, this was a symbolic purification of the cathedral by the iconoclasts.[26]

Further iconoclasm occurred in Kent's cathedrals at the hands of parliamentarian soldiers both on the eve of war in August 1642 and later under the direction of the Mayor of Canterbury, John Lade, in response to a parliamentary ordinance of December 1643. In 1642 soldiers moved the communion table and broke the altar rails in Rochester Cathedral. Similar action was subsequently taken at Canterbury, where the organs were also pulled down and music books and Books of Common Prayer were torn up. Thereafter the Canterbury clergy prudently abandoned elaborate services in the cathedral and retreated to the chapter house, where they read rather than sang a plain service. Culmer was an active participant in the iconoclasm in Canterbury Cathedral authorised by Parliament in December 1643. He recorded that he broke a stained glass window depicting St Thomas Becket, and that images of Christ and the Virgin Mary were comprehensively destroyed by workmen under the direction of the city authorities.[27] The tensions between popular and official civil war iconoclasm have been elucidated in a number of recent studies and it was clearly important to the parliamentarian authorities to gain control over acts of violence which could be interpreted both as mere vandalism and as rebellion against all authority. In the hands of parliamentarian governors and clerics, iconoclasm was acceptable as a tool of further reformation, but in the hands of the soldiery or the general populace it could be seen as a sign of disorder within Parliament's ranks or even as a deliberate assault on its power.[28]

It was not only the cathedral hierarchy who were associated with Catholic tyranny by the parliamentarians. The Prayer Book was also a target across the country and once again objections to it can be traced back to early criticism of the Elizabethan Settlement, when puritans complained that the 1559 version retained many Catholic usages that were not enjoined in the Bible. The royalist Kentish petition of March 1642 thus noted that the Prayer Book was subject to the 'interruptions, scorns, prophanations, threats and force of such men as do daily deprave it and neglect the use of it in divers churches'. One of the charges against Francis Cornwell was that he had preached in June 1641 that 'there is popery' in the Book of Common Prayer. At Cranbrook the moderate episcopalian Robert Abbot was warned in July 1641 that forty of his parishioners planned to demand that he 'lay down the common prayer book or else they will not come to the church'.[29]

The Cranbrook nonconformists were headed by Richard Robson, a substantial clothier, John Elmestone, the schoolmaster, and Edward Bright, the former curate of Goudhurst who had been suspended in September 1640 for not reading the official prayers against the Scots. Robson and Elmestone had both supported the 1640 Kentish Root and Branch petition and all three men were soon to be accused of attending conventicles in the parish.[30] Although in the early 1640s conformists saw such men as dangerous radicals, during the political purges of the war and post-war years they established themselves as figures of some local political and religious importance, and by the end of the decade they were by the standards of the times exercising conservative influence. In the early 1650s Elmestone published a defence of Presbyterianism against the attacks of a local gentleman, Simon Henden of Benenden, who is probably best described as a Seeker.[31] Edward Bright meanwhile had instigated a successful power struggle against a group of local conformist clerics. He branded his replacement at Goudhurst, James Wilcock, as 'popish' not only for using the Prayer Book, but also for wearing the surplice, using the cross in baptism, and kneeling and bowing during divine service. With Parliament's support, he engineered a coup against both Wilcock and Robert Abbot; and by May 1642 he had been appointed as a lecturer not only at Goudhurst and Cranbrook, but also at a third Wealden parish, Brenchley, while his erstwhile opponents were driven out of their parishes. By 1646 Bright had been installed as vicar of Goudhurst, a post he retained until Wilcock reclaimed the living at the Restoration.[32]

Such disputes among the clergy illustrate not only the intense power struggles which took place between conformists and their opponents before the war broke out, but also how as the war progressed the Presbyterian clergy became established, even conservative figures. They also tellingly illustrate the increasingly active participation of laypeople in religious and political affairs. During their battle with Bright, both Abbot and Wilcock were opposed by considerable numbers of local nonconformists. Conventicles in Cranbrook were attended by men and women from the neighbouring Wealden parishes of Goudhurst, Biddenden and Benenden, and included local gentlemen, yeomen, husbandmen, weavers, clothiers, labourers and a mercer.[33] Along with his patron, Daniel Horsmonden, the rector of Goudhurst and Ulcombe, Wilcock had also acted as a witness against a group of a hundred or so local people who were charged with meeting privately in Ulcombe 'for the purpose of denigrating and opposing the king's authority in ecclesiastical causes'. Among this group was John Turner, a chandler of Sutton Valence, who had a long track record of separatist activity dating back at least to 1624, when he had refused to have his child baptised. A great opponent of tithes, Turner had spent fourteen years in prison between 1626 and 1640 for his opposition to the established Church. In the mid-1630s Archbishop Laud had accused him and his associates of influencing some of the 'poorer sort' around Ashford to hold separatist conventicles. Robert Acheson has described him as 'an early and significant torch-bearer for congregationalism in Kent', whose career is valuable in tracing the links between separatism in the 1620s and 1630s and the 'formed' churches of the 1640s and later.[34]

Petitioning and attendance at conventicles were just two of a number of ways in which large groups of laity in Kent registered their discontent with both the established Church and the conformist clergy in the early 1640s. Some laymen and women also went so far as to appropriate one of the key functions of the ministry by preaching. In March 1642 and on several other occasions, the curate at Sevenoaks, William Turner, was interrupted while preaching by James Hunt, a local husbandman who had pursued his calling as a lay preacher from about 1636. Hunt had appeared before the Court of High Commission in 1640 when he was described as a 'fanatic and frantic person ... who took it upon himself to preach and expound the scriptures' while standing on a stone in St Paul's churchyard in London. He was committed by the court to the London Bridewell, where he later claimed to have been imprisoned eight times. From 1641 onwards he set out his beliefs in a number of pamphlets, in which he opposed episcopacy as an unreformed Catholic institution and described the bishops as agents of the devil. In a familiar puritan vein, he also criticised those conformist clergy who could do no more than read from the Prayer Book. Like John Turner, Hunt was also an opponent of tithes, arguing conventionally that, while they were to be paid under the law of the Old Testament, they did not belong to the priesthood of Christ, and that money should only be paid voluntarily to 'true preachers' by their congregations. His writings were, however, to become increasingly repetitive and incoherent as the 1640s progressed and he appears to have had no local following.[35]

Lay preachers like Hunt who had not been formally ordained were seen as difficult to control and regarded with particular hostility by the civil powers in the 1640s. Fear of unregulated preaching also helps to explain the almost universal hostility later encountered by the Quakers, who had no ordained ministry and maintained that all believers who were moved by the Inner Light could speak in public. The ordained clergy of all persuasions saw the activities of lay religious leaders as a particular mark of dishonour; this was reinforced when women were involved, since they were seen as the weaker sex both intellectually and morally. The allegation that women were active within a sect was a long established way of smearing religious opponents that can be traced back to the days of Lollardy and the early Reformation in England. Robert Abbot thus claimed that his opponents in Cranbrook wished to place authority in the hands of the entire congregation, 'both men and women'. Similarly, James Wilcock denigrated Bright's followers as 'Mechaniques only, ignorant and unlearned Tradesmen, Women and Children', whereas he claimed by contrast to have the support of the 'Gentlemen and Scholars' in the parish.[36] At the end of the revolutionary period, the Presbyterian Thomas Danson ridiculed female Quakers for their inability to defend their preaching against the Pauline prohibitions against women speaking in church. He jeered when one unmarried woman argued that St Paul's rules related to married women only and another claimed that, as she was neither a Roman nor a Corinthian, 'what Paul wrote to them, was nothing to her, unless the spirit within her did prompt her to do the same things'.[37]

Despite the fierce criticisms of Danson and others, some women did preach on frequent occasions. In 1641 the preaching of Joan Banford of Faversham and Susan May of Ashford was vilified by an anonymous pamphleteer. In 1646 Thomas Edwards, the Presbyterian apologist and heresiographer, complained of 'a preaching woman, an Anabaptist, who doth meet other women' in the parishes of Brasted and Westerham in Kent.[38] Although the radical Independent minister of Brasted, John Saltmarsh, denied that he encouraged women preachers, other Kent radicals were prepared to allot women a public religious role. Francis Cornwell intimated that women had been allowed to administer communion in the primitive church when he wrote that 'there were women in the first constituted church after the apostolic order: Acts 1: 14 and had a right to the breaking of bread as well as the men'. Richard Coppin, preacher at Rochester Cathedral and suspected Ranter, wrote in 1659 that 'a woman creature may have freedom to speak and answer as a man'.[39]

III

The importance that the parliamentarian authorities gave to the control of preaching was reflected in the policy of clerical ejections, which was initiated by a House of Commons select committee, chaired by Sir Edward Dering, set up in December 1640 to consider ways of replacing 'scandalous ministers', meaning insufficient or Laudian clergy. The Commons had called for its members to supply information about the state of preaching in their counties, and Kent is one of the few counties, along with Herefordshire, where substantial numbers of these parish complaints have survived. Many of the allegedly 'scandalous' priests in Kent were accused of neglecting their cures and rarely or never preaching, while some were accused of aggressively adopting the Laudian innovations of the 1630s, particularly the railed altar.[40]

After war was declared by Charles I in August 1642, Parliament could do little to replace preachers in royalist counties in the west country, the midlands and the north, but there were considerable changes in clerical personnel in the counties under its control around London and in the south-east of England. This was particularly the case in Essex, Suffolk and Kent, where some clerics fell foul of the parliamentary authorities because they had read the declarations and proclamations from the King from their pulpits.[41] There was also a specific purge in Kent after the failed rising there in the summer of 1643, when an estimated four to six thousand armed men gathered around Ightham, Sevenoaks, Aylesford and Faversham.[42] The rebels' central concerns included the desire for the continued use of the Book of Common Prayer, hostility to puritan ministers intruded into parishes by Parliament, and opposition to a recently imposed parliamentary oath of loyalty. After the rapid defeat of these Kent insurgents, seven ministers were sequestrated for encouraging the rebellion.[43]

These continuing ejections opened preferment to a new generation of young radical clerics and to older men whose careers had previously been blocked by their nonconformity. But ministers intruded by Parliament did not necessarily receive a warm welcome in their new parishes. When the Presbyterian naval chaplain Samuel Annesley was intruded into the living of Cliffe at Hoo in 1645, some of his parishioners greeted him armed with 'spits, forks and stones'. The previous year a 'hurliburli' was orchestrated in St James's Church in Dover against Mr Vincent, 'a godly able minister ... sent thither by Parliament'. The tensions that were caused at parish level by such intrusions were particularly clearly illustrated at Minster in Thanet, where Richard Culmer was appointed minister by Parliament in 1645 in place of one of the cathedral prebendaries, Meric Casaubon. Although he was welcomed by a few of his new parishioners, Culmer's Presbyterian ministry was opposed by both local royalists and Independents. The latter were active in lobbying both the county committee and Parliament against him and refused to pay tithes to him. Culmer's traditionalist parishioners, meanwhile, dubbed the *Directory for Public Worship* 'the Round-headed kind of service', and as Culmer was conducting a wedding he was interrupted by the groom, who claimed 'he did not say right'. Relations between Culmer and his 'Prayer Book parishioners' were thus highly confrontational and Culmer declared that 'he would not be chaplain to the worms, to say grace before they go to dinner and feed on the dead corpse'. On one occasion, his unsympathetic refusal to read the burial service at the graveside was met with threats to bury him alive.[44] As well as the issue of the Prayer Book, the pursuit of traditional festive rites and celebrations also divided the parish.[45] Culmer opposed the traditional maypole, and his refusal to preach on Christmas Day provoked an assault on him in the churchyard.

In 1647 Parliament's order that traditional Christmas celebrations should not be observed led to similar confrontations in Canterbury parishes, which then developed into widespread unrest in Kent in the summer of 1648. As the crisis deepened, Culmer used his influence to persuade some of his Thanet parishioners to support Parliament by arguing that parliamentary taxation was necessary and that the army was a safeguard against 'bloody wolves in Ireland, papists, atheists etc'. But the split in his parish was evident as some of his parishioners called for pen and ink to subscribe a petition against Parliament. When the fighting of the second civil war broke out in Kent and Essex in the summer of 1648, Culmer fled to London. He soon returned under the protection of two thousand soldiers commanded by Sir Thomas Fairfax, who quelled the anti-parliamentarian forces at the battle of Maidstone. During his short absence the royalist faction in his parish had obtained the services of a minister who used the traditional service book, but his occupancy proved short-lived as Culmer was reinstated. He continued to experience problems in the parish throughout the 1650s, as some of his parishioners refused to pay tithes, while he was obliged to pay a fifth of his stipend of £200 to the previous incumbent. Like many other intruded ministers, he was finally ousted in 1660 on the return of Meric Casaubon to the parish he had been forced to leave fifteen years earlier.[46]

At the county town of Maidstone another prominent Presbyterian, Thomas Wilson, achieved considerably more success in his ministry than Culmer, principally because he was fully supported by the town's godly elite. He was appointed lecturer in the town by Parliament in 1642, and vicar there in 1644 as a replacement for the royalist Robert Barrell. He had been vicar of the nearby parish of Otham since 1631, where the patron was George Swinnock, a puritan member of the Maidstone civic elite. With the support of a succession of godly mayors, Wilson exercised firm moral and religious control over the town until his death in 1653. Previously 'morris dancing, cudgel playing, Stool-ball, crickets and many other sports' had been allowed 'openly and publicly on the Lords Day', but now Maidstone became a centre of godliness, where the Lord's Day was strictly observed. Although an Independent congregation also grew up in Maidstone, the Presbyterians continued to dominate the town well into the 1650s.[47]

Wilson and Francis Taylor, minister of Yalding, were chosen as the Kent representatives to the largely Presbyterian Assembly of Divines, which met from 1643 to advise Parliament on religious reform. The two men were influential advocates of the Presbyterian agenda at Westminster. Wilson had preached a sermon against Laud to the House of Commons in 1642, in which he argued against the divine right of bishops. Taylor later preached two sermons to Parliament in October 1645 and May 1646, in which he argued for the erection of a Presbyterian Church system and urged the MPs not to succumb to the arguments of the Independents. In the first of these sermons, to the Commons, Taylor argued a clear case for resistance to the Crown, declaring that both the authority of the MPs and the Solemn League and Covenant of 1643 legitimated Parliament's defence 'against the personal command of Princes'. In his second sermon, to the Lords, he claimed that the toleration of the Independent sects would leave scope for '10,000 errors to be taught contrary to God's word'.[48]

Although the abolition of episcopacy by Parliament in 1646 was officially accompanied by the erection of a national Presbyterian Church, there is scant evidence that such a system ever functioned in Kent. The strength of the gathered churches as well as the survival of support for episcopacy may have persuaded the county committee not to press ahead with parliament's plans in the county. Hostility between Presbyterian and Independent clergy also mounted as the first civil war drew to a close and some of the county's Independent leaders were decried by Thomas Edwards in his infamous 1646 work, *Gangraena*, where he recorded the 'errors, heresies, blasphemies and pernicious practices' of the Independents and cast Presbyterianism as religious orthodoxy. Among his targets in Kent were the layman, John Turner, and the clerics John Saltmarsh, Francis Cornwell and John Durant.[49] Saltmarsh had left Kent by May 1646 and served Sir Thomas Fairfax as a chaplain until his death at the end of that year. As we have seen, Cornwell was influential among the Kent Baptists.

John Durant had served initially as a parliamentary naval chaplain before becoming an acknowledged leader of Independency in East Kent. In 1643 he was appointed to a lectureship at St Peter's, Sandwich, through the considerable influence in the county of the Earl of Warwick, Lord Warden of the Cinque Ports from November 1643 until April 1645 and commander of the parliamentarian navy. In 1646 Durant became pastor to an Independent congregation that had recently been founded in Canterbury by nine laymen who had covenanted to 'walk one with another in the exercise of the worship of the gospel'. In 1649 he was made rector of St George's, Canterbury, and in 1656 became one of the six preachers in the town's cathedral. In *Gangraena* Thomas Edwards accused Durant of preaching that the King should be treated as a prisoner in chains after his defeat in the first civil war, and much later he was said to have promoted the Kent petition calling for Charles I's execution. In fact there is no evidence that Durant even signed the petition, although some of the founder members of his Canterbury congregation, including William Buckherst, Zachariah Lee and Josias Nichols, did.[50]

This 1649 petition marked a crucial split between the Independents and the Presbyterians in Kent. Whereas such Presbyterian clerics as Richard Culmer, Thomas Wilson and Edward Bright had signed the 1642 Kent petition calling for further religious reforms, the later petition was signed almost exclusively by Independents. The petitioners included men who had risen to prominence during the 1640s in the urban oligarchies of east Kent towns, such as Sandwich, Canterbury and Hythe.[51] They were headed by

William Kenwricke of Boughton under Blean, who represented Kent in Barebone's Parliament in 1653. Although the members of this assembly were not elected but chosen by Cromwell and the council of army officers, Kent was one county where the Independent church congregations did successfully nominate some of their representatives.[52]

IV

The local dominance of the Independents following the execution of the King did not, however, herald the total exclusion of the Presbyterians from positions of influence in Kent in the 1650s. Instead the spread of radical religious and political ideas in the county associated with the Ranters, Quakers, Muggletonians and Fifth Monarchists, along with the continuing but ill-focused threat from royalism, forced the Presbyterians and Independents into an uneasy alliance throughout the Interregnum. Presbyterian clerics such as Culmer and Francis Taylor continued to officiate in their parishes throughout the 1650s, and in 1655 a group of Presbyterian clerics joined with religious radical, Major-General Thomas Kelsey, to bring the only prosecution in Kent for blasphemy in the period against the suspected Ranter, Richard Coppin.

The Ranters have been the subject of much recent debate among historians. It is clear enough that there was no formal Ranter organisation such as that developed by the Quakers in the 1650s, but J. C. Davis has gone further in arguing that Ranterism as a coherent set of ideas and values did not exist and was the fabrication of the sensational press and the heresiographers of the early 1650s. Ranters were characterised by their opponents as antinomian and pantheistic and were believed to reject both the force of the moral law and the authority of the Bible. Between 1652 and 1656 the cathedral pulpit at Rochester was dominated by two men, Joseph Salmon and Richard Coppin, both of whom have been identified as Ranters or 'near-Ranters' by a number of historians, including Christopher Hill. As Davis persuasively argues, however, the evidence for these identifications is tendentious.

Salmon was a New Model Army chaplain, who was briefly imprisoned for his preaching in Coventry in 1650 at the same time as Abiezer Coppe who, along with Laurence Clarkson, was widely identified by contemporaries as a leading Ranter.[53] After his release he moved to Rochester in 1652, but there is little evidence of any preaching activities there. More is known about his successor, Richard Coppin, who replaced him in 1655. Coppin also had links with Coppe, who had provided a preface for his *Divine Teachings* published in 1649. His preaching at Rochester alarmed the local Presbyterian clergy so much that in October 1655 they set up a weekly lecture in the cathedral as a counter to him. In December of that year a group of local Presbyterian ministers including Walter Rosewell, curate of Chatham, and Daniel French, curate of Strood, engaged Coppin in a four-day disputation. They attacked him as a heretic and blasphemer for stating among other things that all men were potentially saved, that heaven and hell were to be located solely in men's consciences, and that there was no bodily resurrection. While characterising Coppin as a Ranter, they were also concerned to associate him with Catholicism for preaching universal salvation. This was the most high profile disputation to take place in Kent in the revolutionary period and was attended by William Pask, the Mayor of Rochester, Captain Smith, the local military commander, and George Robinson, a local JP and future mayor of the city. After the disputation Coppin ignored an order from the county committee not to preach in the cathedral and was committed to prison by Major-General Thomas Kelsey under the terms of the Blasphemy Ordinance of 1650 – the only recorded use of the act in Kent.[54] Kelsey informed Cromwell that he feared many of the soldiers at Rochester and some of their officers were infected by Coppin's beliefs and asked him to exile the preacher and replace the soldiers.[55] Coppin's printed defence of his beliefs did little to impress the Cromwellian authorities, and over a year later in July 1657 he was committed at the assizes until he paid a fine.[56]

From 1655 onwards local officials were also alarmed by the spread of Quaker beliefs in Kent. Quakers were seen as dangerous social levellers, who encouraged their adherents to preach and address public meetings to spread their subversive views. The first Quaker missions into Kent took place in 1655, when John Stubbs and William Caton travelled to Dover and addressed local congregations there, including the Baptists. They also held meetings at Luke Howard's house, where several were 'convinced of the truth'. From Dover they moved on to Folkestone, Hythe, Romney and Lydd where they met Samuel Fisher and 'several more' who were 'convinced of the Truth of God'. They then moved on via Ashford to the Weald, visiting Tenterden, Cranbrook and Staplehurst. In these last two parishes they encountered 'a very open people', who were ready to receive their message. Caton paints a story of striking success, with meetings being established in most of the places that they visited. On their way to Maidstone, Stubbs and Caton encountered a large Baptist meeting and they then split up to address the separate Presbyterian and Independent congregations in the town. Their reception in the Presbyterian-dominated Maidstone was the most hostile they encountered. Both men were put in the stocks and 'desperately whipped'. After some time without food they were accompanied by parish officers to the outskirts of London. But two or three days later they returned into Kent and travelled to Canterbury, where they were well received by both the Baptists and the Independents and where Caton claimed that another meeting was established.[57] The leading Quaker evangelist, George Fox, also travelled into Kent later that year and visited Rochester and Cranbrook. At Rye he encountered Samuel Fisher and an 'abundance' of Baptists, recording in his journal that 'a great convincement there was that day'. He then pressed on to Dover and Canterbury and back to Cranbrook.[58]

There is also some evidence at this time of support in Kent for Ludowicke Muggleton. He and his cousin, John Reeve, experienced a religious conversion in 1652 and thereafter styled themselves as the two witnesses in the Book of Revelations who would proclaim the Second Coming of Christ.[59] After travelling from London into Kent in 1656, Reeve made contact with a small group of adherents around Maidstone that included a heel-maker named Christopher Hill and the family of a tanner named Thomas Martin who lived in East Malling. Reeve's death in 1658 left Muggleton as the leader of the movement and in 1663 he married Martin's daughter, whom he described as 'very zealous and strong' in her belief of his 'commission of the spirit'.[60] In 1676 it was reported that at Ashford and other nearby places in Kent there were about thirty Muggletonians. At the same time it was reported that there were Fifth Monarchists in the parish of Boughton Monchelsea. Extreme millenarians who believed that the violent overthrow of civil power would precede the second coming of Christ, from the early 1650s Fifth Monarchists were seen by successive regimes as a serious threat to political stability. In 1656 it was believed that their agents were operating in Sandwich and a group was also apparently in existence in Canterbury in the 1660s. Like the Muggletonians, however, they were never a large body in Kent.[61]

V

Despite the spread of such radical religious beliefs in Kent, particularly among the middling sort, there is also strong evidence of a continuing attachment to traditionalism in the county throughout the revolutionary period. In 1642 the royalist Kentish Petition drawn up at the March Assizes called for the quiet enjoyment of the liturgy of the Church of England 'with holy love embraced by the most and best of all the laity'. The petition was largely drafted by Sir Edward Dering and Sir George Strode and was supported by the royalist grouping in the county led by the cavaliers Richard Lovelace and Sir William Butler.[62] We have already seen how Culmer's traditionalist parishioners confronted him over the use of the *Directory* after its introduction in 1645. Most conservatives had little alternative but to worship according to the new service book if their minister adopted it, but some gentry families were able to pay for the private conduct of Prayer Book services. In the 1640s the Fogges of Tilmanstone made use of both the Prayer Book and the new *Directory*. Richard Fogge recorded the christening of his son, Richard, in October 1643 using the Book of Common Prayer 'and signed by ye cross' by Thomas Russell, whom he described as 'a great cavalier'. The christening took place in a chamber over the kitchen at his house at Danes Court, with Sir Thomas Peyton, a leading royalist agent in Kent, and Edward Belke standing as godfathers, and the child's aunt, Ann Fogge, as godmother. By March 1645 the family was using the *Directory* when a daughter, Jane, was christened 'after the new fashion', but when Ann Fogge married Christopher Boys of Uffington in the summer of 1649, 'Mr Hart married them the old way' at Tilmanstone church using the Prayer Book.[63]

John Evelyn similarly recorded the covert christening in the early 1650s of his children and the churching of his wife in the library at his home of Sayes Court in Deptford by Richard Owen, the sequestered minister of Eltham: 'I always making use of him on these occasions, because the parish minister durst not have officiated according to the form and usage of the Church of England to which I always adhered'. Evelyn continued to make private use of the services of Owen and Jeremy Taylor to take communion or celebrate 'solemn feasts'. Alternatively, he travelled to London 'where some of the orthodox sequestered divines did privately use the common prayer, administer sacraments etc'. He also catechised and instructed his family at home 'those exercises universally ceasing in the parish churches ... all devotion now being placed in hearing sermons and discourses of speculative and notional things'. Confessing that he only went to the parish church in Deptford to avoid suspicion that he was a 'papist', in January 1653 he described Thomas Malory, the incumbent at Deptford, as 'somewhat of the independent', but a 'peaceable' man, who preached 'sound doctrine'. He was less impressed in December 1653 when a 'tradesman, a mechanic' stepped up to preach in the church; he had imbibed Fifth Monarchist tenets and argued that 'now the Saints were called to destroy temporal governments; with such feculent stuff'. In the 1650s Evelyn also reported that, as churches were not permitted to open on Christmas Day, his family celebrated the feast at home. In 1657 he was arrested and interrogated by army officers for privately celebrating Christmas Day in London at Exeter House Chapel with a number of other like-minded communicants, though after twenty-four hours in custody he was set free.[64]

VI

The restoration of the Stuart monarchy saw the reinstatement of many of Kent's royalist and Anglican clergy, and around sixty-two intruded and dissenting incumbents were ejected from their livings in the county under the terms of the Act for Confirming and Restoring of Ministers of 1660 and the Act of Uniformity of 1662. Nevertheless, the dissenting tradition also remained strong, and in 1672 licences for nonconformist worship were taken out in fifty places in the county.[65] Four years later the Compton Census revealed that at least fifty-five parishes in the diocese of Canterbury contained Quakers and at least ninety-one contained Baptists; fourteen contained Presbyterians and fifty, Independent congregations.[66] The census cannot reveal the exact numbers of dissenters, as it did not cover all parishes and some incumbents failed to distinguish between different non-conformist groups. It does, however, demonstrate a baseline for the continued presence of nonconformity in east Kent.

This nonconformity would continue to be a major factor in post-Restoration politics and Kent's county and urban elites were subjected to periodic religious purges from the 1660s until the 1680s. For the restored monarchy, the religious beliefs of the inhabitants of Kent were not simply a matter of private conscience, for religious conformity and obedience was once again seen as the cornerstone of civil authority and it was widely feared that religious diversity would also generate political opposition. Such fears were particularly acute in Kent owing to the geographic, strategic and administrative importance of the county. Nonetheless, the strong survival of the dissenting tradition in Kent demonstrates that the religious and political freedoms won by the inhabitants during the 1640s and 1650s would not be relinquished lightly. For the religious debates of the revolutionary period had involved not only gentlemen such as Henry Oxinden, Sir Edward Dering and John Evelyn, but also the shoe-maker, Luke Howard, women preachers such as Joan Banford, as well as many other tradesmen, clothiers, farmers and labourers. The traditional structures of political and social authority exercised by the gentry and the clergy had been challenged as lay men and women negotiated their own forms of religious worship, moving freely between different congregations and even taking on the roles of religious teachers. In Kent, as elsewhere in the country, the English Revolution had released the genie of individual religious liberty, which successive early modern regimes had struggled to keep bottled up before 1640. Despite the repression of the later Stuart period, it would prove impossible to undo the effects of those years in which so many different groups had achieved new levels of self-expression and self-definition.

Notes

1 D. Gardiner (ed.), *The Oxinden Letters, 1607–1642* (London, 1933), p. 257. I am grateful to Richard Eales and Christopher Durston for their comments on this chapter.

2 For the variety of belief in east Kent, see R. Acheson, 'The Development of Religious Separatism in the Diocese of Canterbury, 1590–1660', unpublished PhD thesis, University of Kent, 1983. Partly because of the paucity of documentation, there is no comparable study of the diocese of Rochester in west Kent for this period.

3 J. Eales, 'Kent and the English civil wars, 1640–1660' in F. Lansberry (ed.), *Government and Politics in Kent, 1640–1914* (Woodbridge, 2001), pp. 4–5, 17, 19.

4 M. Zell, 'The coming of religious reform', and M. Zell, 'The establishment of a Protestant church', in M. Zell (ed.), *Early Modern Kent, 1540–1640* (Woodbridge, 2000), pp. 177–244. For Cranbrook see L. Flisher, 'Cranbrook, Kent, and its Neighbourhood Area, c.1570–1670', unpublished PhD Thesis, University of Greenwich, 2003.

5 G. Nuttall, 'Dissenting churches in Kent before 1700', *Journal of Ecclesiastical History*, 14 (1963), 175–89.

6 John Saltmarsh, *Smoke in the Temple* (2nd edn, London, 1646) p. 61. For Saltmarsh, see L. Solt, 'John Saltmarsh: New Model Army chaplain', *Journal of Ecclesiastical History*, 2 (1951), 69–80.

7 Luke Howard, *Love and Truth in Plainness Manifested* (London, 1704), pp. 1–30. For Howard, see Acheson, 'Development of Religious Separatism', pp. 115, 230, 244–50.

8 Samuel Fisher, *Infant's Baptism Maintained: Or a True Account of the Disputation held at Ashford in Kent, July 27 1649* (London, 1650), A2r. For Fisher, see Acheson, 'Development of Religious Separatism', pp. 219–23, 256–9.

9 L. Larking (ed.), *Proceedings, Principally in the County of Kent*, Camden Society, 80 (1862), 235–6, 182–3, 185, 236. For the altar policy, see Kenneth Fincham, 'The restoration of altars in the 1630s', *Historical Journal*, 44 (2001), 919–40.

10 Larking (ed.), *Proceedings ... in the County of Kent*, pp. 25–38.

11 T. P. S. Woods, *Prelude to Civil War 1642: Mr Justice Malet and the Kentish Petitions* (Salisbury, 1980), pp. 77, 80, 81, 83–4, 179, 188, 189.

12 J. Eales, 'Provincial preaching and allegiance in the first English civil war, 1640–6', in T. Cogswell, R. Cust and P. Lake (eds), *Politics, Religion and Popularity* (Cambridge, 2002), pp. 185–210.

13 Ian Green, 'The persecution of "scandalous" and "malignant" parish clergy during the English civil war', *English Historical Review*, 94 (1979), 522–3; Alan Everitt, *The Community of Kent and the Great Rebellion, 1640–1660* (Leicester, 1966), p. 299; A. G. Matthews, *Calamy Revised* (Oxford, 1988), p. xii.

14 J. S. Cockburn (ed.), *Calendar of Assize Records: Kent Indictments Charles I* (London, 1995), p. 438; Francis Cornwell, *The Vindication of the Royal Commission of King Jesus* (London, 1644), p. 7; Acheson, 'Development of Religious Separatism', pp. 212–14.

15 Two contemporary copies of the 1649 petition survive; see Bodleian Library, Tanner MS 57b and Rawlinson MS A298.

16 For radical religious traditions in Kent, see P. Clark, 'The prophesying movement in Kentish towns during the 1570s', *Archaeologia Cantiana*, 93 (1977), 81–90; P. Clark, 'Josias Nicholls and religious radicalism, 1553–1639', *Journal of Ecclesiastical History*, 28 (1977), 133–150, and Acheson, 'Development of Religious Separatism', *passim*.

17 For studies of these counties, see Mary Coate, *Cornwall in the Great Civil War and Interregnum, 1642–6: A Social and Political Study* (Truro, 1963); Jacqueline Eales, *Puritans and Roundheads: The Harleys of Brampton Bryan and the Outbreak of the English Civil War* (Cambridge, 1990); and B. G. Blackwood, *The Lancashire Gentry and the Great Rebellion, 1640–1660* (Manchester, 1978).

18 W. Hunt, *The Puritan Moment: The Coming of Revolution in an English County* (Cambridge, MA, 1983); Anthony Fletcher, *A County Community in Peace and War: Sussex, 1600–1660* (London, 1975); Clive Holmes, *The Eastern Association in the English Civil War* (Cambridge, 1974).

19 *Commons Journal*, vol. 3, pp. 299, 359; *Lords Journal*, vol. 7, p. 10; Patrick Collinson, 'The Protestant cathedral, 1541–1660', in P. Collinson, N. Ramsay and M. Sparks (eds), *A History of Canterbury Cathedral* (Oxford, 1995), p. 200.

20 J. Bulteel, *A Relation of the Troubles of the Three Foreign Churches in Kent* (London, 1645).

21 William Prynne, *Canterburies Doome* (London, 1646), pp. 27, 33, 388–409, 539–43, 504–6.

22 Peter Lake, 'Anti-popery: the structure of a prejudice', in R. Cust and A. Hughes (eds), *Conflict in Early Stuart England: Studies in Religion and Politics, 1603–1642* (London, 1989), pp. 72–106.

23 I am grateful to Tom Freeman for his advice about the figures cited here; see also Zell, *Early Modern Kent*, pp. 242–4.

24 Richard Culmer, *Cathedral News from Canterbury* (London, 1644), pp. 1–3; Larking (ed.), *Proceedings … in the County of Kent*, pp. 119–20. For Culmer, see also J. Eales, *Community and Disunity: Kent and the English Civil Wars, 1640–1649* (Faversham, 2001), pp. 35–43.

25 Culmer, *Cathedral News*, pp. 10–12.

26 J. Walter, 'Abolishing superstition with sedition? the politics of popular iconoclasm in England, 1640–1642', *Past and Present*, 183 (2004), 95, 117–19.

27 *Commons Journal*, vol. 2, p. 841; vol. 3, pp. 299, 359; *Lords Journal*, vol. 7, p. 10; Collinson, 'The Protestant cathedral', p. 200; W. H. Coates, A. S. Steele and V. F. Snow (eds), *The Private Journals of the Long Parliament, 3 January to 5 March 1642* (London, 1982), pp. 222–3; Culmer, *Cathedral News*, *passim*.

28 Walter, 'Abolishing superstition with sedition?', *passim*.

29 For the Kentish Petition, see Woods, *Prelude to Civil War*, pp. 140–4; British Library [hereafter BL], Stowe MS, 184, fol. 43; Cockburn (ed.), *Kent Indictments Charles I*, pp. 420, 448.

30 Larking (ed.), *Proceedings ... in the County of Kent*, pp. 25–6, 90, 142–4; Centre for Kentish Studies, Maidstone, U350/C2/86; Cockburn (ed.), *Kent Indictments Charles I*, p. 449.

31 J. Elmeston, *An Essay for the Discovery and Discouraging of a new sprung schism, raised and maintained by Mr Simon Henden* (London, 1652).

32 James Wilcock, *A Challenge Sent to Master E. B. a Semi-Separatist* (London, 1641), p. 14; A. G. Matthews, *Walker Revised* (Oxford, 1988), p. 209.

33 Cockburn (ed.), *Kent Indictments Charles I*, pp. 449–50.

34 *Ibid.*, p. 439; Acheson, 'Development of Religious Separatism', pp. 142, 158; William Laud, *Works* (New York, 1977), vol. 5, p. 347; John Turner, *No Age Like Unto this Age* (London, 1653).

35 The National Archive: Public Record Office, SP16/434/171; James Hunt, *The sermon and Prophecie of James Hunt* (London, 1641), *A Plain and Brief Discovery of those two beasts that are written Revelation 13* (London, 1643), and *A sermon Gathered and set forth by that Divine Spirit* (London, 1648), pp. 7–8.

36 BL, Stowe MS 184, fol. 27r; Wilcock, *A Challenge*, p. 14.

37 Thomas Danson, *The Quakers Folly Made Manifest to all men* (London, 1664), pp. 58–9.

38 Cited in Acheson, 'Development of Religious Separatism', p. 289. For a recent and comprehensive study of Edwards' work, see Ann Hughes, *Gangraena and the Struggle for the English Revolution* (Oxford, 2004).

39 Hughes, *Gangraena*, p. 201; Cornwell, *The Vindication of the Royal Commission of King Jesus*, p. 15; Richard Coppin, *Michael Opposing the Dragon* (London, 1659), pp. 243–4.

40 *Commons Journal*, vol. 2, p. 54; Larking (ed.), *Proceedings ... in the County of Kent*, pp. 26–38. For Herefordshire, see Eales, *Puritans and Roundheads*, pp. 108–10.

41 John White, *The First Century of Scandalous, Malignant Priests* (London, 1643), *passim*.

42 My account here follows George Hornby's important unpublished research, 'Allegiance in west Kent during the first civil war, 1642–1646'. I am grateful to Mr Hornby for allowing me to make use of this work. See also Everitt, *The Community of Kent*, pp. 187–200.

43 Hornby, 'Allegiance in west Kent', pp. 58–9, 63–80, 97–101, 240–50; White, *The First Century of Scandalous Malignant Priests*, p. 23; Matthews, *Walker Revised*, pp. 209–10, 213–14, 217, 219, 220, 224, 227.

44 Daniel Williams, *The Excellency of A Public Spirit Set forth in a Sermon* (London, 1697), p. 136; Richard Culmer jun., *A Parish Looking Glass for Persecutors of Ministers* (London, 1657), pp. 3, 15–18.

45 For support for the Prayer Book, see Judith Maltby, *Prayer Book and People*

in Elizabethan and Early Stuart England (Cambridge, 1998). For the puritan attempt to suppress festive culture see Christopher Durston, 'Puritan rule and the failure of cultural revolution, 1645–1660', in Christopher Durston and Jacqueline Eales (eds), *The Culture of English Puritanism, 1560–1700* (Basingstoke, 1996), pp. 210–33.

46 Culmer, *A Parish Looking Glass*, pp. 15–18.

47 George Swinnock, *The Life and Death of Mr Thomas Wilson* (London, 1672) pp. 40–1. See also Eales, *Community and Disunity*, pp. 27–34.

48 Thomas Wilson, *Jerichoes Down-Fall* (London, 1643), pp. 6, 10; Francis Taylor, *Gods Covenant the Churches Plea* (London, 1645), pp. 18–20, and *The Danger of Vows Neglected* (London, 1646), p. 22.

49 Hughes, *Gangraena*, pp. 200–13.

50 For Durant, see M. V. Jones, 'The divine Durant: a seventeenth century Independent', *Archaeologia Cantiana*, 83 (1968), 193–204.

51 For the petition, see footnote 15 above.

52 Austin Woolrych, *Commonwealth to Protectorate* (Oxford, 1982), p. 120.

53 J. C. Davis, *Fear, Myth and History: the Ranters and the Historians* (Cambridge, 1986), pp. 31–41; Christopher Hill, *The World Turned Upside Down* (London, 1972), pp. 168–79.

54 Richard Coppin, *A Blow at the Serpent* (London, 1656); Walter Rosewell, *The Serpents Subtilty Discovered* (London, 1656). For Kelsey, see Christopher Durston, *Cromwell's Major-Generals: Godly Government during the English Revolution* (Manchester, 2001).

55 Thomas Birch (ed.), *A Collection of the State Papers of John Thurloe Esq.*, 7 vols (London, 1742), vol. 4, p. 486.

56 J. S. Cockburn (ed.), *Calendar of Assize Records: Kent Indictments 1649–1659* (London, 1989), pp. 233, 267.

57 William Caton, *A Journal of the Life of … Will. Caton* (London, 1689), pp. 14–20.

58 George Fox, *A Journal or Historical Account …* (London, 1694), pp. 150–1.

59 For Reeve and Muggleton, see their entries in the *Oxford Dictionary of National Biography*.

60 T. L. Underwood (ed.), *The Acts of the Witnesses* (Oxford, 1999), pp. 4, 10, 76–7, 81, 93, 193–5, 198.

61 Bernard Capp, *The Fifth Monarchy Men: A Study in Seventeenth-Century Millenarianism* (London, 1972), pp. 77, 215.

62 Woods, *Prelude to Civil War*, pp. 141–2 and *passim*.

63 'A family chronicle of Richard Fogge of Danes Court in Tilmanstone', *Archaeologia Cantiana*, 5 (1863), 112–32.

64 W. Bray (ed.), *The Diary of John Evelyn* (London, 1966), pp. 224–7.

65 Matthews, *Calamy Revised*, p. xii; Nuttall, 'Dissenting churches in Kent before 1700', 179.

66 A. Whiteman (ed.), *The Compton Census of 1676: A Critical Edition* (Oxford, 1986), p. 14.

11

The experience of defeat revisited: suffering, identity and the politics of obedience among Hertford Quakers, 1655–65

Beverly Adams

I

When the Hertford Quaker William Bayly was asked in 1659 to stand surety for his good behaviour, he refused to do other than 'stand in the will of God'.[1] A disregard for secular authority was inherent in the puritan condition, but early Quakers (or, as they called themselves, Friends) carried this to extremes, externalising their disdain with wilful insubordination. Quakers, as a distinct religious group, had been established in Hertford since 1655 and had already embarked on the creation of an exclusive social and spiritual identity. Abrasive and unorthodox in doctrine, they proved more than the Interregnum authorities could tolerate and, taking the brunt of increasing distrust of the radical religious sects, they were persecuted to a greater extent than any other group. Within the county town of Hertford, they and their opponents cultivated potent and conflicting demonologies and by the end of the Interregnum religious and political partisanship had deeply divided the community.

This chapter, which charts the origins of the Society of Friends in Hertford, its struggles with the Interregnum authorities, and its confrontation with the penal code of the early Restoration, has two major themes. Firstly, it will argue that Quakers were not always, as their own propaganda often suggested, *passive* sufferers; rather, by blazing a trail through the penal laws with exemplary defiance they were responsible for waging a campaign that involved active disobedience, challenges to legal devices, and reserving to themselves the benefits of providence. Secondly, it will suggest that Quaker acts of defiance were articulated in two different idioms – spiritual and civic – each expressing a distinct identity. By making a deliberate distinction between these two identities, Quakers drove a wedge into the brittle synthesis of religious and political duty, and undermined the prevailing concept of citizenship by which the state sought to counsel the individual conscience.

II

Hertford's political and religious environment provided an ideal environment for the Quaker 'convincement' of local Protestants. A number of long-term religious developments help to explain the emergence of radical Protestant sects in the 1640s and 1650s. Prophesyings had flourished in the later sixteenth century, and 'sermon-gadding' (the barometer of puritan commitment) had become a county pastime by the 1580s. Following the godly initiatives of the Feoffees for Impropriations in the 1620s, the inhabitants of the county had been fed a diet of populist millenarianism and predestinarian orthodoxy; and after the suppression of the Feoffees, the rise of the Laudians had provoked a bitter process of polarisation and descent into civil war. These trends were reinforced by the events of the 1640s. The county of Hertfordshire was more involved in the civil wars than any other in the Eastern Association, and its county town, which had been staunchly puritan before the conflict, maintained a firm allegiance to Parliament during the civil war years. Throughout the 1640s and 1650s, moreover, when parliamentary appointments to Hertfordshire churches were 'markedly Independent in character', Hertford's churchgoers faced yet greater religious confusion; the thundering ministry of the militant Fifth Monarchist Christopher Feake was followed by a more moderate parish puritanism, and finally they were faced with the challenge of statutory Anglican conformity after 1662.[2]

Renowned as a 'Calvinist heresy-hunter' for his inflexible Presbyterianism and the religious horror stories included in his *Gangraena*, Thomas Edwards was the hard man in the orthodox campaign to reclaim London from the sectaries. A former minister in Hertford, he claimed that the town's spiritual malaise was so severe that the population was vulnerable to any crackpot religious notion. Edwards vented particular hostility against those women of the region who believed they possessed a ministerial vocation, declaring: 'in Hertfordshire ... there are some woman-preachers who ... expound the scriptures in houses, and preach upon texts'. While the decline of church order was in itself deeply shocking to Presbyterians, the fact that women (of whose intrinsic moral and intellectual worth seventeenth-century men were generally unconvinced) were insinuating themselves into this exclusively male preserve was an even greater reason to panic.[3]

III

Liberty of conscience and a refusal to swear oaths or to defer to their social betters were the cornerstones of early Quaker doctrine; if the first of these tenets was a less troublesome concept in the early days of the Interregnum, the others were guaranteed to provoke the authorities. In the traditional framework of authority – a conservative moral construction underwritten by the Church – public duty and individual conscience shared the same moral and intellectual framework, and as the former rested on an idealised *common* good, personal inclination and public obligation were combined.[4] But with the old order torn up by its roots during the 1640s, the integrated framework that had informed both conscience and political loyalty now lacked both intellectual coherence and a normative framework. For the Quakers, there was an inevitable disjunction between public and private duty, and, despite Cromwell's *laissez-faire* religious policy, their enthusiasm for itinerancy, oath refusal and often shocking acts of religious symbolism made them appear ungovernable.

To conservatives it seemed that, along with other wayward and harmful groups, such as Ranters and Socinians, they had 'wonderfully lost their consciences and their wits'.[5] In 1655 and 1656, therefore, orders were issued against vagrancy and a range of social and cultural offences, and in some parts of the country the authorities tendered to Quakers the Oath of Abjuration (intended originally for Catholic recusants) as a means of bringing them to heel.[6] Quakers, however, continued to assemble in increasing numbers, to disturb parish worship, to refuse to take oaths or remove their hats (acts frequently interpreted as contempt of court), and to default on tithe payments.[7] Moreover, in response to their persecution, they were always ready to point to their persecutors' hypocrisy. 'Was not freedom of conscience the great cause of the late wars?' they asked; Christ alone, they maintained, should rule the conscience. For the Quaker Edward Burrough, any attempt by worldly powers to mediate between God and conscience was an offence against 'truth'.[8]

IV

Inspired by the 'Inner Light' and wielding their 'spiritual' weapons with undoubted charisma, from the mid-1650s onwards groups of Quakers sprang up throughout Hertfordshire. In 1655 Quaker meetings were recorded in Baldock and Royston. The same year, after James Nayler had lodged with the town's butcher, Henry Sweeting, and convinced his entire family of the Quaker truth, George Fox registered the existence of a 'fine' meeting in Hertford. At much the same time, the maltster Henry

Stout had his spirit 'broken' by a female preacher in Ware, while his future
wife, Mary Saunders, turned to Quakerism while employed as a maid'
in the Protector's London household. Cromwell and Saunders appear to
have enjoyed a mutual respect; the Quaker chronicler George Whitehead
recounted her intervention with the Protector on behalf of 'suffering
Friends', and Cromwell personally conveyed to her the news that George
Fox had arrived in the capital after release from imprisonment in 1656.[9]

At first, responses to Hertfordshire Quakerism were far from uniform.
Isaac Puller and William Packer, the two Hertford MPs and members
of the county bench during the Interregnum, epitomised the authorities'
confusion over Friends' potential to subvert the state. Puller, a local man
of impeccable godly credentials who was returned to all three protectoral
parliaments, was horrified by James Nayler's Quaker witness in Bristol
in 1656 and favoured his banishment.[10] His parliamentary colleague,
William Packer, an outsider who was appointed deputy major-general for
Hertfordshire in 1656, was far more lenient.[11] But, as Quaker nuisances
multiplied, those like Packer who glossed Quaker intractability with the
'spirit of error' rather than a 'malicious opposition to authority' waned in
influence.[12] In July 1656, as the rule of the major-generals consolidated
its hold on the regions, the Hertfordshire bench was purged, acquiring
fourteen new 'sober and orderly' justices.[13]

As the decade progressed, the names of Hertford Quakers appeared in
the official records with increasing regularity. In July 1657 Henry Stout,
who was chosen to perform jury service for Hertford and Braughing,
refused to be sworn and was fined £5.[14] In April 1658 Henry Feast, an
Essex husbandman who would later join with the Hertford Friends, was
committed to Hertfordshire county gaol until he paid a fine of £5 and
nearly ten shillings in costs for disturbing the minister of Hunsdon church,
an action that had provoked 'uproar' in the congregation.[15] In September
of the same year, another Quaker was held in Hertford gaol and subsequently committed to the house of correction for three months 'for setting
up a paper of truth against a priest'.[16] By October 1658 several more
Quakers were in Hertford gaol; Thomas Harris 'bore testimony' and was
convicted for disturbing ministers, while Nicholas Lucas was imprisoned
for seven months for non-payment of tithes.[17]

As they grew in strength in the east of the county, Friends evoked
considerable popular hostility. The 'rabble' increasingly made them scape-
goats in their communities, and by 1659 Friends were routinely the victims
of physical and verbal abuse. By then, however, they had already developed
a bureaucracy that allowed discrete local groups to identify themselves
as part of a nationwide entity and to coordinate their polemical publications. As a united body, the Hertfordshire Quakers wrote an open letter

to Parliament in 1659 as the guardians of 'the honour and safety of the Commonwealth', asking them to consider whether commissions of the peace should be encouraging attacks on Quakers. They claimed that one Hertfordshire Quaker meeting had witnessed a particularly brutal attack by 'the sons of Belial', aided and abetted by a local justice who encouraged the 'tories' to commit violence. The signatories pointed out that many of them had 'ventured their lives in the late war', and yet did not enjoy the same freedom of worship as other former combatants: 'the true friends of Christ (that cannot be enemies to good government) ... are not only slandered and reviled ... but most cruelly buffeted, beaten and stoned to the shedding of blood'.[18] In the same year, Mary Saunders joined over seven thousand 'handmaids and daughters of the Lord', including 107 from Hertfordshire, in petitioning Parliament against tithes, while the elderly Friend George Huckle was imprisoned for refusing to pay 'smoke money' to his local parish priest.[19] Hertford Quakers were now identified with the seditious opposition as a coherent and visible public menace, and an intercepted letter of July 1659 suggested that local Friends and Anabaptists were arming themselves as political subversives.[20]

V

By the late spring of 1660 the English Revolution was over and the forces of conservatism had triumphed; the only small consolation most radical puritans could take from this turn of events was that Charles Stuart's offer from Breda to allow 'liberty to tender consciences' held out the prospect that the restored monarchy might pursue a programme of religious moderation. In Hertford, the corporation and its judicial system were quickly reappropriated by the restored forces of Church and state. Four days after the proclamation of the King, the corporation ruled that the arms of the Commonwealth in the town hall be replaced with those of the Crown.[21] In September, a former burgess, Joseph Browne, who had been disqualified in 1645 for refusing the Covenant, presented himself at the mayor's court and laid claim to his right of office as a chief burgess. Predictably, the borough court ruled that he had been removed illegally, and reinstated him following the 'willing' resignation of John Prichard.[22] Within a fortnight Browne had been elected Mayor of Hertford.

Much has been written on the Quakers' change of course at the Restoration, not least their articulation of a 'peace principle' designed to convince the government that Friends were radical only in religion and were not politically seditious. Clearly Quakers *were* forced to acknowledge an altered political context but, as Richard Greaves has suggested, the heady outburst of Protestant sectarianism did not evaporate with the

Restoration. While those attached to the objectives of the 'good old cause' were forced to redirect their energies and many Quakers internalised their former 'radical expectation', outwardly there was little change in their behaviour.[23] Hertford Quakers doggedly pursued the same course they had embarked upon before 1660, committing the same offences, developing their doctrines and strengthening their bureaucracy. Both Church and state, however, now determined to confront them.

How were Quaker liberties inhibited by the Restoration state and how were those constraints justified both politically and theologically? The ecclesiastical settlement proved not to be moderate, as Charles had suggested at Breda, but rather political and Erastian. Religious affiliation and public duty were reintegrated to form the irreducible core of loyal citizenship. Moreover, the settlement contained a refurbished theological heart, and the exercise of public authority over private conscience was now to be sustained by a devotional programme of holy living centred on the 'whole duty of Man'.[24] Obedience became the great imperative. Bishop Jeremy Taylor was anxious to point out how during the revolutionary years sovereignty of conscience had led men into a 'bottomless morass of private revelation'.[25] Robert Sanderson, now Bishop of Lincoln, agreed, and declared that for the sake of their consciences subjects were again obliged to observe 'every human law rightly established'. The Protestant sects, which were 'crumbling into fractions and factions, biting and ready to devour one another', should weigh their consciences in relation to the 'public good' and to the 'preservation of Church or Commonwealth in safety ... and order'. It was, he maintained, 'the easiest thing in the world ... for men to pretend conscience when ... not minded to obey'.[26]

Yet there was little consistency in the government approach. The restored King was torn by conflicting impulses: a hatred of zealotry, respect for authoritarian tradition, and the practical demands of his foreign policy.[27] If he personally held the belief that a limited toleration would do far less harm than severe persecution, he also needed to assuage hard-line reactionary sentiments both in Parliament and the Church. As Mark Goldie has shown, there was thus no monolithic opposition to puritanism, no permanent alliance of Crown and altar.[28] Inconsistency of government policy and the patchy local implementation of the penal laws ensured a sporadic, rather than continual, persecution. Nonetheless, those who longed for revenge were given ample ammunition by some radical activists who converted free conscience into a principle of armed resistance. A subterranean network of plotters flourished, and, once Venner's revolt of January 1661 had provided the perfect opportunity to equate nonconformity with treason, the laws against dissent began to multiply.[29] Aware of the danger of guilt by association, later that year six 'God-fearing and sufficient' Quakers from each county promised that their meetings would not be used as a cover for sedition. Guided by the 'peace principle', they declared that if anything was required of them contrary to conscience, they would 'rather suffer than sin by resistance'.[30]

Such promises, however, were disregarded by the government intelligence service, which continued to monitor closely the activities of Quakers with parliamentarian connections. Agents who intercepted their letters were particularly wary of collections of money, fearing that the Quaker habit of mutual aid was a cover for the purchase of arms.[31] As the third anniversary of Oliver Cromwell's death approached in September 1661, the government was concerned that the godly, who were reputed to have forty thousand men 'ready to rise in a moment', might mark the event with a show of force.[32] As a result former New Model Army officers were arrested in Hertford and London, on suspicion of fomenting a 'fresh civil war'.[33]

VI

This account now turns to the culture of Quaker 'suffering' in Hertford and to the evolution of a distinct identity under an invigorated penal code. The surviving sources lean heavily towards Friends' own accounts of their experiences, but, as has been noted by Stephen Roberts in his study of Evesham Quakers, such accounts have a high degree of factual accuracy and can often be corroborated from other sources.[34] To suffer for the sake of conscience was a shibboleth that helped Quakers to achieve a self-conscious identity as a covenanted people. Spiritual struggle was a Christian (and acutely puritan) experience; Quakers anticipated persecution and gained a heightened sense of affirmation in the process. Francis Howgill rallied imprisoned Friends in Hertford and Bristol in March 1661 with the reminder that though they be 'in the war', the triumph would be 'glorious'.[35] But, although they were persecuted in droves, the suggestion that they endured this patiently in the apostolic tradition of 'sheep and lambs in the midst of wolves' requires closer scrutiny. While they expected trouble, they were not necessarily passive victims, and Craig Horle has revealed their canniness in delving into the law, exploiting its loopholes, and lobbying government with irksome regularity.[36]

The question of Quaker *corporate* identity is linked, paradoxically, to their understanding of *individual* conscience. This is an important issue in the wider sense, not only because liberty of conscience has traditionally been equated with *personal* freedom, but because it became a bone of contention within the Quaker movement itself. The early Quaker understanding of an unfettered conscience was not a function of nascent

individualism or a precursor to liberal human rights: 'properly understood, liberty of conscience meant submission to God' and not to 'self'.
For seventeenth-century Quakers, self-interest was actually the negation
of self, and true Christian liberty led not to an abstract freedom but to
submission to God. By subordinating themselves collectively to the Inner
Light, Quakers were claiming elect status as a group. To more orthodox
Protestants, this was a wilful presumption. Furthermore, contemporaries
were sorely irritated at the intimate fellowship which marked Quaker
organisation: their tendency to 'particularise, and sever from the conversation of the honest' savoured of confederacy. Given the contrast
between Nicholas Morgan's finding that Lancashire Quakers retained the
missionary character of the early Friends until well into the 1730s, and
David Scott's contrasting discovery that York Quakers were 'comfortably bourgeois' and integrated into urban society, the *corporate* nature
of Quaker identity in Hertford may hold the key to other aspects of the
town's religious and political development.[37]

Quaker suffering was clearly linked to the character of the judiciary
and its personnel. Chief Justice Hyde claimed at the Hertford Assizes in
1663 that the county bench was often served by 'ignorant justices' given to
'fancy and opinion'.[38] More recently, Craig Horle has uncovered a system
in which the county benches were riddled with the 'amateurish, primitive,
and prejudicial character of local law enforcement'.[39] In Hertfordshire, the
ranks of the JPs at the Restoration included the elder and younger Thomas
Fanshawe, who, clearly exasperated with their lack of power to deal with
intransigent nonconformists, resorted to the Elizabethan and Jacobean
recusancy statutes. This allowed them to tender the Oath of Allegiance to
the monarch and to charge persistent refusers with *praemunire*.[40] Refusal
to swear the oath was a common indictment in Hertford throughout
1660, a judicial ploy to which Henry Stout, Richard Thomas and Henry
Sweeting regularly fell victim.[41] In April 1662, Stout was also presented
at the county sessions for not attending church.[42] This *ad hoc* approach
was soon, however, overtaken by specific legislation aimed at oath-refusal
and alternative meetings of worship. The Quaker Act, which received the
royal assent on 2 May 1662, unleashed a wave of persecution in London
and elsewhere. John Crook, who later joined Hertford Quakers, was the
first to be tried under its provisions.[43]

In October 1662, one month after the Fanshawes had overseen the political cleansing of Hertford corporation under the terms of the Corporation
Act, the borough magistrates expressed reservations about dealing themselves with the town's flourishing Quaker meeting and requested the
county bench to deal with the leading local Friends, Henry Sweeting,
Richard Thomas, John King and Abraham Rutt, the latter two of whom

had just lost their posts as assistant burgesses. In the Friends' own account of the episode, the new borough authorities claimed that Hertford's Quakers were now 'a people too mighty' for their own jurisdiction. The county JP, Sir Thomas Fanshawe, subsequently tendered the Oath of Allegiance to all four, and pointedly exhumed the civil war record of Richard Thomas and his involvement by imputation in the regicide. The prisoners declined the offer of a period of grace in which to consider their position, and a further refusal of the oath gave the jury no choice but to return a guilty verdict, which in Joseph Besse's account, was delivered 'with a faint, low voice'. In their own account, Henry Sweeting and his co-defendants claimed that jurymen and accused had shared a sense of civic solidarity, and that the jury and even some of the more moderate JPs, such as their fellow townsman Henry Chauncy, had sympathised with them and disapproved of the intimidation resorted to by the vindictive Fanshawes. Chauncy, they claimed, had found the task of passing the sentence of *prae-munire* his 'hard misfortune'. The four were subsequently imprisoned for thirty-one weeks over the winter months, a sentence which was commuted the following May following a petition to the King.[44]

The transfer of proceedings to the county bench was undoubtedly a conscious decision to confront Quakers with a more weighty authority. Frustrated magistrates, themselves under scrutiny, were prepared to use any means to make Quakers obey. Hertford corporation had even resorted to buying in information from spies.[45] The reconstituted ecclesiastical courts also now pitched in with their own proceedings and Thomas, Sweeting and Rutt appeared before the archdeaconry court in December 1663 for non-attendance at church. In June 1664 and July and September 1665, they were also presented for refusing to pay church rates.[46] William Fairman, Thomas Prior, Nicholas Lucas and Henry Stout, meanwhile, were presented in January 1664 for assembling in Lucas's 'new meeting house', itself a sign of denominational consolidation.[47] By the mid-1660s Hertfordshire Quakers were experienced offenders; out of 2,405 indictments before the county quarter sessions in this period, non-attendance at church accounted for around a third of the total.[48] Punishments went unrecorded, but it seems safe to assume that the ecclesiastical courts' customary sanctions of penance and excommunication held little meaning for those who already believed the Church of England a corrupt and apostate institution.

VII

By July 1664, the Cavalier Parliament had augmented the penal code against nonconformity with the Conventicle Act. Sir Matthew Hale, the outstanding legal mind of the period, maintained that this new legislation was aimed not at religious meetings but merely at 'seditious conventicles', but his interpretation was superseded by the ruling of the Lord Chief Justice of Common Pleas, Sir Orlando Bridgeman, at the Hertford assizes that the legislation applied to all gatherings 'under colour of religion'.[49] His gloss on the law was a breakthrough in the judicial battle with Quakers and served as a benchmark for local magistrates in subsequent trials. Only six weeks after the act came into force, eight Hertford men (John Blindell, Henry Feast, Jeremiah Herne, Nicholas Lucas, Francis Pryor, Henry Marshall, Samuel Treherne and Thomas Wood) were the first Friends in England to be sentenced to banishment for attending an unauthorised religious gathering.[50] Although he maintained that his intention was to reform rather than punish, Bridgeman relied on circumstantial evidence and even body language to prove that their silent meeting for worship involved conspiracy. Quakers, he claimed, might communicate not by 'auricular sound', but 'by a cast of the eye, or a motion of the head or foot'. Initially, the grand jury found no case to answer, since the worshippers had merely been seated in silence. But, according to the Quaker chronicler, William Smith, they were then intimidated by the bench, and one of the twelve was accused of 'not being purged from his old dregs'. Pressurised to reconsider, they produced a 'true bill', and the trial took its inexorable course to a guilty verdict, Bridgeman directing a conviction on the 'bare proof' of Quaker assembly. The unanimous verdicts were followed by abortive attempts by Bridgeman at conciliation, in which each prisoner was given the option to commute the sentence with a fine. The Hertford prisoners, however, rejected any compromise and the gaoler, William Edmonds, commissioned Thomas May, master of the *Anne* of London, to ship them to the West Indies.[51]

By November 1664, however, the Hertford transportees were still in England, and claiming the intervention of divine providence. No longer aboard the *Anne*, all seven had returned home bearing a certificate from Thomas May, stating that he dared not transport them against their will. 'Providence', he claimed, had 'much crossed' him. Despite repeated embarkations, squally weather and a crew fearful of antagonising God had prevented his setting sail.[52] The prisoners were ordered back to Hertford where, asserting their status as dutiful and loyal Englishmen, they 'thought it expedient' to inform the King that he might find them at home. On the orders of the privy council, they were promptly re-arrested and languished in Hertford gaol for a further seven years.[53]

The Hertford trial and its aftermath had enormous potential for propagandists on both sides. Edward Manning's hostile tract, *The Mask'd Devil*, claimed to be an 'excellent and true description' of these Quaker 'monsters' and how the 'honourable bench ... turned physician' had prescribed a change of air to calm their enthusiasm. In his account, an insurmountable combination of Quaker 'treachery', Thomas May's 'folly' and the sympathy of factious constables in Deal had confounded the attempt at banishment. Moreover, one of the prisoners, Samuel Treherne, had, he claimed, exploited the delay by slipping back to Hertford and acting out a triumphal snub to the authorities, riding about 'like another Nayler at Bristol'. Manning's grudge, however, was probably as much commercial as religious, for he had personally lodged a £700 bond with the Crown to transport the Hertford Quakers. Outwitted by the prisoners and the unhelpful Thomas May, he was forced to lament his 'utter ruin' at the hands of these 'speculative Christians'.[54] The Quakers responded swiftly in print, dismissing Manning's account as 'a very forged lie'. Treherne, they claimed, had not taken advantage of the confusion to slip his leash and return to Hertford on horseback, but had been sufficiently at liberty to walk all the way home from London after which he had been committed to Hertford gaol 'by reason of some blood thirsty men in power'.[55]

VIII

The case created an ugly context for the October county quarter sessions, when Henry Stout, Henry Sweeting and a further nineteen Friends were indicted for a third offence under the Conventicle Act. The county bench, again chaired by Henry Chauncy and including both Fanshawes, encountered another display of Quaker defiance. As in 1662, the shire JPs trespassed on the corporation's jurisdiction and also, in William Smith's account, tampered with the grand jury to exclude the 'more moderate'. But Hertford's Quakers had been briefed by legal experts in the interval since the summer assizes, and the bench now faced a group not of passive sufferers, but well-informed citizens, versed in their rights under English law and willing to be tried by the 'witness of God' in their 'countrymen's consciences'.[56]

Arrested at a silent meeting, the indicted Quakers outlined to a bemused bench their religious practice of waiting in silence 'to receive refreshment' from the Lord. Since a first group of prisoners had been arrested outside the borough, no objection could be levelled at the authority of the court. But a further seven (William Browne, Thomas Crawley, Robert Crooke, Robert Fairman, Francis Hatton, Richard Thomas and Samuel Woolestone) had been arrested within the limits of the corporation, and the Conventicle Act had specifically stated that offences were to be tried where they had been committed. Thus, when asked to plead, the labourer

Robert Crooke entered into a clearly rehearsed dialogue with the clerk of the court, claiming that his status as a royal subject entitled him to be tried by the borough magistrates. Another defendant, Richard Thomas, then elaborated on their rights as inhabitants of the borough. When Fanshawe resorted to precedent, arguing that members of the corporation had been tried by the assizes in August, Thomas responded that the assizes, sitting as a commission of oyer and terminer, encompassed the borough while the quarter sessions did not. Although Fanshawe then denied Thomas the right to 'over rule the court', the determined Hertford brewer proceeded to instruct the court on jury competence, citing Sir Edward Coke as his authority. The bench, however, was unmoved by his legal expertise; Chauncy summed up and after only fifteen minutes and the jury returned a verdict of guilty.[57]

The climax of the day's proceedings came with the trial of Henry Stout. He, too, claimed his accountability only to the borough magistrates; to plead in the county court, he maintained, would force him to breach the privileges of his corporation which he was honour bound to maintain. To prove his point, he came armed with a copy of the Hertford town charter, and was allowed to start reading from its text until the bench realised he had an English and not a Latin copy, at which point they withdrew their permission. The resulting tussle crystallised rival perceptions of Protestant duty, for the restoration of Latin as the language of authority in the early 1660s not only reimposed social distance, but enraged puritans to whom it represented both the language of idolatry and a detested foreign power. Lacking the skill to translate as he read, Stout could not proceed, but he now symbolised not only the proud defender of corporation privilege, but also a patriotic underdog confounded by an elitist establishment.[58]

By proclaiming his civic status, Stout was consciously playing to the gallery. The jurisdiction may have belonged to the county, but the venue in the Hertford market-place was packed with his neighbours and fellow inhabitants. He portrayed himself as a spokesman for all those labouring under an unaccountable local regime, dominated by career politicians, such as the Fanshawes. According to William Smith's Quaker narrative, the trial did not leave the bench unscathed. Smith claimed that while passing sentence, Chauncy appeared 'as smitten of the Lord, and ready to faint away under the sense of his stroke for the wicked works he was about'. The justice may well have been dejected; having already expressed the court's 'particular kindness' for Henry Sweeting, he may have shrunk from banishing his fellow townsmen.

This second trial had functioned as an identity-giving event. That identity, moreover, had been articulated in two distinct idioms: the spiritual and the civic.[59] The county bench continued to prosecute Hertford

Quakers at a steady pace until 1665.[60] Given the absence of the borough Quarter Sessions records for the 1660s, one can only conjecture that the borough magistrates, survivors of the political pruning of 1662, lacked both the will and the moral authority to deal with these men on their own territory. Friends such as Henry Stout were, after all, established tradesmen, 'men of estates and repute', who were vital in this economically fragile community.[61]

William Smith's narratives of the Hertford Quaker trials which endorsed the image of passive suffering were complemented by further stirring publications. The anonymous pamphlet, *The Jury-man Charged*, invoked the hand of providence against jurors who convicted Quaker worshippers without material proof of sedition. The author also exposed the illogical nature of the Conventicle Act, citing countless examples which mocked its provisions. Were the family prayers of a large household in breach of the new law? Were the impromptu prayers of midwives infringing the Church's monopoly over Christian worship? Furthermore, were Quaker meetings of godly fellowship to be equated with meetings for worship? It was, after all, 'common for Quakers ... to visit each other and maybe then to worship'; was this domesticated piety the same as meeting 'under colour of religion'?[62] The Hertford trials, moreover, had created practical difficulties for the government. Thomas May's reluctance to antagonise providence had set a precedent, and in January 1665 the crew of the *Mary Fortune*, like that of the *Anne* before her, being 'smitten by the Lord with a terrible fear', decided they dare not transport 'innocent persons'. Since the forcible removal abroad of Englishmen also risked incurring legal penalties at the other end of the journey, the government opted for the use of merchant shipping for transportation. But, while both Lord Chancellor Clarendon and Bridgeman deemed immediate transportation essential to rid them of 'so many tedious persons', its implementation posed difficulties that the government found hard to circumvent.[63]

IX

How then, did the persecution of Quakers in Hertford relate to the themes discussed at the start of this essay? First, the local context was vital. The town had a vibrant and deep-rooted puritan community; it had been on the front-line during the civil war and after 1660 experienced the vengeful hostility of royalists such as the Fanshawes. From the Quaker perspective, Hertford had been a major focus of activity since the 1650s; the movement's doctrines and bureaucratic procedures were developed and codified in the town, and its adherents there had entered Quaker historiography as high-profile sufferers.

That their demeanour before the courts was essentially passive, however, is not the case. Rather, the Hertford Quakers were provocative witnesses to their faith and identity, rejecting compromises, arrogating to themselves the blessings of providence, and challenging the judicial establishment which interpreted and enforced the penal laws. They also contested the intrusions of the county authorities that deprived them of their civic privileges, and emphasised throughout the moral nature of their actions by attributing them to a godly conscience. They converted every attack into a polemical opportunity, and proclaimed their identity as the reviled people of God with prophetic 'visitations', heart-warming epistles and 'impartial relations' of persecution. Their behaviour throughout was actively defiant.

They did not, however, resist the law from some modern liberal concept of freedom grounded in *self*-determination and innate human rights. Rather they asserted a Christian liberty through which, as both individuals and a corporate fellowship, they might attain spiritual perfection. It is thus probably more appropriate to speak of their 'struggle' than their 'suffering'. The 'struggle motif' was an essential feature of the affective piety that had brought them into being, and they were also 'struggling' against the paternalist moral imperatives of a Church and state that equated public and religious duty. Anxious to be taken seriously as upright citizens as well as individuals who owned an unmediated responsibility for their personal salvation, they claimed that religion was a private matter between God and the individual. Indeed, from the outset they had made a clear distinction between 'those things that are called civil, and such as are called spiritual', and rejected the restored Church's claim to have a pastoral duty to counsel the wayward conscience.[64] Thus, in the course of their bruising encounters with the restored regime and its legal officials, the Hertford Quakers came to reject the Anglican perception of duty and to generate instead their own dynamism and self identity. Thereafter, Quaker energies in Hertfordshire and elsewhere would be channelled into denominational consolidation, mutual aid and corporate discipline.

This dichotomy between the religious and the secular reveals much about the nature of Quaker identity in Hertford. The movement's sense of belonging could be measured along two distinct axes – spiritual and civic – both inward-looking and hostile to outsiders, both societies within societies. Quaker spiritual identity was subsumed into a growing movement whose unorthodox doctrine of the Inner Light forged a sense of shared experience and unity. Their quite separate civic identity, with its enduring puritan heritage, was expressed in a broad hostility to incursions from careerist politicians and those on corporations who pandered to their political agenda. Seen in this light, the claims to civic privilege by Stout,

Thomas and Crooke echoed the popular godly opposition of the 1620s, when puritan members of Hertford corporation had challenged the cosy electoral pact between the Earl of Salisbury and Viscount Fanshawe, and when political invective had been charged with rousing appeals to ancient English liberties.[65]

Quakers were not alone in separating their religious and civic identities. After 1665, the Hertford mayor's court confined itself rigidly to business affairs and the enforcement of social order. Clearly, the town's Friends were integral to the economic life of the community, and if it was now impossible for them to hold office without taking the necessary oaths, they were nevertheless still admitted to the freedom.[66] Similarly, if the penal laws ensured that they could no longer enjoy the full benefits of English citizenship, in Hertford they clearly nonetheless enjoyed a *de facto* toleration in terms of civic experience and continued to join with their neighbours in resisting the encroachments of external authorities. Above all, they experienced this civic identity in parallel with the spiritual solidarity and zeal of a distinct religious movement, combining the social integration of York Quakers with the missionary fervour of Friends in Lancashire.[67] In so doing, they had acquired an identity that reconciled the apparent paradox between the Quaker 'peace principle' and the 'Lamb's War'.

Notes

I should like to record my sincere thanks to John Miller of Queen Mary College, University of London, and to Andrew Barclay, Patrick Little, Jason Peacey and Stephen Roberts of the History of Parliament Trust for their encouragement and for guiding me to some essential source material at the eleventh hour.

1 Bayly was a persistent offender against authority in Hertford after the Restoration; he refused an oath in April 1663, and was gaoled in October 1663 and again the following January for the same offence: see W. Le Hardy (ed.), *Calendar to the Sessions Books and Sessions Minute Books*, Hertford County Records (Hertford, 1930) vol. 6, pp. 81, 94, 100. See also Library of the Religious Society of Friends in Britain [hereafter FHL], Original Record of Suffering [hereafter ORS], fol. 282.

2 Unpublished constituency article for Hertfordshire, History of Parliament Trust; Patrick Collinson, *Godly People: Essays on English Protestantism and Puritanism* (London, 1983), pp. 179, 480; Patrick Collinson, *The Religion of Protestants* (Oxford, 1982), p. 260; *Calendar of State Papers, Domestic* [hereafter CSPD], *1633–4*, p. 344; *Victoria County History of Hertfordshire* [hereafter *VCH Herts.*], vol. 4, p. 351.

3 For Edwards, see Ann Hughes, '"Popular" Presbyterianism', in Nicholas Tyacke (ed.), *England's Long Reformation* (London, 1998), pp. 237–42; and also now Ann Hughes, *Gangraena and the Struggle for the English*

Revolution (Oxford, 2004). For his comments on Hertford, see Thomas Edwards, *Gangraena: A Catalogue of Many of the Errours, Blasphemies and Practices of the Sectaries* (London, 1646), Part 3, preface (unpag.), and p. 84. For the impact of the Revolution on women, see Patricia Crawford, 'The challenges to patriarchalism: how did the revolution affect women?', in John Morrill (ed.), *Revolution and Restoration: England in the 1650s* (London, 1992), pp. 113–14.

4　For more details, see Kevin Sharpe, 'Private conscience and public duty in the writings of James VI and I', in John Morrill, Paul Slack and Daniel Woolf (eds), *Private Duty and Public Conscience in Seventeenth-Century England* (Oxford, 1993), pp. 78, 82; and Collinson, *Religion of Protestants*, p. 251.

5　Blair Worden, 'Toleration and the Cromwellian Protectorate', in W. J. Sheils (ed.), *Persecution and Toleration*, Studies in Church History, 21 (Oxford, 1984), pp. 205–6, 212.

6　Stephen Roberts, 'The Quakers in Evesham, 1655–1660: a study in religion, politics and culture', *Midland History*, 16 (1991), 71.

7　*CSPD, 1658–9*, p. 156.

8　*Ibid.*, p. 148; Edward Burrough, *The Case of Free Liberty of Conscience in the Exercise of Faith and Religion* (London, 1661), p. 5.

9　*VCH Herts.*, vol. 3, pp. 71, 259, vol. 4, p. 356; John L. Nickalls (ed.), *The Journal of George Fox* (London, 1952), pp. 219, 202 n. 2, 274; FHL, Temp MS, 745; FHL, Robson MS, Tr 3, Commonplace Book of Thomas Robson, fol. 94; George Whitehead, *Christian Progress* (London, 1725), pp. 93–4.

10　Unpublished biographical article on Puller, History of Parliament Trust.

11　Christopher Durston, *Cromwell's Major-Generals: Godly Government during the English Revolution* (Manchester, 2001), pp. 28, 208.

12　*CSPD, 1657–8*, pp. 156–7.

13　Durston, *Cromwell's Major-Generals*, p. 78; Thomas Birch (ed.) *A Collection of the State Papers of John Thurloe Esq.*, 7 vols (London, 1746), vol. 5, p. 187.

14　Le Hardy (ed.), *Calendar to the Sessions Books*, vol. 5, p. 492.

15　*CSPD, 1658–9*, p. 162; Le Hardy (ed.), *Calendar to the Sessions Books*, vol. 1, p. 122.

16　*CSPD, 1658–9*, p. 149.

17　*Ibid.*, p. 156; Joseph Besse, *A Collection of the Sufferings of the People Called Quakers*, 2 vols (London, 1753), vol. 1, p. 241.

18　*VCH Herts.*, vol. 4, p. 356; Besse, *Collection of Sufferings*, vol. 1, p. 241; FHL, Tracts 137(35), *To the Parliament of the Common-wealth of England, Now sitting at Westminster* (London, 1659), pp. 1–3.

19　FHL, Tracts 46(3), *These several papers was sent to the Parliament the twentieth day of the fifth moneth, 1659* (London, 1659), p. 55; Edward Burrough, *A Declaration of the present Sufferings of above 140 Persons of the people of God* (London, 1659), p. 8.

20　Birch (ed.), *Thurloe State Papers*, vol. 7, p. 704.

21 Hertfordshire Archive and Local Studies [hereafter HALS], Hertford Borough Records [hereafter HBR], vol. 20, fol. 409.

22 *Ibid.*, vol. 20, fols 228, 410–11.

23 For more details, see Richard L. Greaves, *Deliver Us From Evil: The Radical Underground in Britain, 1660–1663* (Oxford, 1986), p. 227; Richard L. Greaves, 'The nature of the puritan tradition', in R. Buick Knox (ed.), *Reformation, Conformity and Dissent* (London, 1977), p. 273; and Jonathan Scott, 'Radicalism and Restoration: the shape of the Stuart experience', *Historical Journal*, 31 (1988), 457.

24 John Spurr, *The Restoration Church of England, 1646–1689* (London, 1991), pp. 42, 163; John Spurr, 'Religion in Restoration England', in L. K. J. Glassey (ed.) *The Reigns of Charles II and James VII and II* (Basingstoke, 1997), p. 110. The tenor of Anglican devotional literature was encapsulated in Richard Allestree, *The Whole Duty of Man*, first published in 1658. See Spurr, *Restoration Church*, chap. 6.

25 W. K. Jordan, *The Development of Religious Toleration in England*, 4 vols (London, 1940), vol. 4, p. 389.

26 Robert Sanderson, *Nine Cases of Conscience: Occasionally Determined by the late Reverend Father in God, Robert Sanderson, Lord Bishop of Lincoln* (London 1685), pp. 166, 169, 172; Robert Sanderson, *Thirty Four Sermons* (London, 1657), preface, points xxiii, xxiv; Isaak Walton, *The Life of Sanderson* (London, 1678), p. 88. See also K. T. Kelly, *Conscience: Dictator or Guide? A Study in Seventeenth Century English Protestant Moral Theology* (London, 1967), pp. 36–8; and, for the Anglican appeal to Augustine as theological support for coercion, Mark Goldie, 'The theory of intolerance', in O. Grell, J. Israel and N. Tyacke (eds), *From Persecution to Toleration* (Oxford, 1991), pp. 335–48.

27 John Miller, *Popery and Politics in England, 1660–1688* (Cambridge, 1973), p. 110.

28 Mark Goldie, 'Danby, the bishops and the Whigs', in Tim Harris, Paul Seaward and Mark Goldie (eds), *The Politics of Religion in Restoration England* (Oxford, 1990), pp. 75–6.

29 Anthony Fletcher, 'The enforcement of the conventicle acts, 1664–1679', in Sheils (ed.), *Persecution and Toleration*, p. 245 and *passim*; R. L. Greaves, *Enemies Under His Feet: Radicals and Nonconformists in Britain, 1664–1677* (Stanford, 1990), pp. 132–42; see also N. Morgan, *Lancashire Quakers and the Establishment 1660–1730* (Halifax, 1993), p. 61.

30 *CSPD, 1660–1*, p. 361.

31 *CSPD, 1661–2*, pp. 107, 177, 263–4.

32 *Ibid.*, p. 81.

33 *Calendar of State Papers Venetian, 1661–4*, pp. 63–4.

34 Roberts, 'Quakers in Evesham', *passim*.

35 FHL, Swarthmore MSS Transcripts, vol. 7, pp. 211–12.

36 C. W. Horle, *The Quakers and the English Legal System, 1660–1688* (Philadelphia 1988), *passim*. See also J. R. Knott, 'Joseph Besse and the Quaker culture of suffering', in T. N. Corns and D. Loewenstein (eds),

The Emergence of Quaker Writing: Dissenting Literature in Seventeenth-Century England (London, 1995), p. 136.

37 For more details, see Beverly Adams, 'The "durty spirit" at Hertford: a falling out of Friends', *Journal of Ecclesiastical History*, 52 (2001); J. C. Davis, 'Religion and the struggle for freedom in the English Revolution', *Historical Journal*, 35 (1992), 515, 518–19, as well as Davis's earlier contribution to this volume; Margarita Stocker, 'From faith to faith in reason?', in T. G. S. Cain and K. Robinson (eds), *Into Another Mould: Change and Continuity in English Culture* (London, 1992), p. 74; Edward Manning, *The Mask'd Devil, or Quaker Neither Fearing God, nor Reverencing Man* (London, 1664), pp. 3–4; Morgan, *Lancashire Quakers*, p. 280; and David Scott, *Quakerism in York, 1650–1720*, University of York, Borthwick Paper, 80 (York, 1991), *passim*.

38 Scott, *Quakerism in York*, p. 31.

39 Horle, *Quakers*, p. 114.

40 *Ibid.*, p. 49.

41 Besse, *Collection of Sufferings*, vol. 1, pp. 242–3.

42 Le Hardy (ed.), *Calendar to the Sessions Books*, vol. 6, p. 63

43 W. H. Braithwaite, *The Second Period of Quakerism* (York, 1979), pp. 23–4.

44 Henry Sweeting, Abraham Rutt, Richard Thomas and John King, *A Brief Relation of the Persecutions and Cruelties that have been acted upon the People called Quakers In and about the City of London* (London, 1662), pp. 15–16; Le Hardy (ed.), *Calendar to the Sessions Books*, vol. 6, p. 72; Besse, *Collection of Sufferings*, vol. 1, pp. 243–4; *CSPD, 1670 and Addenda, 1660–70*, p. 680.

45 The accounts of the mayor's court for 1662 revealed an expenditure of two shillings 'at the Bell about Quakers' and sixpence at the same venue on 'such as would not go to Church': HALS, HBR, vol. 20, fol. 430.

46 HALS, records of archdeaconry court of Huntingdon, Hitchin division, AHH, 5/19, fols 23–6, 5/20, fol. 2.

47 *Ibid.*, 5/19, fol. 17.

48 See the introduction to Le Hardy (ed.), *Calendar to the Sessions Books*, vol. 6, pp. xxix–xxx.

49 William Smith, A True, Short Impartial Relation ... (London, 1664), p. 4; J. S. Cockburn, *A History of the English Assizes, 1558–1714* (Cambridge, 1972), p. 246; Horle, *Quakers*, p. 107.

50 FHL, ARB (A. R. Barclay) MSS, vols 323–324, fols 88–9.

51 FHL, Swarthmore MS 3, fols 105–6; Smith, *Impartial Relation*, pp. 1–8; H. E., *The Jury-man Charged; or a Letter to a Citizen of London. Wherein is shewed the true meaning of the Statute, Entituled, An Act to prevent and suppress Seditious Conventicles* (London, 1664), pp. 11–12; Besse, *Collection of Sufferings*, vol. 1, p. 245; Horle, *Quakers*, p. 260.

52 Nicholas Lucas *et al.*, *A True and Impartial Narration of the Remarkable Providences of the Living God of Heaven and Earth, appearing for Us his oppressed Servants called, Quakers* (London, 1664); *CSPD, 1664–5*, p. 80.

May's certificate is quoted in Manning, *Mask'd Devil*, p. 12; and Lucas *et al.*, *Remarkable Providences*, p. 8.

53 The National Archives: Public Record Office, PC 2/57, fol. 163r; Besse, *A Collection of Sufferings*, vol. 1, pp. 246–8.

54 Manning, *Mask'd Devil*, pp. 1–23.

55 Lucas *et al.*, *Remarkable Providences*, p. 5.

56 Le Hardy (ed.), *Calendar to the Sessions Books*, vol. 6, pp. 120–1; William Smith, *A Second Relation from Hertford* ... (London, 1673), reverse of title page, and p. 2.

57 Le Hardy (ed.), *Calendar to the Sessions Books*, vol. 6, p. 121; Smith, *Second Relation*, pp. 2–3, 10–11.

58 Stout had been granted the 'liberty' to trade in 'malt and coals' under the mayoralty of the county commissioner, William Turner, in 1658: HALS, HBR, vol. 20, fol. 393; Smith, *Second Relation*, pp. 13–15.

59 Smith, *Second Relation*, pp. 13, 18; FHL, Swarthmore MS 1, fol. 47. None of them was actually sent to the West Indies, but they remained in the county gaol until released by letters patent in 1672: Besse, *A Collection of Sufferings*, vol. 1, p. 250; N. Penney (ed.), *Extracts from State Papers Relating to Friends, 1654–1672* (London, 1910), p. 346; *CSPD, 1671–2*, p. 489.

60 Le Hardy (ed.), *Calendar to the Sessions Books*, vol. 6, pp. 125–6.

61 HALS, HBR, vol. 20, fols 422–3; *VCH Herts.*, vol. 4, p. 357. Henry Stout, Nicholas Lucas and Richard Martin were maltsters; Richard Thomas and William Fairman, brewers; and Henry Sweeting, a butcher: see Violet Rowe, *The First Hertford Quakers* (Hertford, 1970), pp. 49–54. The corporation could not realistically exclude Quakers from the freedom: see A. Greening, '"Needful and necessary men"? Hertford borough freemen, 1640–1715', in D. Jones-Baker (ed.), *Hertfordshire in History* (Hertford, 1991), p. 189 and *passim*.

62 H. E., *The Jury-man Charged*, preface, title-page, and pp. 5–12.

63 *CSPD, 1664–5*, pp. 164, 207, 244, 373, 513.

64 Quoted in Morgan, *Lancashire Quakers*, p. 41.

65 Lawrence Stone, 'The electoral influence of the second earl of Salisbury, 1614–68', *English Historical Review*, 71 (1956), 392; David Underdown, *A Freeborn People: Politics and the Nation in Seventeenth-Century England* (Oxford, 1996), p. 31.

66 For examples, see HALS, HBR, vol. 20, fols 425, 427, 442; vol. 25, fols 6–14.

67 D. A. Scott, 'Politics, Dissent and Quakerism in York, 1640–1700', unpublished PhD thesis, University of York, 1990, pp. 117–20; Morgan, *Lancashire Quakers*, p. 280.

Index

Abbot, George, Archbishop of
    Canterbury 70, 208
Abbot, George, nephew of Archbishop
    208
Abbot, Robert 233–5
Abbott, Robert 108
Abyssinia 29
Acheson, Robert 234
Acontius, Jacobus 53
Act for Confirming and Restoring of
    Ministers (1660) 244
Act for the Relief of Peaceable People
    (1650) 8
Act of Toleration (1689) 15
Act of Uniformity (1662) 15, 168, 244
Albigensians 45
ale houses 120, 168, 208, 210, 214–15,
    217, 220–1
altars 228, 232–3, 236
America, North 2, 57, 121, 210
Ambrose, St 76
Ames, William 83
Amiraut, Christopher 105
Amsterdam 54
Anabaptists 45–6, 61, 102, 108–9,
    181, 186, 189, 190, 194–5, 199,
    208–9, 236, 253
    Dutch Anabaptists 186–7

Angier, John 101
Anglicanism and Anglicans 14, 43, 98,
    106, 131, 145, 150, 152, 158–80,
    262
Annesley, Samuel 237
anti-Catholicism 83, 137–8, 144–5,
    151, 183–5, 232
Antichrist 29, 50, 56, 58, 79, 103, 107,
    183–5, 190, 197, 210
    see also Satan
Antinomians 48, 56, 83, 109, 240
apocalypse 5, 28–30, 78, 184–5, 195
    see also eschatology; millennium
Archbishops of Canterbury 70, 207–8,
    228
Armada Day 164
Arminians and Arminianism 3, 22,
    46, 48–9, 52, 56, 98, 108
army 48, 95, 103, 110, 115, 119, 131,
    190–1, 195, 197, 237, 243
    chaplains 55, 189, 199, 212, 240
    council of army officers 240
    see also New Model Army
Arras College 148
Arundell, Lord 149
Arundell, Sir John 146
Ashe, Simeon 93, 101, 103–4
Ashburnham, John 70

Ashford (Kent) 227–9, 231, 234, 236, 241–2
Ashton, Robert 159
assemblies 95
    Lancashire Provincial Assembly 120, 123, 125, 129
    London Provincial Assembly 123–4, 126
assizes 229–30, 241–2, 256, 258–60
Astley, Richard 145
Astley, Walter 145
Aston, Lady Gertrude 144
atheism 48, 50, 58, 210, 238
augmentations 104–5
Augustine, St 45, 49–50, 61, 76
Austria 29
Aveling, John 139
Axtell, Daniel 194
Aylsford (Kent) 237

Bacon, Francis 29
Baillie, Robert 44, 46, 48, 93–4, 103
Baker, Augustine (Benedictine) 151, 153
Bakewell, Thomas 130
Baldock (Herts) 251
Baltimore, Lord 149
Bampfield, Thomas 215
Banford, Joan 236, 244
banishment 258–9
baptism 12, 99, 102, 161, 163, 166, 176, 227, 234, 243
    believers' baptism 12, 182, 184, 186–8, 196
    infant baptism 56, 182–3, 186–7, 198, 228, 230, 243
    sign of the cross at 234, 243
Baptist polity 181–2
Baptist theology 181–3
Baptists 1, 8, 9, 10, 11, 12, 43, 48–50, 52, 55, 59, 61, 94, 99, 102–3, 108, 151, 181–201 *passim*, 230, 239, 241–2, 244
    Calvinist Baptists 99, 186–7
    General 54–5, 58, 183–8, 191, 195, 199, 227–8

'Independent' Baptists 188
    London Mill Yard Congregation 188
    Particular 55, 183, 185–90, 194–5, 198, 227
    Seventh Day 12, 185–6, 188, 198–9
Barker, Matthew 101, 115
Barkstead, Sir John 24, 220
Barnard, Dr Nicholas 106
Barrell, Robert 238
Bastwick, John 46
Batchelor, John 113
Batcombe (Somerset) 208
Baxter, Richard 105, 108–9, 125, 164, 217
Bayly, William 249
Beake, Robert 216–17
Beale, John 28–9
Beaumont, Agnes 34
Becket, St. Thomas 233
Bedford, Thomas 125–6
Bedford (Herts) 32
Bedingfield, family 140, 146, 150–1
beer 28, 165
    see also ale houses
Belke, Edward 243
Bellasis, Lord 152
bell-ringing 214
Bendenden (Kent) 234
Beoley (Worcs) 140
Berkshire 106
Bermuda 33
Bernard, Richard 208
Bernard, St 76
Berwick 220
Besse, Joseph 257
Best, Paul 58
Beza, Theodore 49–50, 53
Bible 32, 34, 56, 71, 76, 183–4, 185–6, 206, 211, 214, 218, 233, 240, 250
biblical interpretation 71–2, 74–5, 78–9, 121, 183
Biddenden (Kent) 234
Biddle, Hester 71
Biddle, John 53, 58–9, 107, 124

Biddulph, family of Biddulph (Yorks) 145

Bideford (Devon) 113

bishops 3–4, 7, 74, 94, 110, 160, 163, 165, 168–9, 171, 173, 179, 199, 206, 210, 226, 229–31, 235, 254

Bishops' War 4, 44, 74

Blackfriars (London) 208

Blacklo 148–50

see also White, Thomas

Blackloists 148–50, 153

Blandford (Dorset) 165

blasphemy 1, 6, 20, 22, 48, 50–1, 59, 95, 112, 228, 239–41

Blindell, John 258

Bollington (Cheshire) 221

Book of Common Prayer 1, 4, 6, 7, 8, 10–11, 13, 70–1, 112, 161–80 *passim*, 214, 218, 226, 230, 233–5, 237–8, 243, 246

Calendar of 158, 160, 163–4, 166, 168, 172, 174, 176–7, 232, 237, 243

Book of Sports 79–80, 206–7, 213, 232

Booth, Sir George 104

Booth's rising 152

Borlace, Nicholas 146

Boteler, William 59

Boughton Monchelsea (Kent) 242

Boughton under Blean (Kent) 240

Bowles, John 8

Box (Wilts) 221

Boys, Christopher of Uffington 243

Brabourne, Theophilus 206, 213

Bradley (Derbyshire) 117, 127

Braintree (Essex) 216

Bramhall, John, Bishop of Derry 210–11

Brampton 143

Brasted (Kent) 227, 236

Braughing (Herts) 252

Bray (Berkshire) 8

Breda, 253–4

Brenchley (Kent) 234

Bridewell, the London 235

Bridge, William 101

Bridgeman, Sir Orlando, Lord Chief Justice 258, 261

Bridgewater, Earl of 106–7

Bright, Edward 233–5, 239

Brinsley, John 101

Briscoe, Michael 101

Bristol 252, 255, 259

Brooke, Lord 44

Brown, Sylvia 70, 72

Brown, family, viscounts Montague 145

Browne, Joseph 253

Browne, William 259

Brownists 44, 109

Brownrigg, Ralph, Bishop of Exeter 168

Brudenell, Lord 149

Bryan, John 109

Buckherst, William 239

Buckingham, Duchess of 70

Buckingham, Duke of 70

Buckinghamshire 100, 113

Bull, George, Bishop of St Davids 163

Bunyan, John 31–4, 188

Burford 195

Burges, Anthony 127–8, 132

Burgess, Cornelius 26

Burrough, Edward 251

Burroughs, Jeremiah 6, 44, 49, 53

Burton Dassett (Warwickshire) 111

Bushnell, Walter 101

Bushnell, William 221

Butler, Sir William 242

Byfield, Adoniram 101

Cade, Robert 76

Calamy, Edmund 25, 46, 60, 84, 101–2, 104

Calvin, John 45, 49–50, 57, 59, 76, 85

Calvinism and Calvinists 56, 70, 95, 137, 179, 187, 210, 250

Cambridge 108

Cambridge Platonists 43

Cambridgeshire 162, 187

Candlemas, feast of 232

Canterbury (Kent) 165, 227, 229, 231–3, 237, 239, 241–2, 244
Canterbury, Archbishops of 14, 230, 232
capitalism 2
Capp, Bernard 69
Cardell, John 27
Caryl, Joseph 99, 101
Case, Thomas 121
Castellio, Sebastian 53
Casubon, Meric 237–8
catechising and catechisms 9, 89, 120, 122–3, 125–6, 129–30, 218, 243
    Large Catechism (1647) 26, 48, 82–3
    Racovian Catechism 124
    Shorter Catechism (1648) 123
cathedrals 171, 229, 231–3, 236–7, 239–41
Catholicism, Roman 22, 137–57, 166, 185, 208, 233, 241
    see also papists; popery; recusancy
Catholics, Roman 10, 11, 15, 43, 45, 49, 58, 82, 137–57 *passim*, 226, 228, 231, 251
Caton, William 228, 241–2
Cawdrey, Daniel 209, 211
Cawton, Thomas 127
Ceeley, Edward 216
Celsi, Mino 53
censorship 69, 85, 189, 207
ceremony and ritual 3, 44, 94, 161–2, 210, 212, 229
Chamberlen, Peter 188
Chambers, Humphrey 101
chaplains 70, 112, 189, 190, 228, 239–40
    royal 61
    see also army chaplains; naval chaplains
Chard (Somerset) 221
charitable works 206, 214
Charles I 3–4, 7–8, 15, 22, 23, 25, 27–8, 44, 61, 78–9, 81–2, 137–8, 140–1, 147, 152, 165, 170–3, 180, 192, 196, 198, 206–7, 209, 219, 229–32, 236, 239–40

cult of 172
personal rule of 13, 141, 228
Charles, Prince later Charles II 14–15, 99, 141, 146–7, 152, 158, 171–2, 219, 222, 253–4, 257–8
Chatham (Kent) 241
Chauncy, Henry 257, 259–60
Cheevers, Sarah 85
Cheshire 96, 101, 104, 112, 137, 176, 208, 221
Chester 171
Cheynell, Francis 52
Chichester 168
Chidley, Daniel 72
Chidley, Katherine 6, 72–5, 80–1
Chillenden, Edmund 184
Cholmley, family of Brandsby 143
Christmas 11, 163–6, 177, 237, 243
Christology 165
Chrysostom, St John 76
church, primitive 211, 236
church-ales 206–7, 214
church courts *see* ecclesiastical courts
church decoration 229
Church of England 2, 11, 14–15, 73–4, 115–16, 130, 158–80 *passim*, 182–3, 186–7, 199, 206, 226–8, 230, 234, 242–4, 257
    Supreme Governorship of 172–3, 234
    see also Anglicanism and Anglicans
churching of women 177, 243
church officers 74, 173
church property 170–1, 180
church rates 257
Church of Scotland 118, 137
churchwardens and churchwardens' accounts 127, 129, 161, 176, 208, 215–16
Cinque Ports 229, 239
City of London 48, 55
civil war 4, 21, 159, 173–4, 191, 206, 209, 219, 226, 229–33, 250, 253, 255, 261
    first civil war 95, 147, 150, 239

second civil war 144
Clarendon code 15
Clarke, Samuel 85, 101
Clarkson, Laurence 240
classis 1, 94–5, 116–17, 120, 124, 127, 131
clergy 97–108, 115–16, 174, 197
  cathedral 231–2, 237
  conformist 235
  Dissenting 244
  ejected 15, 112, 167, 207, 230, 232, 233, 236–7, 243, 244
  godly 237
  intruded 237–8, 244
  parochial 9, 161–6
  Presbyterian 118–36, 230, 234–5, 237–8, 240–1
  puritan 5, 57, 94, 207, 237
  Roman Catholic 77, 144, 146–50
  stipends 9
  see also chaplains
Cliffe (Kent) 237
Clifton on Teme 140
cloth industry 227
Clubmen Associations 165
Cobbett, Thomas 50
Coffey, John 148
Cokayn, George 27
Coke, Sir Edward 260
Colchester (Essex) 219
Coleman, Thomas 81
Coleman Street Congregation 227
Collier, Thomas 192–3
Collins, An 6, 34, 82–4
Collins, Jeffrey 93, 99–100, 105
Collinson, Patrick 123, 127, 130
colonial settlements 28, 164, 178, 199, 210
Commandments, Ten 22, 26, 48, 89, 205, 207, 209, 212
Commissioners for the Approbation of Public Preachers 98–100, 104
commissions of the peace 253
Committee for Compounding 146
Committee for Plundered Ministers 167

Committee for the Propagation of the Gospel 52
Committee for Religion (Long Parliament) 71
Commons, House of 8, 46, 48, 55, 78, 162, 215, 219, 229, 236, 238
Commonwealth 93, 95–6, 104, 212, 227, 253–4
Communion 80, 117, 121, 126, 128, 166, 171–2, 188, 214, 218, 236, 243
  communion fairs 130
  communion tables 233
  communion wine 127–8, 132
  see also altars; Lord's Supper; mass, the
Compton Census 244
confession, auricular 127
conformists and conformity 4, 12, 116, 131, 158–9, 165, 178, 226, 229, 233, 235, 244, 250
  see also Anglicanism and Anglicans
Congregationalists and Congregationalism 8, 44, 49–50, 52–3, 55–7, 59, 73, 94–5, 97, 101–2, 104–6, 113, 115, 116, 119, 131, 234
conscience 13, 43–4, 46–7, 51, 54–5, 57–61, 73, 93–6, 102, 107, 110, 119, 123, 138, 147–9, 151, 153, 193, 241, 244, 250–1, 253–6, 259, 262
constables 215–16
Constantine, Emperor 56
Conventicles Act (1664) 257, 259, 261
conventicles 60, 231, 233–4, 258
Cooke, John 23
Cooper, Ollive 90
Coppe, Abiezar 240
Coppin, Richard 236, 240–1
Cornwall 146, 165, 231
Cornwell, Francis 230, 236, 239
Corporation Act (1661) 256
Cosin, John, Bishop of Durham 170–3
Cotton, Clement 87
Cotton, John 49–50, 59, 210

Coughton (Warks) 140
Council of the Marches 141
Council of the North 141
Counter-Reformation 70
county committees 142–6, 219, 226,
    229, 237, 239, 241
Court of High Commission 235
Covenanters 4, 44–7
Coventry 103, 109, 163, 216–17, 240
Cowley, Abraham 43
Cranbrook (Kent) 108, 227, 233–5,
    241–2
Crane, Thomas 128, 132
Cranford, James 76, 120, 123
Cranmer, Thomas 158, 160, 162, 177,
    230
Cratfield (Suffolk) 214
Crawley, Thomas 259
Cressy, Serenus (Benedictine) 151
Crofton, Zachary 107, 122, 124
Cromwell, Oliver 5, 9, 14, 19, 20,
    23, 26, 30, 37, 48, 51–2, 59, 64,
    93–4, 97–100, 102–9, 111–12,
    138, 143–6, 148–9, 153–3, 166,
    171, 174, 190–1, 195–6, 215, 219,
    240–1, 251–2, 255
Cromwell, Richard 14, 107
Cromwell, Thomas 171
Crook, John 34, 256
Crooke, Robert 259–60, 263
Croope, John 55–6
Croxdale (co. Durham) 142
Culmer, Richard 232–3, 237–40, 242
Cumberland 108, 141
Cummings, Brian 150

dancing 206, 214, 238
Danson, Thomas 226, 235–6
Dartford (Kent) 228–9
Davis, J.C. 240
Davy, Sarah 35
Deal (Kent) 259
Declaration of Breda (1660) 158,
    253–4
Declaration of Indulgence (1672) 99
deism 56

Dell, William 55, 119, 212
Denne, Henry 187, 195
Deptford (Kent) 218, 243
Derbyshire 111, 117–18, 127
Dering, Sir Edward 229, 232, 236,
    242, 244
Derry, Bishop of 210–11
Devon 102, 112–13, 118, 165
diaries 31, 84–6, 90, 126, 218–22
Digby, Kenelm 149
Diggers 212
Directory for Public Worship (1645)
    1, 7, 8, 70, 160–2, 214, 226, 237,
    242–3
dissent and dissenters 13, 46, 49, 54,
    60–1, 94, 147, 226, 244, 254
divine right of bishops 229, 238
divine right of kings 229
Dorchester (Dorset) 198
Dorset 108, 165, 198
Douai 147, 149
Dover (Kent) 231, 237, 241–2
Dowsing, William 25
Drake, Roger 101, 104, 126, 129
Drogheda 26
Drysdale, A.H. 115–16, 131
Duffy, Eamon 116, 123, 163
Dunbar, battle of 219
Duppa, Brian, Bishop of Salisbury and
    Winchester 168
Duppa, John 72, 187
Durant, John 239, 248
Durham 141, 168, 170
Durham, County 142
Durston, Christopher 99–100
Durston (Somerset) 216
Dury, John 29–30
Dutch War 219
Dyer, Thomas 72
Dyke, Daniel 99

Earls Colne (Essex) 218
East Anglia 11, 140, 142
East Malling (Kent) 242
Easter 11, 158–9, 178
Eastern Association 250

Eaton, Samuel 101, 187
ecclesiastical courts 117, 123, 128, 165, 182, 257
Edgehill, battle of 219
Edward VI 77, 170
Edwards, Thomas 5, 6, 46–7, 49–50, 53, 72–4, 80, 191, 236, 239, 250
Edmonds, William 258
ejectors 9, 59, 97, 99–102, 107, 110, 221
elders 1, 94, 115–16, 118, 120, 127–9
Elizabeth I 2, 77, 140, 166, 227, 231
Elizabethan settlement 199, 233
Elmestone, John 233–4
Eltham 243
embassies
    Spanish 149
    Venetian 149, 217
Engagement (1647) 104, 106
episcopacy and episcopalianism 1, 2, 3, 4, 7, 14, 44, 49, 51, 60, 94, 96, 98, 102, 108–9, 114, 116, 129, 131, 158–9, 168–9, 174, 226, 229, 233, 235, 239
    see also Anglicanism and Anglicans; bishops
Episcopal Church (USA) 166
Erastianism 43, 48, 60, 116, 118, 131, 254
eschatology 5, 184, 193, 242
Essex 100–1, 104, 111–12, 118, 137, 216, 218–19, 231, 236, 238, 252
Essex, Earl of 163
L'Estrange, Hamon 208
Eton 113
Eure, Lord 144
evangelisation and evangelism 9, 121, 124–7, 131, 187, 189, 192, 242
Evans, Katharine 85
Evelyn, John 10, 11, 163, 165–7, 177, 218, 243–4
Evesham 255
Evening Prayer 162, 172
Everard, William 212
Everitt, Alan 230
excommunication 120, 131, 257

Exeter 168, 215
Exeter House (London) 243
exile 11, 22, 146–7, 150, 168–70, 186, 241

Fairfax, family, of Gilling 144
Fairfax, General Sir Thomas 143–4, 147, 238–9
Fairman, Robert 259
Fairman, William 257, 267
fall, doctrine of 56, 82
Fanshawe, family 256–7, 259–60, 263
fasting 5, 25–6, 106, 121, 137, 213
Fauconberg, Lord 152–3
Faversham (Kent) 236–7
Feake, Christopher 250
Feast, Henry 252, 258
feasts and festivals 11, 13, 158, 160–4, 177, 206–7, 217–18, 232, 237, 243, 248
Feoffees for Impropriations 250
Fifth Monarchists 8, 12, 24, 29, 71, 107, 181, 191, 195–9, 240, 242–3, 250
Fisher, Edward 211
Fisher, Samuel 55, 104, 228, 241–2, 245
Fitch, Thomas 106
Flanders 146, 152
Fleetwood, Charles 107
Fleetwood, family of Calwich (Staffs) 152
Fogge, family of Tilmanstone (Kent) 243
Folkestone (Kent) 241
Folkingham (Lincolnshire) 118
Fortescue, Sir Nicholas 151
Fox, George 25, 213, 221, 242, 251–2
Fox, Margaret Fell 85
Foxe, John 232
France 42, 148
Frances, family of Knighton 143
French, Daniel 241
Friends, Society of *see* Quakers
Frith, John 105
funeral liturgies 163–4, 177, 237

Gallican church model 148 , 153
Gardiner, Samuel Rawson 2
gathered church 6, 8, 13, 46, 48, 56, 73, 75, 80, 96, 130, 183, 185, 196, 227, 239
Gee, Edward 101
Germany 29, 194
Ghent 147
Gifford, Humphrey 145
Gifford, Peter 145
Gillespie, George 27, 46–7, 50
Gloucestershire 100, 102–3, 108, 112, 142, 211
Glynn, Sir John 215, 220
Goad, Thomas 70
godly, the 11–12, 22–4, 32, 43–4, 46–9, 53, 69, 75, 77, 95, 97, 102, 104–5, 107–9, 115–18, 120–4, 127, 131, 149, 153, 160–1, 164, 166, 173, 185, 190, 192–3, 196, 198, 207, 209, 214–18, 222, 237–8, 250, 252, 255, 261–3
  see also puritans
godparents 243
Goffe, William 59
Goldie, Mark 254
Gonville and Caius College, Cambridge 55
Goodwin, John 43, 48, 53–7, 60–1, 98, 121, 227
Goodwin, Philip 209–10
Goodwin, Thomas 44, 49, 94
Goudhurst (Kent) 233–4
Gouge, William 208
Gough, William 113
grace, doctrine of 23, 34, 56, 77, 83, 98, 116, 121, 125, 192
Grand Remonstrance (1641) 44, 94
Gray's Inn 215
Great Budworth (Cheshire) 208
Great Tew circle 151
Greaves, Richard 253
Green, Ian 122
Greenhill, William 99, 102, 104
Gregory, St 76
Gunpowder Plot 164, 178

Habington, family 139
  William 140
Hackett, John, Bishop of Coventry and Lichfield 163–5, 167
Hackforth 143
Hale, Sir Matthew 257
Hall, Joseph, Bishop of Exeter and Norwich 168
Halstead (Essex) 104
Hammond, Robert 23
Hampshire 108, 118, 145, 221
Harbledown (Kent) 232
Harlackenden, Richard 104
Harley, Sir Robert 213
Harrington, James 36, 43
Harris, Thomas 252
Harrison, Thomas 19
Hart, Mr 243
Hartlib, Samuel 28–30, 54
Harvey, Christopher 169, 173
Harwick (Kent) 221
Hatton, Francis 259
hell 33, 93, 210, 241
Helwys, Thomas 187
Henden, Simon 234
Henderson, Alexander 46
Henrietta Maria, Queen 70, 137, 147, 150, 207
Henry VIII 71, 171
Herbert, George 35, 73, 169
Hereford 208, 213
Herefordshire 231, 236
heresy 45–53, 56–8, 80, 96, 106–7, 112, 124, 198, 236, 239–41, 250
Herle, Charles 101
Herne, Jeremiah 258
Hertford 13, 249–67 *passim*
Hertfordshire 32, 250
Hesilrige, Sir Arthur 228
Hever (Kent) 229
Heylyn, Peter 207
Higginson, Thomas 228
High Walkers 109
Hill, Christopher 2, 24, 192, 240, 242
Hill, Thomas 108
Hilton, Walter 151

Hirst, Derek 122
Hobbes, Thomas 35
Hobby, Elaine 71
Hobson, Paul 190–1
Holden, Henry 148–9, 151
Holdenby House (Northamptonshire) 79
Holland, Colonel 59
Hollingworth, Richard 101
holy fairs 121
Holy Spirit 20, 23–4, 33, 73, 75, 126, 131, 151, 162, 232, 242
Hoo (Kent) 237
Hooke, Robert 31
Hooker, Richard 151, 162, 174
Hopwood, Edmund 216
Horle, Craig 255–6
Horsmonden, Daniel 234
Horsmonden (Kent) 228
Howard, Luke 227–8, 241, 244
Howard, Philip, Dominican priest 150
Howe, John 108
Howgill, Francis 255
Huckle, George 253
Hughes, Ann 116
humanism 53
Humble Petition and Advice (1657) 9, 108
Hunsdon (Herts) 252
Hunt, James 235
Hussites 45
Hutchinson, Lucy 85
Hyde, Edward, Chief Justice, later Lord Chancellor Clarendon 147, 256, 261
Hythe (Kent) 239, 241

iconoclasm 4, 232–3
idolatry 22–3, 25–6, 45, 48–9, 56, 58, 94, 161, 165, 207, 212, 260
Ightham (Kent) 237
illiteracy 165
Independents 6, 8–9, 35, 43, 47–8, 50–1, 53–5, 59–61, 73–4, 80, 82–3, 93–5, 98–103, 108–10,
119–20, 130, 183, 189, 194, 196, 198, 212, 227, 230, 236–40, 242–4, 250
Inkpen (Berks) 113
Inner Light 235, 251, 256, 262
Instrument of Government (1653) 9, 52, 94–7, 102
Interregnum 9, 11, 145, 153, 229, 240, 249, 251–2
Interregnum church 93–114 *passim*, 169, 183, 198, 220
Ireland 19, 22, 25, 26, 42, 45, 137–8, 148, 238
Ireton, Henry 51, 53
Irish rising (1641) 144
Isle of Wight 113
Ives, Jeremiah 213

Jackson, Arthur 101
Jacob, Henry 187–8
Jago, John 146
James I 3, 45, 131, 206, 229
Jekyll, Elizabeth 90
Jenkyn, William 102, 104
Jenny, George 75–6
Jessey, Henry 99, 188
Jesuits 147–50, 166
Jewel, John, Bishop of Salisbury 45
Jews 29, 54, 58–9, 206, 211–13
Jocelin, Elizabeth 70, 72
Jones, Thomas 208–9
Jordan, W.K. 42–3, 60
Josselin, Ralph 25, 104, 125, 218–20, 222
Julian of Norwich 151
justification, doctrine of 56, 83
Juxon, William 14

Kelsey, Major-General Thomas 240–1, 248
Kempe, Sir Garrett 145
Kenilworth (Warwickshire) 118
Kent 11, 12, 104–5, 108, 221, 226–48 *passim*
Kent county committee 165, 226, 229, 237, 239, 241

Kentish Root and Branch petition (1640) 233
Kentish royalist petition (1642) 242
Kenwricke, William 240
Kidderminster (Worcs) 217
Kiffin, William 192, 194, 197, 227
Killigrew, Anne 86
Kilvington (Yorks) 142
King, Henry, Bishop of Chichester 168
King, John 256
Kirke, Anne 86
Kirk Ireton (Derbyshire) 117
Knatchbull, Mary, Abbess of the Benedictine Convent at Ghent 147
Knighton 143
Knole (Kent) 229

Lade, John 232
laity 7, 10, 56, 94, 97, 99–101, 106, 115, 118, 122, 125, 131, 137–47, 162–6, 168, 170, 218, 228–9, 234, 235, 239, 244
'Lamb's War' 263
Lambe, Thomas 187, 192
Lancashire 9, 95–6, 101, 111–12, 118, 120, 123–5, 139, 141, 152–3, 206, 216, 218, 231, 256, 263
Lanherne (Cornwall) 146
landowners 138–9
Lane, Edward 30
Lanyer, Aemilia 77
last days 27, 56, 184
Last Judgement 21
    see also Second Coming
Latitudinarians 34
Laud, William, Archbishop of Canterbury 4, 14, 31, 71, 79, 137, 207, 228, 231–2, 238
Laudianism and Laudians 3–4, 14, 16, 44, 69, 70, 79, 159–60, 168, 172, 207, 209–10, 229, 231–2, 236, 250
laying on of hands 186
    see also ordination

lecturers and lectures 121, 228, 234, 238–9, 241
Lee, Zachariah 239
Leigh, Dorothy 69, 72
Leicester 121
Lenthall, William 215
Levellers 6, 12, 54–5, 72, 95, 148–9, 181, 191–5, 199, 212
    'Agreement of the People' (1647) 55, 95–7
    Officers' Agreement of the People (1649) 95–7
Ley, John 207–8
Libertarians 210
liberty 47, 54, 58–62, 95, 211, 251, 255–6, 262
licenser 69, 76, 113
Lichfield 163
Lilburne, John 72, 192, 194
Lincoln, siege of 146
Lincolnshire 118
Lindley, Keith 139, 141
liturgy 1, 4, 7, 11, 70–1, 158, 160–6, 172, 177, 218, 242–3
Lloyd [or Llwyd] Morgan 29
Locke, John 61
Lollards 45, 227, 230, 235
London 7, 9, 47, 54, 72, 79, 95–6, 101–2, 104, 107, 112, 118–20, 122–30, 153, 163, 187–9, 191–2, 194–5, 197–8, 207, 212, 218–20, 222, 227, 229, 231–2, 235–6, 238, 241–2, 250, 252, 258–9
    Mayor of London 102, 220
Lord's Day *see* sabbatarianism and sabbath
Lord's Prayer 162
Lord's Supper 120–2, 125–9, 131, 178
    see also Communion; mass, the
Lords, House of 48, 78, 95, 226, 238
Love, Christopher 95, 101–2, 119–20, 127–8, 132
Lovelace, Richard 242
Lucas, Nicholas 252, 257–8, 267
Luther, Martin 45
Lutherans 218

Lydd (Kent) 228, 241

MacCulloch, Diarmaid 159
Mackworth, Humphrey 100
magistrates, civil 5, 14, 44–54,
    57–9, 59, 61, 79, 81, 93, 99, 103,
    118–20, 124, 141, 153, 185, 189,
    210, 215–17, 220–1, 241, 252–3,
    256–61
Mahumetanism (Islam) 51, 58
Maidstone (Kent) 105, 109, 227, 229–
    32, 238, 241–2
  battle of 238
major-generals 59, 99, 219–20, 240–1,
    252
Malory, Thomas 179, 243
Malta 85
Maltby, Judith 3
Malton 144
Manchester 7, 105
Manning, Edward 258–9
Mansfield 105, 109
Mansell, Richard 111
Manton, Thomas 99, 102
Marian persecutions 74, 170, 227, 232
marriage 161, 237, 243
Marshall, Henry 258
Marshall, Stephen 26, 52, 93
Martin, John 170
Martin, Thomas 242
Martindale, Adam 96
Marxism 2
Marston Moor, battle of 143
Mary, Blessed Virgin 146, 232–3
  devotion to 56
Maryland 149, 166
masques 214
mass, the 56, 58, 142, 161, 163
Massachusetts 49–51, 54, 210
May Day 209
May, Susan 236
May, Thomas 258–9, 261
maypoles 214, 237
Mede, Joseph 30
Mennonites 186–7
Mercurius Politicus 103

Metcalfe, John 143
Meynell, family 142–4
Middlesex 220
midwives 261
millennium 29, 57, 181, 184, 193, 195,
    198, 242, 250
Milton, John 27–8, 43, 55, 57–9,
    212–13
Minster (Kent) 237
missions and missionaries 14, 85, 218,
    228, 241, 263
Mold, John 120
monasteries, dissolution of 171
Monck, George 103, 144
Montague, viscounts 145
Moore, Elizabeth 84, 90
Moorfields 220
More, Henry, Jesuit provincial 147
Morgan, Nicholas 256
Mornay, Philippe du Plessis 87
morning exercise 9, 121–2, 126
Morning Prayer 162, 172–3
Morrill, John 1, 115, 158, 174
Morton, Thomas, Bishop of Durham
    168
Moss, Ann 76
'mothers' legacies' 69–70, 85–6
Muggleton, Ludowicke 226, 242
Muggletonians 240
Munster 198
Murphy, Andrew 43

Nalton, James 104
natural law 57–8
naval chaplains 237, 239
Nayler, James 59, 108, 251–2, 259
Nedham, Marchamont 35
Netherlands 29, 42, 54, 59, 186–7
New England 5, 44, 49–51, 54, 146,
    148–9, 210
New Jerusalem 192, 197
New Model Army 7, 22, 48, 81, 95,
    118, 131, 147, 183, 190–1, 194,
    212, 240, 255
New Testament 56, 87, 212–13
Newcastle, Earl of 138

Newell, Elizabeth 164–5, 167
Newman, Peter 139
Nichols, Josias 239
Nichols, Thomas 83
Nominated Assembly 27
non-attendance at church 257
nonconformist and nonconformity
        166, 227, 231, 233–4, 237, 244,
        254, 256–7
Norfolk 101, 105, 112, 140, 142, 146,
        166, 170, 180, 221
Northamptonshire 112
Northumberland 118, 141
Norwich 168, 231
Norwood, Richard 33–4
Nottingham 215
Nye, Philip 49, 53, 94, 99, 101

Oath of Abjuration 142, 145, 152,
        251
Oath of Allegiance 147, 151, 256–7
oaths 256–7, 263
obedience 6, 47, 79, 185, 195–6, 227,
        244, 254, 257
Okey, Colonel 28
Old Testament 49, 51, 56, 59, 87, 207,
        235
Oldenburg, Henry 29
Ongar (Essex) 118
ordination 73, 77, 96, 98, 104, 117,
        168–9, 179, 228, 235
    see also laying on of hands
organs 233
original sin 186
    see also predestination
Otham (Kent) 238
Ottoman empire 29
Overton, Richard 55–6, 148, 192,
        194–5
Owen, John 6, 28, 43, 49–52, 58–9,
        61, 85, 97, 99, 106, 108
Owen, Richard 166, 243
Oxburgh (Norfolk) 140, 146
Oxenbridge, John 113
Oxford 8, 61, 168, 170, 222
Oxford Movement 159

Oxford, University 8, 105
Oxfordshire 195, 218
Oxinden, Henry of Deane (Kent) 226,
        244

Packer, William, Major-General 59,
        191, 252
Padua 151
pagans 50, 54
Pagitt, Ephraim 46
Palmer, Herbert 209, 211
pamphlets 42, 46, 54–5, 58–9, 81, 118,
        120, 208, 235–6, 260–1
pantheism 240
papal authority 56
papacy 147–9, 153
papists 50, 58, 74, 108, 137, 232, 238,
        243
    church papists 152
Paris 29, 146, 148, 151
parish clerk 129
parishes 7, 8, 10, 51, 93, 95–7, 99, 105,
        116–20, 159, 167, 184
Parker, Henry 43
Parker, Kenneth 207
Parker, William 212
Parliament
    Barebone's Parliament (1653) 97–8,
        196, 240
    Cavalier Parliament 257
    first protectoral parliament 19, 52,
        59, 99, 102, 107, 196, 219, 227,
        252
    Long Parliament 1, 4, 7, 11–12, 25,
        45, 71–2, 78, 94, 116, 159–60,
        170, 177, 188–9, 207–9, 213, 226
    Protectorate Parliament 12
    Rump Parliament 12, 20, 52, 95,
        97, 194, 212, 214–15
    second protectoral parliament 22,
        28, 59, 103, 107, 111, 215, 227,
        252
parliamentarians 10, 22, 43, 45, 57
Parr, Susanna 35
Pask, William 241
patriarchy 73

patronage 97, 105, 111, 238
Patshulland 145
Paul, St 125, 129, 235
'peace principle' 253, 255, 263
penal laws 60, 249, 254–5, 257, 263
penance 257
Pepys, Samuel 31, 221–2
Perkins, William 83
persecution 6, 13, 33, 46, 57–8, 62,
    72, 142–4, 174, 185–7, 197–8,
    249, 251, 254–5, 261
    see also Marian persecutions
Personal Rule 13
Peterborough 171
petitions 13, 59, 81–2, 105, 108, 118,
    159, 194, 229–30, 232–4, 238–9,
    242, 246, 253, 257
Petre, Thomas 144
Peyton, Sir Thomas 243
Philips, Katherine 75
Pickering, John 217
plundering 140, 142
pluralism 15, 54
Pocklington, John 207
Pocock, Edward 113
Poland 29, 54, 59
Poole, Elizabeth 6, 82
Pope, Mary 6, 78–82
popery 44, 52, 96, 137–8, 142, 149,
    152, 160–3, 166, 185, 232–3
Pordage, John 106
Portadown 137
Porter, Thomas 106–7
praemunire 256–7
prayer 25, 71, 86, 121, 160, 172
    conferences 214
    contemplative 151
    daily offices *see* Evening Prayer;
        Morning Prayer
    family prayers 261
    free prayer 160
    impromptu prayer 261
    Lord's Prayer 26, 162
    public prayer meetings 117
Prayer Book *see* Book of Common
    Prayer

Prayer Book Protestants 10, 11, 159–
    60, 162, 166, 170
    see also Anglicanism and
        Anglicans; conformists and
        conformity
preachers and preaching 3, 9, 27, 33,
    54–6, 77, 81–3, 93, 97–8, 107,
    111, 115, 117, 119–21, 124–6,
    168, 184–91, 199, 210, 213,
    217–18, 221, 227, 229, 235–6,
    239–41, 243–4, 250
    lay preachers 235
    women preachers 235–6, 244, 250,
        252
    see also sermons
predestination 3–4, 82, 184, 186–7,
    189, 227, 250
preferment 167–8, 237
prelacy 52, 96
Presbyterians and Presbyterianism 5,
    6, 7, 13–14, 15, 43, 44, 46–53,
    55–7, 59–60, 71–3, 75–82, 93–4,
    98–109, 115–36 *passim*, 160, 189,
    191, 193, 196, 217, 226–8, 232,
    234–40, 244, 250
    Scottish Presbyterians 102
Presbyteries, classical 117–18
    congregational 117–18, 123, 131
    see also classis; provincial
        assemblies
Preston, battle of 27
Price, John 121
Pride's Purge 27
Prior, Thomas 257
Pritchard, John 253
Privy council 207, 258
profession, public 9, 10, 12, 93–4, 96,
    100, 104, 107, 109–10
prophecy and prophets 78, 80–2, 85,
    226–7, 250, 262
Protectorate 9, 52, 93–4, 96–8, 100–4,
    107, 109, 145, 149, 152, 196–7,
    227
protectorate council 98–100, 104–7,
    112–13, 197, 219
Protestantism, continental 231–2

providence 19, 22, 26, 35, 78, 195, 249, 258, 261–2
provincial assemblies 117–18, 131
   London Province 124, 129
   see also Synods
Prynne, William 43, 47
Pryor, Francis 258
Pudsey, family 143
Puller, Isaac 252
puritans 3–4, 6, 10–11, 22, 31, 43, 49, 58, 61, 71, 82–3, 94–6, 105, 107–9, 111, 116, 122–3, 131, 140–1, 145, 160, 172, 191, 206–7, 211–13, 216, 220–2, 226–7, 229, 233, 235, 237–8, 248, 250, 253–5, 260–1, 263
   see also godly, the
purity 184–5, 200, 232
Putney 192

Quaker Act (1662) 256
Quakers 1, 8, 10–11, 13, 51–3, 55, 59, 71, 82, 101, 106, 108, 149, 151, 198–9, 213, 216, 218, 221, 227–8, 235, 240–2, 244, 249–67 *passim*
   disobedience and defiance of 249–67 *passim*
quarter sessions 257, 259–61

radicals 10, 13, 44, 57, 148–9, 151, 160, 187, 191–2, 195, 208–12, 227, 229–31, 233, 236–7, 240, 242, 246, 249–50, 253–4
Ranters 32, 236, 240–1, 251
Ratcliff, E. C. 161
Rathmines, battle of 25
Reading, John 61
recusancy 156, 251
   recusancy fines 141, 143–5, 152
   recusancy laws 147, 256
   see also papists; popery; Catholicism, Roman
Reeve, John 242
reform 118, 137, 229, 231, 239, 258
reformation 10, 22, 25, 57, 107, 115–19, 130–2, 212, 230–1

godly reformation 99, 107, 109, 149, 231
   long Reformation 131
   reformation of manners 218
Reformation, the 26, 82, 127, 138, 141, 150, 161, 170, 195, 227, 230, 235
   Edwardian Reformation 170
regicide 19, 23, 27–8, 85, 172, 230, 257
Reigate (Surrey) 118
religious houses 147
religious orders 147–151
   see also Jesuits
republicanism 14
Restoration 10, 14, 28, 60–1, 138–9, 145, 149, 152–3, 159, 168, 170–2, 174, 188, 197–9, 211, 221–2, 234, 238, 244, 249, 253–4, 256
Restoration settlement 14, 60, 168, 254
resurrection, doctrine of 241
Reynolds, Edward 14
Rhode Island 49, 54
Richardson, Elizabeth 6, 70–1
Richardson, Samuel 55–6
ritualism 159
Roberts, Francis 126
Roberts, Stephen 255
Robinson, George 241
Robinson, Henry 54, 58, 61
Roborough, Henry 115
Robson, Richard 233
Rochester Cathedral 233, 236, 240–1
Rochester (Kent) 227, 229, 231, 241–2
Rogers, John 24
Rogers, Nehemiah 111
Rolle, Richard 151
Rolvenden (Kent) 228
Rome 148, 186
Romney (Kent) 241
'Root and Branch' petition (1640) 229
   see also Kent, Kentish Root and Branch petition
Roots, Ivan 168

Rosewall, Walter 241
royalism and royalists 5, 14, 60–1, 78–
    9, 94–5, 97, 102, 105–6, 139–42,
    146–7, 152, 159, 165–6, 168, 170,
    226, 229, 231, 233, 236–8, 240,
    242–4, 261
royalist army 139–43, 146, 152
Royston (Herts) 251
Rushworth, John 143
Russell, Thomas 243
Rutherford, Samuel 5, 46–7, 50, 59,
    61, 75
Rutt, Abraham 256–7
Rye (Kent) 242
Rye (Sussex) 145
Rymer, Ralph 143

St Agnes and St Anne Aldersgate 119,
    133
St Aldates Oxford 8
St Bartholomew-by-the-Exchange 127
St Botolph Aldgate 107, 122
St Bride Fleet Street 130
St Christopher-le-Stocks 120, 123
St Erme (Cornwall) 146
St George Botolph Lane 120
St George's Hill (Surrey) 212
St John, Oliver 27, 48
St Lawrence Jewry 120, 127, 129
St Leonard Eastcheap 115
St Martin's Outwich 125
St Mary Aldermanbury 128
St Peter's Cornhill 81
St Peter Westcheap 126
St Stephen's Coleman Street 55
sabbatarianism and sabbath 1, 10,
    12, 52, 120, 124, 126, 205–25
    passim, 238
sacraments 3, 82, 104, 121, 125, 127,
    129–30, 161–3, 166, 171, 183,
    243
    see also baptism; Communion;
    Lord's Supper; marriage; mass,
    the
sacrilege 11, 171
Saints, the 130, 193, 196, 198

Saladin 107
Salisbury, Earl of 263
Salisbury 168, 195
Saller, William 213
Salmon, Joseph 240
Saltmarsh, Edward 143
Saltmarsh, John 227, 236, 239
salvation, doctrine of 2, 4, 24, 29, 33,
    56, 83, 130, 161, 165, 182–3,
    186–7, 211–12, 241, 262
Salvin, family 142
sanctification, doctrine of 78, 83, 121,
    125–6, 184, 210, 213
San Domingo 21
Sanderson, Robert, Bishop of Lincoln
    254
Sandwich (Kent) 228, 231, 239, 242
Sargeant, John 148
Satan 106, 208, 235
    see also Antichrist
Saturday sabbath 213
Saunders, Mary 252–3
Savoy Confession (1658) 50, 55
Saye and Sele, Lord 44, 48, 51, 226
Sayers, family of Worsall (Yorks) 152
scandalous ministers 99–100, 106, 236
schism 124
Schmidt, Leigh Eric 130
Scilly, Isles of 53
Scotland 19, 22, 42, 45, 74, 93, 103,
    106, 118, 121, 130, 131, 142, 219
Scots' army 106
Scott, David 256
Scott, Jonathan 42
Scroop, Colonel 28
Sealed Knot 152
Seaman, Lazarus 101
Second Coming 21, 28, 242
    see also Last Judgement
sectarianism 128, 131, 188, 197, 199,
    253
sects and sectaries 45–6, 47, 53, 58,
    71, 80, 95–6, 102, 124, 151, 196,
    198–9, 210, 235, 238, 249–50,
    254
Sedgwick, Obadiah 46, 50, 53, 99

sedition 45, 230, 255, 261
Seekers 6, 8, 13, 55–6, 108, 234
separatists 13, 44–5, 72, 74–5, 119, 130, 183, 186–7, 192, 226–7, 234
sequestration 97, 127, 142–4, 147, 152, 168, 226, 230–1, 237, 243
Sequestration committee 143
sermons 9, 23, 25, 26, 27–8, 46, 55, 58, 63, 78, 84, 86, 88, 90, 98, 107, 120, 122, 126, 137, 151, 164, 167, 177, 192–3, 206, 214, 217–18, 229, 232, 238, 243, 250
see also preachers and preaching
Servetus, Michael 45, 49–50, 53
Sevenoaks (Kent) 235, 237
Seventh Day Adventism 188
Shaw, William 115, 118, 131
Sheldon, family 139
Sheldon, Gilbert 14
Sheldon, William 140
Shell, Alison 150
Shepard, Thomas 209–10
Shepherd, Henry 78
ship money 80
Shrewsbury 72
Shrewsbury, Earl of 140
Shropshire 100, 106–7, 112, 217
Sidney, Mary 87
Simpson, John 107
Simpson, Sidrach 99
sin 58, 82, 83, 170–1, 255
Skinner, Robert, Bishop of Oxford and Worcester 168
Skippon, Philip 107
Slindon 145
Smarden (Kent) 230
Smith, Captain 241
Smith, David 107
Smith, William 258–61
Smyth, John 186–7
Society for the Promoting of Christian Knowledge (SPCK) 14
Society for the Propagation of the Gospel in New England 146
Socinians and Socinianism 46, 49, 50–6, 58, 107, 124, 251

Solemn League and Covenant (1643) 7, 23, 45, 93–5, 106, 110, 116, 131, 238
Somerset 108, 112, 118, 208, 216, 221
Somerset House 215
soteriology *see* salvation, doctrine of
Southwell, Anne 77
Southworth, John 149
Spain 23, 42
Sparrow, William 104
Spelman, Clement 170–2, 180
Spelman, Sir Henry 170, 180
Spilsbury, Jonathan 187–8
Spittlehouse, John 213
sports 206, 210, 213, 216, 220–2, 238
Sprigge, Joshua 59
Spurr, John 14, 172
Staffordshire 100, 112, 141, 144–5, 152
Stalham, John 104
Staplehurst (Kent) 241
Stepney 104
Sterry, Peter 27
Strode, Sir George 242
Strong, William 99
Stout, Henry 251–2, 256–7, 259–62, 267
Stowe 111
Strood (Kent) 241
Stuarts 5, 10, 21, 77, 146, 156, 166, 170, 173
Stubbe, Henry 55–6, 60–1
Stubbs, John 228, 241
Sturry (Kent) 228
Suffolk 142, 146, 214, 231, 236
surplice 234
Surrey 118, 212
Sussex 108, 145, 153, 231
Sutton Courtnay 106
Sutton Valence (Kent) 234
Swannington (Norfolk) 221
Sweden 29, 218
Sweeting, Henry 251, 256–7, 259–60, 267
Swinnock, George 238
synods 1, 7, 73, 94, 117

Talbot, family 139
Tankard, Thomas 143
Taylor, Francis 238–40
Taylor, Jeremy 43, 61, 169, 179, 211,
    243, 254
Temple, Richard 100, 111
Tenterden (Kent) 241
Thanet (Kent) 237
Thomas, Richard 256–7, 259–60, 263,
    267
Thomason, George 81, 195
Thorndike, Herbert 43
Thornton, Alice 35
Throckmorton, family 140
Thurloe, John 103, 106
Tillam, Thomas 213
Tilmanstone (Kent) 243
tithes 55–6, 59, 96–7, 99, 128, 170,
    185–6, 191, 193, 210, 234–5,
    237–8, 251–3
tobacco 177
toleration 5, 6, 7, 8, 42, 44, 46–62, 72,
    78, 94, 104, 119, 147–8, 153,
    185, 190–1, 209, 239, 249, 254,
    263
Toleration Act (1689) 60
Tombes, John 99
Topsham (Devon) 113
Tories 14
tracts 81, 207, 211, 230, 258
transportation 259–61
Trapnel, Anna 34, 71
Traske, John 188, 206, 213
treason 231, 254
Treherne, Samuel 258–9
triers 9, 59, 97–9, 102, 104–5, 107,
    111
Trinity, doctrine of 45, 48, 51, 56, 58,
    82, 161
Trinity College, Cambridge 108
Troppe, James 196
Tuckney, Anthony 99
Turks 54
Turner, Sir Henry 162
Turner, John 234–5, 239
Turner, William 235, 267

Tyburn 149
typology 80

Ulcombe (Kent) 234
Underdown, David 165, 175
uniformity 43–4, 49, 51–2, 55, 57, 60,
    231
Uniformity Bill (1662) 162
universalists 48

vagrancy 251
Vane, Sir Henry the younger 28, 48,
    54–6, 59
Venn, Anne 85
Venn, John 85
Venner, Thomas 197–8,
Venner's revolt 254
vestries 120, 123, 127–9
Vincent, Mr 237
Vines, Richard 52, 101, 104, 126–30,
    132
Virginia 164–6, 177, 187

wakes 214
Waldegrave, Sir Edward 139
Waldensians 45
Wales 168
Walker, George 207–8
Wall, Moses 29
Wallington, Nehemiah 115, 125–6
Walsham Alexandra 22
Walter, John 232
Walton, Izaak 174
Walwyn, William 6, 54–6, 58, 192,
    194, 212
Ward, Nathaniel 50
Ward, Samuel 137
Ware (Herts) 252
Warren, Elizabeth 6, 75–9, 81
Warwick 217
Warwick, Earl of 239
Warwickshire 100–1, 111–12, 118,
    140, 169, 216–17
Water Eaton (Bucks) 145
Watkinson, Peter 117
Watson, Thomas 104

Weald (Kent) 227–9, 231, 234, 241
Wentworth, Anne 35
Westerham (Kent) 236
Westminster 4, 55, 81, 167, 220, 231
Westminster Assembly of Divines 7, 26, 27, 45–6, 48, 74, 82, 93–5, 101, 116, 118, 123, 160–1, 212, 214, 238
Westminster Confession 47, 55
Westmoreland 108, 141
Weston (Warwickshire) 140
Weston, Henry 105
West Indies 258, 267
Whalley, Edward 59, 215
Whitchurch (Shropshire) 106–7, 109, 113
White, Thomas 104
White, Thomas (also known as Blacklo) 148–50
  see also Blacklo
Whitehall 107, 231
Whitehall debates (1648) 51, 53, 56, 59
Whitehead, George 252
Whitelocke, Bulstrode 215, 218
Whitsun, 11, 208
Wiersdale, John 117, 127
Wilcock, James 234–5
Wiltshire 101, 108, 112, 165, 221
Williams, Roger 6, 49, 53–6, 58–9, 61, 148
Wilson, Thomas 105, 238–9

Winchester 168
Winstanley, Gerrard 212
Wirksworth (Derbyshire) 117, 124, 127
Wolsey, Cardinal Thomas 171
women 6, 35, 69–90, 144, 166, 199, 234–6, 244, 250, 252, 264
Wood, Anthony 222
Wood, Thomas 258
Woodbridge (Suffolk) 76
Woodkirk (W. Yorks) 217
Woodward, Ezekias 8
Woolestone, Samuel 259
Worcester 139–40, 168
  battle of 107, 146, 219
Worcestershire 108, 139–40, 142, 151, 217, 220
Worden, Blair 42
worship, public 160–2, 183, 206, 208, 210, 212, 214, 218–20, 222, 227, 234, 242
Wrightson, Keith 218

Yalding (Kent) 238
Yarmouth 101, 113
York 103, 256, 263
Yorkshire 138–9
  North Riding 11, 142, 144–5, 152–3
  West Riding 101, 112, 118, 142, 144, 217

Zwingli, Huyrich 57